Employment Rights

A Reference Handbook

RICHARD W. PAINTER and KEITH PUTTICK

Pluto Press

LONDON • BOULDER, COLORADO

First published 1993 by Pluto Press
345 Archway Road, London N6 5AA
and 5500 Central Avenue
Boulder, CO 80301, USA

British Library Cataloguing in Publication Data
A catalogue record for this book is available from the British Library
ISBN 0 7453 0584 9 cased
ISBN 0 7453 0589 X paperback

Library of Congress Cataloging-in-Publication Data
Painter, Richard W., 1952–
   Employment rights / Richard W. Painter and Keith
Puttick.
   440p. 23cm.
   Includes bibliographical references and index.
   ISBN 0-7453-0584-9 (hbk.). – ISBN 0-7453-0589-X (pbk.)
   1. Labor laws and legislation – Great Britain. 2. Labor contract –
Great Britain. 3. European Economic Community – Great Britain.
I. Puttick, Keith. II. Title.
KD3095.P35 1993
344,41'01–dc20
[344.1041]

93-15994
CIP

7 104566 120164 7

Produced for Pluto Press by
Chase Production Services, Chipping Norton
Typeset from author's disks by
Stanford Desktop Publishing Services, Milton Keynes
Printed in the EC by TJ Press

Contents

Abbreviations

AC	Appeal Cases
ACAS	Advisory Conciliation and Arbitration Service
All ER	All England Law Reports
BJIR	*British Journal of Industrial Relations*
CA	Court of Appeal
CAB	Citizens' Advice Bureau
CAC	Central Arbitration Committee
Ch	Law Reports, Chancery division
CLY	Current Law Yearbook
DE	Department of Employment
DSS	Department of Social Security
EA	Employment Act
EAT	Employment Appeal Tribunal
ECJ	European Court of Justice
EOC	Equal Opportunities Commission
EPA	Employment Protection Act 1975
EPCA	Employment Protection (Consolidation) Act 1978
EqPA	Equal Pay Act 1970
HL	House of Lords
HSC	Health & Safety Commission
ICR	Industrial Cases Reports
ILJ	*Industrial Law Journal*
ILO	International Labour Organisation
IRLIB	Industrial Relations Legal Information Bulletin
IRLR	Industrial Relations Law Reports
IT	Industrial Tribunal
KB	Law Reports, King's Bench division
LRD	Labour Research Department Publications
NIRC	National Industrial Relations Court
QB	Law Reports, Queen's Bench division
RSC	Rules of the Supreme Court
TULRA	Trade Union and Labour Relations Act 1974
TULR(A)A	Trade Union and Labour Relations (Amendment) Act 1976
TULR(C)A	Trade Union and Labour Relations (Consolidation) Act 1992
TURERA	Trade Union Reform and Employment Rights Act 1993
WA	Wages Act 1986
WLR	Weekly Law Reports

Preface

In producing a book about employment rights we have also offered a perspective on the way that the employment law system appears to us to be developing. At a formal level this task is made easier by the fact that policy changes are often mooted, or set out in their final form, in published documents, or are widely reported. The relevant chapters therefore contain references to government 'Green' and 'White' Papers, ministerial statements, EC policy declarations and so on.

References are also made to leading cases illustrating the courts' position and shifts in judicial attitudes on key issues. In dealing with legislation, we have been fortunate in our timing of the book's publication in being able to include the effects of the new Trade Union and Employment Rights Act 1993.

As far as earlier stages in the law-making process are concerned, it has been possible, too, to comment on the influences which have prompted changes in the law. Undoubtedly politicians and employment ministers are influenced by media commentary and public reactions on key issues. At one point early in 1993, for example, ministers seem to be wavering on the government's commitment to abolish the Wages Councils in the face of public concern. Public opinion also had some part to play in the government accepting a compromise over the EC directive limiting working hours. An important, and highly influential, factor in recent times has also been the views of right-wing 'think-tanks', which have clearly been behind many recent government initiatives in the employment field.

Underlying everything is the point that economic forces are relentlessly reshaping our society. Thus a combination of factors, including sudden falls in demand for products and services in certain industries, together with a government philosophy of 'non-intervention' has the capacity to produce large-scale unemployment in some regions almost overnight. This was clearly seen with the closure of the Swan Hunter shipyard on Tyneside in May 1993.

Again, companies' falling profitability, and demands for competitiveness, produce demands on government for policies which facilitate cost-cutting measures. As labour costs are a major element in most companies' operations, it is hardly surprising that our economic system demands, and has generally been getting, an employment law regime which makes it easier for employers to reduce such costs, whether through redundancies, cutting wages or making savings in other ways.

Recent events show how these facts are having an effect in both the private and public sectors. In the latter, we are now seeing 'privatisation' as the prime catalyst for massive wage cuts, and erosion of working conditions, affecting tens of thousands of workers – in the health service, local government services and elsewhere in government. As private contractors vie with each other for contracts, workers are often being given a simple choice: accept a new contract or face immediate unemployment.

In one week in April 1993, in Macclesfield, two separate issues illustrated the position perfectly. In one, hospital porters were informed that they would shortly be working for a new private contractor as their existing employer (also a private contractor) had just lost its NHS contract. As the price for keeping their jobs, though, they were required to take a substantial pay cut, lose holiday rights and forego redundancy payments. In the other case, pay cuts and changes in conditions were imposed by a registered charity on its care workers to enable the charity to compete for contracts as part of the 'care in the community' programme, which came into operation throughout the country that month. There is no reason to doubt that what is happening in a town in Cheshire is also happening in every other part of the country.

In the private sector there are, again, numerous recent examples of employers, including major UK companies, cutting their costs in similar ways. As reported in an influential *Panorama* documentary on BBC 1 on 17 May 1993, some of the methods used could loosely be described as 'within the law', for example sacking people before they complete two years' service (which precludes them from receiving the benefits of protective legislation), or re-employing full-time staff on part-time contracts with reduced pay and conditions. The programme also reported, for instance, the use of 'zero hours contracts' whereby staff are expected to be available for work at unspecified times convenient to the company.

Recent months have seen an upsurge in industrial action, including one-day strikes by railway workers worried about threatened job cuts in the lead-up to privatisation. These coincided with other industrial action, including action by bus workers in London. In the bus workers' case there has been the added issue of imposed wage cuts, again due to privatisation measures. At the time of writing British Rail has just given new job security guarantees. Another major dispute, between the teachers and the government over classroom 'tests' of pupils (and the increased workload this involves), has also recently come to a head and resulted in a partial climbdown by the education secretary, John Patten.

Both these disputes have a long-term significance. In particular, they have highlighted the vulnerability of public sector staff when employment disputes have the potential to bring them into conflict with the government. For this reason, as well as prompting an outburst of hysteria by the media and demands for public sector industrial action to be outlawed, they also led to media demands for the courts to intervene immediately. The *Financial Times*, for example, in its leader on 2 April 1993, pushed for British Rail to 'turn to the law' if the strikes continued.

In the case of the teachers, Wandsworth Council did indeed try to stop the teachers' boycott by claiming the action was 'political' rather than 'industrial', and by seeking to show that teachers had a 'statutory duty' to help in the implementation of the tests. Despite the council's best endeavours the action eventually failed in the Court of Appeal.

The issue did, however, raise the question of whether the government might, as a result, use the opportunity to legislate against public sector employees. Sure enough, the then employment secretary, Gillian Shepherd, in a letter leaked to the National Union of Teachers, put forward options for removing unions' legal immunities if their members in the future took action which had the effect of frustrating 'statutory duties'. It is not clear, at the time of writing, how far such changes will be pursued. If they are, they would certainly have a significant effect on public sector workers' rights in many situations.

These and other workplace issues have illustrated the continuing importance to many workers of union membership. However, the UK employment regime still refuses to provide a system which legally *requires* workers' organisations to be recognised for collective bargaining purposes, or which prevents 'de-recognition' whenever the employer wants to do this. In some cases employers have been turning to works councils, as provided for by EC legislation (based on continental models for this form of representation). This will, before long, start to pose a dilemma for UK unions, particularly as works councils, unless their introduction is properly negotiated, can cut across existing lines of representation and be employer-dominated in every way.

The issue of recognition is also tied in with another trend, which is away from collective bargaining and agreements and towards so-called 'personal' contracts. In a significant decision in the Court of Appeal it has been held that employers' inducements (or 'sweeteners') to encourage staff to relinquish union membership and accept a personal contract can amount to discrimination against individuals who wish to retain union membership. The case also made it clear, however, that the judgement did not affect employers rights to de-recognise or to impose changes to contracts (if that is done correctly in procedural terms).

The Trade Union and Employment Rights Act 1993 has, however, thanks to a late amendment, reversed the ground won in the Court of Appeal by once again permitting such inducements. Overall, the 1993 Act is 'swings and roundabouts' in terms of employment rights, as discussed in the text. On the one hand it implements important new rights in areas like maternity leave. On the other, it continues the incremental erosion of trade union rights.

On the Maastricht Treaty, there is still doubt about the UK's position on the Social Chapter. Succumbing to pressure from an alliance between Tory Eurosceptics and the Opposition, the Government have included a new clause in the Maastricht Bill. This states that the Act may only come into force if both Lords and Commons are allowed a vote on the question of adopting the Social Chapter. Apart from making a nonsense of the whole Maastricht process to date, this has opened up the prospect of court action – probably in a judicial review application brought by the Eurosceptics on the right to clarify the position.

The good news, as far as the EC is concerned, is that the other EC member states are now looking for available ways to render the United Kingdom's Social Chapter 'opt-out' a dead letter. In particular, it is likely that they will be looking to legislate under treaty provisions which do not allow the UK to evade the responsibilities which other members accept and implement. What has prompted this has been the government's attempts to entice inward investors, and companies located elsewhere in the EC, to move their operations to the UK, with the promise of lower operating costs and an easier employment law regime.

Finally, we would like to express our thanks to Jackie Pate for all her hard work in helping with the manuscript, Anne Beech for commissioning the project, and Diana Russell for her painstaking editing. Also, thanks to our families for their support while the book was being produced.

We have attempted to state the law as at 1 July 1993.

Keith Puttick and Richard Painter
Stoke-on-Trent, July 1993

PART ONE

Introduction

CHAPTER 1

Employment Rights:
Past, Present and Future

This book sets out to provide a guide to peoples' rights at work. At the outset, however, it is important to understand how the present system of UK employment law has evolved in order to appreciate both how it works and its shortcomings. It is also useful to have an awareness of the likely future direction of employment law.

There are two key considerations. First, the continuation of Conservative government for the foreseeable future has been resulting in 'more of the same', as one commentator predicted immediately after the 1992 general election. In other words, as it was forecasted at that time, there has, indeed, been further weakening of individual employment law rights coupled with yet further restrictions on the legal freedoms of trade unions. The second factor is the EC. At the end of the 1980s it seemed as if UK and EC ideologies and policies were in complete conflict, and that the government would have no choice but to accommodate EC standards and requirements or get out of the organisation altogether. However, recent history has shown that the position is not so simple. The UK's 'opt-out' from the Social Chapter at Maastricht was both a surprise and a disappointment for those who see UK employment law standards lagging behind the rest of Europe. Nevertheless, as we shall see, EC membership has continued to be a potent source of regulation, particularly in the spheres of sex discrimination and equal pay, and in areas like maternity leave and health and safety.

Intervention v. Deregulation:
the Origins of the Present System[1]

Despite the existence for many decades of statutes, such as the Factories Acts dealing with health and safety in factories, and of many judicial decisions in the law governing employment, observers have looked in vain for what they might recognise as 'labour law' in Britain. Britain has never had a labour law code, so that one expert was able to observe in 1959: 'When British industrial relations are compared with those of other democracies they stand out because they are so little regulated by law.'[2] This description of the state's traditional approach

3

to the conduct of British industrial relations, known variously as legal absten-
tionism, voluntarism or collective laissez-faire, was by the 1970s in need of
considerable modification. The droplets of legal intervention discernible in the
1960s assumed torrential proportions during the following decade.

The source of the trend towards regulation can be traced back to a series of Acts
which gave employees certain rights which were enforceable in the new industrial
tribunals: the Contracts of Employment Act 1963 (right to minimum period of
notice and right to receive in writing major terms and conditions of employment);
the Redundancy Payments Act 1965 (employees could claim compensation if their
jobs became redundant); the Equal Pay Act 1970 (equal pay for 'like work'), and
the unfair dismissal provisions of the Industrial Relations Act 1971.

Indeed, the Act of 1971 was a failed attempt to introduce a comprehensive
legal regulation of employment relations in line with the North American
model. With its repeal by the Trade Union and Labour Relations Act 1974, we
saw a return to the previous policy of legal abstention in relation to collective
labour law. A further element in the so-called social contract between the labour
government and the Trade Union Congress (TUC) was the enactment of legislation such as the Employment Protection Act 1975 (EPA) which created a
'statutory floor' of individual employment rights and gave a degree of legal support
for union organisation and collective bargaining. The idea of the 'floor' was to
provide legally guaranteed minimum rights which could then be *improved* upon
at the workplace through the encouragement, extension and use of the collective
bargaining process.

In radical contrast, the legislation of the 1980s and 1990s – the Employment
Acts 1980, 1982, 1988, 1989 and 1990, the Trade Union Act 1984, the Wages
Act 1986 – aim to deregulate so far as employment protection and collective
bargaining are concerned, but impose major legal restrictions on trade unions.

This legislation aims to place major obstacles in the way of the organisation
of industrial action. Strike organisers and trade unions are exposed to court orders
and damages by the narrowing of the statutory immunities from judge-made
liabilities. In this way, secondary industrial action, solidarity and political strikes,
picketing away from the pickets' own workplaces and official action not preceded
by ballot are, in effect, made unlawful. In addition, the reduction of strikers'
dependants' entitlement to supplementary benefit (now income support) and the
widening of the employer's freedom to sack strikers without incurring the risk
of liability for unfair dismissal, have been put in place in order to make individual
workers think twice before withdrawing their labour.

In addition to the civil law, the Public Order Act 1986 redefined and expanded
some of the criminal law offences which were extensively used against pickets
in the 1984–5 miners' dispute. The law and policy relating to collective labour
relations are discussed in Part Six below.

At first sight there would appear to be a contradiction between the neo-liberal
philosophy of the Conservative administration, which essentially believes in keeping

the business of the state and the business of government to a minimum, and the highly interventionist policy it has adopted in relation to trade union reform. There is, in fact, no contradiction. For the free marketeer, the market is the mechanism by which individual wants and desires can be controlled. The only valid function of government is to protect this mechanism from interference. According to this philosophy trade unions maintain a labour monopoly through such practices as the closed shop, and not only distort the market but also infringe the political liberty that the free market offers. The basis of trade union power is seen to be coercion resting on legal privileges which should be revoked.[3]

While the logic of the 'free market' points to the legal restriction of trade unions, it requires that most of the burdens of state intervention are lifted from employers. This is the task of deregulation: to dismantle the legal and bureaucratic controls which, in free market theory, deter employers, especially small employers, from recruiting labour. Deregulation embraces a wide range of policies, including privatisation, the encouragement of low wages for young workers and – of special concern here – the erosion of legal support for collective bargaining and employment protection. Landmarks in the deregulatory process include:

- The abolition of the procedure under EPA 1975 and the Fair Wages Resolution (which originated as far back as 1891), measures designed to establish the 'going-rate' of pay and other conditions in particular industries and fair wages in companies awarded government contracts.
- The removal of persons under the age of 21 from the protection of the Wages Council system, followed by abolition of the system altogether in 1993.
- The repeal of the Truck Acts 1831–1940, a series of statutes which, albeit in a somewhat complicated, anachronistic and piecemeal manner, offered groups of workers a measure of legal protection against arbitrary deductions from pay and the right to payment in cash.
- The removal of restrictions on working hours and conditions of women. Section 7 of the Sex Discrimination Act 1986 removes all major restrictions on women working shifts and at night, overtime restrictions and maximum hours limitations.
- The quadrupling of the qualification period for workers before they can claim unfair dismissal – from 26 weeks in 1979 to two years in 1985.[4]
- A weakening of maternity rights. In particular, firms employing five or fewer employees have been given complete exclusion from the provision that employees have a right to return to work after maternity leave.

The Effects of 'Deregulation'

The policy of deregulation, though significant, has been subject to certain constraints or countervailing pressures.

The curtailment of statutory rights has not prevented, and may even encourage, resort to alternative remedies provided by the common law. For example, recent developments have seen the courts evidence a greater willingness to grant injunctions in order to halt dismissals which take place in breach of a contractually incorporated disciplinary procedure or to prevent a breach of the employer's other obligations under the contract (see *Irani* v. *Southampton & SW Hampshire HA* [1985] ICR 590; *Powell* v. *LB Brent* [1987] IRLR 466; *Hughes* v. *LB Southwark* [1988] IRLR 55, discussed in chapter 13 below). Other cases have seen courts upholding claims for breach of contract against employers based on terms incorporated into the contract of employment from a collective agreement (see *Rigby* v. *Ferodo Ltd* [1987] IRLR 516, discussed in chapter 5).

Furthermore, Conservative governments of the 1980s have been forced, mainly on account of pressures from Europe, to introduce new measures such as the Transfer of Undertakings Regulations, Equal Pay Regulations, the Data Protection Act and the Sex Discrimination Act 1986. EC membership means that UK law is subordinate to the provisions of the Treaty of Rome, the Single European Act and the regulations and directives made under the treaty.

The potency of European regulation can be seen from the landmark case of *Barber* v. *Guardian Royal Exchange Assurance Group* (1990). In what was – for UK employers – probably the most important judgement ever to come from the European Court of Justice (ECJ), the court held that occupational pensions payable under a contracted-out scheme constitute 'pay' under article 119 of the Treaty of Rome, and so must be non-discriminatory in their terms. This means that pensionable ages must be the same for men and women, and benefits payable must be equal. Where a scheme allows a woman to take a pension at the age of 60, a man will have the right to insist on the same option, on the same terms.

As article 119 is directly enforceable in the UK, employers have had to act immediately in order to avoid exposure to industrial tribunal claims. UK discrimination legislation, which allowed discrimination in pension entitlements and benefits, is overridden as a result of the decision in *Barber*.

The relationship between UK and EC law is discussed in greater detail in chapter 10 below.

In a number of areas the government has been under intense pressure to legislate to protect workers' rights where, in the deregulatory environment which has been created, major abuses have occurred. In the pensions field, for example, Robert Maxwell's theft of his employees' pension scheme funds, and the widespread use by employers of such funds for their own purposes, led to an urgent consideration of the pensions system by the House of Commons Select Committee on Social Security and to demands for stricter regulatory legislation.[5]

There is, too, the paradox that the enthusiasm to roll back the frontiers of the state has shifted the burden from the state to the employer. Two examples of this 'reverse deregulation' are the legislation on statutory sick pay and statutory maternity pay, areas of complex interaction between social security and employment protection.

Perhaps deregulation has been most effective in relation to cutting back state support for collective bargaining. The statutory trade union recognition procedure (ss. 11–16 EPA 1975), the limited right to arbitration where it was claimed that the employer was not observing the 'recognised' terms and conditions for the industry (sched. 11), and the Fair Wages Resolution have all disappeared since 1979. New measures in legislation in the Trade Union and Employment Rights Act 1993 is likely to include the removal of the statutory role of ACAS to encourage the development of collective bargaining. A new right for individuals to join the union of their choice will further undermine the collective bargaining system, and destabilise recognition arrangements. Also moves by the EC to finalise draft directives on company law and on information and consultation procedures (the Vredling Directive) were strongly opposed, and this has left the process of introducing EC legislation on rights of participation temporarily in limbo.

So if the underlying trend is still for legislative and common law intervention, despite deregulation, what impact has the law made?

The Impact of the Law

During the 1980s, the law became a major tactical weapon in industrial disputes. Employers and, on occasion, disaffected union members demonstrated a willingness to take or threaten court action. Employers increasingly sought court orders to restrain strikes called without a secret ballot (the most frequent cause of action), but also to prevent secondary action and unlawful picketing. In the face of this legal onslaught, and the removal of their 'blanket immunity' after 1982, unions were forced to centralise authority so as to attempt to avoid liability.[6] Finally, the decisive use of legal tactics in disputes which became media causes célèbres – the *Stockport Messenger*, Austin Rover, News International, the seafarers' dispute and, above all, the miners' strike – provided the clearest demonstration of the law's potency. In the light of these experiences, unions have generally complied with court orders[7] and the TUC has refused to spearhead any campaign of active opposition to the legislation.

While the extensive use of law in industrial disputes is a fairly recent phenomenon, the impact of the employment protection law has been felt since the introduction of the right not to be unfairly dismissed in the early 1970s. Unfair dismissal has been the basis for most industrial tribunal (IT) applications, and it has encouraged significant changes in industrial relations practices. The evidence of surveys and case studies indicates that the dismissal provisions have generally stimulated the spread and formalisation of grievance and disciplinary procedures, enhanced the role and status of personnel managers and employers' associations and encouraged employers, especially larger ones, in adopting more efficient recruitment and discipline practices. One impact claimed for the legislation is, however, rather difficult to substantiate: the negative employment effect of the legislation. This view has provided for a number of changes which have been. wrought to the law since 1979: it has 'neutralised' the burden of proof; introduced the pre-hearing assessment in an attempt to discourage the continuance of claims which are unlikely to succeed; and it has, of course, increased the qualification. period necessary to claim. However, surveys of management attitudes and responses suggest that the legislation has only had a minor impact in discouraging recruitment. It has induced, however, a greater care in selection in order to ensure the right quality of recruits rather than reducing quantity.[8] Later research found that only 8 per cent of firms surveyed expressed reluctance to recruit additional staff on account of the law of unfair dismissal.[9] The most recent survey does no more than confirm the previous findings.[10]

Other areas of law have also had a major impact on both personnel management and collective negotiations. The redundancy laws have facilitated redundancies by encouraging – in consultation with unions – cash payment for jobs. Union demands have usually been confined to the level of payment and a preference for voluntary redundancy. The gender and race discrimination laws have led to the adoption in some places of formal equality policies, though the real impact of the Equal Value Regulations on pay structures is still an open question. It has taken three House of Lords' decisions to restore such potency as the regulations had when promulgated.

The law has also established important health and safety requirements, and extended the development of joint safety committees and safety training. Health, safety and the work environment are a crucial aspect of workplace rights. In this area, the policy of deregulation has clearly failed and, at the instigation of the EC, major changes will be introduced from 1993. A central theme will be the general requirement to design work to accommodate the worker's safety and welfare requirements and for work operations to be 'assessed'. This policy is being progressively introduced through a series of important measures and will eventually cover many potentially hazardous workplace activities ranging from manual lifting operations to the use of visual display units. Among other things, EC law will give workers a right to stop work in hazardous situations. The law is also increasingly recognising employees' rights in relation to the environment, and it is likely that the EC will shortly require union involvement in environment 'audits' and in introducing environmental measures.[11] These, and other important changes, are examined in more extensive detail in chapter 16 of this work.

The impact of these laws measured purely in terms of the effectiveness of the statutory rights in protecting individual claimants has been relatively minimal; in unfair dismissal, for example, the success rate is low (around one-third of all cases which reach tribunal), as is the level of compensation (a median award of £1,773 in 1990/1), and the tribunals, which have generally adopted managerial perspectives on efficiency and reasonableness, are reluctant to order reinstatement (it occurs in only 3 per cent of cases where a remedy is awarded).[12]

Similarly, the law has manifestly not eliminated equal pay or discrimination on grounds of sex or race or union activity. The effect has been rather on management policies and procedures and collective bargaining. Overall, as Hepple observed in 1983, there has been an 'underlying trend towards the jurid-ification of industrial disputes … Matters which were once entirely within the sphere of managerial prerogatives or left to collective bargaining, are now directly regulated by positive legal rights and duties.'[13]

Future Trends

Current Conservative policies, and stated policies for the future, adhere to the deregulation concept. The Employment Act 1989 contained provisions many of which were originally mooted in the 1986 White Paper 'Building Businesses … Not Barriers.'[14] For example:

- With the twin objectives of deregulating the labour market and complying with the EC Equal Treatment Directive (76/207), the Act removes most of the restrictions on the types of work which women and young people under the age of 18 can do. For example, women are no longer prohibited from working underground in mines or cleaning factory machinery.
- Written particulars of disciplinary rules. The Act exempts employers of less than 20 employees from the requirement to include a note specifying any disciplinary rules which are applicable to the employee, a person to whom the employee can apply if dissatisfied with a disciplinary decision, and the manner in which such an application should be made.
- The Act empowers the secretary of state to make regulations authorising the holding of a 'pre-hearing review' in industrial tribunal proceedings, and enabling whoever conducts the review to require either party to pay a deposit of up to £150 'if he wishes to continue to participate in the proceedings'. The government's consultation paper on tribunal procedure envisaged that a party might be required to pay a deposit if their case appears to have 'no reasonable prospect of success' or it seems 'frivolous, vexatious or otherwise unreasonable'. The way in which the amount of the deposit is to be determined, the consequences of not paying it and the circumstances in which the deposit will be refunded or paid over to the other party will be covered in forthcoming regulations.

Further, in the White Paper 'Employment for the 1990s',[15] the total abolition of the already emasculated wages councils was proposed because the government considered that the system may still be inhibiting 'the business developments on which job creation depends.'

But while deregulation continues in the individual employment sphere, the extensive regulation of collective labour law continues. The Employment Law

Act 1988 introduced tighter requirements relating to ballots for industrial action and union executive elections, made the post-entry closed shop impossible to enforce lawfully and prevented unions disciplining those of its members who did not comply with a call to take industrial action.

The Employment Act 1990 reflects the proposals set out in two 1989 Green Papers: 'Removing Barriers to Employment' and 'Unofficial Action and the Law'. Commenting on the new legislation, the then secretary of state for employment, Norman Fowler, stated:

> This [Act] will strengthen the rights of people at work and help to protect the community as a whole against irresponsible industrial action. It tackles three long-standing problems: the closed shop, secondary action and unofficial strikes ... As we move into the 1990s it is essential that industrial relations law is kept up to date and that it continues to provide essential rights for people at work and effective protection against the abuse of industrial power. That has been the consistent purpose of our legislation since 1979 and it is the theme of this new Bill.

The government's continued commitment to the individualisation of employment relations was then clearly emphasised in the 1991 Green Paper 'Industrial Relations in the 1990s', and in the 1992 White Paper 'People, Jobs and Opportunities',[16] where it pledged itself to ensure that 'the aspirations of individual employees to deal directly with their employer, rather than through the medium of trade union representation or collective bargaining', are supported. In the event, the ensuing Trade Union Reform and Employment Rights Act 1993 contains an array of regulatory measures directed at unions' internal management; the supervision of union elections; recruitment and membership; industrial action ballots, and new rights for employers and other interested parties affected by proposed action.

Deregulation versus 'Social Europe'

There is a clear and inevitable conflict between the UK government's policies of deregulation and the interventionist stance adopted by the European Commission in its Charter of Fundamental Social Rights.[17] The charter, which represents a blueprint for the future of European workplace policy, proposes a number of social and employment rights for EC citizens. These are dealt with in more detail later in this book, but it is worth identifying the main principles here:

- The right to freedom of movement throughout the Community, including the right to engage in any occupation or profession on the same terms as those applied to nationals of the host country. This will require harmonisation of the recognition of qualifications and occupational skills across the member states.

- The right to fair remuneration for both full- and part-time workers. The charter requires that 'a decent wage' be established either by law or by collective agreement, and the legal regulation of the withholding or seizure of wages.
- The improvement in the living and working condition of workers in the EC. This includes: the organisation and flexibility of working time, particularly by establishing a maximum duration of working time; regulation of fixed-term, seasonal, part-time and casual work; and of other forms of working such as weekend working, night work, shift work and systematic overtime.
- Every worker residing in the EC shall have the right to annual paid leave and to a weekly rest period.
- Every worker to have the right to have his/her conditions of employment stipulated in a contract of employment save where such conditions are governed by law or collective agreement.
- The right to belong to a professional organisation or trade union, the freedom to negotiate and conclude collective agreements, and the right to take industrial action. However, the charter also states that the establishment and use of procedures to settle collective disputes by conciliation, mediation and arbitration should be encouraged.
- The right to vocational training and leave for training purposes in order to keep pace with technical developments.
- The right to equal treatment for men and women. The charter proposes that action to implement this principle of equality should be intensified in the areas of pay, access to employment, social protection, education, vocational training and career development. Such action shall imply the development of amenities enabling those concerned to reconcile their occupational and family obligations more easily.
- Information, consultation and participation for workers must be developed along appropriate lines and in such a way as to take account of the laws, collective agreements and practices in force in the member states. In particular, these provisions shall be implemented in due time in the following areas:

> when technological changes which, from the point of view of working conditions and work organisation, have major implications for the workforce are introduced into firms;
> in connection with restructuring operations in firms or in cases of mergers having an impact on the employment of workers;
> in case of procedures of collective redundancies or those regarding bankruptcies.

- Every worker must enjoy satisfactory health and safety conditions in the workplace.
- For young people, the right to equitable remuneration and complementary vocational training during working hours for at least the first two years of their working lives. The charter proposes a minimum employment age of 16.
- The right to adequate social protection, including an income sufficient to sustain a decent standard of living in retirement.
- Measures should be taken to ensure the fullest possible integration of people with disabilities into working life by improving the accessibility of workplaces, transport and housing.

The first five draft directives to implement the Social Charter were adopted by the European Commission in late 1990. Dealing with working time, pregnant employees and various aspects of part-time and temporary work, the directives will require significant amendments to UK law if implemented.

The Implementation of the Charter

The Commission's hope was that the charter would be unanimously adopted by the Council of Ministers. It would then form the basis of an action programme which would be binding on member states if adopted.

The United Kingdom government strongly opposed the charter and continues to resist much of the detailed legislation designed to implement it, on the ground that it will lead to excessive regulation and will impede rather than foster the creation of jobs. Indeed, Mrs Thatcher described the charter as 'inspired by the values of Karl Marx and the class struggle.' It was, therefore, unsurprising when at the meeting of the European Council in Strasbourg in December 1989 the UK was the only dissenting voice among the 12 on the question of the adoption of the charter.

However, since the coming into force of the Single European Act in July 1987, certain Community legislation can be adopted by qualified majority voting (QMV) rather than requiring the agreement of all member states. This includes measures which relate to the establishment or functioning of the internal market but, significantly, specifically excludes provisions 'relating to the rights and interests of employed persons' (article 100A of the Treaty of Rome). On the other hand, provisions on 'improvements, especially in the working environment, as regards the health and safety of workers' are covered by QMV (article 118A). Under the QMV procedure, Council members' votes are weighted according to the size of their state's population. The UK, for example, has 10 votes, whereas Luxembourg has only two. A total of 76 votes can be cast, and 54 constitute the qualified majority.

Given the UK government's opposition to the charter, it is unlikely to result in EC legislation unless its content can fit within the scope of the qualified voting majority procedure. Since the scope of that procedure is far from clear, it may require a ruling from the European Court of Justice to establish which provisions of the charter can be implemented with only majority support and which cannot progress without unanimity. Indeed, on several occasions, the UK government has threatened to seek such a ruling.

At the Maastricht summit in December 1991, the UK strongly resisted the expansion of EC legislative activity in the area of social policy. The Treaty on European Union which resulted from the negotiations was signed by the heads of all 12 member states at Maastricht on 7 February 1992. However, the accompanying protocol and agreement which extends the scope of the qualified voting procedure into new areas of social policy will cover only 11 states – the UK being in a minority of one. The basis of the protocol is that all member states apart from the UK 'wish to continue along the path laid down in the 1989 Social Charter.'

In the Council of Ministers, qualified majority and unanimous voting will take place as if the twelfth member state never existed. Controversially, both the UK representatives in the European Parliament and the commissioners from the UK will be able to influence the adoption of legislation in the social field, which would not, however, be applicable in the UK.

The UK's situation is further complicated by the fact that the Commission will retain its powers within the framework of the EC of 12 to propose and press for directives in the social field on the basis of the EC Treaty, that is articles 118A, 100A and 100.

Currently on the table is the much discussed proposal for a directive on working time, which the EC will undoubtedly try to pursue under article 118A on the basis that it is a health and safety measure. The UK has argued that in reality it is a health and safety measure which should be adopted under article 100, which requires unanimity. It remains to be seen, however, whether in the years to come the Commission will continue to rely, as far as possible, on the treaty to have its proposals on social legislation adopted and implemented throughout the entire EC. If the Commission follows this approach, and as the adoption of measures under articles 100A and 118A only requires qualified majority voting in the Council, the UK could still, in principle, be overruled and be required to comply with these directives. In any case, it seems clear that if the Commission anticipates that a social measure which it intends to propose under the agreement of the 11 states might be acceptable to the UK, it will invoke the treaty, presumably article 100, to allow the UK to participate.

In Maastricht, the 11 agreed to use qualified majority voting in the following areas:

- improvement of the working environment to protect workers' health and safety;

- working conditions;
- the information and consultation of workers;
- equality between men and women with regard to labour market opportunities and treatment at work;
- the integration of people excluded from the labour market.

But, unanimity of the 11 will still be required to adopt measures such as social security, protection of workers where their employment contracts are terminated, and representation and collective defence of worker and employer interests. Specifically excluded from the scope of the agreement, however, are pay, the right of association, the right to strike and the right to impose lock-outs, which presumably will continue to be dealt with under article 100 of the treaty.

The Effect on the UK

The protocol expressly states that 'acts adopted by the Council and any financial consequences other than administrative costs entailed for the institutions shall not be applicable to the UK.' But, of course, it is open to a future UK government to 'sign up' to the agreement made under the protocol if it wishes to do so. With the defeat of the Labour Party in the general election of 1992, that appears to be a rather remote possibility.

PART TWO

Individual Rights

CHAPTER 2

The Gateways to Employment Rights

Context

The employment protection legislation was drafted principally with full-time, permanent employees – so-called core workers – in mind. The legislation of the mid-1970s which established the 'statutory floor of employment rights' effectively excluded millions of workers from its protections because they were considered to be self-employed, or failed to qualify through lack of continuity of employment. Indeed, it may well be argued that, if the policy behind the legislation was to protect those workers which collective bargaining could not reach, the groups who were excluded – the 'peripheral workers' – were the ones in greatest need of protection.

It is a paradox that at the very moment the contemporary structure of labour law was erected, the labour market started a rapid transformation, both in terms of composition and structure, leaving even more workers engaged, for instance, as part-timers, casuals, homeworkers, or as part of a government training scheme on the margins of employment protection.

Part-time workers constitute the largest group of peripheral workers. Trends in the UK labour market in recent years show a marked increase in part-time work as full-time work has declined. Labour Force surveys show that about 5 million people (25 per cent of all employees) now work less than 30 hours a week, women constituting around 90 per cent of this total and married women accounting for some three-quarters of all part-timers.[1] Most of the growth in the number of part-time jobs and the increase in part-timers as a proportion of the workforce has resulted from changes in the structure of the labour market. Manufacturing, traditionally employing few part-timers, has declined, while the services sector, which has always engaged a relatively large number, has grown.[2]

While the increase in part-time working since the 1960s may be explained by appreciation by employers of the benefits in terms of lower overheads, increased productivity and greater flexibility engendered by the use of part-time labour, there are serious disadvantages from the worker's point of view, not least the low rate of pay relative to full-time employment.[3] A House of Lords committee which examined the problems of part-time workers made this comment on the part-time worker's vulnerability:

Part-time employees, while contributing significantly to the development of the economy and to the flexibility of the productive system, are as a group still behind their full-time colleagues in regard to wage rates, access to training and the promotion and the provision of other benefits. This is both economically self-defeating and socially unacceptable, not least when it reinforces other types of discrimination such as that between male and female employees.[4]

As will be seen, this economic vulnerability is compounded by the status and working hours requirements of our employment protection law, with the result that a significant number of part-timers will be excluded from rights to redundancy pay, minimum notice periods, statutory guarantee payments, maternity leave, maternity pay or protection against unfair dismissal.[5]

As the use of part-timers increased in the 1980s, this was also paralleled by a marked, though less spectacular, growth in the use of the temporary and casual worker. Research by the Institute of Manpower Studies[6] suggests that three-quarters of employers in most industrial sectors hire temporary workers; the research sample indicates that 7.6 per cent fell within this category. It was found that the proportion had grown since 1980 and was on a rising trend. It appears that newer rationales for the engagement of temporary workers (associated with 'flexible manning' policies) are increasingly seen by employers to be important, though traditional rationales (holiday, sickness and absence cover, etc.) still predominate.

As with part-time work, the vast majority of 'temps' are women (two-thirds) and are concentrated in personal services, semi- and unskilled manual occupations. However, the survey does suggest that a small but growing proportion of temporary workers is to be found in managerial, technical and professional work.

In legal terms, temporary workers are at least as, and perhaps more, vulnerable than their part-time counterparts. Once again, problems of employment status and continuity present themselves, while those engaged on fixed-term contracts may lawfully be required to sign away redundancy and unfair dismissal rights should the employer not renew the contract.[7]

Employee Status

The distinction between contracts of employment and self-employment is of fundamental importance, because only 'employees' qualify for employment protection rights such as unfair dismissal, redundancy payments and minimum notice on termination. Wider protection is provided under the Health and Safety at Work Act 1974 and under the discrimination and equal pay legislation which applies to those both under a contract of service and a contract 'personally to execute any work or labour', so including the self-employed.

Given the fundamental importance of the distinction, it is unfortunate that the formulation of the test of employee status has come from the courts and tribunals rather than from statute. The only guidance on the question in the legislation is so completely circular as to be absolutely useless.[8]

The case law on this subject is confusing and contradictory. Historically, the leading approach was to apply the test of 'control', that is, could the employer control how, when and where the worker was to work – if so, that worker was an employee. However, as nowadays many employees possess skills not held by their employers, control as the sole determinant of status was rejected. Along the way the test of 'integration' was floated, that is, whether the worker was fully integrated into the employing organisation, but the test was never widely adopted. The modern approach has been to abandon the search for a single test and adopt a multifactorial test, weighing up all the factors for and against the existence of a contract of employment to determine whether the worker was 'in business on his own account'.[9]

Factors which are influential include:

- The method of payment (payment on a commission basis is indicative of self-employment).
- The degree of control exercised over the worker. For example, the worker may be subject to a disciplinary code laid down by the employer.
- If the worker supplies his/her own tools and equipment, this may point to self-employment.
- Can the worker hire his/her own helpers and who bears the risk of loss and chance of profit?
- The payment of sickness and holiday pay indicates the existence of a contract of employment.

Recent case law involving the question of the status of temporary and casual workers has seen an emphasis placed on the concept of mutuality of obligation as a possible factor in the equation. In other words, there must be reciprocal obligations on the employer to provide work for the employee and on the employee to accept that work.

The implications of this test for workers with irregular working patterns are highly disadvantageous – at least if it is applied in a strict sense. The dangers are highlighted in the case of *O'Kelly* v. *Trusthouse Forte plc* [1983] IRLR 369. In this case, the Court of Appeal was not prepared to find that 'regular' casual waiters were employees, even though they had a well-established and regular working relationship with Trusthouse Forte. It was held to be quite 'unreal' to maintain that the long-standing arrangement, which involved a reliance by the employer on its regular casuals, and the regulars receiving priority in the allocation of work, involved the essential 'mutuality of obligation' to classify these casuals as employees. Mutuality was lacking because technically they could refuse work when it was offered, even though in practice they did not do so because refusal would result in removal from the regular casual list.

This sort of narrow reasoning is also to be found in the judgement of the Employment Appeal tribunal (EAT) in *Wickens* v. *Champion Employment* [1984] ICR 365, where temps engaged by a private employment agency were not accorded employment status because of the lack of binding obligation on the part of the agency to make bookings for work and the absence of any obligation by the worker to accept them.

A more liberal approach is to be found in the majority judgements of the Court of Appeal in *Nethermere (St Neots) Ltd* v. *Gardiner and Taverna* [1984] IRLR 240. Here, homeworkers making clothing on a piecework basis were accorded employee status on the basis that the regular giving and taking of work over a period of time evidenced the necessary mutuality of obligation. This was so even though the workers were under no obligation to undertake a particular quantity of work and in certain weeks did no work at all. As Lord Justice Stephenson put it:

> I cannot see why well-founded expectations of continuing homework should not be hardened or refined into enforceable contracts by regular giving and taking of work over periods of a year or more, and why outworkers should not thereby become employees under contracts of service.

The confusions which abound in this area are multiplied because of the view that the question of employment status is one of mixed fact and law rather than a pure question of law (see *O'Kelly* v. *THF* above). As a result, the powers of the EAT and Court of Appeal to interfere with decisions of industrial tribunals on status are much reduced and the chances of inconsistency thereby heightened. Those who regretted the adoption of this view, welcomed the House of Lords decision in *Davies* v. *Presbyterian Church of Wales* [1986] IRLR 194, where it appeared that Lord Templeman unequivocally held that whether the claimant was an employee was a pure question of law. That case, in which *O'Kelly* was not referred to, turned entirely upon the construction of a document, whereas *O'Kelly* had to be decided partly on the interpretation of various written documents and partly on inferences to be drawn from the parties' conduct. This difference was seized upon by the Court of Appeal in *Hellyer Bothers Ltd* v. *McLeod* [1987] IRLR 232 in order to distinguish Davies and to continue to apply the *O'Kelly* approach: viz. an appellate court is entitled to interfere with the decision of an industrial tribunal on whether the applicant was employed under a contract of employment only if the tribunal had misdirected itself in law or its decision was one which no tribunal properly instructed could have reached.

More recently, the Privy Council in *Lee* v. *Chung* [1990] IRLR 236 adopted a similar approach to that taken in *McLeod*, holding that, in the ordinary case, whether or not a person is employed under a contract of employment is not a question of law but a question of fact to be determined by the industrial tribunal. *Davies* v. *Presbyterian Church of Wales* was described as an exceptional case where the relationship was dependent solely on the construction of a written document.

After a period of uncertainty, where it was not clear whether the courts would allow the stated intentions of the parties to determine the matter of status, it now appears that the subjective intention of the parties will not override what in other respects has the attributes of a contract of employment.

In *Young and Woods Ltd* v. *West* [1980] IRLR 201, West, a sheetworker, requested that he be treated as self-employed. This was accepted by his employer and, although there was no difference between his working conditions and the 'employees' he worked alongside, doing the same job and under the same level of supervision, he was paid gross of tax. When West's job was terminated, he claimed that he was an employee after all and therefore entitled to claim unfair dismissal. The Court of Appeal held that, despite West's arrangement with his employer, he was really an employee and that the IT had jurisdiction to hear his complaint.

Continuity of Employment

Many workers will be excluded from employment law protections because of the general rule that to count towards a period of continuous employment the employee must work, or normally be required to work, 16 hours a week or more. For those who cannot meet this criterion, they will only cross this threshold of employment law rights after five years' continuous employment at eight hours or more per week.

The provisions relating to continuity are very complex but we outline the principles below.

Continuity: Change of Employer (EPCA sched. 13, paras 17, 18)

Normally only employment with the present employer counts. But there are six circumstances set out in paragraphs 17 and 18 in which a change of employer does not break continuity. These include a transfer which occurs on the death of an employer, a change in the constitution of a partnership which acts as an employer and where an Act of Parliament causes one corporate body to replace another as employer. The two most important situations provided for by sched. 13, however, are given here.

The first is if a trade, business or undertaking is transferred, the period of employment at the time of transfer counts as a period of employment with the transferee. In other words, the transfer does not break continuity (para. 17[2]).

In order for this provision to operate, the business must be transferred as a going concern; a mere sale of the physical assets of the business is insufficient. An example of this distinction is provided by *Woodhouse* v. *Peter Brotherhood Ltd* [1972] ICR 186. In this case the nature of the business changed after the transfer from the manufacture of diesel engines to the manufacture of compressors and steam turbines. The Court of Appeal held that in this situation there was only a transfer of physical assets and not a transfer of a business.

In the important case of *Melon* v. *Hector Powe Ltd* [1980] IRLR 477, Lord Frazer thought that essential distinction between the transfer of a business or part of business and the mere sale of assets was 'that in the former case the business is transferred as a going concern so that the business remains the same business in different hands ... whereas in the latter case the assets are transferred to the new owner to be used in whatever business he chooses. Individual employees may continue to do the same work in the same environment and they may not appreciate that they are working in a different business, but that may be the true position on consideration of the whole circumstances.'

What counts as the essence of the business? In many cases a decisive factor will be the transfer of the 'goodwill', that is, the acquisition of the right to trade with the transferor's former customers. Machines, and other property, do not possess this essential quality. It is also likely that if the product changes after transfer then the 'business' has not been transferred.

In *Crompton* v. *Truly Fair (International) Ltd* [1975] ICR 359, for example, it was held that there was only a change of ownership of the physical assets where a factory, together with its machinery, was sold and was used for the manufacture of men's trousers, whereas the premises had originally been used for the manufacture of children's clothes.

Until recently, this provision was thought only to preserve continuity where the employee is employed in the business 'at the time of the transfer'. Consequently, a gap between the employee's employment with the transferor and employment with the transferee would break continuity. In *Macer* v. *Abafast* [1990] IRLR 137, the EAT adopted an alternative purposive interpretation of the provision and held that periods of employment accrued with the old employer at the time of the transfer could be added to the period of employment with the new employer and that any gap in employment 'which is related to the machinery of transfer' should not break continuity.

In *Macer*, it was admitted that the new owners had deliberately attempted to break the applicant's continuity by creating a gap of more than one week before the transfer transactions commenced. The EAT decided that continuity was preserved and that he was entitled to maintain his claim for unfair dismissal.

In approaching the construction of the provision, the EAT felt that

> the Court should lean in favour of that interpretation which best gives effect to the preservation of continuity of service and hence to the rights of the employee, and to obviate and discourage a tactical manoeuvre which seeks to avoid the clear intention of Parliament.

The second key circumstance providing continuity of employment is that if the employee is taken into the employment of an 'associated employer', the period of employment with the old employer counts as a period of employment with the 'associated employer' (para. 18).

The definition of this concept is to be found in s. 153(4) EPCA, which states that '... any two employers are to be treated as associated if one is a company of which the other (directly or indirectly) has control, or if both are companies of which a third person (directly or indirectly) has control.'

Two major issues arise from this definition. First, 'control' means voting control rather than de facto control. In *Secretary of State for Employment* v. *Newbold* [1981] IRLR 305, Mr Justice Bristow stated: 'In the law affecting companies, control is well recognised to mean control by the majority of votes attaching to the shares exercised in General Meeting. It is not how or by whom the enterprise is actually run.'

Second, the definition has been held to be exhaustive, so that only companies can be associated – local authorities or health authorities fall outside the definition (see *Gardiner* v. *LB Merton* [1980] IRLR 472).

In *Hancill* v. *Marcon Engineering Ltd* [1990] IRLR 51 it was held that the word 'company' in s. 153(4) can include an overseas company if the overseas company can be likened in its essentials to a company limited under the Companies Act. Thus, Mr Hancill was able to count his period of employment with an American subsidiary in order to meet the qualifying period of service for claiming unfair dismissal.

The Transfer of Undertakings (Protection of Employment) Regulations 1981

These complex regulations overlay additional rules which apply where there is a change of employer. They provide for the automatic transfer of contracts of employment, collective agreements and trade union recognition in the case of certain transfers of commercial ventures, impose a duty on employers to inform and consult recognised trade unions and hold any dismissal in connection with such transfers automatically unfair unless it occurs for an 'economic, technical or organisational' reason. This latter aspect of the regulations will be discussed in greater detail in chapter 15 below.

None of the provisions of the regulations operates unless there is a 'relevant transfer' under reg. 3(1), that is, 'a transfer from one person to another of an undertaking situated immediately before the transfer in the UK or a part of one so situated'. An undertaking is defined by reg. 2(1) to include ' any trade or business but does not include any undertaking or part of an undertaking which is not in the nature of a commercial venture'. Under the Trade Union Reform and Employment Rights Act 1993 (TURERA) the definition is extended to cover non-commercial undertakings. This is designed to bring UK legislation into line with EC law.[10] The implications of this change for those workers involved in contracting out of services and compulsory competitive tendering are discussed in chapter 15 below. It would appear that, as under para. 17 (2) of sched. 13, a mere transfer of assets which falls short of a transfer of the undertaking as a going concern will fall outside the regulations.

The Effect of a Transfer on the Contract of Employment
The important change wrought by the regulations is to override the position at common law and provide that a transfer does not terminate the contracts of the employees of the business. Instead, contracts continue with the substitution of the transferee as employer and the transferee taking all the transferor's 'rights, powers, duties and liabilities under or in connection with any such contract' – reg. 5 (1) and (2).

By virtue of reg. 5 (3), however, this transfer of liability will only occur where the employee was employed in the undertaking 'immediately before the transfer'.

Different divisions of the EAT reached different conclusions on the precise interpretation of the phrase 'immediately before the transfer'. This conflict of authority was apparently resolved by the decision of the Court of Appeal in *Secretary of State for Employment* v. *Spence* [1986] IRLR 248 that only when employees are employed at the very moment of a business transfer does the purchaser take over the vendor's liabilities under or in connection with the existing employment contracts. In other words, a business purchaser could not be made liable for dismissals carried out by the vendor before the transfer.

The scope of this decision is now heavily constrained by the judgement of the House of Lords in *Litster* v. *Forth Dry Dock & Engineering Co Ltd* [1989] IRLR 161. The House of Lords helds that liability for a dismissal by the vendor prior to the transfer passes to the purchaser if the employee has been unfairly dismissed for a reason connected with the transfer.

Although reg. 5 (3) provides that liability is to be transferred only where the employee is 'employed immediately before the transfer', in order for the regulations to give effect to the EC Employee Rights on Transfer of Business Directive 77/187 as interpreted by the ECJ, reg. 5 (3) must be read as if there were inserted the words 'or would have been so employed if he had not been unfairly dismissed in the circumstances described in reg. 8 (1)'.

Without such a purposive interpretation, the regulations would, according to Lord Keith, 'be capable of ready evasion through the transferee arranging with the transferor for the latter to dismiss its employees a short time before the transfer becomes operative', thereby leaving the employees, as in this case, with 'worthless claims for unfair dismissal' against an insolvent vendor (see also *P Bork International A/S* v. *Forgeningen af Arbejdsledere i Danmark* [1989] IRLR 41).

The approach advocated by the House of Lords is in two stages. First, it must be determined whether the dismissal by the vendor was unfair within the meaning of reg. 8. If yes, then unfair dismissal liability under reg. 5 passes to the purchaser, even if the dismissal was not, in temporal terms, immediately before the transfer. Second, it is only where the dismissal does not breach reg. 8 that the construction of 'employed immediately before the transfer' laid down in *Spence* continues to apply. So, if the reason for the dismissal is unconnected with the transfer, liability passes to the transferee only if the employee had not been dismissed before the moment of transfer.

Continuity: Periods away from Work

An employee's service may be continuous in a statutory sense even where the employee has been away from work for certain periods.

First, para. 4 of sched. 13 makes it clear that each week during which there is in existence a contract of employment that would normally involve employment for 16 hours or more per week counts as a week of continuous employment. This is so whether the employee is actually at work or not. It follows that periods of absence from work by reason of sickness or pregnancy will count as periods of continuous employment without reliance on any other provision so long as the contract of employment has not been terminated.

Second, even where an employee is away from work and no longer has a contract, service may still be deemed to be continuous in certain situations should the employee eventually return to work. These situations are set out in paras 9 and 10:

(i)   Absence through sickness or injury, provided the absence does not exceed 26 weeks.

(ii) Up to 26 weeks absence wholly or partly because of pregnancy or confinement (for example, where a woman with less than two years service with her employer has been dismissed while absent because of pregnancy and is later re-employed by that employer.

(iii) The whole of statutory permitted absence for leave on the grounds of pregnancy or confinement.

(iv) Absence through a 'temporary cessation of work'. This phrase has caused some difficulty; two decisions by the House of Lords and one of the Court of Appeal have provided guidance on its interpretation. The first authority is *Fitzgerald* v. *Hall Russell Ltd* [1970] AC 984, where it was held that the phrase refers to the cessation of the individual employee's work for some reason: there is no need to show that 'at the same time the whole works would close down or a department was closed down or a large number of other employees were laid off at the same time' (Lord Upjohn).

This decision also states that in order to determine whether the absence is temporary it should be viewed in the context of the employment relationship as a whole. With the benefit of hindsight, we should be able to determine whether the absence was of a transient nature.

The second important House of Lords authority is *Ford* v. *Warwickshire County Council* [1983] IRLR 126. The applicant in that case was a teacher who had been employed by the county council under a series of consecutive short-term contracts, each for an academic year, for a total of eight years. There was, therefore, a break between the end of one contract and the beginning of the next. The House of Lords held that para. 9 (1) (b) could apply in order to preserve the continuity of her employment. In the course of his judgement, Lord Diplock offered the following guidance:

> The continuity of employment for the purpose of the Act is not broken unless and until looking backwards from the date of the expiry of the fixed-term contract on which the employee's claim is based, there is to be found between one fixed-term contract and its immediate predecessor an interval that cannot be characterised as short relative to the combined duration of the two fixed-term contracts.

This approach is undoubtedly of benefit to many workers, such as part-time or temporary teachers, and makes it much more difficult for employers to avoid the employment protection laws by offering a succession of fixed-term contracts. However, it may not be appropriate where patterns of employment are not regular, as they were in Ford's case, but are subject to fluctuation. To look only at a particular period of unemployment and to compare that period with the combination of the periods either side could lead to some unjust results.

This issue arose before the Court of Appeal in *Flack* v. *Kodak Ltd* [1986] IRLR 258. In this case, Mrs Flack had been employed by Kodak in its photo-finishing department over a number of years for periods which fluctuated markedly. Following her final dismissal, she and the other 'seasonal employees' claimed redundancy payments. An industrial tribunal, purporting to follow what Lord Diplock had said in Ford with regard to temporary cessation, rejected their claim. In coming to this conclusion, the IT confined itself to a purely mathematical comparison of the gap in employment falling within the two years preceding the final dismissal with the period of employment immediately before and after that gap. Both the EAT and Court of Appeal thought that this was the wrong approach in the context of this particular case. They were of the view that the correct approach was to take into account all the relevant circumstances, and in particular to consider the length of the period of employment as a whole. While it was true that the only absences from work on account of temporary cessations of work which were relevant for the purposes of redundancy payments and unfair dismissal claim qualifications were those which occurred during the two years prior to the dismissal, the characterisations of those cessations as temporary may be crucially affected by the whole history of the employment. As Sir John Donaldson put it: 'A long gap in the course of a longer period of work extending over many years might well be considered temporary, whereas if the same gap occurred in the course of a shorter period it would not.'

(v) Absence from work 'in circumstances such that by arrangement or custom' the employee is regarded as continuing in the employment of the employer for all or any purposes.

It would appear that in order to fall within this provision, the arrangement or understanding must be established at the time the absence commences (see, for example, *Murphy* v. *A. Birrell & Sons* [1978] IRLR 458). The absences that might be encompassed could be leave of absence arrangements, employees placed upon a 'reserve list' to be called upon as necessary and employees on secondment. A number of commentators argue that the EAT's broad application of the sub-paragraph in *Lloyds Bank Ltd* v. *Secretary of State for Employment* [1979] IRLR 41 is no longer good law following the judgements of the Lords in *Ford*. In the Lloyds case, the EAT held that where an employee works on a one-week-on and one-week-off basis, the weeks which she does not work count towards continuity by virtue of para. 9 (1) (c). This was despite the fact that the side note to paragraph 9 reads 'Periods in which there is no contract of employment'. In the Lloyds case a contract did exist throughout the period of employment. In the Ford case, the House of Lords placed considerable emphasis on the requirement that there be no subsisting contract before para. 9 could operate. On that basis, the authority of the Lloyds case looks decidedly shaky.

Strikes and Lock-outs

If an employee takes part in a strike or a lock-out, the beginning of the period of employment is treated as postponed by the number of days between the start of the strike or lock-out and the resumption of work (para. 15). In other words, the period of the industrial dispute does not count towards continuity, but it does not break it.

Continuity: Changes in Hours of Work

As we have seen, for a week of employment to count for the purpose of calculating continuous service the employee must either actually work (para. 3), or be employed under a contract of employment normally involving (para. 4) 16 hours per week. Employees who cannot meet this criterion will only cross this particular threshold of employment law rights after five years' continuous employment at eight hours or more per week (para. 6).

Workers whose weekly hours fluctuate above and below the hours threshold are not allowed to 'average' (see *Opie* v. *John Gubbins (Insurance Brokers) Ltd* [1978] IRLR 540) and, in general, if weekly hours fall below the relevant eight or 16 hours per week, continuity will be broken and the worker will be back at square one in attempting to qualify for employment protection (see paras 5 and 7 for the two exceptions to this rule).

An important recent decision in this area is that of the House of Lords in *Lewis* v. *Surrey County Council* [1987] IRLR 509, where the House of Lords held that where an employee is employed under separate but concurrent part-time contracts, she is not entitled to aggregate the number of weekly hours worked under each contract for continuity purposes.

The Case for Reform[11]

In this chapter we have examined the complexities surrounding the two major gateways to employment protection and the particular problems they pose for those whose work is temporary, part-time or casual.

Commentators such as Hepple[12] and Leighton[13] have argued for a radical change of approach by our legislators, maintaining that any reform in this area is likely to be frustrated if statutory rights continue to rest on the nebulous concept of the 'contract of service'. Hepple has proposed that the 'contract of service' should be replaced by a broad definition of the 'employment relationship' between the worker and the undertaking by which s/he is employed. The relationship would continue to be based on a voluntary agreement between the worker and the undertaking to work in return for pay, but 'it would be a contract of a new kind, one that encompassed both the intermittent exchange of work for remuneration and the single continuous contract.'

Hepple accepts that this protection should exclude genuinely independent workers, those 'in business on their own account', but argues that there can be no watertight legal definition of who is 'independent'. He proposes a statutory presumption that the worker is covered by the legislation, with the burden of proof on the employer should it be alleged that the worker is independent.

The EC Draft Directives on Atypical Workers

In 1990 three draft directives on atypical workers were published. One of three – concerned with the health and safety of temporary workers – was adopted on 25 June 1991, and the Health & Safety Commission has now published draft regulations to implement the directive in the UK. The other two draft directives on part-time and temporary work have not been discussed since the Council meeting in November 1990, and further progress appears unlikely given the UK's strong opposition to the measures which are aimed at, inter alia:

• Ensuring that part-time workers are afforded the same entitlements to annual holidays, dismissal allowances and seniority allowances as full-time employees, in proportion to the total hours worked (article 4 of the draft directive with regard to distortions of competition – the article 100A Directive)

- Ensuring that:

    (a) national laws provide for a limit on the renewal of temporary employment relationships of a duration of 12 months or less for a given job so that the total period of employment does not exceed 36 months;

    (b) provision is made for some form of equitable allowance, in the event of an unjustified break in the employment relationship before the term fixed.

It will be seen that the atypical worker directive on distortions to competition would, if implemented, require the UK to make legislative changes to ensure that part-time employees can qualify under its employment protection legislation. In the majority of member states, legal protections apply to full-timers and part-timers on an equal basis.

Given the lack of progress in relation to the implementation of the draft directives, the Equal Opportunities Commission (EOC) sought judicial review of the validity of the statutory thresholds in the UK employment protection legislation governing qualification to claim unfair dismissal and redundancy payments.[14] The EOC argued that, as 90 per cent of employees working fewer than 16 hours per week are women, the statutory provisions are contrary to EC equal pay laws. The argument was founded on the premiss that different treatment of workers depending on the number of hours per week which they work is indirectly discriminatory and not capable of objective justification (for a more detailed discussion of the law in this area see chapter 10 below).

The High Court held that statutory redundancy pay and unfair dismissal compensation fell within the definition of pay under European law, and that the provisions were indirectly discriminatory because of their adverse effect on women. However, it was held that the government was able to justify the provisions on grounds of social policy. The Court accepted the government's argument that to remove or reduce the hours threshold would place additional burdens on employers and lead to fewer job opportunities for those wishing to work less than 16 hours per week. In other words, the court unquestioningly accepted government rhetoric that more liberal employment protection laws would have a negative employment effect. As we saw in the introductory chapter above, there is absolutely no empirical evidence to support this assertion. Indeed, the econometric analysis work of Disney and Szyszczak suggests that, rather than decreasing the demand for part-time employees, an extension of employment protection to those working less than 16 hours per week would not lead to a rise in unemployment among this group of workers.[15] The EOC's appeal against this decision was rejected by a majority of the Court of Appeal, on the grounds that the EOC did not have standing to bring proceedings against the secretary of state and that judicial view was not the appropriate mechanism for determining whether the UK is in breach of Community law. In the court's view what the EOC should do is support test cases in industrial tribunals.

This was sufficient to dispose of the appeal, but two of the Lord Justices expressed diametrically opposed views as to whether the statutory exclusions are objectively justified. Lord Justice Hirst agreed with the divisional court that they were. On the other hand, Lord Justice Dillon, in a powerful dissenting judgement, stated:

> I can see no *evidence* that abolishing the five-year threshold of continuous employment for part-time workers to be able to claim redundancy pay or compensation for unfair dismissal will cause any significant reduction in the availability of part-time employment. On the contrary, recent history in relation to other discriminatory measures underlines that according women the equal status which is justly their due has not led to the dire results which were foretold by the prophets of doom. In addition, I am much impressed by the fact that no other Member State of the European Community has a comparable threshold for workers working not more than 16 hours per week or thereabouts who want to claim such benefits.[16]

CHAPTER 3

Job Applications and Recruitment

Job applicants, candidates for interview and new starters are generally in an extremely weak position at the recruitment and commencement stage. The prevailing philosophy is that employers should have unrestricted discretion in the recruitment process and in offering terms of employment. This is particularly the case in relation to the fixing of pay levels, and it was the fair wage elements in the EC's Social Charter that were a key reason for UK employers' attacks on the charter in 1989 and on the Social Chapter of the Maastricht Treaty in 1992.

As far as selection procedures and appointments are concerned there is no legal right to be interviewed or, if interviewed, appointed to a job you have applied for, even if you are clearly the best candidate in terms of qualifications and experience. At common law employers are entitled to refuse to give employment, or to go on employing someone, even where they have based their decision on mistaken information, or act for malicious or improper reasons.[1] This position has only been marginally changed by legislation, particulary legislation against race and sex discrimination. There are still other important criteria, such as age, used by employers to impose job qualifications which can preclude well-qualified people from employment and promotion opportunities, and which are often patently unfair. In some employment sectors, such as education, it is now not uncommon to be precluded from appointment for being 'over-experienced', for instance if you are a teacher whose experience and position on the salary scale makes it too expensive for a school to appoint you and stay within its budget limits.

General

Restrictions on an employer at the recruitment stage, and rights for job applicants and new starters, operate through one or more possible sources, and these are discussed below.

National and Local Collective Agreements

These are relevant if there are union-agreed minimum pay scales and conditions at the workplace where you would be working. In particular an agreement may specify the rate of pay and terms on which staff appointed to a particular post, with particular experience and so on, should start. If you are appointed on *worse* conditions than that the union will usually want to ensure the agreement is operating correctly. If a letter of appointment or other evidence of the conditions of employment provide for the terms of collective agreements to apply to the employment, then a failure to honour those terms could be a breach of contract (see further chapter 4 below).

Legislation on Recruitment

Equal pay and discrimination and equal opportunities law (see chapters 10–12 below) include rules restricting employers' discriminatory practices. Employers, particularly in the public sector, frequently state that they are 'equal opportunity employers', and have policies on this – but this does not increase their *legal* liabilities.

Wages Council Orders

Pending the repeal of Part II of the Wages Act 1986 by TURERA, s.35, in some industries minimum pay rates may still apply.[2] Where these operate the pay rates in the order will be the correct contractual rate.[3]

Employment Agencies and Business Regulations

If you are going through an employment agency the agency must provide information about the job's pay and conditions, and comply with other standards on fees charged, contents of advertisements, and so on.[4]

Disability Legislation

The rights of workers with disabilities are minimal, and at the recruitment stage they are particularly inadequate. Companies employing more than 20 staff are supposed to ensure at least 3 per cent of their workforce are persons with registered disabilities (Disabled Persons (Employment) Act 1944), and 1980 regulations require companies to include statements in their directors' reports on their employment policies on workers with disabilities. The Wages Act 1986 enables employers to pay wages at below Wages Council order rates without requiring a permit (as was required under the earlier 1979 legislation). Given the vulnerability of these workers and the comparative ease with which they can be 'fairly' dismissed during the induction period for 'under-performance' (or even much later if their illness 'disturbs' the business),[5] protective legislation is long overdue).[6] (see further chapter 12 below).

'Rehabilitation' of Offenders Rules

Under the rules in the Rehabilitation of Offenders Act 1974 previous convictions can become 'spent' after the specified rehabilitation period. For sentences of up to six months imprisonment the period is seven years, and for sentences of between six and 30 months it is 10 years. Fines are subject to a five-year period. Sentences of over 30 months cannot be spent, and certain occupations like nurses and doctors, teachers and social workers are outside the scope of the Act. If you do not come within such an excepted category, a spent conviction need not be declared in job applications and questions on forms enquiring about previous convictions do not have to be answered. Questions about convictions can be answered in the negative. There is no sanction in the Act, though, or specific protection if an employer discriminates against an ex-offender before the employment begins. If you bring a tribunal complaint for unfair dismissal *after* commencement, and you are otherwise eligible to claim, you could succeed if all the employer is relying on is a spent conviction.[7] On the unfair dismissal aspects, see further chapter 14 below.

Workers from Overseas

EC nationals, and since 1 July 1992 non-EC spouses of EC nationals, are not subject to work permit requirements or other restrictions on working or setting up a business in the UK. This also applies to citizens of the European Free Trade Association (EFTA) countries (Sweden, Norway, Iceland, Finland, Austria, Switzerland) after 1 January 1993. Non-EC nationals are subject to work permit and other requirements. Guidance can be obtained from the Department of Employment and job centres, but the main criteria for obtaining a work permit are that you have special skills and experience needed for a job, and that if you are offered a job an EC worker would not be deprived of employment. To be eligible you must come within one of the relevant categories of employee (such as 'key' worker, employment in the national interest, senior executive). Business people and company representatives may also be permitted entry under the immigration rules. Working without a work permit when one is required is extremely risky. Apart from the action that can be taken by the immigration authorities, the employment contract is 'illegal', which means there may be no employment protection, dismissal will be fair, and so on. Conditions can be imposed on work permits and a breach of conditions can lead to the permit being revoked.

Legislation against Discrimination on Union Grounds

It is unlawful to refuse to employ a person on union membership grounds, or for employment agencies to refuse to provide their services on such grounds.

The legislation, the Trade Union and Labour Relations (Consolidation) Act 1992, ss. 137 and 138, is based on proposals in a consultative paper 'Removing Barriers to Employment' (1989). A key policy objective was directed against workplace arrangements where new staff are expected either to join a union, or to pay the equivalent of union dues to charity. The scope of the legislation is wider than that, however, and makes anti-union discrimination unlawful. A refusal to employ is unlawful, in particular, if it is because a person:

- is, or is not, a union member;
- does not agree to become, or to cease to be, a union member;
- is unwilling to accept a requirement to make payments, or suffer pay deductions, for not being in a union.

Another part of the legislation (s. 137 [4]) is directed against 'labour supply' arrangements whereby a union supplies workers to employers from among its members. If a non-member applies and is refused a job where this arrangement operates it may be presumed that the refusal was because s/he was not a member.

'Refusal to employ' occurs, or can be presumed to occur, in a variety of situations, such as refusing to entertain or process an application, including union-related conditions in an advertisement, or attaching unreasonable conditions to a job offer.

Industrial tribunal complaints can be made and compensation paid up to the same limits that apply to unfair dismissal compensation. Unions and 'third parties' can be joined as defendants in a tribunal claim.

Other Legal Requirements

In addition to the legislative points referred to here, there may be other legal requirements affecting employers and new starters. These can derive from contract rules (in particular rules concerning the formation of an employment contract), or from legislative and administrative requirements.

Advertisements and Job Offers

Advertisements are subject to standards as to accuracy and content set by advertising standards bodies and the media themselves, as well as to the criminal law and anti-discrimination legislation. The contents of an advertisement can also cause an employer problems in other ways. Collective agreements may restrict, or impose conditions on, job advertising – for example, by requiring a job to be advertised or filled *internally*, or requiring it to be advertised on the same terms that existing job-holders are employed. The contents of a job advertisement are not, in contract terms, normally regarded as an 'offer' which can thereupon be formally 'accepted'. The advertisement is usually just the start of a 'negotiating' phase. Advertisement terms could, however, become 'contractual' – that is, any specific details on pay, hours and other conditions could be treated as terms of the contract which the employer can be held to. This could be the case where, for example, there is no subsequent letter of appointment modifying what is promised in the advertisement, or the conditions on which you are employed are unclear after you have started.[8] If no written statement of terms is issued, as is required within 13 weeks of commencement (two months under the Trade Union Reform and Employment Rights Act 1993), the contents of the advertisement could be referred to when asking a tribunal to determine what your terms are (see chapter 4 below).

In legal terms an employment contract is not formed until an offer of terms, which must normally include the main terms dealing with the most important aspects of the job such as pay,[9] has been made and that offer has been accepted. Without those key elements of offer and acceptance there is no contract. It is important to confirm acceptance formally by letter. Although tribunals and courts will accept other evidence, such as appearing for work or starting a job, a letter of acceptance avoids complications.

In practical terms there is usually no problem provided a letter of appointment, or statement of terms, is issued confirming the details of what has been agreed. These should make it clear whether the employment is 'permanent' (that is, it will continue indefinitely, subject to termination by notice or other legal reasons), or whether it is for a 'fixed term'.

Validity of Employment Contracts

Employment contracts are subject to the same rules as other contracts, for example they are invalid if misrepresentations are made by one side, or if performance is impossible either because of the fault of a party or because of a factor outside anybody's control. 'Non-performance', or breach as it is better known, is discussed in chapters 4 and 5 below.[10] One problem, which is important because of the effect it can have on a worker's employment, is 'illegality'. This is particularly relevant to workers in occupations where the scope for employers to break the law is increased. Employees often bear the consequences of this in employment terms.

Legislation can have the effect of making an employment contract void or unenforceable, for instance if a job requires a licence and one has not been obtained. Work permits have already been referred to but there are many other examples which render the contract void. The exact consequences of illegality will depend on the particular legislation, and the circumstances in each case.

If a contract is illegal from the start, as for example where it is agreed that wages will be paid in cash or as 'expenses' to avoid tax, employees will normally not be allowed to rely on the contract. In practical terms this means you could not sue to recover any arrears of pay that are due, or to enforce other parts of the contract. If an *employer* sets up a pay system which defrauds the Inland Revenue, but without telling the employees concerned, an employee may still be able to rely on the contract, but only while s/he is unaware of what has been going on. This was decided in an unfair dismissal case where the EAT decided the claim could only be maintained if the applicant did not know that the wages system was being run fraudulently.[11]

'Conditional' Job Offers

A job offer can be made conditional; for example, if you have said in interview that you have a particular qualification the employer might make it a condition of the employment offer that you produce evidence of this before starting. References operate in this way, and reference requirements have now become such a normal practice that it is always wiser to assume that a job offer is always going to be subject to the new employer receiving satisfactory references before allowing you to start. For this reason it is always advisable not to resign from an existing job until it is clear that this last hurdle has been safely jumped. Unfortunately, there is a decision which confirms that it is for the new employer to decide if a reference is satisfactory or not.

Example
Mr Wishart was offered a job as information officer at the National Association of Citizens Advice Bureaux 'subject to the receipt of satisfactory written references'. The reference referred to his absenteeism record, which included 23 days off in the preceding year. The offer was withdrawn. The court decided the offer was conditional and the employer was entitled to decide the condition had not been satisfied.[12]

Existing or previous employers are not legally obliged to provide a reference, unless this has been stipulated in a termination agreement – something which is more common with senior staff or as part of a termination package. If a reference is given by your employer the reference can contain an assessment of your record and performance, and include views about aptitude, suitability, and so on for the job applied for. The employer has a 'qualified privilege' in respect of statements made about you, but this would *not* extend to views which are malicious and false, which could amount to defamation. Unfortunately, though, it would appear that you cannot sue the employer in negligence in the preparation of a reference. In the leading case on this the judge described the reference as being so bad as amounting to the 'kiss of death' to the applicant's career in insurance. He held that points in the reference suggesting, or implying, that the applicant was dishonest had been negligently included. The Court of

Appeal, however, held that employers do *not* owe a duty of care based on negligence, and the case failed.[13]

As far as the prospective employer's *use* of references is concerned there is no legal protection available if the information relied on is unfair or inaccurate. This raises the issue of employers' use of organisations which hold 'black-lists' of people on the jobs market, and whether such use should be banned, or at least made subject to accuracy requirements. A further problem that is developing is the increasing insistence of new employers on access to medical records to verify statements in applications about absenteeism and health. As it is now possible to get access to doctors' records (Access to Medical Reports Act 1988), employers may try to require you to obtain access to your records and allow them to read them for their vetting purposes. You have a right to see records, and to query their contents before the employer sees them.

As well as general legal requirements that apply to the keeping of personnel data (that could be used for reference and other purposes), for example in the Data Protection Act 1984, employers are also subject to confidentiality restrictions. This means that data provided to an employer, for instance on application forms marked 'confidential', or obtained in other ways during the employment, should not be divulged to third parties unless this is authorised by the worker concerned, or by law.[14]

Withdrawal of Job Offers

As soon as there has been acceptance a contract comes into operation. If the employer does not allow you to start work (or if you do not begin) there is technically a breach of contract, and an action for damages is normally possible. In practice it is not usually worth an employer's while suing in such cases because the amount of damages that can be recovered is limited, and the damage suffered is not likely to be serious in most cases.

On the other hand the withdrawal of a job offer can be extremely serious for an employee, especially if you have given up another job on the strength of the employer's promise. In such cases the exact amount of damages obtainable (or compensation that can be demanded in settlement of legal proceedings) will depend on the particular circumstances. It may be very limited, and amount to no more than the equivalent pay for the notice period required to terminate the contract. If a specific period of employment was envisaged when the contract was made, it could be the equivalent of what would have been payable under the contract. This is particularly relevant to fixed-term contracts.

In a leading case a company offered jobs and higher pay to staff working for another company. They were told the jobs would last for six months. After they accepted and left their jobs the offers were withdrawn. It was held that compensation should be awarded and this should be based on the representations made about the promised employment. Compensation was payable based on the likely period of employment, but was reduced to take into account a proportion of pay that would have been paid for the climatic conditions they would have been working in had they actually commenced employment (the new jobs were in the Shetland Islands). The representations had, said the court, amounted to a separate, or 'collateral' contract between the workers and the employer.[15]

Internal Appointments and Promotions

The exact terms on which internal appointments and promotions are made, and the procedures that apply, will usually depend on any collective agreements or arrangements that the employer operates. Once interviews have taken place and an appointment has been made employers are not usually entitled to withdraw an offer, and other dissatisfied applicants will find it difficult to challenge the decision.

Example

Mrs Powell worked for Brent Council, and she applied for and got promotion to a post as a principal benefits officer. She was told on the telephone by a senior officer that she had been selected. Meanwhile another candidate started a claim under the grievance procedure. The council decided there had been a breach of the equal opportunity code of practice. Mrs Powell was told she would not be appointed, and the job was due to be re-advertised. She successfully claimed that she had been appointed to the post, and obtained a temporary injunction stopping the post being advertised or filled pending a decision whether she had been properly appointed.[16]

CHAPTER 4

The Contract of Employment

As we saw in the last chapter, a contract of employment is usually formed as soon as the employer's job offer has been accepted. The exact time it comes into operation may depend on any arrangements made about starting dates, working out the notice period of your existing job and similar matters.[1]

In the rest of this chapter we will look at what employment contracts consist of and the various ways in which terms and conditions can become part of the contract. Before doing this it is worth considering the role of the employment contract and its effectiveness in protecting workplace rights.

Contractual 'Rights'

In the United Kingdom context, unlike other employment systems, the contract of employment is the central feature of individual employment law and it deals with key things like pay, working hours and holiday entitlements. In practical terms the majority of employment disputes are concerned with what is actually *in* the contract, that is what has been agreed and whether it has been effectively included, as well as the *scope* of its terms.[2] If disagreements are not resolved disputes can be dealt with in an adversarial system of industrial tribunals and courts. In fact most workers do not make much use of the courts during their employment, largely because of the costs, uncertainties about the likely outcome and the problems of pursuing disputes with employers while still working for them.

Despite these problems and the other difficulties which stem from the contract system's dependency on the adversarial system of courts and tribunals, for most people the contract does represent an important safeguard of their employment rights. Similarly, in the collective sphere, collective agreements are an important formal written record and a bench-mark by which unions can gauge their success. As well as a form of protection of workplace rights they are a spring-board for future negotiations and collective organisation for advancing members' interests. Some trade union commentators see the negotiation of collective terms and their incorporation into the individual contract of employment as unions' central role.[3]

Contractual Rights in Practice

How significant, though, are contract terms in practice in safeguarding employment rights? Although it is very important to have a written statement confirming rights, and this provides the essential legal basis for guaranteeing them, in practical terms the observance of workplace rights depends heavily on non-legal considerations, such as goodwill, economic pressures on the employer's business, the existence and effectiveness of a union organisation (if staff are in a union), and so forth. It is also worth remembering that there can be various aspects of a job which are not dealt with by the contract at all and rights and obligations may rely on assumptions and 'understandings' rather than on any sort of formal definition. Although most employers make sure that contracts give them all the disciplinary power they need, larger employers will also rely on a much wider range of employment 'human resource management' practices to get workers to do what they want.[4]

Even where all the factors are present which suggest that employment rights are securely established in detailed individual contracts and collective agreements, and these are reinforced by strong union organisation, this is no guarantee that an employer will not try to 'roll back' contractual provisions, and rights which developed during the employment relationship. The point was clearly shown in May 1991 when Rolls Royce unilaterally decided that it would not be paying wage rises provided for in contracts and collective agreements. Employees were then sacked and simultaneously offered re-engagement on new terms - which did not include the right to a pay increase! An employer's readiness and ability to do this, assuming it is done correctly in legal terms (see chapter 13 below on termination) came as a considerable shock to many people at the time. In another case[5] employers removed the right to union representation when 'personal contracts' were introduced. The EAT refused to protect this entitlement by treating it as 'action short of dismissal' on grounds of union membership when there were good grounds for doing so.

The courts have, in several instances, co-operated in the process of compulsorily moving employees out of collective arrangements, to personal contracts, and in dismembering recognition and bargaining agreements. One aspect of their approach has been to differentiate between rights and duties which arise from the relationship between the employer and *employee*, and those concerning the employer and *union*. This has led to some curious and patently flawed results.

In one case[6] a newspaper group derecognised the National Union of Journalists and decided to replace collective arrangements, and the unions' members' contracts, with new personal contracts. Acceptance of the change by the staff concerned was coupled with an inducement in the shape of a pay award. But it also entailed losing a range of union-related rights, including the right to have increases and contract improvements determined through the medium of the union. The EAT refused to accept this as 'action short of dismissal' relating to union membership. The action, said the EAT, was not directed at the members *individually*, as opposed to action affecting the *union*, and was not therefore within the scope of the provisions.

Notwithstanding that the contract contains explicit guarantees on such matters as pay rises, promotion, overtime, union representation and so forth, the reality is that because an employer will generally have a stronger hand throughout the employment such rights can remain highly tenuous. There is a variety of legal and non-legal explanations for this, which are discussed further in other chapters, but as an introductory point it is worth identifying some of the key stages at which a person's employment rights can be vulnerable. In the first two years of service an employee runs a gauntlet of possible dismissal because the two-year 'qualifying period' for going to an industrial tribunal will not have been established. This means that changes in employment conditions during that period could not, for example, be challenged in a constructive dismissal claim (although other court action may be possible). Another period during which contractual rights can be extremely vulnerable is during a 'reorganisation' of the employer's business, when significant changes to rights under employment contracts can often be justified in tribunal proceedings (see chapter 5 below).

The time at which work entitlements are particularly at risk, of course, is when an employer's business is in financial trouble, or caught up in insolvency procedures. At that time the management may well have been displaced, and employment responsibilities may have switched to 'administrators' and others. An increasingly important phase for many people and one which can impact severely on a job, is when a new employer takes over. This is often the cue for a new management to introduce changes and reinterpret existing contractual arrangements, working practices and procedures.[7]

Underlying everything is the point that for many workers their contract of employment can often contain terms which are highly disadvantageous, even to the point of being outrageously unfair. This can be seen with things like powers to deduct pay for lateness, imposing compulsory overtime, requiring changes of work base at short notice, powers to deduct pay for 'bad workmanship' and 'under-performance' and so forth. This is due, of course, not to the contract system itself,[8] but to the imbalance in bargaining power which is usually inherent in the employment relationship. There are few minimum safeguards that have to be included in an employment contract and there is no legal test of 'reasonableness' (unlike other areas of contract rights such as consumer transactions)[9] which operates to prevent exploitative terms. It is, no doubt, this aspect of an employer's and employee's 'freedom of contract' which is particularly attractive to some employers and it is a feature of UK employment which was strongly defended by the government at the Maastricht Treaty discussions in 1991, when the UK opted-out of the Social Chapter requirements designed to establish minimum rights.[10]

The government has flagged its philosophy that 'individual dealings' are superior to legal intervention and 'distant negotiation between employers and unions' in its own 'UK Social Charter'.[11] This also emphasises a need for greater flexibility in employment relationships and a determination to resist EC moves on such things as compulsory maximum working hours. These developments are potentially very far-reaching (especially if they translate into legislation and practice). The issues of flexibility and pressures on employees to adapt to employers' changing requirements themselves are not new.[12] An important survey by ACAS in 1987,[13] identified a wide range of pressures on employers which are forcing changes to the conventional employment contract model, and on most employment issues, including pay systems, hours, job mobility and general working practices.

Finally, the difficulties in enforcing contractual rights must be borne in mind. There are various reasons for this. Some are to do with the absence of legal aid for legal assistance and representation for industrial tribunal claims. Others include the problem of having to sue an employer, and jeopardising your job and the goodwill that may exist. This is a practical consideration affecting many non-union workers and an important concern for those who are threatened with the removal of rights to union membership or workplace representation.

Contract Terms and Conditions

Employment contract details are rarely all contained in a single written document which sets out each side's rights and obligations. Only in a small minority of cases, notably senior managers and certain groups like sales staff who might have a detailed 'service agreement', might this be the position. For the majority of employees this is not the case and a typical contract of employment can derive from a variety of possible sources. These include:

- verbal statements and promises
- statutory written statements
- written evidence
- collective agreements
- rule-books, notices, and the like
- custom and practice
- implied terms

Verbal Statements

A contract of employment can be based entirely on a verbal arrangement and there is generally no requirement that it must be evidenced in writing. This means that you would be able to rely on an informally made agreement for most purposes. For example, you could ask the county court for an order that you should be paid for any work done;[14] or for damages if the job does not materialise.

Similarly, you can base claims in the industrial tribunal on a verbally agreed contract although you would, of course, have a harder job establishing what was agreed (on Form IT1 when you apply, see chapter 22 below, or later when you are in the tribunal hearing) than if you were able to produce written evidence.

In practice the question of what is in the contract usually depends on a mixture of verbal and written evidence, and failing that the court or tribunal may be willing to infer agreement on certain points. The courts have, however, laid down stricter limits on how far they will go in helping the parties in this way by maintaining that it is not their job to write or rewrite contract terms.[15]

Statutory Written Statement

Except where the job continues for less than a month, or normally involves employment for less than 8 hours per week, an employee must, within 2 months of starting work,[16] be given a written statement of the terms of his/her employment which contains:

(i)   the names of the employer and the employee
(ii) the date when the job began
(iii) the date on which continuous employment began (taking into account any employment with a previous employer that counts towards that period).

The statement must contain particulars which are accurate as at a specified date which is not more than 7 days before the statement is issued. It should also contain the following particulars:

(a) The scale or rate of pay, or the method of calculating pay.
(b) The intervals at which remuneration is paid (for example, weekly or monthly).
(c) Any terms relating to hours of work, including normal working hours.
(d) Any terms relating to holidays, public holidays and holiday pay; sickness and injury (including any provision made for sick pay); pension and pension schemes.
(e) The length of notice which is required to be given or which should be received to terminate the job.
(f) The title of the job which the employee is employed to do, or a brief description of the work involved.
(g) The period of employment if it is not permanent, or date it ends if it is for a fixed term.
(h) The place(s) of work.
(i)   Any collective agreements which directly affect the terms of the employment.
(j)   Details of any employment for more than one month outside the UK.

The details in points (i)–(iii) and paras. (a)–(c); (d) as it relates to holidays and holiday pay; (f) and (h) must be given in one document, the 'principal statement'.

Other details can be given in 'instalments' by the end of the two month period. The statement must normally also include details of disciplinary and grievance rules and procedures.

- Details of any further steps which result from a disciplinary or grievance application.
- A statement of whether a 'contracting-out' certificate is in force for the employment.

Most statement requirements could, before TURERA, be satisfied if the particulars were contained in another document, such as a collective agreement, to which you could be referred. The law now requires most information to be communicated *directly* in the statement itself.

Status of the Statement

It is important to note what the legal status of the statutory statement is. If you sign it, not just as a receipt but as if it were a contract in itself, it is possible that a tribunal could treat the document in the same way as a written contract.[17] Otherwise the statement should only be regarded as *evidence* of what was agreed. The practical significance of this is that if you do not agree that the statement accurately records what was actually agreed, or if the position has changed since the employment began, you could challenge it or raise the issue when it comes up in a tribunal or in court proceedings.[18]

If there is a later change in any terms of the kind referred to the employer must issue a further statement, giving particulars of the change, in most cases 'at the earliest opportunity', but in any case not longer than one month after the change (section 4, as substituted by TURERA). This requirement does not give an employer the right to make changes which have not been properly agreed. Unfortunately, it is not unusual for employers to try to introduce changes by simply issuing such amending statements, and then expecting staff not to object. See further on such changes in chapter 5.

Going to a Tribunal

You can ask a tribunal to decide what particulars ought to be included in a statement:

- if one has not been issued;
- if you disagree with what you have been given;
- if a change has not been properly notified.

Disagreements over the terms which ought to have been included in a statement often arise when the job is ending, or has already ended. In this case it is important to note that applications must be brought within 3 months of termination.

Written Evidence

If no statutory statement has been issued, or it is inaccurate, other written evidence of what has been agreed may be available. Examples include letters of appointment, internal memos and job advertisements.

Advertisements can be particularly important if they offer entitlements which, for one reason or another, are not repeated in the formal offer or statement of terms. For example, an advertisement which offers participation in a profit-sharing scheme as part of the remuneration package may well be creating a contractual right - even if the point is not repeated in later documentation.

Collective Agreements

Incorporating Terms by 'Reference'
The contents of documents like collective agreements are often expressly 'incorporated' into the contract. For example, a written statement may state that you will be working in accordance with the employer's published conditions of service and that those conditions may be subject to change from time to time in accordance with any new collective agreement made. If it does say that, or a similar form of words is used, any changes in such conditions will usually mean your own terms and conditions will automatically be amended (although it will still be necessary to provide an up-dated written statement).

Before a collective agreement is changed agreement will usually have been reached beforehand between the union and employer (or employer's organisation). But prior agreement is not always essential before changes are legally effective. In particular it may not be required if the particular service condition has not become part of a worker's contract of employment and there are no other legal constraints on the employer withdrawing or altering a benefit.

Example
Employees of a local authority were employed according to the authority's published terms of service, and in this particular case the changes did not require prior agreement with the union representing the authority's staff before they could be made. It was held that the council could, therefore, unilaterally withdraw a non-contributory life assurance scheme.[20]

Crossing the 'Bridge'
The process by which terms of documents are incorporated in this way is sometimes described as a 'bridge' between the individual worker's contract and the document in question. Unfortunately in some cases this system clearly operates to the worker's disadvantage, as in the last example. It is important to note, though, that rights which *have* become part of the individual contract of employment may well be protected from change unless the individual's consent

is given or his/her union agrees the change. Those rights may have 'crossed the bridge' from another document, or may have been part of the contract since the employment began.

Example

Mr Robertson's appointment letter said that incentive bonus scheme conditions would apply to workers in his type of employment. A collective agreement dealt with the actual calculation of bonus payments. Later he received a statutory statement which said that any bonus which may become due would be calculated by reference to the rules of the scheme in force 'at the time'. The part of the collective agreement containing the scheme was later terminated (which the employer could do by simply giving notice to the union of its termination). The corporation thereupon stopped paying bonuses, and Mr Robertson and his colleagues suffered a significant pay cut as a result.

He successfully sued in the county court and on appeal the employer argued that his right to bonus ended when the agreement was terminated. This argument was rejected. The appointment letter had created a contractual right, and even if the employer could terminate the *collective* agreement Mr Robertson's right to bonus, which was in his own contract, went on. The employer could not, therefore, simply stop paying.[21]

Although this case was an example of how employment rights which are (or have become) part of the individual's contract may survive such actions of an employer, a problem remains, and it is one which has important implications for many workers whose employment rights are contained in collective agreements. This is that such rights will always be vulnerable so long as collective arrangements and procedures remain legally unenforceable.[22]

It may sometimes suit workers and their unions to have a situation in which employers are unable legally to enforce many of *their* rights under a collective agreement, but this can clearly operate both ways as a double-edged sword.

For further discussion of incorporation of collective agreements, see chapter 19.

Other Methods of Incorporation

If there is no express provision made in the individual contract of employment which incorporates a collective agreement or other document, can incorporation be achieved by other means?

In an attempt to rationalise, at least in legal terms, the industrial relations practice whereby work arrangements are collectively made and then automatically applied to individual workers, a number of approaches have been put forward. No one approach is entirely satisfactory and often in cases where courts or tribunals have seemingly accepted incorporation as a matter of course the basis on which they have done so is far from clear.

Incorporation by Implication

In some cases collectively agreed work arrangements are applied to individuals on the basis that this can be *implied*. This is obviously easier in situations where the tradition, in a workplace, of making and applying collective arrangements in this way is well established. This is based on the assumption (although the point is not always clear) that an implied term can be found in the individual contract that the particular collective term or arrangement can apply, and that it is appropriate for incorporation.

Although there can be significant problems involved in the practical application of this process, and in particular there does not seem to be a clear rationale for why some collective terms are capable of incorporation while others are not, the practice has been established for some while.[23]

The following leading case illustrates some of the difficulties that can occur.

Example

Workers at Standard Telephones and Cables plc (STC) were made redundant and argued that this was in breach of contract as the company had failed to select staff on the basis of LIFO (last in first out) as provided for by a collective agreement. This procedure was, they said, incorporated into their individual contracts and the failure to follow it entitled them to claim damages. The judge decided that the statutory statements did not expressly incorporate the provisions of the agreements which established length of service as the criterion for selection. He accepted that incorporation could be implied, but this required evidence that this was intended by the parties to the contract. He did not consider such an intention could be inferred from the evidence, including the agreements and other documentation, nor did he believe the redundancy provisions were 'apt' for incorporation.[24]

Collective Agreements as 'Custom'

One authoritative labour lawyer, partly in an attempt to advance the case for more extensive incorporation of collectively agreed procedures and rights, suggested that collective agreements operate, in relation to the individual contract, as a form of 'crystallised custom'.[25] Put simply, this approach proceeds on the basis that individual contracts can include terms and conditions which are normally followed as workplace custom and practice.

It is difficult to see, though, how most modern collective arrangements operate in the same way as customarily established terms (see the section on custom and practice below) and despite its attractions the concept has not become established in practice as a means of demonstrating incorporation.

Agency

Another possible way in which incorporation is sometimes explained is on the basis of 'principal' and 'agent'. So long as the employee (the principal) gives the union (the agent) power to negotiate and make contractual terms, it might be said that the union has power to make and change its members' conditions, and this may make an express clause or other mechanism unnecessary.

Although this relationship does explain many problems in this area, and may be relied on in some cases, it cannot be adopted as a general basis for incorporating collective terms whenever there is no express incorporation clause. For one thing, a union may not necessarily enjoy agency rights for all the workers it 'represents'. This is illustrated, for example, by the fact that in many workplaces the union may well 'negotiate' for non-union staff and members of other unions as well as its own members. But it generally does so, not as an agent but because the individual contracts of those non-union and other staff state that their terms will be in accordance with the collectively agreed arrangements that the union negotiates. Alternatively, it is generally understood that the employer simply applies those arrangements in practice to such staff once they have been agreed.

There is another practical problem in relying on agency as a medium of incorporation. This is the possibility that members may well want to withdraw their authority from the union. In this case the result may be that any collective agreements that are made will not apply to that member as they have not been incorporated effectively into his/her contract.[26]

Rule-Books, Notices and the Like

Workplace rules and notices are ways in which the employer can exercise managerial power, but they do not necessarily amount to terms of a contract. They are used in different ways and for a variety of purposes at most workplaces, and their status will depend on a number of factors.

Their contents might already have been agreed, for example as a collective issue. In this case they could, in appropriate cases, be treated as if they had been incorporated into individuals' contracts and thereby acquire contractual force. Alternatively, the statutory statement or engagement letter might have said that particular issues, such as holidays, sick pay, pay arrangements, will be as set out in notices and work rules. Obviously this will give the employer considerable flexibility in making and changing important conditions.

Even without such a specific reference in the contract, some workplace conditions might have become so well known that they acquire contractual force. An example of this was a case where sick pay arrangements were posted on a works noticeboard.[27]

Apart from these possibilities, notices, circulars and rules can generally be regarded as no more than information or, at best, management instructions. In the latter case these can nevertheless be important, as in some circumstances ignoring them might well amount to a breach of the contractual obligation to carry out employers' orders.

Custom and Practice

Terms can be incorporated into a contract on the basis of custom and practice, either in the particular industry or in the workplace itself. With workers increasingly getting written statements of terms which cover most of their workplace rights and duties this mode of incorporation is becoming less relevant. There have, though, been recent examples of employers seeking to rely on what they have claimed to be established practice, usually to try to justify action like pay deductions or downgradings.

In order to succeed it must be shown that the practice is well established and generally accepted, although it is an arguable point whether the worker concerned must necessarily be aware of the practice on commencing work.[28] In the modern employment context the argument that an employer has not applied the alleged practice consistently, or on the basis that it is an established managerial right, may be significant. In one case[29] a 'chargeman' was demoted and had his pay cut, and the employer tried to justify this by pointing out that this had been done before with the agreement of the individuals concerned. It was held that this did not entitle the employer to take such action. The previous occasions did not, in themselves, establish a managerial *right* in such cases.

Implied Terms

An important kind of contractual term is one which can be *implied*. Although most workers' terms will be dealt with in one written form or another there may well be aspects of the employment relationship which have not been specifically dealt with, or which are not dealt with in any of the ways already mentioned. In this case a court or tribunal may fill the gap or omission by deciding what the contract *ought* to say in order to make it workable or meaningful. In one case, for instance, the House of Lords ruled that there should be an implied term requiring the employer to inform workers of any rights they have under collective agreements or arrangements, or other conditions which could give rise to personal benefits and of which they might otherwise not be aware (such as options under employees' pensions schemes).[30]

Broadly speaking implied terms come within one of two possible categories. The first comprises terms which are implied in the *particular* employment relationship. This would include terms which are 'necessary' and which the parties might have agreed on had the point been considered. For example, it has been held that an implied right to sick pay existed in a case, but that this should only be for a limited period rather than for as long as the employment lasted.[31]

In practice, courts and tribunals bring to bear a wide range of policy considerations in deciding such points, including their own view of the particular case and what they perceive to be generally desirable. In one case, for example, it was held that an implied right to an annual salary rise was not 'reasonable' and had not been established on the particular facts. But this finding was reinforced by the view than an implied right to annual pay rises ought not to be regarded as established in industry.[32]

A second way of implying terms derives from implications which can be made in *general* about what is appropriate in the employment relationship. On this basis a number of important terms may be held to exist unless they are ousted or modified by expressly agreed arrangements. Employers' duties under this head include the obligation to pay wages and to take reasonable care of employees' safety. In certain cases there may be an implied duty to provide some types of staff with work, for example people who need to maintain their work skills or business connections. Such duties may, however, be modified or even completely removed by express clauses. For instance, an employer may include in the contract a term permitting suspensions without pay, or short-time working without pay. Or, as is increasingly common with performance-related pay systems, contracts may specifically exclude implied pay rights. It is now quite normal for more senior staff to be subject to so-called garden leave clauses. These override implied rights and may, if valid, entitle their employer to send them home without work until their employment comes to an end.

Apart from the likelihood that employers will have substantially modified the position by express clauses, there may well be judicial interventions which override any rights which a worker might otherwise have. For example, what had hitherto been assumed to be a well-established right to continue to be paid wages without interruption until the contract is terminated, has been modified and held to be subject to the principle of 'no work, no wages'. Essentially this meant, in the case in question,[33] that as the worker concerned was not working 'normally' (due to industrial action), the normal obligation to pay wages would be suspended.

The importance of implied terms will become particularly clear when we come to look at the right not to be unfairly dismissed and constructive dismissal. In both cases it may be necessary to rely on breaches by the employer of implied terms, for example to maintain the elements of 'mutual trust and confidence' essential in working relationships.

Employees' duties are generally more onerous and are more rigorously applied in practice. The most important implied terms include the duties:

- to obey orders (see chapters 13 and 14 below for examples);
- to show 'fidelity' (a term which may be broken in a wide variety of ways; see chapter 9 for examples);
- to exercise reasonable care in carrying out duties during the employment;
- to co-operate.

Carrying out Employment Obligations

Once a job has started it will be immediately governed by the contract and the terms which have been created in the above ways. Both the employer and employee are required to perform the contract in accordance with those terms, and in a reasonable way.

'Reasonableness' in this context is usually taken to mean doing things in a way that the parties themselves would have expected when the employment terms were agreed. The point is illustrated, for example, by cases where the courts have taken action against workers working to contract or to rule.[34] Or where they have ruled that an employer had abused a power to require overtime working by habitually demanding that staff work unacceptably long hours, as in the junior hospital doctors' case.[35]

Finally, it is important to realise that employment contracts are quite likely to undergo significant changes. In the next chapter we must consider the practical problems that this can entail.

CHAPTER 5

Workplace Change

Most people's jobs are likely to be affected by change at one time or another. In many cases, though, the changes will be regarded by the law as within management's control and therefore usually outside the scope of legal protection. Examples of this include management decisions to alter the physical working environment, by rearranging office accommodation, moving staff around and so forth. Staff changes, like promotions, are likewise normally entirely a matter for management. For many workers, particularly if they are not in a union, there may be little or no rights whatsoever to participate in important areas of workplace decision-making, however much the decisions and resulting changes impact on their working lives. Although draft EC legislation providing for European-style works councils is expected, and this will include increased rights to information and consultation on workplace change,[1] it will be mainly directed, to begin with at least, at larger companies with operations in at least one EC country.[2]

The Relevance of the Contract

In the last chapter we saw how workplace rights and obligations can become contractual, and how this is the basis on which rights and obligations can become legally enforceable. Unless your rights *are* in your contract there is an increased danger that they can be rolled back or eroded at any time.

In practice, in the UK context, there are many 'rights' which workers could quite reasonably claim are, or by practice have become, established 'entitlements'. Unfortunately, if it came to the crunch, many of these would be treated by the courts as 'non-contractual' – and therefore fully susceptible to change without prior agreement. In the present employment environment, and given the inherent imbalance in bargaining power between employers and workers, it is unlikely that many of the areas in which 'management discretion' operates could ever be properly protected through the medium of the contract of employment. It is therefore as important now as it ever was to look to all other ways, including union organisation at the workplace, collective agreements and legislation to provide such protection. Although trade unions, through the collective bargaining system and participation, have traditionally had a key role in the process of change,[3] EC systems of consultation do not necessarily give

52

unions such an important role.[4] There are a number of EC draft directives that will provide important minimum safeguards and block imposed changes in areas which, for many workers in the UK, would never otherwise be adequately dealt with. These include minimum rest periods and holidays; maximum hours for weekend and night work; and rights concerning the work practices of part-timers and temporary staff.

The Courts' Approach to Workplace Changes

Before discussing the issues in detail, it is worth making several general points about the current legal approach to workplace change. In particular, it is immediately apparent that the law places more emphasis on some aspects of the employment relationship than on others. You are more likely, therefore, to get protection (or financial compensation) for changes to your pay or other monetary entitlements than for changes to the way in which your job is organised or performed. It is also apparent that the courts are unwilling to give their protection to certain union-related rights in practice. For example, the EAT has refused to treat the removal by an employer of a right to union representation as 'action short of dismissal' when personal contracts were introduced.[5] To some extent this just reflects the low priority which the law has given employees' rights compared with the emphasis it has given to the needs of the owners of an enterprise. It is this issue, which UK company law has never addressed, that lies behind draft proposals in EC legislation to require worker involvement in boards and management structures.[6]

Despite the illogicality of differentiating between different types of change like this, the courts have attempted to rationalise their approach in several ways. First and foremost, decisions to impose change, and the choice of means for implementing them, are frequently justified as being part-and-parcel of management's 'prerogative to manage'. Rather like the royal prerogative, management prerogative is one of those curious features of the UK workplace scene which nobody really understands, but which has nevertheless acquired an almost mystical quality. To the extent that it can be defined, it means that management has the sole discretion to make decisions on certain ill-defined matters. Even if other parties' views might be heard, at the end of the day these are entirely within management's exclusive control. Second, an employer's need for 'flexibility', particularly in relation to business reorganisations, is considered to be of paramount importance, even if it means that contractual rights may suffer. As can be seen from the business reorganisation cases, this approach has meant that industrial tribunals can, and do, routinely place a higher priority on an employer's business needs than on the rights of the employees affected.

These points look set to go on being important features of employment law in the 1990s. From the courts' point of view the right of management to introduce change is accompanied by a corresponding duty to accept change, and help to make it work.[7] This position is underpinned by the view that employment contracts are substantially different in nature from other kinds of contracts. For example, it is said that, unlike other kinds of contract, they cannot remain 'static' and the parties must therefore accept the need for flexibility in their interpretation. The practical consequence of this, as we shall see, is that it is employees who are called upon to shoulder the negative consequences of their employers' changing business needs. Such a requirement to accept enforced changes, imposed unilaterally by one contracting party to another, would of course be completely unacceptable in commercial or other contract situations.

Changing Working Conditions

Non-Contractual Conditions

Changes can be made to non-contractual conditions without prior agreement and without giving rise to any legal redress. The withdrawal of a discretionary bonus, for example, would not involve the infringement of any legal rights.[8] Except in exceptional circumstances where the employer's conduct (and the *way* in which changes have been carried out) could be said to amount to constructive dismissal[9] there is little that can be done in such situations.

'Contractual' Conditions

If the entitlement or condition *is* contractual, though, there are a number of possibilities that must be considered. These are that:

- the contract may, in fact, already permit such changes;
- any change may require agreement;
- the change might be lawfully achieved by terminating the contract and substituting new working conditions;
- the employer might fairly dismiss you, and avoid paying compensation.

Permitted Changes

It may well be allowed under the contract for an employer to make the changes in question. It is obviously to an employer's advantage to make sure that contracts and job descriptions are worded in such a way that they enjoy maximum flexibility in the sort of work that can be required, and *how* it is to be done. If there is any doubt about this the courts' policy is to look at what the employer *could* ask you to do under your contract, and not just what you have actually been doing since you started.[10]

In the leading case on the introduction of new technology the same approach was adopted:

Example

Clerical and tax officers at the Inland Revenue worked on the administration of the PAYE system. When the system was computerised the Inland Revenue Staff Association initially wanted to co-operate. Its attitude changed when no guarantees were given that there would not be redundancies. The staff thought that the Inland Revenue was not entitled to require them to work with the new computerised system. They tried to get a High Court order to confirm that, and to ensure that they would continue to be paid while not using the new system. It was held that, although the job content of some jobs would be changed by the new requirements, they were still within the terms of the original job descriptions. Although the jobs would be done in a different way, they were still the same jobs. Until the staff were prepared to adapt to the new requirements the Inland Revenue was entitled to stop paying them.[11]

Implementing Permitted Changes

Even if the contract does allow an employer to make changes in your working conditions, those changes should be implemented in a reasonable way which makes it possible for you to carry them out. If the employers do not do this their conduct can amount to a breach of the implied contractual duty of confidence and trust that is in every employment contract.[12]

Unfortunately, although this is an important principle which could offer some protection against the worst effects of one-sided contracts, its scope in practice is often very limited.

Example

Mr White worked in the rubber mixing department of a factory. He asked to be moved to lighter work but this was refused. His attendance record deteriorated and, after a warning, he was later moved to another department where he had to accept a significant drop in pay. His contract had a 'job flexibility' clause which read: 'The Company reserves the right, when determined by requirements of operational efficiency, to transfer employees to alternative work and it is a condition of employment that they are willing to do so when requested.' The industrial tribunal decided that this power was subject to two implied conditions, namely that the transfer should be exercised in a reasonable way and that there should be no pay cut without prior agreement. As the company had broken those terms Mr White had been constructively dismissed. The EAT reversed this decision. If there is an express power to transfer it is wrong to make that power subject to a 'reasonableness' requirement. The employer would only be acting wrongly if, for example, there were insufficient grounds to justify the move or the decision was 'capricious'. On the pay point they ruled that as long as employers act within their rights any loss of income involved will not involve a breach of contract.[13]

Changes by Agreement

If the entitlement or working condition in question is provided for, or regulated, by the contract (and it is not possible to make changes), the employer will need to vary that contract. Variation can only be achieved by agreement, either with the individual concerned or through the collective bargaining process. For example, the change could be formally agreed either on a one-to-one basis or as part of a wider deal affecting other workers (see chapter 19 below, on collective agreements).

In practice changes are often agreed as part of a package of new arrangements, and in order to make the variation legally effective something will usually have to be offered in return by the employer. In law this is known as 'consideration' and without it the change could be legally ineffective. For example, if you verbally agree to come in to work earlier than usual without extra pay, time off in lieu, or some similar arrangement, the employer would find it difficult to claim that such an agreement amounted to a formal change in your conditions. It is for this reason that employers usually include a pay rise, or other tangible benefit, as part of any package involving changes – for instance where they are seeking individuals' agreement to new personal contracts (as discussed in the previous chapter).

In some circumstances, though, the law *presumes* that there has been agreement. This might occur where you have not objected to a change, or your agreement could be inferred from your conduct. It is therefore essential that you do not give the appearance of accepting changes you do not want to agree to. As long as you make clear your objections to a proposed or imposed change you will be able to avoid this risk (see the section on terminating and replacing the contract below). In another case it was held by a tribunal that agreeing to be laid off on a previous occasion did not prevent the worker concerned from arguing that the employer was not legally entitled to lay staff off on a later occasion.[14]

Formal Notification of Changes

Employers are required to notify individuals affected by any changes by issuing a written statement to them giving particulars 'at the earliest opportunity' and, in any event, not later than one month after the changes are made.[15]

Terminating and Replacing the Contract

One option which may be open to an employer who wants to make changes is to terminate the existing contract by giving the required notice, and then offer new terms and conditions under a new contract. An example of an employer attempting this, but withdrawing from it under pressure, was Rolls Royce in 1991. There are, however, many less well-publicised examples of how employers have done this successfully.

For such action to be legally effective, though, the employer must make it clear that the contract is being terminated. It is not enough to simply notify employees of change.

Example

Six school canteen workers employed by Hertfordshire County Council received letters giving them notice that their contracts would be changed with effect from a given date. The changes included a reduction in pay. The letters, from the county education officer, went on to say: 'I hope you will continue in the meals service.' The staff carried on working but made it clear, through their union, that they did not accept the changes. It was held that the employer's action did *not* have the effect of terminating their employment. It merely confirmed the employer's intention to break the contract. By carrying on work, it could not be implied that the women concerned had accepted a new contract. They were therefore entitled to be paid their arrears of wages due under their contract.[16]

In a later case the House of Lords confirmed that workers faced with a unilaterally imposed change can elect whether to accept the change or reject it.

Example

Workers at Ferodo Ltd were told that their wages were to be cut following the company's failure to agree these with their union. They carried on working under protest. It was held that their contracts did not automatically end when the new terms were imposed. As they had not agreed to the changes, and had continued to protest about them, they were entitled to be paid arrears of wages.[17]

A reduction in pay without agreement can be treated as a breach of contract on the more general ground that it undermines implied trust and confidence.[18]

Responding to Imposed Changes

In theory, the position as described in the last section, and the case examples referred to, look easy and suggest that all you have to do is refuse to accept any proposed changes and sit tight on the basis that the law will protect your interests. The reality is of course that workers can be put under great pressure, and a refusal to accept changes may result either in threats of dismissal, or in being forced to resign.

Although the exact rights you have will depend on the circumstances of the particular case, there are several possibilities for responding to an employer's action in trying to impose new working conditions. If the contract was terminable on notice, and you have not been paid for the notice period, you will normally be entitled to compensation for that loss. In chapter 14 of this book unfair dismissal claims, including constructive dismissal, are discussed in further detail. There may also be scope for a redundancy payment if the change means that the job being done has come to an end. Compensation may in such cases be enhanced by an unfair dismissal element.

Claiming Unfair Dismissal

The difficulty with unfair dismissal claims is that employers can often successfully defend claims on the basis that they have acted reasonably in proposing new terms, and therefore tribunals can, and do, decide that the dismissal is 'fair'.

Example

Mr Harper was employed by Chubb Fire Security Ltd as a sales representative. Sales declined and he was offered new contract terms which involved a pay cut, and which required him to cover a different area. He was sacked after refusing the new terms. The tribunal held the dismissal to be unfair. The employers won on appeal. The EAT said that what mattered was the reasonableness of the *employer* in dismissing Mr Harper. Specifically, they formulated the question as follows: 'Was Chubb acting reasonably in dismissing Mr Harper for his refusal to enter into the new contract? In answering that question the industrial tribunal should have considered whether Chubb was acting reasonably in deciding that the advantages to them of implementing the proposed reorganisation outweighed any disadvantage which they should have contemplated Mr Harper might suffer.' The case was therefore returned to the tribunal for reconsideration.[19]

Claims for unfair dismissal, including cases where employers have forced changes on staff as part of reorganisations, company restructuring exercises and so on, are discussed in detail later, in chapters 13 and 14.

CHAPTER 6

Reductions in Work

Lay-off and Suspension

Employers hit by a downturn in business will want to reduce their operating costs as quickly as possible and to do this will be looking to cut their wages bills. In some industries and areas of work this is habitually done through redundancy – that is, by dismissals which may be justified in legal terms by a reduction in the employer's labour requirements (see chapter 15 below). In other situations, though, employers will opt for more temporary measures; in particular, lay-off or suspension. This has the advantage, if the employer is legally able to do it, of keeping the workforce together and at the same time paying reduced wages or no wages at all.

An employer is not entitled to lay you off work, reduce your pay or otherwise substantially change your working conditions, unless there is an express or implied power to do so in the contract, or in a collective agreement, industry custom or other recognised instrument. The principle that an employer's contractual obligations continue, despite difficulties in performing those obligations, will normally mean that wages should continue to be paid, even if there is a reduction in the work you are given to do.

In practice, though, most employers try to make sure that contracts and collective agreements do give them the right to lay staff off, or introduce short-time working, or take other temporary measures. Arrangements will also, usually, be in force to reduce pay, by restricting it either to the level of the minimum statutory 'guarantee payments' that must normally be paid by law (see below), or to levels which are better than the statutory requirements. Even if an agreement *appears* to give the employer powers to lay off or reduce earnings you are entitled to challenge whether those powers can be used in the particular circumstances.

Example

Workers were laid off and their normal wages withheld. This was done, despite normal work being available, because of an industrial dispute. The employer decided the situation was covered by lay-off powers in the national agreement. The agreement provided for guaranteed employment and pay, but it also said that the guarantee could be suspended if there was a dispute. The workers claimed that there could be no suspension under the provision while there was work available which they could do. The claim succeeded. The agreement did not give employers a general right to suspend and there was no customary right in the industry giving them such a power. Normal wages should therefore have continued without interruption.[1]

Transfers and Other Changes

Employers may be able to introduce changes in working conditions on a temporary basis, for example by requiring staff to transfer to other work. Depending on what the contract says this may or may not involve a change in wages or other working conditions.[2]

Responding to Unauthorised Changes

If an employer tries to lay you off, or put you on short-time working or similar, when there is no power to do so you are entitled to bring a claim for constructive dismissal.[3] Rather than opting to leave and claiming unfair dismissal (or possibly redundancy: see chapter 15 below), with results that are unpredictable, it may in some circumstances be better to continue in the job and insist on being paid. If you are not paid, or are underpaid, you should seek legal assistance with a view to suing for breach of contract. The claim should obviously cover any arrears of wages due, but it might also include compensation for things such as lost opportunities to earn commission or overtime. There may also be express or implied obligations of other kinds which could have been affected - for example, the opportunity to practise or develop skills in your particular profession or field.

Even if your employer is entitled to lay you off or keep you on short-time working, there may be scope for bringing a redundancy claim if this is protracted for four consecutive weeks, or six weeks in a 13-week period. (See Chapter 15 in this book on redundancy.)

Statutory Guarantee Payments

Payments under the statutory scheme[4] can be claimed from your employer if:

- you have been continuously employed for not less than a month ending with the day for which payment is being claimed (or you have been continuously employed for *three* months if you are only employed on a fixed-term contract of three months or less or are doing a job which is not expected to go on for more than three months); and
- there is a diminution in the requirements of the business for the work you are employed to do; or

- there is any other occurrence affecting the employer's business relating to the work you do.

'Occurrences' for this purpose would include problems like power failures and interruptions in the supply of raw materials and parts, but the legislation specifically disqualifies anyone who is not working because of:

- strikes, lock-outs and other industrial action involving other staff, or employees of an associated employer; or
- a refusal to accept suitable alternative work, or to carry out reasonable requirements for ensuring their services are available.

The entitlement is normally calculated by multiplying the guaranteed hourly rate – a week's pay divided by the hours normally worked – by the number of hours of the workless day. There is, in any case, a maximum level of entitlement for each workless day.[5] This can be paid for a maximum of only five days in any three month period. Any contractual pay paid on a workless day will reduce the employer's obligation to make guarantee payments. Other sources of income (for example, private insurance scheme payments) do not affect the statutory entitlement.

Court Action and Tribunal Complaints

If wages or other entitlements are due and have not been paid a claim in the county court will usually be appropriate. If guarantee payments are due and have not been properly paid a claim should be made to the industrial tribunal within three months of the workless day.

CHAPTER 7

Pay

Wages Rights and the Law

For most workers wages are by far the most important part of the job.[1] The problems which can occur will be considered in relation to each stage of a job, that is:

- at recruitment;
- during the employment;
- on termination.

Before doing this, it is necessary to refer to the relevance of employment status, and to the various wages systems which are commonly in operation.

Employment Status and Wages

The key feature of most jobs is that in return for the performance of services wages will be paid, usually at agreed weekly, monthly or other intervals. In practice this system applies to most employees – and it also operates for many workers with contractor, or self-employed status. If there are differences, then they are likely to be, first, that the pay intervals may not be so regular. In fact in a contractor's employment there may just be a one-off payment. Second, contractors are often responsible for their own tax and national insurance deductions. Apart from these differences the legal ground rules on pay are generally the same whatever a worker's status. Those rules will depend, first and foremost, on what is provided for in the contract.

As far as legislation on pay is concerned, a worker's rights will – as with other rights – depend on whether the employment status involved brings her/him within the particular statutory protection in question. This might mean, for example, that a non-'employee' would be excluded from the chance to bring an unfair dismissal complaint if his/her wages were unilaterally reduced. In the case of pay, however, it is worth noting at the outset that the scope of the main Act dealing with wages, the Wages Act 1986, is much wider than most other employment legislation. It applies to people working under a contract of service (employees), *or* under 'any other contract' whereby somebody undertakes to do or perform personally any work or services.[2]

Pay Systems

There are a number of pay systems in operation and each system has its own characteristics. These have an important bearing on pay rights and obligations, and on how the courts and tribunals deal with them.[3] The two most important and commonly used systems are time rates and payment by results.

Time-rated Pay

The main feature of this system is that you are paid at the agreed rate provided for in the contract and that rate must continue to be paid *without variation* and irrespective of the quality of your work performance, and without reference to productivity, output, and so on. Most people's pay comes within this category, although it is increasingly common for pay to include other elements, such as discretionary bonuses or performance-related pay.

Payment by Results (PBR)

In this case earnings *will* vary over a given period, and PBR systems will link the level of earnings to whatever performance criteria are in the contract. PBR systems all require some form of performance assessment. That system may operate by using objectively ascertainable criteria (such as the number of 'pieces' produced per hour in the case of piecework). Otherwise it may lay down criteria which give management much wider discretion in ascertaining whether performance targets have been met (for example, where performance bonuses are payable to groups of employees following an assessment of their contribution to company profits).[4]

In most cases PBR systems are used to supplement wages. This is a feature of most commission systems, although for groups of workers, like sales staff, who are employed on commission the guaranteed pay salary element is usually only a small part of their total earnings. Most employers operating PBR systems will try to build into those systems as much flexibility as possible to give themselves the freedom to introduce changes to their schemes, for example by altering conditions of eligibility, the methods of calculation, targets to be reached and so on. Such flexibility is becoming very common in the pay of white-collar staff in Japanese and European companies.[5]

If the earnings include a PBR element there are a number of problems that can arise. These include a lack of opportunity to meet performance targets (or otherwise satisfy the criteria for entitlement), underpayment, and unilateral alterations in the computation methods which the employer uses. In quite a few cases people complain that they have never really been clear what the perform-ance standards of the job have been since the job began! These problems, and the legal issues they raise, will be considered in this chapter.

To begin with, though, it is necessary to look at the basic wages law principles that apply to most jobs.

Wages at the Recruitment Stage

The wages for a job are often decided on before the appointment is made. For this reason it is not usually realistic, in most people's cases, to talk about wages terms being 'negotiated'. Nevertheless, any promises or statements made, whether at the interview or before, and whether in writing or just verbally, may be important, as they could be enforceable if there is sufficient evidence to rely on later. So the advertisement for the job could be decisive, for example, if there are arguments later.[6] If your letter of appointment states that you will receive a particular benefit that may well give you a contractual right to that benefit, whatever happens later.[7]

In the absence of specific agreement the law may imply a duty to pay expenses, or cover any costs[8] involved in carrying out a job. This cannot be relied upon with any certainty, and it is safer to clarify the position at the outset. The right to be paid any costs or expenses incurred is limited to what is reasonable.

Even if wages have not been agreed, as long as it was implicit that wages would be paid the court would be able to decide what is a reasonable wage.[9] What the law cannot do, though, is decide whether the wages which *have* been agreed are adequate,[10] even if they are obviously unfair. Low pay can be supplemented by state benefits, including family credit, housing benefit and council tax benefit.[11]

Once an offer has been made and accepted, and the job has begun, the employer's wages obligations will begin. If, following acceptance of a job offer, the employer tries to withdraw, there may be scope for legal action to obtain compensation. There is the danger, of course, that having resigned from your existing job on the strength of an offer of a new job, the latter never materi-alises. The leading case on this[12] is discussed in chapter 3 above.

Wages Problems during the Employment

The Obligation to Pay Wages

Once the job has started the employer is obliged to pay the agreed wages, at the correct rate, at the correct time, and as otherwise provided for in the contract. That obligation will normally continue until the contract ends. The main exceptions to this are where wages conditions are varied (see pp.54–8), or if you are laid off (see pp.59–61) or suspended without pay (see p.59). Otherwise a departure from what has been agreed will usually amount to a breach of contract.

Example
Mr Mooney's contract as a salesperson entitled him to a salary plus 1 per cent commission on sales. The company decided to change this to a commission paid on sales over a specified target figure. This was held to be a breach of contract entitling him to claim for constructive dismissal, particularly as it was unclear at the time of the change what the effects would be on Mr Mooney's earnings.[13]

As well as not reducing pay, or changing the basis on which pay can be earned, an employer should not make it impossible or difficult for the agreed level of earnings to be achieved. If it has been agreed, or it was understood when the job began, that a particular level of earnings could be earned, then this is what must be paid. If there is a dispute over non-payment, compensation for any lost earnings will be based on this principle.

Example
A photo-journalist was employed by *Picture Post* on a retainer of £10 per week, and on the basis that he would be paid for the photographs and other work accepted for publication. It was held that he should have been given six months' notice, instead of the two weeks he actually received. In assessing his compensation for wrongful dismissal the court took into account what the parties envisaged he would have been able to earn in that six-month period.[14]

Non-payment of Wages; Delays in Payment

Non-payment of wages may occur for a number of reasons. If it is due to delay, any serious delay, or repeated delays, may entitle you to immediately leave and claim unfair dismissal. This was the case, for example, where a barmaid's weekly wages for the week ending 28 June were not received until 5 July (and those due for 12 July did not get paid until 7 August).[15] On the other hand a delay might not be sufficiently serious to enable a claim to succeed; for example, where the causes are outside the employer's control or are not tantamount to treating the employment as at an end.[16]

The most practical step to take, in most cases, if confronted with a delayed payment is to write to your employer requiring payment. If this does not produce results, it may then be advisable to start a claim in the county court for the money due.

Non-payment might also be deliberate; for example, where the employer says staff are not working 'normally'. Although the principle 'No work: no pay' may be relied upon by employers in appropriate situations, it will *not* be relevant where action like a work-in or work to contract does not involve a breach of contract. Nor will it apply where the employer allows somebody to carry on working in their normal way. In a leading case, which has already been referred to in the context of lay-offs, the worker concerned was able to take advantage of this principle. In this case the duty to pay wages may remain unaffected.

Example

Mr Bond was a maintenance setter in an engineering factory. Following a dispute over bonus pay arrangements the setters, including Mr Bond, refused to work on certain machines but otherwise worked normally. Although they had 'withdrawn their co-operation' the employer allowed them to carry on working. Later the company informed them not to come in to work unless they were going to work normally. The dispute was later settled but the employer refused to pay Mr Bond for five days he continued to work, and for two other days when the company's action prevented him working. It was held that under his contract, and the relevant collective agreements, he should have been paid for four of the days he had been allowed to work *and* for two days when he was ready and willing to work but the only thing preventing him working was the company's action.[17]

Pay Increases

Whether you have a right to an increase or not will depend on what your contract says, or on what has been agreed since the job begun. Employers are sometimes not averse to forgetting about promised pay rises, and digging their heels in when it comes to upgrading and other forms of increases. In all cases, though, the question depends on the precise wording of your terms of employment, or on the effects of any relevant collective agreement which deals with pay upgradings and the like.

The courts, for their part, have also tended to interpret contracts, and apply collective agreement provisions on pay enhancements, in a very restrictive way. In one leading case, for example, a lecturer paid on the Burnham national agreement saw her workload expanding rapidly, and assumed that she was entitled as of right to a regrading and pay increase. The court, however, took a totally different view. Even if the prescribed work load for a higher grade had been passed there was not an *automatic* right to be regraded.[18]

Annual Pay Rises

Employers organisations in Britain are generally opposed to any general enti- tlement to annual pay rises,[19] and the courts have also pronounced that there is no general legal right to such a rise.[20] Despite this limitation, there may well be scope for insisting on a pay rise if, for example, other comparable staff have received one, or it would be reasonable to infer a right to one in the particular circumstances – for instance where you have been taking on a greater workload or responsibilities. Unfortunately the courts and tribunals have only gone so far as saying that an employer should not act unfairly in refusing a pay rise, or should not act arbitrarily or capriciously so as to break the implied duty of mutual trust and confidence.[21] In another case a *Daily Mail* journalist managed successfully to challenge his employer's refusal to pay him an increase (which had been paid to other staff), because he had refused to accept a new personalised contract. His challenge was based on EPCA s.23, on the basis that he was being penalised for his trade union membership and activities (by insisting on maintaining his rights under a collective agreement).[22]

Other Rises, Bonuses, Additional Payments

Unless your contract, or a collective agreement, gives you a clear contractual right to this type of payment it will be extremely difficult to force the employer to make it. Unfortunately many arrangements are, in fact, non-contractual and therefore unenforceable. This was the position in a leading case where the promise was to pay salary plus such bonus, if any, as the directors would 'from time to time determine'.[23] Another case illustrates the problem of maintaining the *value* of any pay increases that have been made:

Example
A headteacher's extra duties and responsibilities were rewarded by additional pay. That payment was fixed at 62 per cent of the payments made to assistant teachers. Later the level of the assistant teachers' payments were increased, but the authority refused to award a proportionate rise. The court held that, as the payment was only 'discretionary' (and had not become a contractual entitlement, for example by being regularly paid) the head was unable to insist as a legal right on its value being maintained.[24]

Correct Payment – Itemised Statements

As a way of trying to ensure that workers can check they have been paid correctly, EPCA[25] requires an employer to provide a written statement that itemises the pay which is due, either before or at the time of payment. The statement must show, specifically:

- the gross amount;
- any variable or fixed deductions from the gross amount;

- the net amount payable (including details of any part payments) if the net amount is being made in different ways.

In the case of fixed deductions the employer is entitled, instead of detailing the deductions separately on each occasion, to give an aggregate amount if a 'standing statement' of the various deductions has been provided. Such statements must be updated if necessary and reissued every 12 months. Deductions must, in any event, be authorised (either by law or by the contract), and this is discussed further in the next section.

If a proper itemised statement has not been issued a complaint can be made to an industrial tribunal. The tribunal can:

- decide what particulars should be included;
- award an amount representing the aggregate of all unnotified deductions within the 13 weeks prior to complaint.

Deductions

Wages Act 1986 Restrictions

The Wages Act 1986[26] prohibits an employer from making a deduction from wages, or from receiving a payment, unless:

- the deduction, or payment, has statutory authority (tax and national insurance would come into this category), or is authorised by the contract; or
- there is prior written agreement to it by the worker concerned.

Wages for this purpose are any sums payable to a worker in connection with his/her employment, including bonuses, commission, holiday pay and other payments referable to the employment. It also includes guarantee payments, and other entitlements like statutory sick pay and maternity pay.[27] Payments in the nature of a non-contractual bonus are specifically treated as wages (and are to be treated as payable on the day payment is made). Certain payments are not, however, 'wages' and are not therefore subject to the rules on deductions. These include advances under a loan arrangement, expenses, pensions, redundancy or other payments related to retirement, and other payment which is not paid as a result of the employment.

To deal with situations where it is not clear why there has been a shortfall in pay (for example, where an itemised statement has not been provided) the Act treats any situation in which the total amount paid is less than the total amount payable as a deduction. There is an exception to this if the deficiency is due to an error made in working out the gross wages.[28]

Disputes over Entitlement

Non-payment of wages may, however, be due to an employer maintaining there is no contractual entitlement to the amount claimed. In this case it may be necessary to lodge a claim in the county court for breach of contract to claim any arrears of pay, as the industrial tribunal may not have jurisdiction to deal with a complaint. Or, alternatively, the tribunal may only be able to deal with *part* of the claim for wages due.

Example
Ms Delaney was summarily sacked from her job as a recruitment consultant and given a cheque for £82 as a payment in lieu of notice. Later the cheque was stopped after her former employer claimed she had removed confidential information, and that this meant she could have been dismissed without notice. They also failed to pay her £55.50, representing £18 in commission and £37.50 in holiday pay.

She complained to the industrial tribunal, claiming that all these non-payments amounted to deductions. The tribunal, though, held that as the £82 payment was not 'wages' under the Act, it had no power to deal with that part of the claim. It did, however, award £55.50 in respect of the commission and holiday pay. This decision was upheld following appeals to the EAT, Court of Appeal and House of Lords. The payment in lieu of notice was, in effect, money representing damages for terminating the contract wrongly, that is without proper notice. It could not be classed as wages, as it related to a period after the termination of employment, and the matter could only be dealt with by the county court. On the other hand the commission and holiday pay were clearly money payable under the contract, and by section 8 (3) of the Act the non-payment of it amounted to a deduction.[29]

Other Remedies

An unlawful deduction or non-payment can, of course, have other legal consequences. As well as being the basis of a possible claim for constructive dismissal it may in some cases, particularly for higher paid employees, be appropriate to start a wrongful dismissal action (see chapters 13 and 14 below).

Exceptions

There are a number of important exceptions to the rules prohibiting deductions and payments.[30] The practical effect of this is that disputes over deductions or payments must be dealt with in the county court (or High Court in the case of larger claims).

These exceptions are:

- deductions made, or payments received, in relation to overpayment of wages or expenses;
- deductions, or payments, as a result of statutory disciplinary proceedings (something that is relevant to certain public sector workers, particularly in the emergency services);
- deductions required under statutory procedures, like attachment of earnings orders;
- payments to third parties authorised by a worker (in a signed and dated document) to be made on his/her behalf. This only applies if the authorisation is 'current'. Authorisations are normally effective for three years or until they are revoked, or the employers stop operating a 'check-off' system. Authority for the deduction of union dues would end if the employer is notified in writing that union membership has ceased;[31]
- deductions, and payments to the employer, resulting from industrial action (for example, where the employer wants to recoup wages paid during a dispute;
- deductions made with prior written agreement for the purposes of satisfying court or tribunal orders.

Retail Workers' Protection

The 1986 Wages Act was designed to give workers in retail employment extra protection, particularly as employers in the retail sector have long been accustomed to recouping losses for stock shortages by imposing penalties on their workers. This generally takes the form of deductions from wages or demands for payments.

Although the Act is a long way short of what is needed, and at the end of the day still allows employers considerable powers, the additional protection it provides does give some protection, either by:

- limiting the amounts of wages that can legally be deducted (or which can be the subject of payments to the employer); or
- staggering the times when deductions and payments are possible.

The starting point is that, as with other workers, any deduction (or payment received) must be authorised by law or by the contract.

Deductions for cash shortages or stock deficiencies can be made on a pay day, but the deduction (or payment required) must not exceed 10 per cent of the gross wages payable on that day. Any balance that is still owed must be carried forward to subsequent pay days, and the 10 per cent limit will apply on each of those successive days.[32] Unfortunately, though, there is no restriction applicable to a retail worker's 'final instalment' of wages, and a worker could in this case be subject to substantial deductions and demands for payment. The obvious point here is that the legislation in effect, gives the green light to employers to sack workers and avoid these limitations.[33]

Time Limits and Other Requirements

Deductions or demands must be made within 12 months of the cash shortage or stock deficiency being established by the employer. If a series of deductions is being made in relation to a cash shortage or stock deficiency, the employer need only make the first deduction within the 12-month period. If the shortage or deficiency was not reasonably 'discoverable' the period will only start to run from when it *was* reasonably discoverable.

As far as payments are concerned, any payment is unlawful unless:[34]

(i) there has been previous written notice of the total amount claimed by the employer; and

(ii) the following main requirements have been met, namely that the demand for payment is:

- in writing on a pay day;
- not made earlier than the next pay day after the day the worker is notified of the full amount due;
- not made outside the 12-month period after the shortage or deficiency was discovered (or should reasonably have been discovered);
- not in excess of 10 per cent of gross wages on the particular pay day.

On the last point, it is possible that the employer might try to make a combination of deductions and demands for payments on a particular pay day. In this event the 10 per cent limit applies to the total value of such deductions and demands.

Tribunal Complaints

Complaints of infringements of the Wages Act should be made to the industrial tribunal within three months of the deduction being made, or the payment being received. The tribunal can order the employer to pay back any money due.[35]

Overpayments

If you are mistakenly overpaid, the employer's ability to recover it depends on a distinction which the law makes between overpayments resulting from 'factual' errors – for example, miscalculations, wrong information – and errors made because the law has been misunderstood.

Factual errors will normally mean the overpayment can be recovered. Legal errors will make it more difficult. In some circumstances, namely where employees have been led to believe they are entitled to the money and have acted on the misunderstanding to their detriment (by spending it, or taking on debts expecting to use it, for instance), the employer may be prevented from recouping the payment.[36]

If wages are paid in advance and the employer tries to recover them, its success will depend on what the contract provides. In many cases, though, this will be down to whether or not an obligation to repay can be inferred from the circumstances in question. It is not uncommon, for example, for sales staff to be overpaid commission or expenses which have not been earned by the time they are sacked. In such cases it has been held that there is no implied obligation to repay.[37]

Pension Benefits as 'Pay'

A sizeable amount of workers' pay is tied up in company pension schemes. It is estimated that at least £12 billion a year is contributed by employees to such schemes. In return for this employees expect to receive benefits in the form of an occupational pension on retirement, and other financial benefits. Such benefits have long been regarded by unions and the TUC as deferred remuneration, and they are an important supplement to state basic and earnings-related pension arrangements (SERPS). The importance of occupational pension arrangements is underlined by the fact that most of them are contracted out of the state system, and are expected to provide alternative guaranteed minimum pension rights.

Unfortunately, for a combination of reasons, UK law does not give full recognition to the fact that it is workers' contributions that substantially fund such schemes. In practice, employers have a substantial degree of control over funds' assets, the investment of those assets (including 'self-investment' in the employer's business), and in the use of 'surpluses' which schemes generate. Employers will in many cases have a disproportionate degree of control in the administration of the schemes and deciding on the benefits to be paid (and how they are to be paid), the increases in benefit entitlements, and so on. The exact extent of control will depend on the terms of the trust deed setting up the particular scheme. Regulations require employers to disclose information to employees, including scheme details, leavers' entitlements and options available to beneficiaries, and to provide information about trust rules and the work of trustees.

What is more important, the present pensions law framework gives little protection against mismanagement of schemes and the misuse and misappropriation of their assets. Following the Robert Maxwell fiasco, when over £400 million-worth of funds went missing from Maxwell company schemes, the House of Commons Social Security Select Committee in 1992 called for urgent changes. In particular, it called into question the use of trusts and trust law as an effective means of protecting employees' and ex-employees' interests.

The government has not been in any hurry to take action. This is not surprising given the reliance of UK employers on scheme funds as a ready source of corporate finance, and the importance of fund surpluses to companies. Apart from that, many employers dispute employees' rights to participate in schemes' management, and do not necessarily recognise assets or surpluses as employees' and scheme members' property.

Despite public alarm, the government merely set up a committee, chaired by Professor Roy Goode, to 'review' the position. It has carefully avoided, to date, making any commitments to changes in the pensions system,[38] and it remains to be seen what recommendations the Goode Committee makes in 1993 and what action the government takes in response to them.

A detailed description of pension scheme law, and the payment of schemes' benefits, is outside the scope of this book.[39]

CHAPTER 8

Holidays, Sickness and Time Off

Holidays

Although employers must include any details of holiday entitlements in the statement of terms (see chapter 4), there is currently no obligation to give workers holiday leave. Even if leave is given there is no legal obligation, unless this is provided for in the contract or a collective agreement, to pay holiday wages or other payments. While bank holidays and recognised public holidays are customarily accepted by most employers as holiday days, this is not obligatory and employers do not have to pay their staff for them.

The EC has made non-binding recommendations suggesting minimum holiday entitlements for workers.[1] Unfortunately though, legislation setting minimum requirements for all workers is still awaited, and will eventually be part of the Social Charter Action Programme.

In practice many employers do accept the importance of paid annual holiday leave, and individual contracts and collective agreements usually contain detailed provisions giving employers control over when leave is taken and making payments conditional on compliance with the conditions laid down.[2]

Most complications on holiday issues concern the operation of leave arrangements, and payment problems (note, for example, the case example on p.69 on the withholding of holiday pay on termination). This point is also illustrated by a county court case:

Example
Mr Tucker and other members of the TGWU at a car plant were opposed to seeing changes made to their existing holiday arrangements. In particular they objected to losing two recognised holiday days, the August bank holiday and New Year's holiday, in order to get a week off after Christmas from 27 December to 31 December. The company assured them in writing that statutory holidays would not be transferred except by mutual agreement between management and all the unions represented at the plant. The works committee later agreed the proposed new arrangements, but Mr Tucker and his colleagues still objected and confirmed that they intended to take holidays on the August bank holiday and the New Year holiday. In a later county court action to claim unpaid holiday pay it was held that they were not obliged to

accept changes to their holiday arrangements. Management had neither an express nor any implied right to change holiday terms without their consent. Although a collective agreement enabled staff to be required to take public holidays on dates agreed between the company and the unions, the undertaking given required any changes made to be approved by *all* the unions at the plant, and this had not happened[3].

Sickness Absence

If you are unable to attend work as a result of sickness or injury your rights to time off and pay will usually be dealt with by your contract. Although most workers are now covered by such sickness and injury arrangements,[4] there can be problems if no express arrangements have been made or if they are unclear.

Apart from unusual circumstances such as long-term illness or injury that affects performance of the job, short-term absence does not entitle employers to threaten dismissal or put pressure on their staff to return to work (see pp.000-000). As a general principle unavoidable absence does not bring an employment contract to an end. But, in the absence of any agreed sick pay terms, the question of whether your right to be paid wages should continue while you are away, or whether you should get some other kind of sick pay, will depend on whether this is *implied*. Although a right to sick pay cannot just be assumed there might be a variety of reasons why it should be implied, such as existing workplace practices, whether it has been paid before, and whether other staff normally receive it.[5]

Statutory Sick Pay

If sickness or injury absence continues for four or more consecutive days of incapacity for work employers may be required to pay statutory sick pay (SSP). SSP is a flat-rate benefit which is treated for tax, national insurance and other purposes as income. The main exclusions from entitlement are people who are:

(i) Over pensionable age.
(ii) Working under a contract for less than three months.
(iii) Sick when they are due to start a new job.
(iv) Pregnant and within their maternity pay or allowance period.
(v) Not at work due to a trade dispute where they work, except where they do not participate or have a direct interest in the dispute.
(vi) Paid less than the statutorily defined earnings limit.

SSP is not paid for absence of less than four days, but social security benefits and, in particular, state sickness benefit may be available in this case or where you are excluded for other reasons.

Details of entitlements are in guidance leaflets available from the DSS or job centres,[6] and these should always be referred to, but the key points[7] are that:

- You must be incapable as a result of disease, or bodily or mental disablement, from undertaking the work you can be expected to do under your contract.
- The day of incapacity claimed for must be within a 'period of incapacity' of four or more consecutive days. Periods of incapacity can be treated as continuous if they are within a fortnight of each other.
- You can qualify even if you are only part-time.
- The period of SSP entitlement for the year has not ended. SSP is paid for up to 28 weeks in any period, or in any year (after that you should claim for invalidity benefit and other state sickness benefits). SSP is currently paid at a maximum weekly rate of £52.50 (on earnings over £190 per week), or at £45.30 (on earnings of over £54).
- SSP does not have to be paid if you have not met the necessary certification procedures, including completion of a sickness claim form or continuing sickness form. In order to claim back the SSP they have paid out (from the national insurance payments they collect) employers must keep proper certification and other records.
- Although employers can require notification of absence due to sickness, there are restrictions on what can be required – for example, medical evidence does not have to be given at the same time as notification, and notification cannot be required, if you are away for more than a week, at more than weekly intervals.
- You can appeal if SSP has not been properly paid.[8]

Employers' Sickness Schemes

Employers may well operate their own sick pay schemes which pay normal earnings or improve on the basic SSP level. Such payments will reduce or wipe out the employer's obligation to pay SSP.

Time Off

The starting point for considering time off is that employees are normally required to be ready and available for work at all times during their working hours. If the job requires any time away from the workplace, then a right of absence for that purpose might be implied. Apart from that possibility, specific permission to be away should be obtained.

Although there are several statutory rights to time off which have been superimposed on this contractual position, those rights are mostly limited to work-related activities like trade union functions and health and safety committee work. Outside commitments, with the exception of public duties and jury service, have never figured very highly. A central feature of EC social legislation has been concerned with reconciling work obligations with family and domestic commitments. This was one of the reasons why the Conservative government opted out of the Social Chapter of the Maastricht Treaty in December 1991.[9] In the UK context the only serious commitment in this area has been in relation to maternity leave (see below), and even this does not compare very favourably with arrangements available in other countries.[10]

Nor have the courts' and tribunals' approach to time off for non-work related reasons been very favourably disposed to workers' needs. They have been reluctant to place even domestic emergencies ahead of what they see as an employer's workplace priorities.

Example

Mrs Warner worked as a shop assistant in Stourport. Her son had been taken ill, suddenly, with diabetes and when he was allowed out of hospital, on a Saturday, she expected to be able to be with him on his arrival home to supervise his insulin injections and meals. She tried unsuccessfully to get the day, or even just the morning, off. She left work and later tried to get some compensation for unfair dismissal. Her claim was rejected. There was no entitlement to time off, even in an emergency, that could be implied into all employment contracts. Mrs Warner's lawyer tried to argue that in this day and age an employer should sometimes have to cope with the effects of an employee's domestic emergency.[11]

It was suggested, though, by the EAT that a right to time off could be more readily implied in the case of larger organisations where the effects of a person's temporary absence may not be so significant as with a small employer.

Union Officials

If you are an official of a trade union, and the union is recognised by your employer (see chapter 19 below on recognition), you are entitled to reasonable time off during working time to carry out your duties.[12] The exact amount of time is whatever is 'reasonable in all the circumstances' having regard to the ACAS Code of Practice on Time Off for Trade Union Duties and Activities, no 3. The Employment Act 1989 limited the scope for time off under this head, largely because the government thought the existing provisions were being applied too generously.

Time off is now restricted to the time which an official needs:

(a) for any duties which, as such an official, are concerned with negotiations on anything listed in s.178(2) of the Trade Union and Labour Relations (Consolidation) Act 1992. This would include, in particular, employment terms and conditions, physical conditions at the workplace, the allocation of work, recruitment and dismissal issues, and disciplinary problems;

(b) for other duties s/he may have as an official which are concerned with the issues covered by s.178(2), *and* which the employer has agreed can be undertaken by the union;

(c) to undertake industrial relations training which is relevant to carrying out the duties within point (a) above, and which has been approved by the union or the TUC.

You must be paid for time off as an official on the basis of what would have been your normal pay on the day in question; if your pay varies with the amount of work you do it is calculated by reference to your average hourly earnings.[13]

If time off is refused, or you are not paid, a complaint can be taken to an industrial tribunal.

Union Activities

Union members are entitled to unpaid time off for union activities, or if they are acting as representatives, if the union is recognised by the employer.[14] The activities which this important right covers are organisational activities. As the Code of Practice, para. 21, states: 'To operate effectively and democratically trade unions need the active participation of members in certain union activities.' It goes on to refer to things like voting at workplace union elections, and occasions when it is reasonable for a union to hold urgent meetings during working hours. Members should also, it states, be able to attend official policy making bodies of the union during working time.

In practice many employers are prepared to agree detailed arrangements on time off under this head (and in relation to union officials) which can take into account local circumstances. This is recommended in the Code, and is obviously advantageous from the union's point of view.

Tribunal complaints can also be brought for refusals under this head.

Safety Representatives and Committees

Safety representatives appointed by the union under the Health and Safety at Work Act 1974 (see chapter 16 below) must be given paid time off to carry out their functions under the Act – consultation with the employer, monitoring hazards and compliance with safety arrangements, for instance. This is laid down by the Safety Representatives and Safety Committees Regulations 1977, but important guidance is also given in the HSC Codes of Practice on 'Safety Representatives and Safety Committees' (1978) and 'Time Off for the Training of Safety Representatives' (1978).[15]

Safety representatives must also be given paid time off to attend safety courses. Whether such training is necessary is not just for the employer to decide. It will usually depend on whether or not it is reasonable for particular representatives to go given their responsibilities.[16]

The Trade Union Reform and Employment Rights Act 1993 gives greater protection to representatives against victimisation in respect of their work. See further on this in chapter 16.

Public Duties

There are a number of public duties for which an employer must give unpaid leave. The time off must be 'reasonable in all the circumstances', having regard to the functions in question, the time off already taken and the effects on the employer's business.[17] The duties include: Justice of the Peace, local authority membership, statutory tribunals, National Health Service trusts and health authorities, school managing or governing bodies, and prison and other penal institutions' boards of visitors.

Redundancy and Job-hunting

If you have had two years' continuous service and have been made redundant, you are entitled during the period before your notice runs out (see p.255) to reasonable time off to look for work and to arrange training to help your future employment prospects.[18]

Jury Service

If you are summoned for jury service your employer is bound to let you attend (Juries Act 1974), and you will receive travelling, subsistence allowances and payments for lost earnings in accordance with fixed rates.

Pregnancy

Maternity leave arrangements are a key factor in ensuring that women get equal opportunities with men at work and in the jobs market. It is also the right of women, and men sharing responsibilities in relation to childcare, to be able to reconcile work and home commitments fairly. This is implicit in the equal treatment clause (clause 16) of the EC Charter of the Fundamental Social Rights of Workers.

UK maternity leave legislation has, to date, contained significant limitations on the exercise of maternity leave rights, and still makes no provision for paternity leave. EC Directive 92/85 has improved on UK legislation, notably by removing service requirements as a precondition for leave and by providing for contractual entitlements to continue during the leave period. The exception to this is pay. Although there will be no reason why arrangements should not be made with an employer for normal pay to continue during the leave, EC rules only provide for minimum pay in line with sick pay (see below). The legislation sets *minimum* standards which can be improved on in collective agreements and individual arrangements, whether in relation to pay or any other aspect of maternity rights.

The current legal entitlements are in the EPCA, ss. 33–8A, and 39–44, as inserted by TURERA, ss. 23–5 and schedule 2.

Antenatal Care

If you are pregnant you are entitled to *paid* leave to go to antenatal classes.[19] This right is not dependent on previous service.

Maternity Leave Period

All women employees are entitled to a maternity leave period, and this right is available as soon as the employment has begun. The period will usually begin on the date specified in the notice of leave required to be given to the employer at least 21 days beforehand (ss. 34 and 36). If your baby is born prematurely, the leave period will begin on the date of birth.

Maternity leave will normally continue for 14 weeks from when it begins, or until childbirth, and may continue in any case where a woman is prevented from resuming work under health and safety prohibitions relating to childbirth (s. 35). For women who have been continuously employed for a period of not less than two years at the beginning of the eleventh week before the expected week of childbirth, and who are also entitled to a 14 week leave period, there are additional rights to leave although the rights during that extended leave are less than those during the basic 14 week period (see further below). The extended period operates for 29 weeks after the beginning of the week in which childbirth occurs (s. 39).

To claim the basic 14 week leave period the employer *must* also be informed in writing at least 21 days before the leave period begins, or, if that is not practicable, as soon as is reasonably practicable, that: (a) you are pregnant, and (b) of the expected week of childbirth (or the date when the baby was born). The employer is also entitled to ask for a medical certificate showing the expected week of childbirth (s. 37). If the *extended* period is also claimed the employer *must* also be told that you intend to exercise your right to return to work. The employer must be given written notice of your intention to return to work at least 21 days before the date of return. Further information on claims requirements should be obtained from DE and DSS offices.

As far as pay and benefits are concerned, the legislation states that a woman is 'entitled to the benefit of the terms and conditions of employment which would have been applicable to her if she had not been absent (and had not been pregnant or given birth to a child)' (s. 33), that is, all contractual rights and benefits continue during the leave. In the case of pay, however, unless the contract of employment or collective agreement provides for normal pay or some other entitlement, pay will only consist of Statutory Maternity Pay (SMP), as provided for under pre-TURERA arrangements. Up-to-date guidance on the SMP payable should be obtained from DE and DSS offices.

Returning to Work

A key issue in maternity rights is the position when the maternity leave period ends and a woman wants to return to work. Under the basic 14 week entitlement all women who take advantage of their statutory rights are entitled to resume work on the same conditions they previously enjoyed (subject only to a requirement to give 7 days notice if the return is earlier than expected). This is *not*, however, the position for anyone who carries on into the extended period of leave. In particular an employer is not obliged to take you back in exactly the same post you previously held, although the conditions must be no less favourable than those you had when you went on leave, for example in terms of seniority and pay (s. 39).

Redundancy Rights

Rather than being immediately dismissed if her job is made redundant during the maternity leave period, a woman is entitled to be offered any suitable available vacancy that exists. The job must be suitable in terms of what it requires the woman to do, and should not be on terms which are substantially less favourable than under her previous contract (ss. 38 and 41). On redundancy generally see chapter 15.

Unfair Dismissal

All women, following the changes made by TURERA, have the right not to be sacked on grounds relating to pregnancy or childbirth. Dismissal would automatically be 'unfair' in a number of circumstances (EPCA s. 60, as substituted by TURERA, s. 24), including:

- Dismissal at the end of the leave period for reasons related to the pregnancy. Among other things, employers may not dismiss on grounds that a woman is unable to do the job.
- Dismissal for claiming leave and leave-related rights.
- Redundancy, either where selection is because of pregnancy (or taking leave), or where a suitable vacancy has not been offered when this was available, as an alternative to redundancy.

See also chapter 14 on unfair dismissal.

Suspension on Maternity Grounds

The 1993 Act extends the rights of women who are suspended on health and safety grounds, and who are at risk from dismissal. At present women can be fairly dismissed on such grounds, notably where continued employment would contravene statutory restrictions on working. As well as a right to suitable alternative work, suspension will be an option for women who are pregnant, have just given birth or are breastfeeding. Suspended employees will be entitled to normal pay unless suitable alternative work has been refused. You will be able to take a complaint of non-payment to an industrial tribunal.

CHAPTER 9

Conflicts of Interest, Competition and Confidentiality

The implied duty of 'fidelity', which can operate to an employer's advantage in relation to industrial action (see chapter 20), is also the basis of other important obligations to employers. These are generally concerned with situations where an employee's activities, usually during work time but possibly at other times as well, are considered by the law to be in conflict with the employer's business interests. The exact scope of these obligations will always depend on the particular circumstances in each case, and on the type of business concerned, but it is possible to identify the key principles involved.

In some cases employers may insist on express terms in the contract in order to increase the protection they have – for example, to prohibit business links with other companies, or to prevent contacts with customers, or to curtail attempts to recruit other staff in the organisation after the employment ends. Such terms can be highly restrictive and it is only in a limited number of areas, such as employee inventions and designs, that statutory rights and protection have been introduced. There are also certain limits that the courts have introduced which will be considered in this chapter.

Responsibility for Property, Money

Employees are obviously subject to the ordinary criminal law, and in particular this means potential liability for appropriating an employer's property, putting in dishonest expenses claims and other activities which could be interpreted as theft.[1] The duty of fidelity, which is implied into all employment relationships for this purpose, will also make employees liable to reimburse an employer, either if the property is obtained dishonestly, or if they do not take sufficient care of it, for example if negligence when looking after it results in it being stolen. In the leading case a bank manager was held to be personally responsible for not using sufficient care and skill in giving customers credit facilities without checking their credit worthiness.[2]

Any property or money to which an employer is entitled must be accounted for. This would include money or funds in any other form which should be coming into the employer's business. This point is illustrated in the case of receipts from shop sales. Shopworkers are required to account for these immediately and can have pay deducted to make up for any stock shortages and till deficiencies for which they are responsible (see pp.70–1 on restrictions on employers' rights to deduct and demand payments). As well as accounting to the employer, there is also the risk of dismissal or disciplinary action as in the case of a shopworker borrowing money from the till without authority.[3]

Working for Other Employers

Some employers try to impose tough restrictions on working for other employers, and might even try to bar it altogether. Others may not object, particularly if 'moonlighting' or other part-time work supplements the low wages they pay. Not surprisingly, though, employers with trade secrets, customer lists or other information or special interests to protect will be more likely to try to restrict their staff working for competitors or having outside interests.

In-service Restrictions

Employees are normally free to do what they want in their spare time, that is, outside their normal working hours. There are examples, though, of employers successfully preventing staff working in their spare time where the work is done for a competitor and there is scope for that work resulting in damage to the employer's business in some way, such as revealing to competitors information about secret manufacturing processes.[4] If there is no risk of this kind then an employer is *not* entitled to restrict such part-time work.

Example

Mr Froggatt was sacked from being an 'odd-job man' (as his job was described in the tribunal), after being employed for nearly five years. The employer found out that other workers had been working for a rival upholstery company, and because Mr Froggatt had also been going to the other company's premises assumed he had also been working there. The dismissal was held to be unfair. The fact that the other company was in competition with the employer did not, in itself, mean the employees could be stopped from spare-time working, or that they could be dismissed for doing so. It had to be shown that such work actually damaged the employer, and the nature of Mr Froggatt's work for the rival company did not contribute very seriously to the competition between the companies. Nor did it interfere with any of the work for the employer, such as overtime obligations.[5]

If you are subject to an *express* term in your contract restricting part-time work this may be effective in preventing such work, especially if the work also happens to be for a competitor. In the case example above, the result might have been different if the employee was subject to an express clause, for example making overtime compulsory, as there would then have been a conflict between the employer's requirements and the part-time work. Express restrictions are more commonly used to limit the activities of more senior staff.

Restrictions on Ex-employees

Employers are more restricted in their ability to prevent *ex*-employees working. In fact the position changes as soon as notice to leave is given, or if you simply leave a job to work elsewhere. Although there are exceptional cases where people have been stopped by a court order from working for a rival organisation before the required notice has expired, and where there is an express bar on working for competitors, the courts will not usually make such orders unless significant harm would be caused to the former employer's business.[6] It is increasingly common for employers to put 'garden leave' clauses in contracts, particularly for more senior staff or people in jobs where they have access to confidential data or know-how. Such clauses prescribe long notice periods, and by requiring notice to be worked out (even when you might not be required to do anything) all the in-service restrictions continue to operate. A court may well refuse to enforce this kind of clause, particularly once it is clear the employment relationship is at an end.

Restraint clauses cannot be enforced by an employer if the employer has broken the contract, for example by forcing you to leave or giving insufficient notice.

Restrictions on Working

If an employer wants to restrict you working for other organisations after your job has finished, there will have to be a valid 'restraint' clause in your contract. The general rule is that you are free to work anywhere you want after finishing, and the fact that you might work for a competitor, or even set up a business competing with the ex-employer, is irrelevant. The only basis on which the law permits restraint clauses in some cases is where they are clearly necessary to prevent *unfair* competition, particularly if there has previously been access to confidential data, customer lists, personal contacts with clients and so on that could be unfairly exploited. In practical terms it is the ex-employer's job to try to enforce a restraint, such as by trying to obtain an injunction or damages and the court will expect the employer to demonstrate why the clause is necessary.[7]

To be valid and enforceable a clause must be reasonable in terms of:

- duration;
- what it restricts;
- geographical scope;
- 'public interest' requirements;
- maintaining free competition, and people's right to use their work skills.

On this basis, a restraint that tries to bar activities that could not cause any damage to the ex-employer, or which covers geographical areas where the ex-employer clearly does not operate, is likely to be invalid. There is no 'going rate' by which it is possible to say the time specified in a clause is too long, but clauses stipulating restraint for over 12 months may well be treated as excessive or unnecessary.

Information and Know-how

There may be restrictions on an employee using information required during a job as a result of the implied duty of fidelity. The reasons for this are not always clear but they include a number of factors. First, there is the general principle that people should not collect, disclose or use such information, if the result is to harm their employer's interests. Second, the law gives certain types of 'sensitive' information special protection. Although employers do not necessarily have any formal proprietorial right over such information (such as the rights that copyright or a patent right would give them), the protection can still be very extensive.

While employers can have trade secrets and operational data which it is not unreasonable for them to want to protect, employees also have important rights, in particular the right to make use of, and develop, the knowledge, experience and skills which have been gained in their jobs. Unfortunately, the problem of reconciling these conflicting demands has not been resolved very well by the present rules.

As with spare-time work, and the rules on working for competitors, the law will enforce in-service restrictions more readily than restrictions after the job has come to an end. In practical terms this means, for example, the implied duty could be used if you canvass your employer's business contacts on your last day in the job so that you can get work from them when you set up on your own.[8] Taking copies of the employer's customer list would also be a clear breach.[9] Express clauses, particularly if they make it more clear what is being restricted, will obviously strengthen the employer's hand.

The key principles have now been laid down in a leading Court of Appeal case. In this case,[10] the company employed a sales manager to assist its operations, which included breeding, slaughtering and selling poultry. The manager gained useful sales and other information which he then used when he went into business on his own account, selling chickens from refrigerated vans. There was no express term limiting what he could do after he left. The company claimed he had broken an implied duty of confidentiality, specifically by making use of details about customers and their requirements, the best routes to their locations and the prices the company charged.

After considering the exact scope of the rules about competition with employers and ex-employers, and the type of information involved, the court rejected the employer's claim. The information was not so confidential that it could be covered by an implied prohibition on its use. In particular, the information concerned could not be classed as a trade secret and a number of important points were made which would be relevant in other competition situations.

In the first place there will obviously be situations in which the information is simply not important enough to be classed as confidential. It is possible, though, for employers to make it clear, either in an express clause or through some other means, that specific types of information *are* to be treated as confidential. Misusing such information *while the job continues* is likely to amount to a breach of contract. Employers may also try to extend restrictions by including restraint clauses in the contract. In practice such clauses are difficult to enforce.

The court referred to other factors which may assist in deciding whether a confidentiality requirement will operate, including:

* the kind of employment the employee is in – some jobs obviously involve the use of data which can clearly be highly confidential;
* whether the information itself could be of a kind which is a trade secret or requires the same kind of protection;
* whether the information in question can be separated from other information freely available for an employee to use.

Patents and Copyright

Employees' rights to exploit or benefit from their inventions and designs were very limited until legislation improved the position. The usual presumption was that anything done in the employer's time belonged to the employer. In some cases employers could even lay claim to the results of work done in employees' own time.

The Patents Act 1977, s. 39, makes it clear that an invention will only belong to the employer if:

* it is made in the course of normal duties, or duties specifically assigned, and the invention could reasonably be expected to derive from that work; or
* it is made in the course of normal duties and, at the time of the invention, there is any special obligation to further the employer's business interests.

In effect this means that unless you are employed to invent or design things and actually do such work, or you have some other special obligations under your contract, for example because of the seniority of your job, the invention is *your* property.[11] Where the employer successfully patents an invention the Act may still provide for compensation if it is of 'outstanding benefit to the employer' and it is 'just' that compensation should be paid. It may also be payable if any benefits received are inadequate (s. 40). Compensation is based on a 'fair share' of the benefits from the invention.

'Authorship' rights in an employee's work will usually depend on who owns the copyright in the work in question. This is relevant to written material, designs and software programmes, among other things. In this case anything produced in the course of your employment will normally belong to the employer.[12] The position depends on the particular contract of employment, and it is always advisable to clarify the exact contractual position (either when the job begins, or before doing the work concerned), even if you are involved in working in your own time.

PART THREE

Discrimination

CHAPTER 10

Equal Pay

Background

A victim of sex discrimination may have possible legal remedies under:

- European Community Law
- The Equal Pay Act 1970
- The Sex Discrimination Act 1975

In recent years the impact of Community law has substantially increased as a result of radical decisions of the European Court of Justice in such cases as *Barber* v. *Guardian Royal Exchange Assurance Group* [1990] IRLR 240 and *Foster* v. *British Gas plc* [1990] IRLR 353. As we shall see, Community law will override own domestic law in the event of a conflict. Indeed on two occasions the UK government has been hauled before the European Court by the European Commission because it failed to comply with its obligations under the Treaty of Rome.

In *EC Commission* v. *United Kingdom of Great Britain and Northern Ireland* [1982] IRLR 333, the UK was held to have failed fully to implement Council Directive 75/117/EEC on equal pay. The government was forced to amend the UK's legislation on equal pay in order to comply with the ruling, and to allow equal value claims in addition to claims based on 'like work'. In *EC Commission* v. *United Kingdom* [1984] IRLR 29 the ECJ ruled that British law on sex discrimination did not comply with EC standards because among other things it did not apply non-legally binding collective agreements and that its exemptions regarding small firms and private households were too wide. Once again the government had to introduce legislation, the Sex Discrimination Act 1986, in order to accommodate both that ruling and the ECJ's decision in *Marshall* v. *Southampton and South West Hampshire Area Health Authority ('Teaching)* [1986] IRLR 140, where it was held that the imposition of discriminatory retirement ages for men and women offended the Equal Treatment Directive 76/207.

If the complaint centres on unequal terms and conditions of employment (whether about pay or not) then there may be a remedy under the Equal Pay Act (EqPA). However, the complainant must be able to point to a person of the opposite gender who is treated more favourably – there is no such thing as the hypothetical man or woman under this legislation.

If there is no remedy under the EqPA, then a possible claim under the Sex Discrimination Act (SDA) should be investigated. This Act covers a wide range of discriminatory practices as well discrimination in employment. Within the employment field, it covers not only those in employment but also applicants for jobs. It also makes unlawful discrimination on grounds of marital status within employment. The law relating to discrimination is discussed in the next chapter.

European Community Law

The Treaty of Rome

The general rule is that the articles of the treaty cannot be enforced directly by the individual citizen against a member state. The citizen must wait for the government to legislate and transform its international treaty obligation into domestic law. There are, however, some exceptions to this rule and the European Court of Justice has held that article 119 of the treaty (dealing with equal pay) creates a directly enforceable right for the individual (see *Kowalska* v. *Freie und Hansestadt Hamburg* [1990] IRLR 447).

Article 119 states:

Each Member State shall ... maintain the application of the principle that men and women should receive equal pay for equal work.

For the purpose of this Article, pay means the ordinary basic or minimum wage or salary and any other consideration, whether in cash or in kind, which the worker receives, directly or indirectly, in respect of his employment from his employer.

Equal pay without discrimination based on sex means:

(a) that pay for the same work at piece rates shall be calculated on the basis of the same unit of measurement;

(b) that pay for work at time rates shall be the same for the same job.

The Directives

The treaty is supplemented by directives made by the Council of Ministers. Under art. 189 of the treaty, a directive is 'binding as to the result to be achieved' but the form and method of achieving the result is left to the individual member state.

In certain circumstances, however, a directive may be held to be directly enforceable. In *Van Duyn* v. *Home Office* [1975] 3 All ER 190, it was held that a directive *could* be enforceable by an individual and that this depended on whether the directive was 'clear, precise, admitted of no exceptions, and therefore of its nature needed no intervention by the national authorities.'

A good example of a directive found to have a direct effect is to be found in *Marshall* v. *Southampton and South West Hampshire Area Health Authority (Teaching)* [1986] IRLR 140. Miss Marshall had been employed by the Health Authority for 13 years before being dismissed shortly after she reached the age of 62, despite the fact that she had expressed a willingness to continue her employment as a senior dietician until she reached the age of 65. The sole reason for her dismissal was that, as a woman, she had passed 'the normal retirement age' applied by her employers to female employees. The ECJ held that the dismissal of a woman solely because she had reached the qualifying age for state pension where that age is different for men, constituted discrimination on grounds of sex contrary to the Equal Treatment Directive (76/207). The directive was held to be directly enforceable by the individual against the member state, who in this case was also the applicant's employer (a 'vertical' direct effect). However, a directive could not have been relied on had the employer been in the private sector. This is because directives are enforceable only against the state and its organs; they have no 'horizontal' direct effect against private individuals or organisations.

While it is clear that directives can only be enforced against bodies which are 'organs or emanations of the State', there was, until recently, some doubt as to the scope of this phrase. In *Foster* v. *British Gas* (1990) IRLR 354, the House of Lords referred the matter to the European Court for a ruling. The ECJ was prepared to give a wide definition of these terms. It held that a directive that has direct effect may be relied upon in a claim against a body, whatever its legal form, which has been made responsible for providing a public service under the control of the state and has for that purpose special powers beyond those which result from the normal rules applicable in relations between private individuals. This broad approach means that local government, universities and colleges and nationalised industries all clearly now fall within the potential scope of direct effect.[1]

Equal Pay: Background

When the UK joined the EEC in 1972, the Equal Pay Act 1970 was already on the statute book, although it did not come into force until 29 December 1975. The five-year delay was to give employers time voluntarily to review and alter their pay structures. The Act enabled workers to claim equal pay with colleague of the opposite gender if their work was the same or broadly similar. But it gave no remedy if the work was of equal value, unless the jobs had been rated as equivalent under a job evaluation scheme. In *Commission of the European Communities* v. *United Kingdom of Great Britain and Northern Ireland* [1982] IRLR 333, the Commission alleged that the UK equal pay legislation did not comply with the 'Equal Pay' Directive (75/117). The ECJ held that the UK had not adopted 'the necessary measures' and there was 'at present no means whereby a worker who considers that his post is of equal value to another may pursue his claims if the employer refuses to introduce a job classification system'. As a result of this decision the government was forced to introduce the Equal Pay (Amendment) Regulations 1983 (SI 1983 No. 1794) in order to allow equal value claims to be brought. These regulations were accompanied by new and complex procedural rules designed to govern equal value claims before an industrial tribunal.

This complexity, together with the width of the employer's defence (discussed below), raises serious doubts as to whether the government's response adequately implements the 'Equal Pay' Directive and the ECJ's decision. Indeed, the Equal Opportunities Commission has described the current equal pay laws as 'a paradise for lawyers, a hell for women' (see *Equal Pay for Men and Women – Strengthening The Acts*, 1990).

The Meaning of Pay

Under the Equal Pay Act, claims are not purely restricted to those concerned with unequal wages or salaries; a claim may be brought in respect of *any* term in a woman's contract of employment which is less favourable than that of her male comparator. On the other hand, under Community law, the right only applies to pay or remuneration but is not restricted to contractual entitlements and 'comprises any other consideration, whether in cash or in kind, whether immediate or future, provided that the worker receives it, albeit indirectly, in respect of his employment from his employer' (*Garland* v. *British Rail Engineering Ltd* [1982] IRLR 111 p. 115, per the ECJ).

The European Court has adopted a wide interpretation of 'pay'. In *Garland*, the ECJ took the view that concessionary travel facilities constituted 'pay' and that 'pay' included indirect benefits of this nature which continued to be provided after retirement. In *Worringham and Humphreys* v. *Lloyds Bank Ltd* [1979] IRLR 440, it was held that contributions to a pension scheme paid by the employer in the employee's name were part of the employee's 'pay' for the purposes of the treaty. In *Kowalska* v. *Freie und Hansestadt Hamburg*: 33/89 [1990] IRLR 447, the ECJ held that severance payments made to workers fell within the meaning of 'pay' under art. 119, such payments being viewed by the court as 'a form of deferred remuneration to which the worker is entitled by virtue of his employment, but which is paid to him at the time of the termination of the relationship'. Thus when a collective agreement provided that severance payments were paid to full-time employees but not to part-timers, the applicant was able to present statistical evidence to show the provision indirectly discriminated against women and was contrary to art. 119.

Discrimination in the provision of payments made by employers required by certain legislative provisions may also be caught by art. 119, as illustrated by the

German case of *Rinner-Kuhn* v. *FWW Spezial-Gebaudereinigung* [1989] IRLR 493. Under German national law, whether a sick employee should continue to be paid was subject to a minimum working hours requirement. In reality fewer women would therefore avail themselves of the provision. The ECJ concluded that art. 119 applies to national legislation unless the member state can show that the legislation is justified by objective factors unrelated to any discrimination on grounds of sex.

It is therefore clear from this decision that art. 119 can be relied upon to challenge pay-related national legislation which may have the effect of excluding women from employment protection rights.

These two German cases, together with a third (*Bilka-Kaufhaus GmbH* v. *Weber von Hartz* : 170/84 [1986] IRLR 317), clearly establish that indirect discrimination in pay is unlawful. Indirect discrimination occurs when an ostensibly gender-neutral condition or requirement prejudices a substantial proportion of women compared to men. In *Bilka-Kaufhaus*, for example, the exclusion of part-time workers from an occupational pension scheme was held to fall within the ambit of art. 119 and the benefits provided under such a scheme were 'pay' for the purposes of the article. If the employer seeks to justify a pay practice which in fact discriminates against women workers, the employer must 'put forward objective economic grounds relating to the management of the undertaking. It is also necessary to ascertain whether the pay practice in question is necessary and in proportion to the objectives pursued by the employer.'

More recently, and more radical still, is the decision in *Barber* v. *Guardian Royal Exchange Assurance Group*: C262/88 [1990] IRLR 240. In what is – for UK employers – probably the most important judgement ever to come from the ECJ, the court held that occupational pensions payable under a contracted-out scheme constitute 'pay' under art. 119 of the Treaty of Rome, and so must be non-discriminatory in their terms. This means that pensionable ages must be the same for men and women, and benefits payable must be equal. Where a scheme allows a woman to take a pension at the age of 60, a man will have the right to insist on the same option, on the same terms.

As art. 119 is directly enforceable in the UK, employers had to respond immediately in order to avoid exposure to industrial tribunal claims. The court did, however, seek to limit the impact of its decision by ruling that it did not have retrospective effect. This means that any existing employee is entitled to insist on a non-discriminatory pension age, and anyone who has already instituted a discrimination or equal pay complaint will be entitled to have it determined on the basis of *Barber*. UK discrimination legislation, which allowed discrimination in pension entitlements and benefits, is overridden as a result of the decision in *Barber*.

The court also held that redundancy benefits, whether contractual, statutory or voluntary in nature, also constitute 'pay' – so that these must also be offered to women and men on entirely equal terms.

The *Barber* decision also adopts the approach already taken by the House of Lords in *Hayward* v. *Cammell Laird Shipbuilders Ltd* [1988] IRLR 257 that where there is found to be unequal contractual term, the employer cannot argue that regard should be had to the whole of the remuneration package in assessing whether there is unequal pay. Each of the terms of the contract should be considered separately and individually.

Who Can Claim Equal Pay?

- The Act applies not only to 'employees' but also to anyone who is employed under 'a contract *personally* to execute any work or labour' (s. 1[6]). Therefore, unlike the rights to claim unfair dismissal, redundancy payments and the like, self-employed workers are given protection provided 'the sole or dominant purpose of the contract is the execution of work or labour by the contracting party'.[2]
- Again in contrast to many of the other employment rights, there is no qualifying period or minimum period of hours.
- Most of those workers in the employment of the Crown are covered.
- Employees are generally excluded if they are not in employment at an establishment within Great Britain.

Exclusions

There are three contractual terms which remain unaffected by the 'equality clause':

(a) Terms affected by compliance with the law relating to women's employment. The importance of this exception has been much diminished by the removal by the SDA 1986 of those parts of the Factories Act 1961 which regulated the hours of work of women. This process of deregulation was taken further by the Employment Act 1989 which removed a whole range of restrictions on the types of job which a woman could do. Indeed, the same statute lays down the general principle that any legislation passed prior to SDA 1975 shall be of no effect in so far as it imposes a requirement to do an act which would amount to direct or indirect sex discrimination.

(b) Terms giving special treatment to women in connection with pregnancy or childbirth. This allows employers to provide maternity leave without risking an equal treatment challenge from their male workforce.

(c) Terms related to death or retirement, or to any provision in connection with death or retirement. The significance of this exception has been much reduced as a result of the influence of EC law. First, the SDA 1986 now makes it unlawful to provide for differential retirement ages as opposed to pension ages. Second, the decision in *Barber* renders unlawful any differential treatment paid under an occupational pension scheme. Finally, under the Social Security Pensions Act 1975 it is unlawful to deny either gender equal access to an occupational benefits scheme.

The Right to Equal Pay

The Comparator

Before embarking on an equal pay claim, it is crucial that the female applicant can identify a man with whom to compare herself. If there is no man whose contract can be compared to that of the woman, then she will have no chance in her equal pay claim. This is because, in contrast to a claim under the Sex Discrimination Act, the applicant is not allowed to compare herself with a hypothetical male.[3]

The woman may select the comparator of her choice; it is not the job of the industrial tribunal to reject her choice and select a comparator who appears to the tribunal to be more appropriate.[4] Where an applicant cannot name her comparators, she is not barred from bringing a claim as long as she can show the prima facie case. The industrial tribunal can order discovery of the relevant names.

Under the Equal Pay Act, it was necessary to show that there was a time when her comparator and she employed contemporaneously on like work, work rated as equivalent or work of equal value. Once again our domestic law has proved to be narrower in scope than Community law. As a result, even if a woman cannot show that her comparator was in contemporaneous employment, she may bring a claim under art. 119 as opposed to the Equal Pay Act. This was established in the important case of *Macarthys Ltd* v. *Smith* [1980] IRLR 210.

Mrs Smith became trainee manageress of the stockroom on 21 January 1986, and manageress on 1 March. She claimed equal pay with her predecessor as stockroom manager, a Mr McCullough, who had left on 20 October 1975. The majority of the Court of Appeal held that she could not succeed in her claim under the Equal Pay Act because its wording clearly required contemporaneous employment. However, the court was less certain as to whether she could bring her claim using art. 119 and they referred that issue to the ECJ. The ECJ held that under the Treaty of Rome Mrs Smith could compare herself with a predecessor.

A final constraint in terms of choice of comparator relates to the fact that the woman must be able to show that the comparator is in the 'same employment'. This will not be problematic if the applicant is employed at the same establishment as the comparator. However, if she is employed by the same or an associated employer but at a different establishment, then she has no claim unless common terms and conditions of employment are observed at both establishments either generally or for the relevant class of employee.

In *Leverton* v. *Clwyd County Council* [1989] IRLR 28, the phrase 'same employment' was given an expansive definition by the House of Lords, offering to applicants the prospect of an enlarged pool from which to choose comparators. In this case the applicant and her comparators were employed under the same collective agreement at different establishments – she being a nursery nurse and they being clerical staff. Although there was a difference in the hours worked and the holidays received, the House of Lords concluded that the correct construction of s. 1 (6) called for a comparison between the terms and conditions of employment observed at the establishment at which the woman was employed and the establishment at which the men were employed, and applicable either generally, as in this case, or to a particular class or classes of employees to which both the woman and men belonged; she was therefore in the 'same employment' for the purpose of s. 1 (6). In effect the issue is whether the applicant would have been employed under the same contract had she been doing the same job at her comparator's establishment.

Grounds on Which Equality can be Claimed

There are three different types of comparator on which to base the claim:

(a)   the man employed on like work with the applicant;
(b)   the man employed on work rated equivalent to that of the applicant; *and*
(c)   the man employed on work which is of equal value to that of the applicant.

Like Work

This is defined as work which is the same or of a broadly similar nature where the differences (if any) between the applicant does and what her comparator does are not of practical importance in relation to terms and conditions of employment (s. 1 [4]).

In *Capper Pass Ltd* v. *Lawton* [1977] ICR 83, the EAT stated that a two-stage inquiry should be adopted in determining whether people were engaged in like work. First, is the work the same, or, if not, is it of a broadly similar nature? To this latter question a broad approach should be adopted, without a minute examination of the differences between the jobs. Second, if the work is broadly similar, are the differences of practical importance?

Mrs Lawton was a cook providing lunches for up to 20 directors in a company director's dining room. She was held to be entitled to pay equal to that earned by two male assistant chefs who provided 350 meals per day in the company canteen.

In *Electrolux Ltd* v. *Hutchinson* [1986] IRLR 410, the EAT stated that in order to amount to a difference of practical importance it must be shown that, as well as being contractually obliged to undertake the additional different duties, the duties are actually performed to a significant extent.

In this case, men and women worked on the same track in the manufacture of refrigerators and freezers, but while all the men were paid on Grade 10, 599 out of the 600 women received rather lower wages on Grade 01. The company argued that the men had additional contractual obligations: they had to transfer to totally different tasks on demand and work overtime as and when required. The EAT focused on how frequently the men *did* the work; how often they were required to work on a Sunday; and what kind of work they did in those unsocial hours. The EAT came to the conclusion that in reality the work was like work.

The Time the Work Is Done

The orthodox view is that tribunals should ignore the time when the work is done in comparing the two jobs. In *Dugdale* v. *Kraft Foods Ltd* [1977] ICR 48, the applicant sought equality with a male night-shift worker and it was held that they were employed on like work. The EAT held that 'in the context of the Equal Pay Act ... the mere time at which the work is performed should be disregarded when considering the differences between the things which the woman does and the things which the man does' (Judge Phillips, p. 53). It is the nature of the work which must be considered. The tribunal went on to say that it remains permissible to pay an unsocial hours bonus or night-shift premium to the men as long as the basic pay remains the same.

The *Dugdale* decision was distinguished in *Thomas* v. *NCB* [1987] ICR 757, where the EAT held that female canteen assistants employed during the day were *not* engaged in like work with a male employed alone and at night. The effect of this decision is to make the time when the work is done relevant to the consideration of like work if it results in additional responsibility; for example, as in this case, working alone.

Additional Responsibility

A factor such as responsibility may be decisive where it can be seen to put one employee into a different grade from another with whom comparisons are being made. In *Eaton Ltd* v. *Nuttall* [1977] IRLR 71, a male production scheduler handling 1,200 items worth between £5 and £1,000 in cash and a woman scheduler handling 2,400 items worth below £2.50 each were held not to be engaged on broadly similar work – an error on the part of the man would be of much greater consequence.

Conversely (or perhaps perversely), it has been indicated that if a woman's work is more onerous or responsible than a man's, she may not be considered to be engaged in like work, even if she is less well paid (see *Waddington* v. *Leicester Council for Voluntary Services* [1977] ICR 266). An applicant in this situation is now able to bring an equal value claim since the decision of the ECJ in *Murphy v. Bord Telecom Eireann* [1988] IRLR 267.

Work Rated as Equivalent

A woman may claim equal pay with a man even though she is not doing like work, if her job has been 'rated as equivalent' to that of the man. The work will be rated as equivalent if the jobs of the comparator and applicant

> have been given an equal value, in terms of the demand made on the worker under various headings (for instance, effort, skill and decision) on a study undertaken with a view to evaluating in those terms the jobs to be done by all or any of the employees in an undertaking or group of undertakings, or would have been given an equal value but for the evaluation being made on a system of setting different values for men and women on the same demand under any heading (s. 1 [5]).

In *Bromley* v. *H & J Quick Ltd* [1988] IRLR 249, the Court of Appeal held that in order to fall within s. 1 (5), a job evaluation study must be 'analytical' in the sense that it must analyse the jobs covered by it in terms of the demands made on the worker under various headings (such as points assessment or factor comparison). Therefore, job evaluation studies based on 'felt fair' comparisons of 'whole jobs' (such as job ranking, paired comparisons or job classification) will not suffice and will not prevent the applicant bringing an 'equal value' claim under s. 1 (2) (c).

If no job evaluation has been carried out, under this part of the Act, there is no legal requirement for the employer to conduct one. It was, of course, this flaw in the legislation which lead to the introduction of the Equal Pay (Amendment) Regulations 1983. They purport to implement the Equal Pay Directive 75/117 by enabling an employee to insist that a job evaluation study should be carried out.

Work of Equal Value

An equal value claim is allowed if the applicant is engaged in work which, not being work in relation to which the provisions on like work or work rated as equivalent apply, 'is, in terms of the demands made on her (for instance under such headings as effort, skill and decision), of equal value to that of 'her comparator – s. 1 (2) (c).

In *Pickstone* v. *Freemans plc* [1988] IRLR 357, the House of Lords refused to accept that the presence of a man doing like work to Mrs Pickstone prevented her from making a claim for equal pay for work of equal value using another man as a comparator.

Lord Keith considered that to accept this construction of s. 1 (2) (c):

> would leave a gap in the equal work provision, enabling an employer to evade it by employing one token man on the same work as a group of potential women claimants who were deliberately paid less than a group of men employed on work of equal value with that of the women. This would mean that the UK had failed yet again to fully implement its obligations under art 119 of the Treaty and the Equal Pay Directive and had not given full effect to the decision of the European court in *Commission of the European Communities* v. *UK*. It is plain that Parliament cannot possibly have intended such a failure.

The Procedure in Equal Value Claims

The complex procedural rules governing an equal value claim are now contained in the Industrial Tribunals (Rules of Procedure) Regulations 1985 (SI 1985 no. 16) 2 sched. The sequence of the claim is set out in figure 10.1.

The procedure for lodging a complaint with the industrial tribunal under the equal value provisions is largely the same as under the original Act; that is, proceedings may be instituted by the applicant while she is still employed by the respondent employer or within six months of the termination of her employment (s. 2 [4]). A copy of the originating application is sent to ACAS, which must endeavour to promote a settlement. Furthermore, the industrial tribunal may hold a pre-hearing assessment and, if the contentions of one of the parties appears to have no reasonable prospect of success, it may give a warning as to costs if the case if the case is taken further.

At the full hearing, the tribunal must invite the parties to apply for an adjournment for the purpose of seeking a settlement (reg. 12 [2A]). Assuming that no settlement has been reached and before proceeding further, the tribunal must consider whether it is satisfied that there are no reasonable grounds for determining that the work is of equal value – s. 2 (A) (1) (a). The idea behind this provision is that only hopeless cases would be weeded out and that if there is an arguable case of any kind, the claim should proceed with any doubt resolved in favour of the applicant.

Where the two jobs have already been evaluated under a job evaluation scheme as unequal, the tribunal must dismiss the application if 'there are no reasonable grounds for determining that the evaluation contained in the study was made on a system which discriminates on grounds of sex' (s. 2A[2], that is, whether 'a difference or coincidence between values set by that system on different demands under the same heading or different headings is not justifiable irrespective of the sex of the person on whom those demands are made' (s. 2A[3]).

Where the applicant has overcome the obstacles presented by the filtering process described above, the employer may then ask the tribunal to consider the defence

Figure 10.1: Sequence of an Equal Value Claim

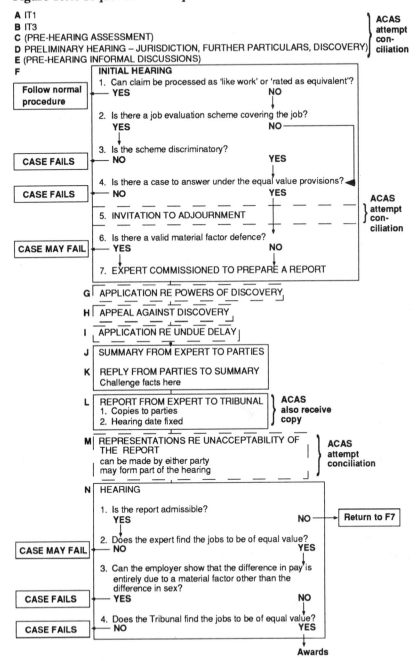

Source: *Equal Treatment for Men and Women: Strengthening the Acts* (EOC, 1990).

that the difference in pay is genuinely due to a material factor which is not a difference in gender (reg. 8 [2E]).

If the 'genuine material factor' defence is raised by the employer at this stage and rejected, it may be raised again after an independent expert's report has been received on the equal value claim. However, following the decision of the industrial tribunal in *Hayward* v. *Cammell Laird Shipbuilders Ltd* [1984] IRLR 463, it seems that employers who wish to put forward the genuine material factor defence should raise it at this preliminary stage. The employers in that case did not pursue the defence at the initial hearing and, as a result, were unable to raise it at the hearing following reception of the independent expert's report. We give a detailed examination of the material factor defence below.

With the exception of the cases where the tribunal decides that the claim is hopeless or that the genuine material factor defence is established, the tribunal must require an expert drawn from a panel nominated by ACAS, to prepare a report. The expert is obliged to take into account all information supplied to her/him and to send to the parties a written summary of the information and representations (rule 7A[3]). In addition, rule 7A (3)(d) places the expert under a duty to 'to take no account of the difference of sex and at all times to act fairly'.

Failure to comply with any of these requirements may lead to a tribunal finding that the expert's report is inadmissible – rule 7A (8) (a). In addition, the report may not be admitted if the conclusion contained in the report is one which, taking due account of the information supplied and representations made to the expert, could not reasonably have been reached; or if for some other material reason (other than disagreement with the conclusion that the applicant's work is not of equal value or with the reasoning leading to that conclusion) the report is unsatisfactory.

The procedure provides a number of avenues for the obtaining of information which may lead a tribunal to decide not to admit a report. The tribunal itself may, at any time after it has received the report, require the expert to explain in a reasoned written reply any matter contained in his/her report or to give further consideration to the question. A copy of the expert's reply must be sent to each of the parties and they must be allowed to make representations (rule 7A [10]).

In addition, each party, having been sent a copy of the expert's report, may make representations and call witnesses on the question of admissibility. The expert is compellable as a witness and may be subject to cross-examination. Furthermore, any party, after giving reasonable notice to the tribunal and any other party, may call one expert witness who may also be cross-examined (rules 7A [9], 8 [2B]).

If the tribunal rejects the report, it must commission a new one and the whole process must begin again. If, on the other hand, the report is admitted, it is ultimately for the tribunal to decide whether or not the jobs are of equal value. At this stage, the tribunal may still hear evidence from experts or other witnesses, but the rules introduce an important limitation. No party may give evidence or question any witness on any matter of fact on which a conclusion in the expert's report is based (rule 8 [2C]). The only exceptions to these restrictions are where the matter of fact is relevant to, and raised in connection with, a genuine material factor defence; or where a party's refusal to comply with a tribunal order for information or documents has prevented the expert from reaching a conclusion on the equal value issue (rule 8 [2D]).

Even where the conclusion of the expert is not shown to be unreasonable and is admitted into evidence, this does not mean that the industrial tribunal is obliged to accept its conclusions.

In *Tennents Textile Colours Ltd* v. *Todd* [1989] IRLR 3, the following guidance was provided by the Northern Ireland Court of Appeal:

- The burden of proof remains at all times with the applicant, and is not transferred even if the expert's report favours the applicant. (This can pose a major difficulty for the applicant if the tribunal cannot decide whether to follow the independent expert's report or that produced by the employer's expert. An applicant may be forced to commission her own expert report with all the attendant cost and complexity.)
- Conversely, the applicant is under no greater burden of proof if the report of the independent expert is not favourable to her case.
- The tribunal may reach a conclusion opposed to that of the independent expert without concluding that the report is obviously wrong; the normal burden of proof on the balance of probabilities is applicable.
- The findings of fact made by the expert are not binding. It can be argued that they are wrong, unreliable or that some are more important than others. The power of challenge exists despite the limited grounds for challenging the report before it has been admitted into evidence.

How Equal Is Equal Value?

There are conflicting views on this question. In *Wells* v. *F. Smales & Son (Fish merchants)* (IT unreported; see 2 EOR 24 [1985]), the expert's report had concluded that nine out of 14 claimant fish packers were engaged in equal or higher value work than a male labourer. The remaining five claimants' jobs had received scores ranging from 79 per cent to 95 per cent of the score accorded the job of the comparator. While accepting all the expert's findings of fact, the industrial tribunal adopted a broad brush approach and concluded that all of the claimants were engaged in work of equal value in that 'the differences between them and the comparator are not relevant nor make real material differences.'

This approach should be contrasted with the much narrower view adopted by the industrial tribunal in *Brown* v. *Cearns & Brown Ltd* ([1985] IRLIB 304), where the expert's report concluded that the applicant's work was worth 95 per cent of her comparator's. The IT declined to hold that the work was of equal value as 'it was not of precisely equal value'.

As we have seen, it is now clear that 'equal' includes 'higher'. Therefore, a woman employed on work of higher value than her male comparator may make an equal value claim (*Murphy* v. *Bord Telecom Eireann* [1988] IRLR 267).

The Genuine Material Factor Defence

It is a defence in equal pay cases if the employer can show that the variation between the woman's contract and the man's contract is genuinely due to a material factor which is not a difference in gender (s. 1 [3]). In the case of like work or work rated as equivalent claims, that factor *must* be 'a material difference between the woman's case and the man's', whereas in the case of equal value claims the factor 'may be such a difference'.

Following the decision of the House of Lords in *Rainey* v. *Greater Glasgow Health Board* [1987] IRLR 26, it would now appear that, despite this difference in wording, the ambit of the defence is probably the same in all three types of equal pay claims. In this case the major issue relating to the scope of the defence was whether the material factor justifying the difference in pay could encompass 'market forces': 'Given that men have traditionally been able to demand higher rewards in the labour market, the acceptance of market force arguments has serious implications for the degree of protection offered by the equal pay legislation.'[5]

In *Clay Cross (Quarry Services) Ltd* v. *Fletcher* [1979] ICR 1, the Court of Appeal held that the phrase 'difference between the woman's case and the man's' meant that only factors relating to the 'personal equation' of the employees could constitute a defence to a like work claim. As a result, it was not acceptable to defend a variation in pay on the grounds that the male clerk had been the only suitable candidate for the job and could only be persuaded to take it with the offer of more money than that paid to the existing female clerk. As Lord Denning put it: 'If any such excuse were permitted, the Act would become a dead letter. Those are the very reasons why there was unequal pay before the statute. They are the very circumstances in which the statute was intended to operate' (at p. 4).

Subsequently, as we have seen, pressure from the EC forced the government to introduce the equal value claim. Given its free market philosophy, the government was concerned that the *Fletcher* approach would prevent employers paying the market rate for labour. Therefore, in reluctantly introducing the equal value claim, it took the opportunity to change the wording of the material factor defence. The substitution of 'must' by 'may' was designed to allow the 'market forces' argument as a defence in equal value claims.

The government need not have worried because in *Rainey* v. *Greater Glasgow Health Board* [1987] AC 224, the court took the *Fletcher* interpretation of the scope of the defence in like work and work rated equivalent claims was unduly restrictive.

Mrs Rainey, a prosthetist employed by the NHS in Scotland, claimed equal pay with a male prosthetist, Mr Crumlin, who earned over £2,000 a year more. Mrs Rainey and Mr Crumlin had broadly the same qualifications and experience, but Mr Crumlin had been recruited from private practice, where salaries were much higher, in order to establish a prosthetic service within the NHS. Mrs Rainey, who had been recruited directly from the NHS, had her salary determined according to the appropriate Whitley Council scale; Mr Crumlin's salary was based upon agreements between his union and private contractors. All those paid at the higher rate were men and, with one exception, all those on the lower rate were women. It was conceded that they were engaged on 'like work' within s. 1 (4) of EqPA.

The industrial tribunal found that there was a genuine material difference other than gender within s. 1 (3), because each was paid according to a different pay scale because of their different mode of entry into the NHS. Mrs Rainey's appeals to the EAT and Court of Session, Inner House, were dismissed. Mrs Rainey also unsuccessfully appealed to the House of Lords. The House of Lords held that a genuine material difference should not be limited purely to personal factors between the man and the woman, but could include extrinsic ones such as economic factors, provided that they could be justified on objective grounds. In Mrs Rainey's case it had been shown that it was essential to pay a higher salary to prosthetists recruited from private practice in order to obtain the personnel necessary to establish the new prosthetic service in the NHS and this constituted a genuine material difference other than a difference of gender.

Some Examples of Genuine Material Factors

Location

Employees who work in London may be paid more in order to compensate them for the higher cost of living in the capital or may be expected to work fewer hours.

In *Navy, Army and Air Force Institutes* v. *Varley* [1976] IRLR 408, Mrs Varley, a female clerk employed in Nottingham, claimed to be entitled to the same shorter working hours as male clerks employed in London. Both male and female clerks in Nottingham worked for the same number of hours (37). NAAFI workers in London (of either gender) worked a 36-hour week. It was held that the different places of employment constituted a material difference.

'Red-circling'

In cases of reorganisation or regrading employers will often transfer workers from a higher grade job to one of lower status but preserve their wages at the previous higher rate. This is known as 'red–circling', and as a result workers will often find themselves in the same grade and doing the same job alongside workers who are paid more. Depending on the circumstances, red–circling may amount to a material difference between the cases of particular men and women.

In *Snoxell* v. *Vauxhall Motors Ltd* [1977] IRLR 123 EAT, Mrs Davies and Miss Snoxell were quality inspectors at Vauxhalls. Though doing the same work as men, they were on a lower grade and paid less. In 1970 the job of quality inspector was downgraded. All the existing female quality inspectors and all new entrants to the job were put into the lower grade. But the men who had been on the higher grade were red–circled and retained their higher wages. In 1976 the women claimed parity. The EAT held that the employers could not shelter behind the red–circle defence. It could not be a genuine material difference if it owed its existence to past sex discrimination – which was the situation in this case.

Where employers seek to establish the red–circle defence, they must do so with respect to every employee who, it is claimed, is within the circle. If an employer subsequently lets an outsider into the red circle, the defence will probably fail because the woman will find it easier to demonstrate that the original reason for the red circle is not the real reason why she is being treated less favourably (*United Biscuits* v. *Young* [1978] IRLR 15 EAT.

In assessing the validity of the defence, it is relevant for an industrial tribunal to take into account the length of time which has elapsed since the red circle was introduced, and whether the employer has acted in accordance with good industrial relations practice in the continuation of the practice (*Outlook Supplies Ltd* v. *Parry* [1978] IRLR 12 EAT).

Part-time Work

A crucial issue in the equality debate is whether it is legitimate to discriminate against part-time workers in terms of pay and conditions. This is a key issue because over 90 per cent of all part-time workers are women, so differential treatment of part-time workers is indirect discrimination against women. Can part-time work constitute a genuine material difference?

In *Handley* v. *H Mono Ltd* [1979] ICR 147, a female machinist, working a basic 26-hour week at £1.61 per hour, claimed an equal hourly rate to a man employed on like work who worked a 40 hour week at £1.67 per hour. It was held that there was a material difference between her case and his because part-time workers contributed less to productivity. His machine was fully utilised for 40 hours per week, whereas hers was used for 26 hours only and remained idle when she was not at work.

This decision can be read as accepting the difference in part-time and full-time work as itself legitimating unequal treatment. However, in *Jenkins* v. *Kingsgate (Clothing Productions) Ltd No. 2* [1981] IRLR 388 EAT, it was held that it was not sufficient for the purposes of s. 1 (3) for the employer to show that he had no intention of discriminating on grounds of sex or that he intended to achieve a legitimate objective. Section 1 (3) should be understood as imposing on the employer the burden of proving that a variation in pay between a man and a woman employed on equal work is objectively reasonably necessary in order to achieve some objective other than an objective related to the gender of the worker.

This view has now been sustained by the decision of the ECJ in *Bilka-Kaufhaus GmbH* v. *Weber von Hartz*: 170/84 [1986] IRLR 317. In this case it was held that, under art. 119, a policy which has the effect of creating a pay differential between men and women undertaking like work – in this case, giving occupational pension rights to full-time workers only – may only be justified if 'the means chosen for achieving that objective correspond to a real need on the part of the undertaking, are appropriate with a view to achieving the objective in question and are necessary to that end'.

Differential Grades

It would appear that a pay difference resulting from a different grade or pay scale will be justified provided that the payment schemes do not discriminate on grounds of gender.

In *Waddington* v. *Leicester Council for Voluntary Services* [1977] IRLR 32, Mrs Waddington was recruited as a community worker and paid under the national scale for social workers. She was put in charge of an adventure playground project and a playleader, a man, was appointed to assist her. His salary was paid according to the scale for youth leaders and community centre wardens. Both salary scales were nationally negotiated. The male playleader, despite being responsible to Mrs Waddington, received a higher salary. The EAT sent the case back to the industrial tribunal in order reconsider whether they were employed on like work (see above). However, they also commented they had first thought that, in any event, Mrs Waddington's claim must fail under s. 1 (3) because of the operation of nationally negotiated pay scales, but again they left this for the industrial tribunal to decide on the ground that evidence might be forthcoming which showed an element of discrimination in the practical operation and application of the scale.

In *Reed Packaging Ltd* v. *Boozer* [1988] IRLR 333, the complainants were employed as dispatch clerks and paid in accordance with the staff pay structure negotiated with ACTSS. They brought a claim comparing their work with that of a male dispatch clerk paid £17 a week more on the basis of a pay structure for hourly paid workers negotiated with GMBATU. The EAT held that the employers had made out a defence under s. 1 (3). There had been no suggestion that either of the two pay structures was sexually discriminatory and there was no reason why the fact of separate pay structures could constitute a material factor defence. As a result, pay as determined in accordance with separate pay structures was 'an objectively justified administrative reason' for the unequal pay.

This has been the subject of the following powerful criticisms:

> Such an approach is plainly superficial: the fact that each pay structure operates internally without bias does not explain why there were two pay scales nor why she was on one and he on another.[6]

> If, as is common, the manual workers are mainly men and the staff workers are mainly women, the fact that the manual workers are paid more for the same work would seem to be a classic illustration of indirectly discriminatory pay since in order to receive higher pay for work of equal value you must be covered by the manual worker agreement, a requirement which has a disproportionately adverse impact on women. On this reasoning, to hold that the mere existence of the two schemes is itself an 'objectively justified administrative reason' for the inequality is a distortion of the concept. There is no 'objective justification' rather it is precisely the kind of administrative convenience that, in accordance with the *Bilka-Kaufhaus* test should no longer suffice as a defence.[7]

The judiciary continue to ignore the power of these arguments and this is glaringly and most recently illustrated in *Enderby* v. *Frenchay Health Authority and Secretary of State for Health* [1991] IRLR 44. This was a test case concerning equal value claims by speech therapists. The applicants claimed that they were employed on work of equal value with male principal grade pharmacists and clinical psychologists employed in the National Health Service whose salary exceeded theirs by about 60 per cent.

At the industrial tribunal, the employers denied that the work was of equal value, but argued, in any event, that the variation in pay was genuinely due to a material factor: the separate negotiating structures by which the pay for the relevant professions was determined. The employers argued that there was no sex discrimination within the professions or in the negotiations. They pointed to the fact that speech therapists had been considered in the past to be a profession auxiliary to medicine and had been treated as such in the national negotiations, whereas clinical psychologists had been treated as comparable to scientists such as physicists and biologists.

The applicants pointed out that the speech therapists, as well as the other professions which had been treated as auxiliary to medicine, were overwhelmingly composed of women. There was a far greater proportion of men in the higher grades in the comparator professions. It was accepted that the negotiations had not been conducted with the deliberate intention of treating women less favourably, but it was argued that the salaries of speech therapists were artificially depressed because of the profession's predominantly female composition. It was argued that the employer's pay policy indirectly discriminated against women in that the outcome of negotiations had an adverse effect upon women and was not justifiable.

The industrial tribunal dismissed the complaints and the EAT dismissed the complainant's appeal. The EAT upheld the industrial tribunal's view that the employers had established a material factor defence by showing that the variation in pay 'arose because of the bargaining structure and its history which was not discriminatory, and from the structures within their own professions which were also non-discriminatory'. Collective agreements were to be properly considered under the headings of genuine material factors or justification under EC law. The EAT could not accept the appellant's submission that a collective agreement can never justify the difference in pay even if it is untainted by gender.

It is hard to accept this reasoning. EC law requires that any difference in pay must be justified in *objective* terms, and yet surely collective bargaining is a subjective decision-making process. Rubenstein produces the following powerful analogy:

> Suppose the different rates of pay were determined unilaterally by the employer. Would it be a sufficient defence for the employer merely to say 'we had a committee which considered pay and this is the result they arrived at?' Of course not. So why should the mere fact that the outcome is arrived at by a multilateral committee including legal representatives change its legal character? If the result is discriminatory, the addition of further parties to the decision merely adds to the number of wrongdoers. It cannot possibly change whether a wrong has been done.[8]

It is hoped that this and other aspects of the reasoning in *Enderby* will be overturned when the case is heard by the Court of Appeal. Before hearing Dr Enderby's appeal, the Court of Appeal has requested a ruling from the ECJ on whether the fact that the two groups are covered by separate collective bargaining arrangements, which are not in themselves discriminatory, can justify the pay inequality between groups (see [1992] IRLR 15).

Indeed, the ECJ has shown itself prepared to look behind superficially gender-neutral pay structures. In *Handels-OG Kontorfunktionaernes Forbund i Danmark* v. *Dansk Arbejdsgiverforening (acting for Danfloss)* [1989] IRLR 532, a Danish trade union claimed that the pay practices of Danfloss were in breach of the Equal Pay Directive. In accordance with a national collective agreement, the employer used a job classification system to establish basic pay for each grade. Within the grade, however, the collective agreement allowed the employer to give increments on the basis of the employee's flexibility – defined as including capacity, quality of work, autonomy and responsibilities – and on the basis of training and seniority.

The union demonstrated that within a pay grade the average pay of men was 6.85 per cent higher than that of women and said that therefore the system was discriminatory, contrary to EC law.

The court held that in respect of 'flexibility', it was acceptable for an employer to reward the 'quality of work' done by an employee, because this was totally neutral from the point of view of gender. If the application of such a criterion did result in systematic unfairness to female workers, that could only be because the employer applied it in an 'abusive manner', it being 'inconceivable that the work carried out by female workers would generally be of a lower quality'. Therefore, the employer may not justify 'quality of work' as a basis for additional increments where it systematically works to the disadvantage of women.

Where flexibility refers to the adaptability of the worker to variable work schedules and places of work, this criterion may also operate to the disadvantage of female workers who, as a result of 'household and female duties', may have greater difficulty in organising their time flexibly. In such a situation the employer must show that adaptability is important to the specific duties of the particular worker and objectively justifiable. Similar considerations were held to apply in relation to additional pay for vocational training.

The court took a different approach in relation to seniority. In its view, even though the criterion of seniority, like that of vocational training, may result in less favourable treatment of female workers, seniority goes hand in hand with experience which generally places workers in a better position to perform their duties. Therefore, it is permissible for the employer to reward it without the need to establish the importance which it takes on for the performance of the specific duties of the particular workers.

The effect of this important decision is that merit pay systems which in practice work to the disadvantage of women can be attacked as unlawful. The ECJ also held that the burden of proof rests on employers to show that their pay practices are not discriminatory and are justifiable.

Remedies

In order to make an equal pay challenge the worker must apply to an industrial tribunal. If the claim is successful the applicant may recover arrears of pay for a period of up to two years prior to the date on which proceedings were started. An order for the payment of damages rather than back-pay will be made where the employer has broken a term of the contract not directly related to pay, such as a term relating to holiday entitlement.

An employer may apply to an industrial tribunal for a declaration of the rights of the employer and employee where there is a dispute about the effect of an equality clause (s. 2 [1A]). The secretary of state has the power to bring proceedings on behalf of the employee where it is not reasonable to expect her to bring the proceedings herself (s. 2 [2]). To the best of our knowledge, this power has never been exercised.

EqPA s. 2 (4) does provide that no claim may be brought before a tribunal unless the applicant has been employed by the employer in the six months preceding the date of the application to the tribunal. It was assumed that this was a general time limit, applicable to all equal pay claims. But in *British Railways Board* v. *Paul* [1988] IRLR 20 EAT, the EAT held that the six-months cut off in s. 2 (4) only applies when there has been a reference of the complaint to the tribunal by the secretary of state. So it would appear that for the vast majority of claims there is no time limit. Nevertheless, given that the EAT's interpretation of the section in the *Paul* case was somewhat novel, it may be safest to advise workers to claim within six months of leaving work – just in case this interpretation is rejected.

Collective Enforcement

Prior to the coming into force of the SDA 1986 a collective agreement containing differential provisions for men and women could by EqPA s. 3 be referred to the Central Arbitration Committee at the request of any party to the agreement or the secretary of state. EqPA s. 3 has now been repealed by the SDA 1986 which provides that collective agreements (whether legally enforceable or not) are deemed automatically unenforceable and void in so far as they provide for the inclusion in a contract of employment of a provision which contravenes EqPA s. 1. But this provision does not provide individuals, such as prospective employees, with a remedy (SDA 1975, s. 77; SDA 1986, s. 6).

Again, European law offers a more effective approach. In *Kowalsa* v. *Freie und Hansestadt Hamburg* [1990] IRLR 447, the ECJ held that terms in a collective agreement which indirectly discriminate against women – for example, by favouring full-timers over part-timers – can be challenged directly under art. 119. The court also rejected the employers' argument that the correct approach is to declare the term void and leave it to the parties to find a solution – the remedy adopted by UK law. Instead, the court took the view that workers should be treated equally proportionate to their hours of work. So in this case part-time workers were entitled to the severance payments available to the full-time workers on a proportionate basis.

Clause 25 of TURERB seeks to remedy the defect in UK law by allowing individuals to challenge in an industrial tribunal the validity of terms of a collective agreement which *may* be applied to them where the terms may contravene the principle of equal treatment.

The Effectiveness of the Legislation

After the SDA came into force in 1975, it did appear to have some initial effect in reducing the gap between male and female pay. Women's earnings as a proportion of men's rose from 63.1 per cent in 1970 to a peak of 75.7 per cent in 1977. But no further inroads have been made and, despite the legislation, women's average earnings have remained stubbornly at around 74 per cent of men's for the last decade. The ineffectiveness of the legislation in mirrored in the number of claims made each year (see table 10.1). Claims under the Act declined rapidly to reach an all-time low of 35 in 1983. The introduction of the new equal value claim in 1984 did increase claim activity but the success rate has remained low (see table 10.2).[9]

Table 10.1: Equal Pay Act – No. of Claims Filed

Year of filing	*1977*	*1978*	*1979*	*1980*	*1981*	*1982*	*1983*	Equal Value Amendment	*1984*	*1985*	*1986*	*1987*	*1988*	*1989*
No.of claims filed	751	343	263	91	54	39	35		70	302	1691[1]	1970[2]	552	1029[3]

Sources: 1977–1985 EOC Annual Reports; 1985–1986 *Employment Gazette*; 1987–1989 ACAS Annual Reports.
Notes: 1. Includes several hundred claims against British Coal. 2. Includes 1,336 speech therapists. 3. Includes two large multiple claims.

Table 10.2: Outcome of Decisions in Cases Filed under Equal Value Amendment

Year of filing	*Won*[1]	*Dismissed*[2]	*Settled*[3]	*Withdrawn*	*Not heard*[4]	*Total*
1983		2	1			3
1984	4	9	1		2	17
1985	3	9	9	1	1	24
1986	6	18	6	2	3	34
1987	3	3	5	1	3	16
1988	1	6	1	2	5	13
1989	2	5			3	10
Total	19	52	23	6	17	117

Source: EOC monitoring of decisions.
Notes: 1. 14 went to ACAS expert; of remainder four won under like work; one won under EEC law. 2. 11 went to ACAS expert. 3. 13 went to ACAS expert. 4. 17 went to ACAS expert.

Defects in the Legislation

Procedural Complexity and Delay

As has been noted earlier, the Equal Value Amendment Regulations are massively complex. During the House of Lords debate on them Lord Denning described them as 'beyond compare ... no ordinary lawyer would be able to understand them ... the industrial tribunal would have the greatest difficulty and the Court of Appeal would probably be divided in opinion.' This prediction has proved accurate, with the lack of clarity in the regulations causing delay in processing complaints. Indeed the president of EAT felt moved to observe that the delays are 'scandalous and amount to a denial of justice to women seeking a remedy through the judicial process'(see *Aldridge* v. *British Telecommunications plc* [1990] IRLR 10 EAT). EOC monitoring of the legislation has shown that on average less than 20 claims have been decided each year in the period 1984–9. This and the average length of time of 17 months for a claim to go through the full procedure show the problems created by the legal maze.

In their report 'Equal Pay For Men and Women: Strengthening the Acts' (1990), the EOC put forward a series of proposals aimed at simplifying and speeding up the procedure and increasing access to justice. These include:

- Requiring members of ITs to have specialised training in the identification of gender bias in pay structures and collective agreements.
- Cases involving important questions of fact or law to be transferred straight to the EAT for initial hearing upon the application of both parties or on the initiative of the IT, and with the consent of the EAT.
- The requirement for an IT to determine that there are no reasonable grounds for the equal value should be abolished, as it operates as an 'unjustified fetter on individuals seeking access to the legal process'. ITs already have sufficient powers to 'weed out' hopeless claims – such as striking out a claim because it is 'frivolous or vexatious', or through the pre-hearing assessment review/assessment procedure.
- An employer's job evaluation study should no longer operate as a bar to an equal value claim.

  > At present an existing job evaluation scheme such as is described in s. 1 (5) of the Equal Pay Act, namely a study which is analytical and covering the jobs in question, acts as a bar to a claim if there are no reasonable grounds for determining that it is based on a sex discriminatory system. This provision covers a study which may have been in existence for several years and which is unlikely to have been introduced for the purpose of eliminating sex discrimination from the pay structure. It is more likely to reflect traditional expectations of employees and employers with a tendency to undervalue women's work, and as a result may well contain

hidden and unintentional sex discrimination which is very difficult to identify without the most searching enquiry.[10]

- Some independent experts should be appointed on a full-time basis and there should be a chief independent expert charged with the responsibility of setting standards, providing initial and continuing training, publishing guidelines on job evaluation, reviewing the equal value procedures, ensuring that the investigations are completed within the agreed timescales.
- Independent experts, within 14 days of receiving an equal value question from the IT, should provide written notification of the estimated time for completion of their report.
- Parties should be required to respond to an independent expert's invitation to supply information or to make comments or representations within a period laid down by statute.
- Independent experts should be granted access to employers' premises within 14 days of making the request and ITs should have the power to make an order for access.

The Material Factor Defence

As stated earlier, the decision of House of Lords in *Rainey* permits the market forces argument to be used by an employer in all equal pay claims (that is, in like work cases as well as in equal value cases). If this concept is applied in a largely unrestricted manner, it will undermine the equal pay legislation. After all, the very raison d'être of the equal pay legislation is that men are more powerful actors in the labour market than women. While the EOC does not propose the removal of the market forces defence, probably on the grounds that it is too well embedded in both UK and EC law for it to be removed, the Commission does argue for certain restrictions on the scope of the material factor defence. First, the employer should be under a statutory obligation to justify a differential pay practice by showing that it corresponds to a real need on the employer's part, is appropriate with a view to achieving the objectives pursued, and is necessary to that end (the *Bilka* test). Second, the employer should be obliged to show that the whole of the pay inequality has been caused by the material factor or factors relied on. This was not the approach favoured by the EAT in *Enderby* v. *Frenchay Health Authority and Secretary of State for Health* [1991] IRLR 4. Finally in this context, the EOC proposes that the use of the material factor defence should only be permitted on one occasion and then only after there has been a finding of equal value.

The Lack of Collective Enforcement Mechanisms

The Act does not provide for an application to be made by a representative or a class or group of employees; it only provides a remedy for the individual employee. Similarly, although trade unions may lend their support to individual equal pay claims as a way of pressurising employers to revise discriminatory pay structures, employers are under no legal obligation to do so; they may prefer to meet the cost of each individual equal pay claim as it arises. The current situation places the industrial tribunals under quite unnecessary administrative strains in dealing with multiple applications from individual members of the same bargaining group (for example, the application by *Enderby* was one of 1,395 equal value application from speech therapists). It also acts unfairly against other employees engaged in the same or broadly similar work, because they will be forced to institute equal pay claims unless the employer is prepared to extend the tribunal's decision to them.

In order to remedy this state of affairs, the EOC proposes:

- There should be a statutory requirement that all employees in the same employment as a successful applicant who do the same or broadly similar work should be entitled to the same award including back-pay.
- Where the source of the pay discrimination is a term or provision in a pay structure or collective agreement the respondent employer should notify the industrial tribunal within a specified period that the term or provision has been modified or removed.
- Industrial tribunals or a similarly constituted body should be given jurisdiction to determine allegations of discrimination in the terms of collective agreements and pay structures on the application of any interested party including the EOC.
- Such a body should be empowered to make orders for the modification or removal of sex discriminatory terms in collective agreements and pay structures.[11]

The 'Hypothetical Male'

A major flaw in the Act is the fact that it provides no remedy for the woman whose work is undervalued but who has no male colleague who is in the same employment and engaged on like work, work rated as equivalent or work of equal value to her own. She cannot compare her situation with that of the 'hypothetical man' and what he would have been paid to do the work. As a result the Act does not begin to tackle the root of the problem. Women's employment is largely segregated and certain jobs are seen as 'women's work'. These jobs tend to be low paid and badly unionised and lack male comparators.

The EOC advocates the replacement of the Equal Pay Act and Sex Discrimination Act with a unified Equal Treatment Act. One benefit of the merger would be a legislative code which would be less complex and more accessible. But another advantage would be the importation of the 'hypothetical male' comparator – allowed in sex discrimination cases – to equal pay claims. The statutory comparisons – like work, work rated as equivalent and equal value – would remain the normal concepts under which the vast majority of equal pay cases would be decided.

Nevertheless, the adoption of the test of discrimination from the Sex Discrimination Act under which the criteria may not only be that employers treat the underpaid woman less favourably than they actually treat a man but also that they treat her less favourably than they *would* treat a man, would permit a wider range of comparisons to be made. This alternative to the three statutory comparisons would be invoked only as a last resort in exceptional circumstances.

CHAPTER 11

Race and Sex Discrimination

Discrimination has been long established in employment and yet legislation seeking to outlaw it has been introduced relatively recently.

Racial discrimination in employment was brought within the scope of the law for the first time by the Race Relations Act 1968. Under the Act, the Race Relations Board was given the power to investigate complaints of discrimination in employment and, if conciliation failed, to initiate civil proceedings. The Race Relations Act 1976 provided the victim of racial discrimination with direct access to the ordinary courts and tribunals without the necessity of seeking the approval of a government-appointed agency. Moreover, the Act encompassed not only direct discrimination but the more subtle forms of indirect discrimination.

It might be expected that the passage of the wider-ranging 1976 Act would make discrimination much less common. In fact, many studies of recruitment and of the position of black workers during the 1970s and 1980s have demonstrated continuing discrimination in employment. For example a survey conducted over 1984/85 found that one-third of employers directly discriminated against black and Asian applicants.[1]

Similarly, in relation to sex discrimination, despite the legislation and at least some attitudinal change, the idea that there is 'women's work' and 'women's wages' remains firmly rooted in our society. As we saw in the previous chapter, the Equal Pay Act has not managed to close the earnings gap between men and women and women's work continues to be concentrated in traditionally low-paid and low-grade occupations.[2]

Of course, it would be naive in the extreme to expect that legislation by itself can eradicate discrimination. Nevertheless, as Steve Anderman has argued:

> it is possible for legislators to take a more or less robust view of the use of legislation to produce social change ... [I]n shaping the content of the legislation the concern of legislators is not to remove discrimination at all costs. There is in their minds a trade-off between the desirability of helping women to achieve greater equality of treatment and opportunity and the effect of social regulation on industry.[3]

In this chapter, we argue that the content of the legislation and the way the judges have interpreted it evidence a marked reluctance to intervene in management decision-making in the interests of helping to bring about social change.

Where to Find the Law

The law relating to discrimination is to be found in two principal statutes, the Sex Discrimination Act 1975 (SDA) and the Race Relations Act 1976 (RRA). As was seen in the previous chapter, sex discrimination in pay and other contractual terms is dealt with separately under the Equal Pay Act 1970 (EqPA 1970), as amended by the Equal Pay (Amendment) Regulations 1983. Both the SDA and RRA encompass discrimination in employment, education and in the provision of goods and facilities, services and housing – though this chapter will focus on the employment field.

A 'Code of Practice for the elimination of racial discrimination and the promotion of equal opportunity in employment' came into effect on 1 April 1984. The Code of Practice was made by the Commission for Racial Equality (CRE) under RRA 1976 s. 47. The Equal Opportunities Commission issued a similar 'Code of Practice for the elimination of discrimination on the grounds of sex and marriage and the promotion of equality of opportunity in employment' under SDA s. 56A, which came into effect on 30 April 1985. The Codes of Practice lay down guidelines for good employment practice, but they are not legally actionable themselves. However, the Codes are admissible in evidence at a hearing and an industrial tribunal can 'take into account' any relevant provision in reaching its decision.

As stated in the previous chapter, the UK's law on sex discrimination has been much affected by the influence of the standards laid down by the European Community. Like the EqPA, the SDA was the subject of a successful complaint by the Commission to the ECJ that the UK had fallen short of the standards required by the Equal Treatment Directive (76/207) (*EC Commission* v. *United Kingdom of Great Britain and Northern Ireland*: 165/82 [1984] IRLR 29). As a result of both this case and the subsequent decision of the ECJ in *Marshall* v. *Southampton and South-West Hampshire Area Health Authority (Teaching)*: 152/84 [1986] IRLR 140, the SDA 1986 was passed in an attempt to bring the UK law in line with EC standards. Further movement towards compliance is evident in certain of the provisions of the Employment Act 1989.

Sex and race discrimination have received a specific focus in the legislation, but, of course, there other reasons why people are victimised. In the following chapter we will examine employers' duties to people with disabilities, and discrimination against gay men, lesbians and those workers with AIDS or who are HIV positive. Discrimination against workers because of membership/non-membership or participation in the activities of a trade union is covered by TULR(C) 1992, ss. 146, 152 and is discussed in our chapters on unfair dismissal and collective bargaining.

Sex and Race Discrimination: Who Is Covered by the Legislation?

The rules relating to discrimination in employment cover not only those who work or seek to work under a contract of employment but also those under contract personally to execute any work or labour (self-employed workers).

Individuals engaged in government training schemes have been held not to fall within this definition (see *Daley* v. *Allied Suppliers* [1973] IRLR 14) but, as a result of revisions to both discrimination statutes, any person providing or making arrangements for the provision of training facilities is now covered (RRA 1976 s. 13 as amended; SDA 1975 s. 14 as amended).

Contract workers supplied by an agency – for example, office temps and certain construction workers – are within the scope of the legislation (SDA s. 9; RRA s. 7). The law makes express provision for such workers because it will usually be the client for whom the temp works – as opposed to the agency with whom the temp is 'in employment' – who will have most control over working conditions.

The Acts extend the umbrella of protection beyond those bodies with which the worker is 'in employment' to include:

- Trade unions and employers' associations (RRA s. 11; SDA s. 12) – it is unlawful to discriminate in the terms on which membership is offered, refused or varied, in the way in which access is provided to benefits, facilities and services or in subjecting them to any detriment.
- Qualifying bodies (RRA s. 12; SDA s. 13) – it is unlawful for a body which can confer an authorisation or qualification which is needed for, or facilitates, engagement in a particular profession or trade to discriminate against a person by refusing or deliberately omitting to grant an application, or by withdrawing or varying the terms upon which the authorisation or qualification is awarded. Examples of such bodies might be the Law Society, British Medical Association and even the British Judo Association when exercising its discretion to grant a referee's licence (*British Judo Association* v. *Petty* [1981] IRLR 484).
- Employment Agencies (SDA s. 15; RRA s. 14) – it is unlawful to discriminate by deliberately denying an employment agancy's services, or in the terms upon which it offers its services, or in the way in which it provides its services. The definition of employment agency in the legislation is wide enough to encompass a university careers office and state employment services, in addition to private profit-making concerns.

- Partnerships (RRA s. 10; SDA s. 11) – partners must not discriminate against a woman partner nor against a woman seeking a partnership. This provision used to apply only to partnerships of six or more but this was removed by the SDA 1986. The six or more rule continues to apply in the context of race discrimination.

Geographical Limitations

In order to qualify to bring a case, the complainant must be employed at an establishment in Great Britain. So a worker who works wholly or mainly outside Great Britain cannot claim (SDA s. 10; RRA s. 8). The exclusion does not apply to employment on board a ship registered in Great Britain, or to employment on an aircraft or hovercraft registered in Britain and operated by a person who has his/her principal place of business, or is ordinarily resident, in Britain, unless the work is done *wholly* outside Great Britain.

In *Haughton* v. *Olau Line (UK) Ltd* [1986] IRLR 465 CA, the employers were based at Sheerness and the worker spent the majority of working hours on a ship outside UK territorial waters. She was held to be outside the coverage of the Sex Discrimination Act because the ship on which she worked was German-registered.

In *Deria* v. *The General Council of British Shipping* [1986] IRLR 108 CA, Somali seamen were refused employment on a British ship requisitioned for service during the Falklands War. The vessel unexpectedly completed its voyage in Southampton rather than Gibraltar, as originally planned. The Court of Appeal construed the section as meaning that 'employment is to be regarded as being at an establishment in Great Britain unless the employee does or is *to do* his work wholly outside Great Britain.' The seamen's claim was excluded, notwithstanding that the ship actually sailed in British waters, since it was not contemplated that those who were employed would work within territorial waters when the applicants were refused employment.

Discrimination and Third Parties

Liability for unlawful discrimination is not confined to the discriminator him/herself.

Vicarious Liability

Principals are liable for the acts of their agents carried out within the scope of their authority and employers are liable for unlawful acts of discrimination by employees committed in the course of their employment (SDA s. 41; RRA s. 32). For example, if you claim that the personnel officer of Capital plc discriminated against you in a job interview, you can sue both the officer and the company. An employer will not be liable for acts which are clearly outside the employee's course of employment. In order to decide if this applies, the courts have to determine whether an act was merely an unauthorised or prohibited mode of carrying out an authorised act (if so, the employer is liable) as distinct from an act which is outside the sphere of employment (no vicarious liability). So, for example, in *Irving* v. *Post Office* [1987] IRLR 289 CA, the Post Office was not vicariously responsible under the Race Relations Act for racially abusive words written on an envelope by a postman, since the postman was not acting in the course of employment. The act of writing on the envelope did not become part of the manner in which the postman performed his duties merely because he did it while on duty. His employment provided the opportunity for his misconduct, but the misconduct formed no part of the performance of his duties, was in no way directed towards the performance of those duties, and was not done for the benefit of his employer.

In addition, employers have a statutory defence if they can show that they took such steps as were reasonably practicable to prevent the commission of an act (SDA s. 41 [3]; RRA s. 32 [3]). Certain commentators and, indeed, the Commission for Racial Equality have questioned why employers need this additional protection, seeing it as open invitation to dismiss claims on the basis of very limited preventative action on the part of the employer. A prime example of this tendency is the decision in *Balgobin* v. *London Borough of Tower Hamlets* [1987] IRLR 401 EAT, discussed below in the section on sexual harassment.

Aiding and Abetting

A person who aids another to commit an unlawful act of discrimination is treated as having committed an unlawful act of 'the like description'. Employees or agents who cause their employer or principal to be vicariously liable are treated as if they aided their employer's or principal's unlawful act. For example, if you are the victim of sexual harassment you can sue both the harasser and your employer.

A person has a defence to aiding if it can be shown that s/he acted in reliance on a statement by the discriminator that the act which was aided was not unlawful and that it was reasonable to rely on that statement.

Other Unlawful Acts

False or Misleading Statements
A person who knowingly or recklessly makes a statement to another that a particular act would not be unlawful, is guilty of a criminal offence and is liable on conviction in a magistrates' court to a fine not exceeding level 5 on the standard scale (RRA s. 33 [4]; SDA s. 42 [4]).

Pressure to Discriminate

Direct or indirect pressure to induce or attempt to induce a person to discriminate is unlawful (RRA s. 31 [1], SDA s. 40). The inducement can take the form of either a threat or a promise. An attempted inducement is not prevented from being unlawful because it is not made directly to the person in question, provided that it is made in such a way that the other is likely to hear it. So if A, the works manager, tells B, an employee, that another employee, C, will be sacked unless B discriminates against D, an Asian, in selecting candidates for a job, A is guilty of an unlawful act. Enforcement of this provision is vested in the EOC and CRE.

Instructions to Discriminate

It is unlawful for one person who has authority over another, or in accordance with whose wishes that other person is accustomed to act, to instruct him/her to perform a racially or sexually discriminatory act or to procure or attempt to procure the doing of such an act (RRA s. 30; SDA s. 39). Once again, enforcement of these provisions is the sole responsibility of the EOC and CRE.

Advertisements

An employer must not cause to be published an advertisement which indicates, or might reasonably be understood to indicate, an intention to discriminate (SDA s. 38 [1]; RRA s. 29).

In relation to sex discrimination it is provided that the use of a job description with a sexual connotation (such as 'waiter', 'salesgirl', 'postman', or 'stewardess') shall be taken to indicate an intention to discriminate, unless the advertisement indicates an intention to the contrary.

Only the EOC or CRE can bring proceedings in respect of discriminatory advertisements.

There are two exceptions to the rules against discriminatory advertising:

(i)   where it is an advertisement for employment outside Great Britain which discriminates other than by reference to colour, ethnic or national origins (RRA s. 29 [3]);

(ii) where the advertisement is for a job in which there are genuine occupational qualifications for employing a person of a particular race, colour, ethnic or national origin or sex.

Discrimination Is Unlawful if Based upon:

(a)   Racial grounds (RRA ss. 1, 3)
(b)   Gender (SDA ss. 1, 2)
(c)   Marital status (SDA s. 3)

Racial Grounds

'Racial grounds' are defined as any of the following grounds: colour, race, nationality or ethnic or national origins.

Case law suggests that 'ethnic origins' is a wider concept than 'racial origins' and brings groups within the scope of the Act who would otherwise be unprotected. So in *Mandla (Sewa Singh)* v. *Dowell Lee* [1983] AC 548, the House of Lords finally decided that Sikhs constituted a distinct ethnic group. The word 'ethnic' did not require the group to be distinguished by some inherited racial characteristic.

Lord Fraser provided the following guidance:

> For a group to constitute an ethnic group in the sense of the 1976 Act, it must, in my opinion, regard itself, and be regarded by others as a distinct community by virtue of certain characteristics. Some of these characteristics are essential; others are not essential but one or more of them will commonly be found and will help to distinguish the group from the surrounding community. The conditions which appear to me to be essential are these: (1) a long shared history, of which the group is conscious as distinguishing it from other groups, and the memory of which it keeps alive; (2) a cultural tradition of its own, including family and social customs and manners, often but not necessarily associated with religious observance. In addition to these essential characteristics the following characteristics are in my opinion relevant; (3) either a common geographical origin, or descent from a number of common ancestors; (4) a common language, not necessarily peculiar to the group; (5) a common literature peculiar to the group; (6) a common religion different from that of neighbouring groups or from the general community surrounding it; (7) being a minority or being an oppressed or dominant group within a larger community, for example a conquered people (say, the inhabitants of England shortly after the Norman Conquest) and their conquerors might both be ethnic groups ... A group defined by reference to enough of these characteristics would be capable of including converts, for example people who marry into the group, and of excluding apostates. Provided a person who joins the group feels himself or herself to be a member of it, and is accepted by other members, then he is, for the purposes of the Act, a member.

This test was applied in *CRE* v. *Dutton* [1989] IRLR 8, where the Court of Appeal had to determine whether gipsies were a racial group. It concluded that using the narrower meaning of the word 'gipsies' as a 'wandering race of Hindu origin' rather than the larger, amorphous group of 'travellers' or 'nomads', the evidence was sufficient to establish that gipsies are an identifiable group defined by reference to ethnic origins. The evidence was that gipsies are a minority with a long-shared history and a common geographical origin. They have certain customs of their own. They have a language or dialect which consists of up to one-fifth of Romany words in place of English words. They have a repertoire of folk tales and music passed from one generation to the next.

Discrimination on the grounds of religion is not *expressly* covered by the Act[4] but a number of religious groups may fall within the definition of an ethnic group following the approach adopted in *Mandla*.

In *Seide* v. *Gillette Industries Ltd* [1980] IRLR 427 EAT, it was held that 'Jewish' could mean a member of a race or a particular ethnic origin as well as a member of a particular religious faith, and can therefore fall within the scope of the Act.

More recently, however, in *Crown Suppliers (PSA)* v. *Dawkins* [1991] IRLR 327, the EAT was not prepared to accept that a refusal to offer a job to a Rastafarian because he would not cut his hair was discrimination against an ethnic group. In the EAT's view, Rastafarians were no more than a religious sect and as such were not sufficiently distinct from the rest of the Afro-Caribbean community. Moreover, because they had been in existence for only 60 years they did not possess a 'long-shared history' – the first essential of the *Mandla* guidelines. Dawkins' appeal was subsequently rejected ([1993] IRLR 284, CA).

It will be seen from the definition that discrimination based on religion is not expressly covered. It is only in Northern Ireland with the Fair Employment (Northern Ireland) Acts 1976, 1989 that legislation seeks to address this form of prejudice.

Sex

As with the Equal Pay Act, the SDA applies equally to discrimination against men and women (SDA s. 2[1]).

Marital Status

SDA s. 3 makes it unlawful to discriminate against a married person in the field of employment. It remains lawful, however, to discriminate against a person because they are single.

Types of Discrimination

The main heads of claim for the complainant under the RRA and SDA are either direct discrimination, indirect discrimination or victimisation.

Direct Discrimination

This occurs when one person treats another less favourably, on the grounds of gender, marital status or race, than s/he treats or would treat a person of another gender, marital status or race.

Unlike the EqPA which requires an actual comparator, the SDA and RRA allow comparison to be made with how a hypothetical person would have been treated.

After a period of uncertainty, it is now clear that direct discrimination not only covers intentionally hostile acts of bigotry but also acts which, although not driven by a hostile motive, nevertheless result in less favourable treatment due to gender, race or marital status.

As Anne Morris and Susan Nott observe:

> To allow motive to justify directly discriminatory behaviour detracts from any attempt to achieve equality of opportunity since it legitimises and perpetuates gender-based prejudice. If direct discrimination were acceptable on the basis that, for example, an employer genuinely believed that one woman working in an all-male workshop would find life very difficult, this would frustrate attempts to eliminate discrimination. Indeed, the deep-rooted assumptions that can lead to a woman receiving less favourable treatment may not be regarded by the person who holds them as discriminatory, and, arguably, the practical effect of allowing a consideration of motive would be to reduce dramatically the number of instances of direct discrimination.[5]

In *R* v. *Birmingham CC ex parte EOC* [1989] IRLR 173, the House of Lords formulated a simple test for establishing direct discrimination as follows:

(i) Was there an act of discrimination? If the answer is in the affirmative:

(ii) But for the complainant's gender (or race), would he/she have been treated differently?

In *James* v. *Eastleigh BC* [1989] IRLR 318, the Court of Appeal failed to apply the test expounded in the Birmingham County Council case and it required another trip to the House of Lords to clarify matters.

Eastleigh Council allowed free swimming for children under the age of three and for persons who had reached the state retirement age. Mr and Mrs James were both aged 61 and both were retired. When they went swimming Mr James had to pay whereas Mrs James had free admission. Mr James alleged this was a breach of s. 29 (1) (b) of the SDA (discrimination in the provision of a service). The Court of Appeal held that there was no act of direct discrimination within s. 1 (1) (a). In order to establish direct discrimination 'one must look at the reason why the defendant treated the plaintiff less favourably, not to the causative link between the defendant's behaviour and the detriment to the plaintiff'. In this particular case it was accepted by the court that the reason for adopting the policy was 'to aid the needy' and was therefore not on the grounds of gender.

Mr James' appeal to the House of Lords was upheld (see [1990] IRLR 289). The majority of the House of Lords laid down a 'but for' causative test for determining whether there had been direct discrimination – that is, 'would the complainant have received the same treatment from the defendant but for his or her sex.' The determinative question is *whether* gender is the ground for the alleged decision; *why* the employer discriminated is irrelevant.

Sexual Harassment

Successive surveys of women's experience have shown that sexual harassment in the workplace is widespread. Commenting on the empirical data documenting the incidence of sexual harassment at work in the EC member states, Michael Rubenstein concludes that:

> sexual harassment is not an isolated phenomenon perpetrated by the odd socially deviant man. On the contrary it is clear that for millions of women in the EEC today, sexual harassment is an unpleasant and unavoidable part of their working lives.[6]

Despite the significance of this problem, there is no specific reference to 'sexual harassment' in the legislation. Indeed, it was not until the mid-1980s that it was firmly established that sexual harassment constituted direct discrimination under the SDA. This recognition came in *Strathclyde Regional District Council* v. *Porcelli* [1986] IRLR 134, the first case on sexual harassment to reach the appellate courts. The complainant, Mrs Porcelli, was a laboratory technician employed by the regional council in one of its schools. She claimed she had been unlawfully discriminated against when she had been compelled to seek a transfer to another school because of a deliberate campaign of vindictiveness against her by two male colleagues, some of it of a sexual nature. She claimed that the regional council was vicariously responsible for the behaviour of the two men.

The industrial tribunal, while accepting that the men's behaviour had been extremely unpleasant, rejected her application. The tribunal was of the view that a man who had been disliked would have been treated equally badly, although the tribunal agreed that the unpleasantness would have been of a different nature.

The EAT rejected this argument and allowed Mrs Porcelli's appeal. The council's appeal to the Scottish Court of Session was dismissed. According to the court, even if only some of the treatment complained of was sexually oriented, there was less favourable treatment on grounds of sex. What mattered was the treatment, not the motive for it, and therefore if any material part of the treatment included elements of a sexual nature to which the woman was vulnerable, but a man would not be, then she had been treated less favourably on grounds of her sex. It was also held that conduct falling short of physical contact could still constitute sexual harassment.

Mrs Porcelli was eventually awarded £3,000 damages for the injury to feelings and stress which she had experienced.

In *Bracebridge Engineering* v. *Darby* [1990] IRLR 3, it was concluded that a single act of a 'serious' nature will support a claim of sexual harassment. Employees committing such acts may well be acting 'within the course of their employment', which in turn makes their employer responsible. In addition any failure to act on the part of the employer, such as a failure to carry out a serious investigation of the complaint, may allow the complainant to treat herself as constructively dismissed.

In many cases, the victim of sexual harassment will be victimised if she has rejected sexual advances. She may be passed over for promotion or dismissed. In other cases, she will find the situation intolerable and seek a transfer, as in Porcelli, or resign, as in Darby. But what is the position if she stays at work and makes a complaint to a tribunal? As we shall see, SDA s. 6 requires a victim of sex discrimination to suffer a 'detriment'. If there is no retaliation against her or she fails to resign, does she suffer a detriment within the meaning of the Act? In *De Souza* v. *Automobile Association* 1986] IRLR 103 – a racial harassment case discussed below - the Court of Appeal took the view that harassment will be unlawful if the reasonable employee could justifiably complain about her working conditions or environment. It is not necessary that the result of the discrimination was either a dismissal or some action by the employee such as leaving employment or seeking a transfer.

So far so good, but there are other decisions by the courts and tribunals which are far less supportive to victims of sexual or racial harassment.

In *Snowball* v. *Gardner Merchant Ltd* [1987] IRLR 397, a female catering manager alleged that she had been sexually assaulted by her male district manager. During her cross-examination, she denied that she had talked freely to her fellow employees about her attitude to sexual matters – it was alleged that she had described her bed as a 'play-pen' and mentioned her black satin sheets in conversation with colleagues. It was held by the EAT that the respondent employer could call witnesses in support of the allegation. The view was taken that the evidence was relevant not only to Ms Snowball's credibility but also for the purpose of deciding whether she had, in fact, suffered any detriment or injury to feelings.

This decision has attracted a welter of criticism on the grounds that it has opened the door to the kind of evidence about a woman's moral character and sexual attitudes which has caused so much resentment in rape cases. It is hard to see why a woman's consensual sexual behaviour should be relevant to assessing the degree of hurt she suffers from uninvited and unwanted sexual advances from her boss or a fellow employee. Faced with the prospect of being cross-examined about her sex life, many women will be deterred from making a complaint of sexual harassment.

A similarly offensive attitude to women is to be found in *Wileman* v. *Minilec Engineering Ltd* [1988] IRLR 144, where a victim of harassment was awarded the derogatory sum of £50 based on the fact that the tribunal was allowed to take into account the fact that, on occasions, the applicant wore what were described as scanty and provocative clothes to work. Mr Justice Popplewell stated:

if a girl on the shop floor goes around wearing provocative clothes and flaunting herself, it is not unlikely that other work people – particularly the men – will make remarks about it; it is an inevitable part of working life on the shop floor. If she then claims that she suffered a detriment, the Tribunal is entitled to look at the circumstances in which the remarks are made which are said to constitute that detriment.

In other words if you wear 'provocative' clothes at work you are 'asking for it'. Yet the way a woman dresses should surely be irrelevant where she has made it clear that the conduct complained of is unwelcome.

We have seen earlier in the chapter that an employer can avoid liability for an act of discrimination committed by an employee in the course of his/her employment by establishing that all such steps as are reasonably practicable have been taken to prevent the conduct in question. The decision of the EAT in *Balgobin and Francis* v. *London Borough of Tower Hamlets* [1987] IRLR 401 suggests that the standard expected of an employer in order to successfully raise the defence is not particularly onerous.

In this case, Mrs Balgobin and Mrs Francis were employed as cleaners in the canteen area of a hostel run by Tower Hamlets. The women complained that between June and October 1985 they had been subjected to sexual harassment by a male cook. Until they complained, management was unaware of the harassment. An inquiry was held in October 1985 into the complaint, but the management was unable to determine the truth of the matter. Thereafter, the two women and the cook continued to work together.

While accepting that sexual harassment had occurred, the majority of the EAT rejected the women's arguments that the employer had produced no evidence that it had taken such steps as were reasonably practicable to prevent the male cook's behaviour. Management did not know what was going on; was running the hostel with proper and adequate supervision of staff; had made known its policy of equal opportunities and, in the majority's view, it was 'very difficult to see what steps in practical terms the employers could reasonably have taken to prevent that which occurred from occurring'. This rather complacent view was reached even though there had been no evidence that the employees had received any training or guidance in the operation of the equal opportunity policy or informed that sexual harassment was unlawful.

Furthermore, the EAT rejected the women's second argument that the employers had discriminated against them by requiring them to continue working with the male cook after the inquiry had been held. The women had not been treated less favourably, for example, than a male to whom homosexual advances had been made.

The EC Council of Labour and Social Ministers adopted a resolution relating to sexual harassment at work (Resolution No. 6015/90). In November 1991, as part of its third action programme on equal opportunities, the European

Commission adopted a Recommendation and Code of Practice on the protection of the dignity of women and men at work. The Recommendation asks member states to

> take action to promote awareness that conduct of a sexual nature, or other conduct based on sex affecting the dignity of women and men at work, including conduct of superiors and colleagues, is unacceptable if:
>
> > (a) such conduct is unwanted unreasonable and offensive to the recipient;
> > (b) a person's rejection of, or submission to, such conduct on the part of employer or workers (including superiors or colleagues) is used explicitly or implicitly as a basis for a decision which affects that person's access to vocational training, access to employment, continued employment, promotion, salary or any other employment decisions;
> >
> > and/or
> >
> > (c) such conduct creates an intimidating, hostile or humiliating work environment for the recipient.
>
> and that such conduct may, in certain circumstances, be contrary to the principle of equal treatment within the meaning of [the Equal Treatment] Directive 76/207/EEC.

A Commission Recommendation cannot of itself give rise to legal right or liabilities. However, in *Grimaldi* v. *Fonds des Maladies Professionelles* [1990] IRLR 400, the ECJ ruled that national courts must take such non-binding measures into account, in particular to clarify the interpretation of other provisions of national and Community law. Consequently, an employee who brings a claim of sex discrimination as a result of being the victim of sexual harassment will be able to refer to the Recommendation and Code of Practice in support of her case.

The Code recommends that senior management should develop and communicate a policy statement which should:

- expressly state that sexual harassment will not be permitted or condoned;
- set out a positive duty on managers and supervisors to implement the policy and to take corrective action to ensure compliance with it;
- explain the procedure which should be followed by employees subjected to sexual harassment at work in order to obtain assistance;
- contain an undertaking that the allegation will be dealt with seriously, expeditiously and confidentially, and that complainants will be protected against victimisation;
- specify that disciplinary measures will be taken against employees guilty of sexual harassment.[7]

Racial Harassment

This can take the form of violence or ostracism and will amount to direct discrimination. Racial insults will also generally amount to racial harassment.

However, the complainant may experience greater difficulty in establishing a claim if the insulting remarks are not addressed directly to him/her but are overheard. This is illustrated by the decision in *De Souza* v. *Automobile Association* [1986] IRLR 103, where the Court of Appeal took the view that merely overhearing a racial insult would not amount to less favourable treatment unless the person making the statement 'intended the complainant to either hear what he said or knew or ought reasonably to have anticipated that the person he was talking to would pass the insult on or that employee would become aware of it in some way.'

Pregnancy-related Dismissals

Currently, if a woman has two years' continuous service, a dismissal on the grounds of pregnancy or a connected reason is automatically unfair and the question of how the employer would have treated anyone else is irrelevant (see chapter 14). On the other hand, if a woman does not have the necessary qualifying service she can still challenge a pregnancy dismissal by way of the sex discrimination legislation. An initial difficulty here is the fact that SDA s.5(3) requires that when comparing how a man would have been treated the comparison must be such that 'the relevant circumstances in the one case are the same or not materially different'. This provision persuaded the majority of the EAT in *Turley* v. *Allders Department Stores Ltd* [1980] IRLR 4 to hold that a pregnancy-related dismissal was not unlawful discrimination because there is no masculine counterpart to pregnancy. More recently, this approach has been rejected and a woman could succeed if she could show that a man in comparable circumstances (such as one who was going to be absent on grounds of sickness) would have been treated better than she was: *Hayes* v. *Malleable Working Men's Club* [1985] IRLR 367.

While the recognition of pregnancy-related dismissals as direct discrimination is to be welcomed, the reasoning used to gain that protection – comparing the treatment of a healthy pregnant woman with a sick man – is unfortunate to say the least.

This issue resurfaced in *Webb* v. *EMO Air Cargo Ltd* [1991] IRLR 124. Ms Webb was employed to replace another employee, Ms Stewart, during the latter's pregnancy. She was informed of this at interview. Two weeks after starting work, Ms Webb discovered that she too was pregnant. She informed the company and was dismissed. Her complaint of sex discrimination was rejected by both the IT and EAT. Applying the test in *Hayes*, it was held that the company had not treated Ms Webb less favourably than it would have treated a man who had been recruited for the same purpose, but who had then informed the company that he would need a comparable period of leave.

A better approach to the problem was adopted by the ECJ in *Dekker* v. *Stichting Vormingscentrum voor Jong Volvassen (VJW-Centrum) Plus* [1991] IRLR 27, where the court held that unfavourable treatment on grounds of pregnancy is direct discrimination on grounds of gender. The Court reasoned that pregnancy is a condition unique to women, so that where it can be shown that unfavourable treatment is on the grounds of pregnancy, that treatment is, by definition, on grounds of gender. A reason which applies 'exclusively to one sex' is in effect inherently discriminatory. Since discrimination on grounds of pregnancy is discrimination on grounds of gender per se, there is no need to compare the treatment of a pregnant woman with that of a hypothetical man.

The import of this decision would appear to be as follows. An employer who refuses to hire (or promote) a woman who is otherwise suitable because she is pregnant or for a reason based on her pregnancy is directly discriminating. Because the discrimination is directly on grounds of gender, it is not capable of being justified. In the court's view, a decision not to hire a pregnant woman because of the financial consequences of her maternity absence should be regarded as being made principally for the reason that the woman is pregnant. That is a reason which can apply to only one gender. Such an act of discrimination cannot be justified on the grounds of the financial consequences for the employer of the woman taking maternity leave. (Since Mrs Dekker was already pregnant when she applied for the job, VJV believed that its insurers would not reimburse the payments that it would have to make to her when she was on maternity leave. If this were the case, VJV would not have been able to afford to employ anybody to provide maternity cover and would be understaffed as a result.)

The court also held that the absence of male candidates for the job was immaterial. According to the ECJ, if the reason for the employer's decision 'resides in the fact that the person concerned is pregnant, the decision is directly related to the applicant's sex. Viewed in this way it is of no importance ... that there were no male applicants.'

It should follow that, to the extent that supremacy must be accorded to the European Court's decision, the comparative approach to pregnancy discrimination that like must be compared with like, followed by the EAT in *Webb*, is no longer good law and should not be followed by the ITs. This is because it is a fundamental principle of EC law that national courts are bound to interpret national law in the light of the aim of an EC Directive as interpreted by the ECJ.[8]

Amazingly, this was not the approach taken when the Webb case reached the Court of Appeal [1992] IRLR 116. The court held that dismissal of a pregnant woman for a reason arising out of, or related to, her pregnancy can in law be, but is not necessarily, direct discrimination. Direct discrimination would only occur if the IT were satisfied that a man with a comparable condition would not have been treated in the same way. Dekker's case was distinguished on the facts, an unconvincing attempt being made to limit the effects of Dekker to a failure to offer a job to someone who was the best applicant and most able to do the job.

The Court of Appeal instead relied on the decision of the ECJ in another case – *Handels-og Kontorfunktionaeremes Forbund i Danmark (acting for Hertz)* v. *Dansk Arbejdsgiverforening* [1991] IRLR 31 – in which the ECJ held that the dismissal of a woman on grounds of absence due to an illness which arose from pregnancy was not necessarily discrimination on grounds of gender.

After the expiry of her statutory entitlement of 24 weeks' maternity leave from the date of birth, Mrs Hertz was off work for 100 days within a year due to illness arising out of her pregnancy and confinement. This resulted in her dismissal on the grounds of her absence. It was claimed that this offended the equal treatment principle. The ECJ was of the view that, while it was up to member states to provide a period of maternity leave which allowed women workers to recover from the normal after-effects of pregnancy and childbirth, in regard to an illness occurring after the end of maternity leave there was no reason to distinguish an illness caused by pregnancy or childbirth from any other illness, since though certain illnesses only affect one gender, men and women are equally affected by illness overall. If a woman worker is dismissed because of a pregnancy-related illness but a sick man would have been treated in the same way, there is no breach of the principle of equal treatment.

But *Hertz* was an unusual case with facts which bear little resemblance to *Webb*. Moreover, as in the Dekker case, the ECJ held that a woman is protected by the principle of equal treatment from dismissal because of her absence during pregnancy and any maternity leave to which she has a right under national law.

Ms Webb pursued an appeal to the House of Lords, where it was decided that the SDA 1975 does not, on the face of it, make it unlawful for an employer to dismiss a woman because she is pregnant and needs time off work, if a male employee who needed time off work would also be dismissed. The Lords accepted, however, that the EC Equal Treatment Directive may deem such a dismissal to be viewed as direct discrimination, and has requested the ECJ for a ruling on the question.[9]

These issues will have less significance as a result of TURERA, which allows all employees, irrespective of their length of service, a right not to be dismissed on the grounds of pregnancy or childbirth.

Stereotyping

Those who discriminate frequently act on the basis of racial or gender stereotypes. Where the decision is based on such generalised assumptions it may be attacked as unlawful discrimination. For example:

- a refusal to employ women with children because they make unreliable employees (*Hurley* v. *Mustoe* [1981] IRLR 208);
- the dismissal of a woman based on the assumption that husbands are breadwinners (*Coleman* v. *Skyrail Oceanic Ltd* [1981] IRLR 398);

- refusal to second a woman on a training course in the London area, where her husband was employed, because it was assumed that she would remain in London when her course finished and not return to her work in Wales (*Horsey* v. *Dyfed CC* [1982] IRLR 395),
- a refusal to deploy a West Indian prisoner on kitchen work because he showed 'the anti-authoritarian arrogance that seems to be common in most coloured inmates' (*Alexander* v. *Home Office* [1988] IRLR 190).

Rules on Dress

The courts and tribunals allow employers a wide measure of discretion in controlling the image of their establishments, including the appearance of their staff, especially when those staff come into contact with the public. For example, in *Schmidt* v. *Austicks Bookshops Ltd* [1977] IRLR 360, a rule prohibiting women from wearing trousers at work was not discriminatory where the employers treated both male and female staff equally, with rules governing the appearance of both genders.

In *Kingston & Richmond Area Health Authority* v. *Kaur* [1981] IRLR 337, a prohibition on a Sikh nurse wearing trousers as part of her uniform was held not to be a racially discriminatory rule. The employers were justified in operating the rule because the form of uniform was governed by a statutory rule and the employers could not lawfully permit any variations.

The Employment Act 1989 provides a limited and specific exception in relation to Sikhs and the wearing of turbans. Section 12 provides that a Sikh working on a building site is exempt from the normal statutory requirement to wear a safety helmet. Employers in the construction industry, therefore, will commit an act of discrimination if they impose such a condition or requirement on Sikhs. Only Sikhs are given this exemption.

Indirect Discrimination

Direct discrimination is aimed at overt and intentional acts of prejudice. However, many forms of discrimination operate in a more subtle and indirect manner. An employer may formulate rules or requirement which, although applying to both genders and all racial groups, actually operate to the disadvantage of one gender or one group. In other words, indirect discrimination consists of acts or practices which are fair in form but unequal in impact: institutional racism or sexism.

Whether unlawful indirect discrimination has taken place depends on the answers to the following four questions:

(i) Has a requirement or condition been applied equally to both genders, marrieds and unmarrieds, or all racial groups? If yes ...

(ii) Is the requirement or condition one with which a considerably smaller number of women (or men), marrieds or persons of a particular racial group can comply compared to those of the opposite gender, unmarrieds or persons not of that racial group? If yes ...

(iii) Has the requirement or condition operated to the detriment of the complainant because s/he could not comply with it? If yes ...

(iv) Can the employer show the requirement or condition to be justifiable irrespective of the gender, marital status or race of the person in question?

Once a prima facie case has been made out by the complainant the burden of proof shifts to the employer to show that requirement or condition was justifiable irrespective of the gender, marital status or race of the person to whom it applies. The *intention* of the employer is irrelevant in establishing liability, though no compensation will be payable if the industrial tribunal is satisfied that the employer did not intend to discriminate.

An interesting application of the concept of indirect discrimination can be seen in *Greater Manchester Police Authority* v. *Lea* [1990] IRLR 372. In this case, the EAT confirmed an IT ruling that, by operating a recruitment policy which generally excluded those in receipt of an occupational pension, the police authority was guilty of indirect discrimination against a male applicant. The EAT was of the view that the scheme was indirectly discriminatory on grounds of sex since, looking at the 'appropriate pool for comparison' (the economically active population of Great Britain), more men (4.7 per cent) than women (0.6 per cent) were in receipt of such a pension, and the policy was not objectively justifiable.

Requirement or Condition
Although some of the case law on the meaning of these words suggests a liberal interpretation, other decisions are highly restrictive.

Some examples of requirement or conditions:

- a redundancy procedure with the trade union which provided for part-time workers to be dismissed first, before applying a last-in first out criteria to full-timers (*Clarke* v. *Eley (IMI) Kynoch Ltd* [1982] IRLR 482 – indirect sex discrimination);
- an age bar operated by the Civil Service which limited candidates for the post executive officer to those in the $17^1/2$ to 28 age range (*Price* v. *Civil Service Commission* [1977] IRLR 291 – indirect sex discrimination);
- a policy that candidates for a job should not have young or dependent children (*Hurley* v. *Mustoe* [1981] IRLR 208 – indirect marital discrimination);
- a refusal to hire persons living in Liverpool 8 where 50 per cent of the population were black (*Hussein* v. *Saints Complete House Furnishers Ltd* [1979] IRLR 337 – indirect racial discrimination).

This list of examples provide some guidance as to the range of practices which have been held to establish a prima facie indirect discrimination. But, on occasions, the employer may express a 'preference' which may or may not amount to an outright requirement and, in *Perera* v. *Civil Service Commission* [1983] IRLR 166, the Court of Appeal held that this could not amount to indirect discrimination.

In this case, a barrister from Sri Lanka was rejected for a legal post in the civil service. The selection committee assessed all applicants according to a number of criteria: age, practical experience in England, ability to communicate in English and so on. Perera argued that these were 'requirements or conditions', but the court did not agree. None of them were absolute 'musts', without which an applicant could not succeed. The court reasoned that, for example, a applicant whose ability to communicate in English was poor might nevertheless be successful if s/he scored highly on the other factors. The only relevant condition was that the applicant was a barrister or solicitor and this Perera fulfilled.

Perera was applied in *Meer* v. *London Borough of Tower Hamlets* [1988] 399. Mr Meer, who is of Indian origin and a solicitor with local government experience, applied for the job of head of the legal department with Tower Hamlets. Of 23 applicants, 12 were selected for 'long-listing', Mr Meer not being one of them. The criteria for long-listing was: age, date of admission as a solicitor, present post, current salary, local government experience, London government experience, Inner London government experience, senior management experience, length in present post, and Tower Hamlets' experience. All four of the applicants who had Tower Hamlets' experience were placed on the long-list. Mr Meer contended that this was a requirement or condition which indirectly discriminated against those of Indian origin contrary to s. 1 (1) (b) and s. 4 (1) (a) of the RRA. The CA held that the lower courts were correct in concluding that the criterion relating to Tower Hamlets' experience was not a 'must' and was not therefore a 'requirement or condition' within the meaning of s. 1 (1) (b).

The implication of this approach is that employers are given a wide prerogative in matters of selection and promotion, as long as they do not express the criteria in terms of *absolute* bars to selection or promotion. Employers will not be held to have indirectly discriminated if they can argue that, although the criteria applied may have a disproportionate effect on women or a racial group, these would be waived in the case of an individual who has exceptional compensating qualities. Angela Byre has observed: 'this approach risks undercutting the entire indirect discrimination concept, since it may often be possible to cite offsetting factors or theoretical exceptions to a basic rule even though they are unlikely to occur in practice.'[10] For this reason both the EOC and the CRE have proposed that the wording of the Act be expanded and clarified to make it clear that any *practice or policy* having an adverse impact upon one gender/racial group or married persons should amount to indirect discrimination.[11]

The uncertainties surrounding the phrase 'requirement or condition' are vividly highlighted by comparing the conflicting approaches adopted in the next three cases.

In *Home Office* v. *Holmes* [1984] IRLR 299, a civil servant who asked to return to work on a part-time basis following the birth of her second child was told that there were no part-time posts available. The EAT held that the obligation to work full-time was a 'requirement' within the meaning of s. 1 (1) (b) of the SDA and indirectly discriminated against women. The EAT also expressed the view that words like 'requirement' and 'condition' are plain, clear words of wide import and there was no basis for giving the words a restrictive interpretation in the light of public policy.

This broad-brush approach, however, was not adopted by the EAT in *Clymo* v. *Wandsworth London Borough Council* [1989] IRLR 241. After having a baby, Ms Clymo, a branch librarian, wanted to job share with her husband, a senior assistant librarian. Both were employed by Wandsworth but at different libraries. The council had a policy of allowing job sharing in the library service for lower-level jobs. Wandsworth refused to allow Ms Clymo to job share with her husband.

The EAT, upholding the decision of the IT, concluded that the employer had not applied a requirement or condition of full-time working; to work 'full-time' was the nature of the job. The EAT also expressed the view that it was not for the tribunal to decide whether a particular job was one which by its nature required full-time work. The decision was one for 'an employer, acting reasonably, to decide – a managerial decision – what is required for the purposes of running his business or his establishment'.

Fortunately, the *Clymo* reasoning was not followed by the Northern Ireland Court of Appeal in *Briggs* v. *North Eastern Education and Library Board* [1990] IRLR 181. Mrs Briggs, a school teacher, was required to undertake extra-curricular teaching duties as part of her contract in a promoted post. Following the adoption of a baby daughter, she requested that she be relieved of her after-school obligations. Her request was granted but only on the basis that she would take a demotion. Mrs Briggs alleged indirect sex and/or marital discrimination on the basis that the requirement of after-school attendance had a significant adverse impact on women and married people. It was held that the after-school attendance stipulation was a 'requirement' or 'condition'.

Preferring the approach adopted in *Holmes* to that in *Clymo*, the court was of the view that the fact that the nature of the job requires full-time attendance does not prevent there being a 'requirement'. (Having managed to overcome this hurdle, Mrs Briggs lost her case on the basis that the after-hours requirement was justified.)

Can a Considerably Smaller Proportion of the Protected Group Comply with the Requirement or Condition?

The courts and tribunals have offered no clear guidance on what proportion constitutes 'considerably smaller'. In the United States many courts have adopted the 'four-fifths rule' – that is, adverse impact is established if there is a 20 per cent difference between the groups under comparison. Indeed, the Commission for Racial Equality has proposed that we should adopt the four-fifths rule in this country.

It would appear that the phrase 'considerably smaller proportion' covers the situation where *no* members of a particular group can comply with the condition or requirement (*Greencroft Social Club and Institute* v. *Mullen* [1985] ICR 796).

The complainant must produce evidence – usually in statistical form – to support adverse impact. On the other hand, the EAT has suggested that it is not good policy to require elaborate statistical evidence to be produced.[12]

A recurring problem in establishing indirect discrimination lies in respect of the selection of the pool for comparison. In *Pearse* v. *City of Bradford Metropolitan Council* [1988] IRLR 379, Ms Pearse, a part-time lecturer, was unable to apply for a full-time post at Ilkley College, where she worked, because the only persons eligible to apply were full-time employees of the local authority. She submitted statistics showing that only 21.8 per cent of the female academic staff employed in the college were employed full-time compared with 46.7 per cent of male academic staff who could comply with the full-time working requirement. The EAT concluded that Ms Pearse had not selected the correct group for comparison. The correct pool for comparison would have been those with the appropriate qualifications for the post, rather than those eligible. Ms Pearse's statistics related to the latter and therefore she failed in her claim.

Consistency of approach in relation to appropriate pools of comparison is hindered by the fact that in *Kidd* v. *DRG (UK) Ltd* [1985] IRLR 190 it was held that the choice of pool was an issue of *fact* within the discretion of the tribunal, which would not normally be open to challenge by appeal unless it was a perverse choice.

Moreover, the phrase 'can comply' has been given a generally wide interpretation. In *Mandla* v. *Lee* [1983] IRLR 209, it was stated that it should be read as reading 'can in practice' or 'can consistently with the customs and cultural conditions of the racial group' rather than meaning 'can physically' so as to indicate a theoretical possibility. Similarly, in *Price* v. *The Civil Service Commission* [1977] IRLR 291, the EAT stated: 'It should not be said that a person 'can' do something merely because it is *theoretically possible* for him to do so; it is necessary to see whether he can do so *in practice*.'

So, in the Mandla case it would have been theoretically possible for a Sikh to remove his turban in order meet the school's uniform requirements and, in the Price case it was theoretically possible for a woman not to have children in her 20s in order to be able to comply with a civil service entry age maximum of 28 years. But in neither case was it a practical possibility.

Has the Condition or Requirement Operated to the Detriment of the Complainant?

It is insufficient to show that a condition or requirement is indirectly discriminatory; the complainant has to also show that s/he has been disadvantaged by it. The main purpose of this particular hurdle is to prevent hypothetical test cases from swamping the tribunals.

The time to determine whether the complainant has suffered a detriment is the time when the complainant has to comply with the requirement or condition. As we saw earlier, in *Clarke* v. *Eley (IMI) Kynoch Ltd* [1972] IRLR 482 a 'part-timers first' redundancy selection procedure was held to be indirectly sex discriminatory. The employers unsuccessfully tried to argue that the women could have avoided the detriment by becoming a full-time worker at some point in the past. This was held to be irrelevant; the women suffered detriment because at the time redundancy selection rule was applied they could not undertake full-time work.

Can the Employer Justify the Condition or Requirement?

At this stage, the onus of proof switches from the complainant to the employer. The employer has to show that the requirement or condition which has been applied is justifiable irrespective of the gender, race or marital status of the person to whom it is applied.

In the early days of the legislation, the courts and tribunals adopted a narrow approach to the scope of this defence. In *Steel* v. *The Post Office* [1977] IRLR 288, the EAT stated: 'it cannot be justifiable unless its discriminatory effect is justified by the *need, not the convenience*, of the business or enterprise.'

But the justification test was subsequently weakened and became more generous to the employer. In *Ojutiku and Oburoni* v. *Manpower Services Commission* [1982] IRLR 418, two of the judges in the Court of Appeal took the view that it was not essential for an employer to prove that a requirement was necessary and 'If a person produces reasons for doing something which would be acceptable to right-thinking people as sound and tolerable reasons for so doing, then he has justified his conduct.' (Lord Eveleigh). This diluted test was subsequently taken to be the correct one by industrial tribunals.

The third judge in *Ojutiku*, Lord Justice Stephenson, articulated a test based on the approach adopted in *Steel*:

> The party applying the discriminatory condition must prove it to be justifiable in all the circumstances on balancing the discriminatory effect against the discriminator's need for it. But that need is what is reasonably needed by the party who applies the condition.

After a period of uncertainty, the Court of Appeal in *Hampson* v. *Department of Science* [1989] IRLR 69 has now made it clear that it is the test set out by Lord Justice Stephenson which should be adopted in future. As a result, the test for justified indirect discrimination resembles that applied to determine whether unequal pay is justified under EqPA s. 1 (3).

It will be seen that the test for justification requires a balance to be struck between the discriminatory effect of the condition and requirement and the needs of the employer. Therefore, the greater the discriminatory effect, the more compelling the business need must be in order to come within the defence. It also follows there the requirement or condition will not be justifiable if there is a less discriminatory alternative for the employer to achieve the aim.

While the return to the narrower test for justification is to be welcomed,[13] there is still much scope for judicial discretion. As Anne Morris and Susan Nott observe: 'The difficulty is that in balancing the employer's needs against those of a woman who has suffered discriminatory treatment, corporate needs may automatically assume greater weight.'[14]

Victimisation

A separate form of discrimination identified by RRA s. 2 and SDA s. 4 is that of victimisation.

The legislation makes it unlawful to treat anyone less favourably than another by reason that s/he has:

(a)   brought proceedings against the discriminator or against any other person under the RRA, SDA or EqPA;

(b)   given evidence or information in connection with proceedings brought by any person against the discriminator or any other person under the RRA, SDA or EqPA;

(c)   otherwise done anything under or by reference to the RRA, SDA or EqPA in relation to the discriminator or any other person;

(d)   alleged that the discriminator or any other person has committed an act which (whether or not the allegation so states) would amount to a contravention of the RRA, SDA or EqPA.

The provisions also cover the situation where the 'discriminator knows the person victimised intends to do any of those things, or suspects the person victimised has done, or intends to do, any of them'.

There is no protection where an allegation which leads to adverse treatment is both false and not made in good faith.

These provisions were enacted in order to protect those employees who took action under the legislation, or who intended to do so, from a hostile response from their employer – a not infrequent reaction. Alice Leonard's survey of successful sex discrimination and equal pay complainants found that:

Many applicants reported that workplace relationships deteriorated as soon as they filed their case, particularly with employers and managers. Some even reported ill-feeling with fellow workers, and a few were subsequently avoided or insulted in public. For several the situation became untenable: they left their jobs, some before the hearing, and some afterwards. Even worse, a number of applicants actually stated they were dismissed or made redundant because they had brought a case.[15]

Jeanne Gregory's later survey of women who were unsuccessful in their claim paints a similarly depressing picture, with 60 per cent of respondents reporting a deterioration in relations both inside and outside work.[16]

Recent developments in the case law cast serious doubts on the effectiveness of the provisions on victimisation. It would appear that it is not sufficient for complainants to show that they were victimised because they brought proceedings against their employers under the discrimination legislation: they have to go further and show that they would not have been victimised for bringing proceedings under a different statute.

This is illustrated in *Cornelius* v. *University College of Swansea* [1987] IRLR 141. Mrs Cornelius, a personal secretary, alleged that she had been sexually harassed by her boss, the college's finance and estates officer. As a result, she was transferred to a post as secretary to the director of a new arts centre. After three months in the new post, she complained that she did not like it and requested to be returned to her old job. When her request was refused, she commenced proceedings against her employer under the SDA. These claims were unsuccessful because it was held that they were lodged out of time.

While awaiting the outcome of an appeal against the IT's finding, Mrs Cornelius again requested a transfer back to her former post. She was informed that no action would be taken until the outcome of her appeal was known. At this point, she made a fresh IT application, this time alleging that the second refusal to transfer was victimisation of her for commencing the earlier complaint of discrimination. The Court of Appeal, in rejecting her claim, stated that the actions of the college were those they would have taken pending the outcome of *any* legal proceedings and were not specifically related to the fact that Mrs Cornelius had lodged a complaint under the discrimination legislation.

A similar approach is to be found in the reasoning of the Court of Appeal in *Aziz* v. *Trinity Street Taxis Ltd* [1988] IRLR 204. In this case, the taping of conversations by a taxi-driver in order to acquire evidence of racial discrimination was found to be an act done 'by reference to' the discrimination legislation. However, his expulsion from the taxi-driver co-operative when his recording activities were discovered was held not to be victimisation. The complainant had to show that he was treated less favourably because of his actions in gathering evidence for a claim under RRA. This was held not to be the case; the members of the co-operative would have voted for the expulsion of any member who had made secret recordings, whatever their purpose, because it was a gross breach of trust between members.[17]

Both the CRE and EOC have argued that this approach seriously undermines any protection offered by the legislation against victimisation and they have proposed that the provisions should be amended to make clear that any person suffering detriment as a result of anything done or by reference to the discrimination legislation will be the victim of discrimination.[18]

The Scope of Protection against Discrimination

The discrimination legislation makes it unlawful to discriminate at every stage of the employment relationship: advertising vacancies (discussed above), hiring workers, offering promotion, training or fringe benefits, dismissing workers or 'any other detriment'. In order for there to be a detriment, a reasonable worker must take the view that by reason of the acts complained of s/he was disadvantaged in the way s/he would have to work (*De Souza* v. *Automobile Association* [1986] IRLR 103). Some acts are regarded as too insignificant to constitute a 'detriment'. For example, in *Peake* v. *Automotive Products Ltd* [1977] ICR 968, the Court of Appeal took the view that a rule allowing women to leave five minutes early was not a detriment.

Where Gender or Race Is a Genuine Occupational Qualification (GOQ)

An employer is permitted to discriminate on grounds of gender in any of the following circumstances (SDA s. 7):

- The essential nature of the job calls for a man on grounds of his physiology; for example, to work as a model. But greater strength and stamina alone are insufficient as qualifications.
- A man is required for authenticity in entertainment. So a film director is not required to interview actresses for the male lead in his film.
- Decency or privacy requires the job to be by a man either because there are men 'in a state of undress at the workplace' (for example, the job of lavatory attendant) or because the job involves physical contact and customers or employees might reasonably object to such contact from a member of the opposite sex. But note that the employer cannot use this exception if there are enough other employees of the appropriate gender to carry out these 'intimate' duties. So in *Etam plc* v. *Rowan* [1989] IRLR 150, a man claimed that he was discriminated against when he was refused employment as a sales assistant in a woman's dress shop. The employer's argument that the job fell within the decency and privacy exception was rejected. The EAT found that, while a sales assistant may be required to work in fitting rooms and to measure women who are uncertain of their size, it would have been possible to ensure that those aspects of the job could have been done by one of the 16 existing female employees without undue inconvenience.[19]

- The job requires workers to live in, there are no separate sleeping and sanitary facilities and it is unreasonable to expect the employer to provide them.
- The job involves working or living in the private home and needs to be held by a man because objection might reasonably be taken to allowing a woman either the degree of personal or physical contact with a person living in the home or the knowledge of the intimate details of such a person's life.[20]
- The job is at a single-sex establishment where persons require supervision or special care and it is reasonable to reserve the job for a person of the same gender – for example, a prison officer.
- The job-holder provides individuals with 'personal services' promoting their welfare, education or similar needs, and those services can 'most effectively' be provided by a man – for instance, a social worker or probation officer.
- The job needs to be held by a man because it is likely to involve work abroad in a country whose laws and customs are such that the job can only be done by a man – for example, work in the Middle East.
- The job is one of two which are held by a married couple – such as a public house manager.

An employer is allowed to discriminate on the grounds of race in the following circumstances (RRA s. 5):

(i) For reasons of authenticity:

- in entertainment – for example, an actor.
- in art or photography – for example, a model.
- in a bar or restaurant with a particular setting – for example, a waiter or waitress in an Indian restaurant.

(ii) The holder of the job provides persons of that racial group with personal services promoting their welfare, and those services can most effectively be provided by a person of that particular racial group.

In *Lambeth LBC* v. *CRE* [1990] IRLR 231, the Court of Appeal confirmed that the use of the word 'personal' in the GOQ exception appears to require direct contact between the provider of that service and the client. Therefore, the words are not apt to cover managerial or supervisory posts where there is no face-to-face contact. Consequently, the council's advertisement restricting two managerial posts in its Housing Benefit Department to those of Afro-Caribbean or Asian origin was unlawful.

It is clear that even if only some of the duties of the job fall within the GOQ provisions, it will still be lawful to discriminate in filling the post (RRA s. 5 [3]; SDA s. 7 [3]). In *Tottenham Green Under-fives' Centre* v. *Marshall (No. 2)* [1991] IRLR 162 EAT, it was held that being of Afro-Caribbean origin was a GOQ for a post as nursery worker because an ability to read and talk in dialect was a 'personal service' even though it was not the most important attribute of the post-holder. As long as the tribunal is satisfied that the duty is not a sham or so trivial it should be disregarded, it is not for the tribunal to evaluate the importance of the duty.

As with the gender GOQs, the above exceptions do not apply if the employer already has employees of that racial group who are capable of being deployed on such duties and it is reasonable to expect such deployment without undue inconvenience.

Reverse Discrimination

As we have seen above, both discrimination statutes impose strict restrictions on the occasions when gender or race is perceived to be a legitimate criterion for appointing somebody to a job. In general terms, positive or reverse discrimination is unlawful in Britain. The limited exceptions to this position do not relate to selection for a post but are restricted to the following:

(a)   training boards, employers and trade unions may discriminate in training afforded to members of one gender if during the preceding 12 months there were, in respect of the particular job for which training is being given:

    (i)   no persons of the favoured gender/race doing the job; or
    (ii) the number was comparatively small (SDA ss. 47, 48; RRA ss. 35, 37, 38);

(b)   training bodies may favour persons who appear to be in special need of training because of periods for which domestic or family responsibilities have excluded them from regular full-time employment (SDA s. 47[3]);

(c)   trade unions and other similar bodies may reserve seats on elected bodies to members of one gender (SDA s. 49), and organise a discriminatory recruitment campaign, if, during the preceding 12 months, the organisation has no women members or comparatively few (SDA s. 48 [3]).

Enforcing your Rights

Claim in Time

A complaint must be presented to an IT before the end of the period of three months beginning when the act complained of was committed. The IT has a discretion to hear a complaint which is presented out of time if, 'in all the circumstances of the case, it considers it just and equitable to do so' (SDA s. 76 [5]; RRA s. 68 [5]).

If the act of discrimination continues over a period, the time limit runs from the end of that period (SDA s. 76; RRA s. 68[7]). For example, in *Calder* v. *James Finlay Corporation Ltd* [1989] IRLR 55, EAT, a woman was refused a subsidised mortgage on the ground that the benefit was only available to male employees. She left employment eight months after the refusal of the mortgage but lodged her discrimination complaint within three months of the termination of her job. The EAT held that her claim was not out of time. The failure to allow her access to the subsidised scheme was a continuing act of discrimination which lasted up to the day she ended her employment.

Proving Discrimination

Questions of proof are crucial to the outcome of many claims under the legislation. In cases where direct discrimination (or victimisation) is alleged, the burden of proof is on the complainant. It will be only in very few cases that the complainant will have clear proof of discrimination. In the usual case, s/he will need to rely on circumstantial evidence in an attempt to persuade the IT to infer that discrimination has taken place.

The difficulties facing those alleging direct discrimination have been recognised by the courts and tribunals, as has the fact that the explanation for the employer's action is best looked for from the employer. In *Khanna* v. *Ministry of Defence* [1981] IRLR 331, Mr Justice Browne Wilkinson stated:

> The right course in this case was for the Industrial Tribunal to take into account the fact that direct evidence of discrimination is seldom going to be available and accordingly in these cases the affirmative evidence of discrimination will normally consist of inferences to be drawn from the primary facts. If the primary facts indicate that there is discrimination of some kind, the employer is called on to give an explanation and, failing clear and specific explanation being given by an employer to the satisfaction of the Industrial Tribunal, an inference of unlawful discrimination from the primary facts will mean the complaint succeeds.

In *Noone* v. *North West Thames Regional Health Authority* [1988] IRLR 195, Dr Noone, a Sri Lankan, applied and was interviewed for the post of consultant microbiologist with two other candidates. The qualities considered by the appointments committee were training, qualifications, experience and personality. Despite superior qualifications, experience and publications to those of the successful candidate, Dr Noone was not appointed. The CA concluded that there was sufficient evidence to infer discrimination on racial grounds. Lord Justice May said:

For myself I would have thought that it was common sense that if there is a finding of discrimination and of a difference in race and then an inadequate or unsatisfactory explanation by the employer for the discrimination, *usually* the legitimate inference will be that the discrimination was on racial grounds. [our emphasis]

The use of the word 'usually' may be seen as something of a retreat from the *Khanna* approach which had been understood to mean that (i) if there is a difference in race (or gender) (ii) less favourable treatment (iii) an unsatisfactory explanation by the employer, then the IT *should* infer race (or gender) discrimination.[21]

Success rates in direct discrimination cases are low[22] and the CRE, EOC and European Commission have all proposed modifications to the burden of proof in discrimination cases. Such a change would mean that once the applicant proves less favourable treatment in circumstances consistent with grounds of sex or race discrimination, a presumption of discrimination should arise which would require the respondent to prove that there were grounds for that treatment other than sex or race discrimination. The UK government has blocked a proposed EC directive aimed at achieving this modification.

In indirect discrimination cases, the burden of proof is on the worker to show that there is a requirement or condition with discriminatory impact and which is to his or her detriment because s/he cannot comply with it. However, if the employer seeks to claim that the requirement or condition is justifiable, it is for the employer to prove it. If indirect discrimination is established, the burden is on the employer to show that it was not intentional, so that damages should not be awarded (see the section on compensation below).

The Questionnaire Procedure

The difficulties of proving a discrimination complaint are given some limited recognition by the legislation. Individuals who consider that they may have been the victim of discrimination can issue a questionnaire to the proposed respondent to help them decide whether to bring a claim and, if so, to present their case in the most effective way. The respondent is not compelled to reply to the questions, but if the respondent deliberately and without reasonable excuse does not reply within a reasonable period, or replies evasively, then an IT can draw any reasonable inference from that fact. (SDA s. 74; Sex Discrimination (Questions and Replies) Order 1975 (SI 1975 no. 2048); RRA s. 65; Race Relations (Questions and Replies) Order 1977 (SI 1977 no. 842).

Useful questions might relate to:

*   the number of men and women in particular posts and in the workforce as a whole;

- in the case of a failure to recruit or select for promotion, the breakdown by gender of the applicants at the various stages of the appointment process.

Discovery

An IT may, on the application of either side to the proceedings, order disclosure of a document which is relevant to those proceedings. As with the questionnaire procedure, this is a valuable means by which the complainant can develop his/her case.

The House of Lords has set out the following guidance to ITs on how to exercise their powers to order discovery:

- the information necessary to prove discrimination cases is normally in the possession of the respondents, so making discovery essential if the case is to be fairly decided;
- confidentiality of the material is not, of itself, a reason for refusing discovery, but is a factor to be considered. In the case of confidential documents the court or tribunal should examine them to see whether disclosure really is necessary, and if so to consider whether it is possible fairly to preserve confidentiality by covering up the irrelevant parts;
- the test in both the courts and the tribunals is whether discovery is necessary for fairly disposing of the proceedings or for saving costs. (*Science Research Council* v. *Nasse; Leyland Cars Ltd* v. *Vyas* [1979] ICR 921 at p. 933).

Besides grounds of confidentiality, the employer may attempt to resist a request for discovery on the grounds that it is oppressive. For example, it may require the provision of material which can only be made available with difficulty and at great expense; or the effect of the discovery would be to add unreasonably to the length and cost of the hearing.

The value of discovery to the complainant's case can be seen in *West Midlands Passenger Transport Executive* v. *Singh* [1988] IRLR 186, where the Court of Appeal held that, in attempting to establish direct discrimination, the complainant was entitled to the discovery of statistical evidence which was relevant to his claim. In this particular case, the evidence was a schedule showing the number of white and non-white persons who applied for posts of traffic supervisor with the employers, categorised as to whether or not they had been appointed, covering the two-year period prior to his own unsuccessful application for promotion.

Remedies

On an individual complaint to an IT the following remedies are available if the tribunal considers them 'just and equitable' (RRA s. 56; SDA s. 65).

- declaration
- compensation
- recommendation of action to be taken

Declaration

This is an 'an order declaring the rights of the complainant and the respondent in relation to the act which the complaint relates' (RRA s. 51[1][a]; SDA s. 65[1][a]). This order is not enforceable but may have a persuasive influence on the employer.

Compensation

Compensation may be awarded for:

- actual losses, such as expenses and wages
- future losses of wages and benefits
- injury to feelings

In addition, in cases where the employer has acted maliciously, insultingly or oppressively, the plaintiff can ask for aggravated damages.[23]

No compensation can be awarded for indirect discrimination unless the employer *intended* the discrimination to occur. The EOC has argued that the distinction between intentional and unintentional discrimination is inappropriate. Indirect discrimination has been outlawed since 1975 and well publicised among employers. There are no longer convincing grounds why employers should avoid compensation because their discriminatory practices were unintentional.[24]

The amount of compensation which may be awarded is subject to a statutory maximum (£11,000 in 1993/4) but, as with unfair dismissal awards, the typical award does not begin to approach that amount.[25]

Until recently, the courts and tribunals have shown a marked reluctance to award anything but a purely nominal amount to compensate for injury to feelings. Indeed, as we have seen, sexual harassment cases such as *Wileman* v. *Minelec Ltd* and *Snowball* v. *Gardner Merchant Ltd* bear eloquent testimony to the reluctance of predominantly white, male, middle-aged and middle-class tribunals to put a serious value upon injury to feelings. Two decisions of the Court of Appeal in 1988, however, offer the prospect that in future tribunal awards under this head will be more substantial. In *Alexander* v. *Home Office* [1988] IRLR 190, the Court of Appeal awarded £500 for injury to feelings to a black prisoner who had been the victim of race discrimination by prison officers. Lord Justice May stated: 'Awards [for injury to feelings] should not be minimal because this would tend to trivialise or diminish respect for the public policy to which the Act gives effect.' In *Noone* v. *North West Thames Regional Health Authority* [1988] IRLR 195, a case we discussed earlier, Dr Noone was awarded £3,000 for injury to feelings – a sum described by the Court as at the top end of the bracket.[26]

Given the uncertainties surrounding the appropriate levels of compensation and the marked disparities in awards made by different ITs, the EOC has proposed that any finding of unlawful discrimination should be marked with a basic minimum award (similar as for unfair dismissal) of £500 or four weeks' pay, whichever is the higher, and that a compensatory award including injury to feelings should be additional. This amount should be adjusted annually.[27] While this approach would block the tendency on the part of certain ITs to make derisory awards, we are still left with a maximum compensation limit which is unrealistically low.[28]

One possible route to increased compensation may be via EC law. In *Marshall v. Southampton and South-West Hampshire Area Health Authority (No .2)* [1990] IRLR 481, CA, the IT concluded that, as Mrs Marshall's claim was brought against her employer under art.6 of the Equal Treatment Directive and the relevant EC case law suggested that compensation for breach should have a deterrent effect, the tribunal could award compensation in excess of that set by UK legislation. Consequently, it awarded Mrs Marshall £19,405, together with interest on the damages which amounted to over £7,000. Unfortunately, the EAT and Court of Appeal adopted a much more cautious approach. The EAT held that interest was not payable on compensation awards made for sex discrimination.[29] The Court of Appeal held that the provisions as to compensation in art.6 are not sufficiently precise or unconditional to have direct effect and, therefore, national compensation limits were not overridden. As at mid-1993, the matter is on appeal to the House of Lords, which in turn referred it to the ECJ.

Recommendation

An IT may make a recommendation for specific action, but the scope of the tribunal's action is limited. In particular, there is no general power to order an employer to discontinue a discriminatory practice, other than in relation to the individual complainant.

If the respondent fails to comply with the recommendation, the IT can increase any compensation previously awarded, subject to the statutory maximum; or, if previously the IT did not award compensation, then it may do so (SDA s. 65[3][a]; RRA s. 56[4]).

The strength of the recommendation as a restraint on an employer's behaviour has been diluted by restrictive interpretations of the scope of the remedy by the judges. In *Noone v. North West Thames Regional Health Authority (No .2)* [1988] IRLR 530, the Court of Appeal held that an IT had exceeded its powers in recommending that an applicant who had been the victim of a discriminatory selection procedure should be appointed to the next suitable post which became available. It was felt that such positive discrimination would be unfair to other applicants for that post and such action could of itself amount to direct discrimination.[30]

In addition, in *Irvine v. Prestcold Ltd* [1981] IRLR 281, the Court of Appeal held that an IT's power to make recommendations for the taking of action does not include the power to make a recommendation that the employer increase the complainant's wages. Money issues were best addressed when the IT decided whether to exercise it power to award compensation.

The Commissions and their Role in Enforcement

The Equal Opportunities Commission (EOC) and the Commission for Equality (CRE) have the following, broadly similar, duties in their respective spheres of operation:

- to work towards the elimination of discrimination;
- to promote equality of opportunity between men and women and racial groups, and to promote good race relations;
- to keep under review the working of the equal opportunities legislation and, as and when necessary, to propose amendments.

Members of the commissions are appointed by the home secretary. The commissions are financed from public funds but operate independently of the Crown. Both commissions must publish annual reports.

In order to carry out their duties, the commissions have the power to act in various ways:

- They may assist applicants in the bringing of complaints of discrimination if the case raises a question of principle or it is unreasonable to expect the complainant to deal with the case unaided.
- They may undertake or assist research and education activities and may also issue codes of practice.
- They may conduct formal investigations for any purpose connected with the carrying out of their duties, and this may lead to the issue of a non-discrimination notice to call a halt to particular discriminatory practice. This aspect of their work is worthy of closer attention.

Formal Investigations

The commissions may conduct a general investigation or an investigation into the activities of a particular person or body. They must conduct an investigation if so required by the secretary of state. There are very detailed procedural rules regulating the steps to be followed in conducting a formal investigation. These requirements have been made more stringent as a result of judicial interpretations, the cumulative effect of which unnecessarily restrict the commissions' role.

A formal investigation cannot take place until terms of reference have been drawn up and notice has been given of the investigation. In the case of a 'general' formal investigation general notice is sufficient, but where the investigation relates to named person the commissions must notify those named. In addition, in a named person investigation, where the commission believes that unlawful discrimination is present, the named person has the right to make oral or written representations and be supported by legal representation.

Since the judgement of the House of Lords in *R* v. *CRE ex parte Prestige Group plc* [1984] IRLR 355, the power of the EOC and CRE to carry out formal investigations has been considerably narrowed. The Lords held that the CRE could not investigate a named person or organisation unless it believed that such a person or organisation might be acting in breach of the law. The effect of the *Prestige* judgement is to require the Commission to have sufficient evidence to found a belief before it can commence a named person investigation. The limiting effects of this requirement have been described by the EOC as follows:

> There are many situations which give rise to concern that equality of opportunity is being denied, for example where a high degree of job segregation between men and women occurs, but where, in advance of an investigation, there is no evidence as to the reasons why this has come about on which a belief relating to unlawful acts could be based. This is particularly likely to be the case where indirect discrimination is occurring as a result of certain practices and procedures. It is also important to note that, where a particular institution has a monopoly or near monopoly position, the Commission could not conduct a general investigation and is thus precluded from investigating its activities at all unless it can form a belief that unlawful acts may have occurred.[31]

In the circumstances, therefore, it is hardly surprising that both the EOC and CRE have argued for a legislative amendment so as to overturn the *Prestige* decision.

Once the formal investigation is underway, whether or not the Commission has any power to compel the attendance of witnesses and the production of evidence depends on whether it is a general or named person investigation. In the former case, the Commission only has the power to serve notice requiring information where it is authorised by the secretary of state. In a named person investigation each commission has the power to require information and evidence and this can be enforced by court order.

On completion of investigation, the commissions are required to prepare a report of their findings which must be published or made available for inspection. They are also obliged to make recommendations which appear necessary in the light of their findings. These recommendations may be directed at any person with a view to promoting equality of opportunity; or at the secretary of state relating to changes in the law.

Non-discrimination Notices

If, in the course of a formal investigation, the Commission is satisfied that a person is committing an unlawful discriminatory act, the Commission must issue a non-discrimination notice (RRA s. 58; SDA s. 67). A notice lasts for five years. The Commission can stop further ('persistent') discrimination within these five years by obtaining an injunction (see below).

A notice can be issued if someone has:

- committed an act of direct or indirect discrimination;
- applied an actual or potential discriminatory practice;
- published an unlawful advertisement;
- issued instructions to discriminate;
- put pressure on an employer to discriminate.

A non-discrimination notice requires the recipient

- not to commit any discriminatory acts;
- to change his/her practices in order to comply with the point above;
- to inform the Commission that s/he has made the changes and what they consist of;
- to take reasonable steps, as specified in the notice, to tell people concerned about the changes;
- to provide information so that the Commission can verify that the notice has been complied with; and
- to give information in a specified form and by a certain date.

Before it issues a non-discrimination notice, the Commission must tell the proposed recipient of its intention, give its reasons, give him/her at least 28 days to make written and/or oral representations, and take these into account.

After a non-discrimination notice has been served on him/her, the recipient has six weeks to appeal to an industrial tribunal. It was originally assumed that the appeal was an appeal against the specific requirements of the notice, rather than an opportunity to reopen the case. However, in *CRE* v. *Amari Plastics Ltd* [1986] IRLR 252, the Court of Appeal took the view that the recipient is entitled to contest not only the Commission's requirements as set out in the notice, but also any of the facts relied upon by the Commission. This rerun of the case merely adds to an already unduly cumbersome and lengthy procedure. Lord Denning was moved to remark that the legislative provisions were 'a spider's web spun by Parliament, from which there is little hope of escaping'.

Persistent Discrimination

If, within five years of a non-discrimination notice becoming final, it appears to the Commission that unless restrained the person concerned is likely to commit more unlawful acts of discrimination, it may apply to a county court for an injunction restraining that person from doing so. However, if the employer has not appealed against the non-discrimination notice, the employer must first test the legality of the notice before an industrial tribunal. This is a final tortuous twist in a massively cumbersome procedure. The complexities surrounding the formal investigation process go some way to explaining why the commissions have made relatively limited use of their powers.

CHAPTER 12

Other Forms of Discrimination

Discrimination against Homosexuals

No law in the UK specifically prohibits discrimination on grounds of sexual orientation. As a result, the question arises as to the extent to which the laws of unfair dismissal and sex discrimination offer protection to gay men and lesbians.

A Remedy under the Sex Discrimination Act?

This legislation is unlikely to be of much help. Employers who refuse to hire a man because of his sexual orientation will be able to shelter behind the argument that they would not have recruited a woman with similar sexual inclinations. However, if the employer refuses to employ any men because of the sexual orientation of a proportion of them this will be direct discrimination. For instance, Dan Air operated a policy of not employing male air stewards. The company argued that a large proportion of male cabin staff were homosexual and sexually promiscuous and that it was concerned about the AIDs risks to its passengers. This was clearly a case of direct discrimination against men and the EOC issued a non–discrimination notice requiring Dan Air to change its recruitment policy (EOC 1987).

Unfair Dismissal

There are relatively few reported cases concerning unfair dismissal on the grounds of homosexuality. The decisions which have been reported display a lack of understanding and, on occasion, hostility towards gay men and lesbians.

The decision in *Saunders* v. *Scottish National Camps Ltd* [1980] IRLR 174 is a prime example. The employee was a maintenance worker at a children's camp. He was dismissed when his employers discovered his homosexuality. He contended that he was able to keep his private life entirely separate from his job and a psychiatrist gave evidence to the IT that his sexual orientation did not create a danger to the children. The dismissal was held to be fair on the basis that a considerable proportion of employers would take the view that the employment of a homosexual should be restricted, particularly when an employee is required to work in proximity to and contact with children. This decision, formed in the face of expert evidence, merely serves to reinforce stereotypical assumptions about gay men. We have seen that operating on the basis of racial and gender stereo-typing will amount to unlawful discrimination but apparently the law of unfair dismissal offers little protection against blind prejudice.

A particular difficulty is that it will often be relatively easy for employers to argue that there was some additional factor, over and above mere homosexual-ity, which prompted them to dismiss. For example, in *Boychuk* v. *H. J. Symons Holding Ltd* [1977] IRLR 395, the EAT upheld an IT's decision that it was fair to dismiss a woman for insisting on wearing a 'Lesbian's Ignite' badge at work. The rationalisation was that a reasonable employer 'on mature reflection' could reasonably have decided that the badge would be offensive to customers and fellow workers. It was not necessary for the employer to wait until business was disrupted or damaged before taking action. As we have seen, employers are given a wide prerogative in terms of dress requirements they can impose on their employees.

The majority of the case law relates to the dismissal of gay men who have been convicted of sexual offences. In *Nottinghamshire County Council* v. *Bowly* [1978] IRLR 252, a schoolteacher with almost 30 years' service was convicted of an offence of gross indecency with a man in a public place and was dismissed from his post. The IT found that the dismissal was unfair because 'there was no satisfactory evidence of any incident suggesting a risk to pupils.' The EAT allowed the employer's appeal, emphasising that the role of the tribunal is not to decide what *it* would have done in such circumstances, but to decide whether the employers had behaved reasonably in dismissing Mr Bowly. According to the EAT, 'provided they approach the matter fairly and properly and direct themselves correctly, the disciplinary Sub-Committee cannot be faulted in doing what in *their judgement* ... is the just and proper thing to do' (our emphasis).

Workers with HIV or AIDS[1]

As with gay men and lesbians, there is no specific legislation offering employment protection to those workers who have contracted AIDS or who are HIV positive. In the US, a number of states have introduced specific legislation to prevent AIDS/HIV sufferers from being discriminated against and from being required to undergo AIDS screening tests.[2] During the passage of the Employment Act 1990 through the House of Lords, the government resisted an attempt to introduce a clause which would have made it unlawful to discriminate against AIDS/HIV sufferers in this country. The government's preferred approach is to encourage employers voluntarily to adopt policies towards AIDS and to educate their workforces as to the non-existent risk of infection in the vast majority of work situations.[3] In the absence of specific legal protection, AIDS/HIV sufferers are forced to rely on general employment law provisions.

Discrimination at the Point of Recruitment

With the exception of the law forbidding trade union, gender and race discrimination, employers have a wide prerogative in terms of deciding which workers they employ. As a result, AIDS/HIV sufferers generally have no remedy when they experience recruitment embargoes.

Refusal to employ a candidate for reasons related to AIDS may amount to indirect gender or race discrimination in certain cases. For example, a refusal to employ anybody from a country where the disease was rife would amount to unlawful indirect race discrimination in the absence of justification.

It has also been suggested that a recruitment ban on AIDS/HIV sufferers amounts to indirect discrimination against men, given that the statistical evidence to date shows that AIDS disproportionately affects men. Even if this argument is correct, the employer can still utilise the defence of justification and much will depend on the nature of the occupation. Stronger cases of justification can be made out if the employment is in the medical and emergency services or if the work is to be carried out in a country which requires workers to pass an AIDS test.

Questions at Interview and HIV Screening Tests

It is also lawful to ask job candidates questions about their health records and ask them to undergo medical examinations and have blood tests. Where the job applicant lies about his/her medical condition and is subsequently employed, the employer may well be justified in dismissing the employee when the misrepresentation is subsequently discovered.

Employers can write into the employment contract the power to require an employee to submit to periodic medical checks. However, unless the employer has included such a clause, the worker can legitimately refuse to undergo the test. Even if the employer has the power under the contract to require general medical tests, an attempt to introduce an HIV test as part of the general medical check-up may be seen in most cases as a unilateral extension of the contract and unlawful. An exception would be certain 'high-risk' jobs involving the provision of health services where there is a recognised risk (albeit small) that the virus may be communicated other than by sexual contact. In such occupations, the courts might infer a term in the contract of employment that the employee must undergo an HIV test.

Working Conditions and Dismissal

The government guidance pamphlet 'Aids and the Workplace' emphasises that HIV infection is not of itself sufficient to justify dismissal. Employees with AIDS-related illnesses should be subject to the same procedures and treated no differently than a worker with any other form of illness (see chapter below on unfair dismissal).

In the relative few occupations where a worker with AIDS/HIV is seen to constitute a health risk to others, dismissal may be justified under 'some other substantial reason', although an employer should first consider deploying the worker in alternative work before terminating the contract.

In other situations, the employer may try to justify the dismissal on the grounds that other workers refused to work alongside the employee. In *Buck* v. *The Letchworth Palace Ltd* (1987)(IT 36488/88, 3.4.87), the dismissal of a cinema projectionist was upheld as fair because, following a conviction for gross indecency, other projectionists refused to work with him. The other projectionists 'viewed his behaviour with disgust, and also feared that their shared toilet facilities might become contaminated with the AIDS virus. Despite the fact that there was no evidence that the employee had actually contracted AIDS, the IT stated that this was not 'a case where the employers took notice of unreasonable prejudices on the part of their employees'. While acknowledging that the fellow workers may have overreacted, the IT held that the employers had acted reasonably in responding to the fears of Buck's fellow workers.

Brian Napier has argued that as a matter of public policy the law should not countenance the approach adopted in *Buck*:

> In the United States, for example, it has been established as a general rule that co-worker or customer preference is not a sufficient defence for an employer who commits a discriminatory act against his employee. But there is no such equivalent legislation in Britain, and there is no real support for this point of view in the cases dealing with unfair dismissal.[4]

Workers with Disabilities

Recent research estimates that there are 2.3 million adults with disabilities below pension age in Britain. Of these, only 31 per cent are in paid employment, compared with 69 per cent for the general population, with the length of unemployment twice that for the general population.[5] Workers in employment who have disabilities earn on average one-fifth less than the average rates. Despite this clear evidence of discrimination, we still lack an effective set of legal guarantees of the rights of such workers.

Under the 1944 and 1958 Disabled Persons (Employment) Acts, employers have a very limited obligation to employ a percentage of persons with registered disabilities, but there is no specific law against discrimination. Indeed, in practice relatively few employers comply with the quota - only 27 per cent in 1986. There have been only 10 prosecutions (eight of them successful) since 1947.

Companies which employ more than 250 workers per week must include in their annual report a policy statement about the employment of people with disabilities, although the company is under no legal obligation to have any specific policy beyond meeting the quota (Companies Act 1985, 7 sched. 9). There is a Manpower Services Commission Code of Good Practice on the Employment of Disabled People, but this also is not legally binding.

Obligations to Recruit People with Registered Disabilities

Employers with 20 or more employees must employ workers with registered disabilities as 3 per cent of the workforce. Such workers must be employed for at least 30 hours a week, although someone working between 10 and 30 hours counts as half a worker.

Under the legislation, a 'disabled person' is a person who, on account of injury, disease or congenital deformity, is substantially handicapped in obtaining or keeping employment (or undertaking work on his or her own account) of a kind which would be suitable for his or her age, experience and qualifications were it not for that injury, disease or deformity (DPEA s. 6[1]).

It is purely voluntary for persons with disabilities to apply for registration on the Department of Employment's register. The disability must be likely to continue for at least 12 months. Applications are considered by disablement resettlement officers. Entry on the register – and possession of the so-called green card – shows that the registered person is capable of entering into and keeping some form of employment.

A person can be disqualified from holding registration if s/he is in prison, a full-time in-patient at a hospital, sanatorium or similar institution, or of 'habitual bad character' (Disabled Persons [Registration] Regulations 1945 [SR & O 1945 no. 938] para. 6).

Government departments and the NHS are not covered by the Disabled Persons (Employment) Acts but they have agreed to be bound by the quota scheme.

It is a criminal offence to:

- offer work to a person who is not 'registered disabled' if the quota has not been fulfilled;
- dismiss a worker so registered without reasonable cause if the employer would then be below the quota; and
- fail to maintain records to show whether the quota has been complied with.

Employers can apply on a 12-month basis for an exemption on the ground that the quota is too large having regard to the circumstances of the employment.

They can also apply for a permit to count workers with disabilities who are not registered.

In addition, the secretary of state can designate specific classes of employment as particularly suitable for workers with disabilities. So far, passenger electric lift and car park attendants have been so designated. Any employer of any given size who gives designated employment to a person who is not registered with a disability commits a criminal offence, unless the employer has obtained an exemption permit from the secretary of state. Persons with registered disabilities employed in such reserved occupations do not count towards the fulfilment of the employer's statutory quota.

Obligations to Provide Access and Facilities for Workers with Registered Disabilities

Under the Chronically Sick and Disabled Persons Act 1970, factory, office and shop employers are obliged to provide access to and within premises, car parking and sanitary facilities for disabled workers, but only in so far as it is practicable and reasonable to do so.[6]

Unfair Dismissal

There is no rule that the dismissal of a person with a disability is automatically unfair, and even a dismissal which is a criminal offence under the 1944 Act will not necessarily be unfair. The ordinary law of unfair dismissal applies. In *Post Office* v. *Husbands* (1980) EAT 432/80, the EAT stated:

> If an employer knowingly takes a disabled person into his employ, he must have regard to that fact and any decision to dismiss must fairly take into account both the disability itself and the basis on which the person has been employed.

So, for example, in a collective redundancy situation where selection is based on standards of work performance, an employer should specifically consider the individual situation of a worker, disability or not (*Hobson* v. *GEC Telecommunications* [1985] ICR 777, EAT).

Whether it is fair to dismiss a worker for failure to disclose a disability during recruitment will depend on all the circumstances such as the nature of the work, safety risks and whether the employee deliberately misled the employer. See *O'Brien* v. *Prudential Assurance Co* [1979] IRLR 140, EAT.

Reform

The weakness of the existing employment protection laws for workers with disabilities has prompted calls for a legislative model which would parallel that adopted in relation to gender and race discrimination. Such legislation is to be found in the US, Canada and Australia. The advantage of this approach is that it would offer rights to people with disabilities, independently of registration, in recruitment and selection, terms and conditions of employment and job security. However, as Brian Doyle has argued, it will also be necessary to consider what forms of positive action or positive discrimination might be included in such legislation. According to Doyle, intervention would be necessary on at least three levels. First, any reform must contain a degree of positive action, such as contract compliance, affirmative action planning, equal opportunity management audits, reasonable accommodation and outreach requirements. Second, disability rights will also have to be guaranteed in areas beyond employment, such as education, transport, income maintenance and public access. Finally, a degree of reverse discrimination, especially in employment, might be countenanced on behalf of those for whom full integration in a competitive society is perceived as impossible because of the severity of their disabilities. In this context, there is a role for a strengthened reserved occupation and quota scheme.[7]

At the time of writing, the Civil Rights (Disabled Persons) Bill has been given its third reading in the House of Lords and commenced its path through the Commons. The Bill has little chance of becoming law unless the government is prepared to allocate it parliamentary time.

The Bill would make it unlawful for employers to discriminate against employees and job applicants on the ground of disability, either directly or indirectly. Victims of discrimination would have a right to complain to an industrial tribunal. A Disablement Commission would fulfil a similar role to that played by the EOC and CRE in the areas of gender and race discrimination.[8]

PART FOUR

Job Loss

CHAPTER 13

Terminating the Contract

Termination Involving Dismissal at Common Law

- dismissal by notice
- dismissal for fundamental breach
- wrongful dismissal

Termination Not Involving Dismissal

- death or dissolution of the employer
- frustration
- expiry of fixed-term contracts
- mutual agreement

Terminations Deemed to be Dismissals by EPCA

- an act of the employer or an event affecting the employer (including death, dissolution of a partnership, or winding up of a company) which has the effect of terminating the contract automatically at common law will be deemed to be a dismissal for the purposes of redundancy but *not* for an unfair dismissal claim (EPCA s. 93)
- termination of the contract by the employer with or without notice (EPCA ss. 55[2][a] and 83[2][a])
- the failure to renew a fixed-term contract (EPCA ss. 55[2][b] and 83[2][b])
- where the employee terminates the contract, with or without notice, in circumstances such that s/he is entitled to terminate it without notice by reason of the employer's conduct: 'constructive dismissal' (EPCA ss. 55[2][c] and 83[2][c])

Terminations Involving a Dismissal at Common Law

Dismissal with Notice

The general principle is that either party to the contract of employment can bring it to an end by giving notice to the other. Once notice is given, it cannot be withdrawn unilaterally.

If the contract is for a fixed period, then the employment cannot be lawfully terminated before the end of that period unless, of course, the employee is in breach of contract or unless the contract provides for prior termination by notice.

The length of notice required to bring a contract to an end should be expressly agreed by the parties. If no notice is expressly agreed then the law requires that 'reasonable notice' should be given with the length depending on such factors as the seniority and status of the employee.

Statutory Minimum Periods of Notice

Apart from any contractual provision for notice, an employee is entitled to a statutory minimum period of notice. The employer must give one week's notice to an employee who has between one month and two years' service and then not less than one week's notice for each year of continuous service up to a maximum of 12 weeks for 12 years. In return, the employee must give at least one week's notice of resignation once employed for more than a month (EPCA s. 49).

The minimum notice provision does not:

* prevent either party from waiving the right to notice;
* affect the right of either party to terminate the contract without notice in response to a serious breach of contract by the other (see below); or
* prevent the employee accepting a payment in lieu of notice.

Dismissal with Pay in Lieu of Notice

Employers will often decide that it is in their interests not to require dismissed employees to work out their notice. At best such workers will lack motivation and at worst they may try to find a way of getting their own back! When such workers are given pay in lieu of notice, the law regards this as the payment of damages for wrongful dismissal.

Summary Dismissal for Fundamental Breach

The conduct of the employee may be viewed as sufficiently serious to justify immediate termination of employment without notice. In this event, the employee will lose entitlement to both contractual or statutory minimum notice.

Theft of or wilful damage to the employer's property, violence at work, dishonesty and other criminal offences will normally justify instant dismissal. Disobedience to lawful and reasonable orders may justify instant dismissal but not in every case – all the circumstances must be considered. The same applies to the use of obscene language, as can be seen from the rather colourful case of *Wilson v. Racher* [1974] IRLR 114 CA.

Philip Wilson was the head gardener on Mr Racher's estate. He was dismissed following an incident in which Racher accused Wilson of shirking his work and in the course of the ensuing argument Wilson used obscene language. The court found that he had been wrongfully dismissed because his outburst had been provoked by an unfair accusation by this employer.

Terminations which May Not Amount to Dismissal

Frustration

'Frustration' is a legal concept which, if it applies, brings the employment contract automatically to an end. As a result, the employer does not have to go on paying you wages, or to pay you compensation for unfair dismissal, redundancy, or the like.

In order for frustration to apply, there are two essential factors which must be present:

(i)   There must be some event, not foreseen or provided for by the parties to the contract, which either makes it impossible for the contract to be performed at all, or at least renders its performance something radically different from what the parties envisaged when they made the contract; and

(ii)   the event must have occurred without the fault of either contracting party. Frustration will not operate if it was 'self-induced' or caused by the fault of a party.

Events which have been held to frustrate the contract include the following:

* the conscription of the employee to national service
* internment as an enemy alien during wartime.

However, frustration arguments have been most frequently employed in the cases of long-term absence through sickness or through imprisonment.

Sickness

In relation to sickness absence, a number of principles will be relevant in deciding whether a contract is frustrated. In *Williams* v. *Watson's Luxury Coaches* [1990] IRLR 164 the EAT usefully summarised the relevant principles in deciding whether a contract is frustrated through sickness as follows:

* the court must guard against too easy an application of the doctrine, more especially when redundancy occurs and also when the true situation may be dismissal by redundancy;
* although it is not necessary to decide that frustration occurred on a particular date, nevertheless an attempt to decide the relevant date is a far from useless

exercise as it may help to determine in the mind of the court whether it is
a true frustration situation;

- there are a number of factors which may help decide the issue, including
the length of the previous employment; how long it had been expected
the employment would continue; the nature of the job; the nature, length
and effect of the illness or disabling event; the need of the employer for the
work to be done, and the need for a replacement to do it; the risk of the
employer acquiring obligations in respect of redundancy payments to the
worker who has replaced the absent employee; whether wages have
continued to be paid; the actions and statements of the employer, particularly whether the employer has sought to dismiss the sick employee and
whether it is reasonable, in all the circumstances, to expect the employer
to keep the job open any longer;

- the party alleging the frustration should not be allowed to rely on the frustrating event if that event was caused by the fault of that party.

The case of *Notcutt* v. *Universal Equipment Co Ltd* [1986] IRLR 218 provides
a good illustration of the operation of the frustration doctrine. Mr Notcutt had
been employed by the same relatively small company as a skilled worker for some
27 years. In October 1983, when two years from retirement age, he suffered a
coronary and was thereafter off work. His employer for a time sub-contracted
his work on a temporary basis, but this was not wholly satisfactory and, by July
1984, decided to take on someone else if Mr Notcutt was not going to return
to work. With Mr Notcutt's permission, the employer sought a medical report
from his GP. In that report, the doctor said that he doubted whether Mr Notcutt
would ever work again. As a result Mr Notcutt was given 12 weeks' notice of
dismissal.

Mr Notcutt took legal advice and was informed correctly that under EPCA
he was entitled to sick pay during the notice period, notwithstanding that
ordinarily under his contract he was not paid when off sick. He lodged a claim
to that effect in the county court. Ultimately, the Court of Appeal decided that
the county court judge was correct in finding that Mr Notcutt's contract of
employment had been frustrated by an illness which would have probably
prevented him from working again. The contract, therefore, was not terminated
by the employers and Mr Notcutt was not entitled to sick pay during the notice
period.

Imprisonment

In the past imprisonment was thought to be 'self-induced' frustration. More
recently, however, the Court of Appeal has ruled that a custodial sentence of
six months *did* have the effect of frustrating a four-year apprenticeship contract
which still had 24 months to run. It was felt that it was the sentence passed by
the trial judge – as opposed to the employee's criminal conduct – which was

the frustrating event. Consequently this was not a case of self-induced frustration (*F.C .Shepherd & Co Ltd* v. *Jerrom* [1986] IRLR 358).

The courts have provided very little guidance as to how long a sentence of imprisonment has to be in order to frustrate the contract. In *Harrington* v. *Kent County Council* [1980] IRLR 353, a sentence of 12 months' imprisonment was found to have frustrated the contract, even though the sentence was later quashed on appeal.

In *Chakki* v. *United East Co Ltd* [1982] ICR 140, the EAT was of the view that in imprisonment cases, whether frustration had occurred could be determined by answering the following questions:

(1) Looking at the matter from a practical commercial point of view, when was it necessary for the employers to decide as to the employee's future and as to whether a replacement ... would have to be engaged?

(2) At the time when the decision had to be taken, what would a reasonable employer have considered to be the likely length of the employee's absence over the next few months?

(3) If in the light of his likely absence it appeared necessary to engage a replacement, was it reasonable to engage a permanent replacement rather than a temporary one?

While frustration arguments may well succeed in exceptional cases, the courts are generally reluctant to apply the doctrine. In *Williams* v. *Watson's Luxury Coaches* (above, p. 165), the EAT attributed this judicial caution to the view that the doctrine can do harm to good industrial relations, as it provides an easy escape from the obligations of investigation which should be carried out by a reasonable employer. It is therefore better for the employer to take dismissal action.

Fixed-term and 'Task' Contracts

The expiry of a fixed-term contract is regarded as a dismissal. Such a contract must have a definite starting and finishing date, although there may be provision for earlier termination by notice within the fixed-term period (*BBC* v. *Dixon* [1977] IRLR 337). This protection offered to those on fixed-term contracts represents a limited recognition on the part of those who drafted the legislation that any other approach would invite employers to employ large sections of their workforce under such arrangements and so avoid liability for unfair dismissal and redundancy payments.

However, this protection is very limited for two reasons. First, a dismissal of a worker who comes to the end of a 'temporary' contract may, in the circumstances be held to be fair as 'some other substantial reason' (see later). Second, s.142 of EPCA states that where an employee is employed for a fixed term of a year or more s/he may agree in writing to exclude any right to claim unfair dismissal and, if employed for two years, any right to redundancy also, should the contract not be renewed at the completion of its term.

Moreover, the courts have made a distinction between a fixed-term contract, deemed to be a dismissal under the legislation, and a contract for the completion of a particular task, at the end of which there is no dismissal A 'task' contract is discharged by performance of the particular task and cannot give rise to a dismissal – for example a seafarer engaged for a particular voyage or a worker hired to paint a house.

In *Brown* v. *Knowsley Borough Council* [1986] IRLR 102 the distinction between a fixed-term contract and a contract to perform a particular task was extended to cover contracts terminable on the happening or non-happening of a future event. In that case a further education college lecturer, having been previously employed under a number of fixed-term contracts, was then employed under a one-year temporary contract from 1 September 1983 which was expressed to last only so long as sufficient funds were provided by the Manpower Services Commission (MSC) to support the course she taught. On 3 August 1984 she was given written notice that, as MSC funds had ceased to be available, her employment would terminate on 31 August 1984. The applicant's claim for a redundancy payment was rejected by the IT and EAT on the basis that there had been no dismissal and that her contract was terminable on the happening or non-happening on a future event – the withdrawal of MSC sponsorship.

Termination by Mutual Agreement

As with other contracts, a contract of employment may be terminated by the mutual consent of the parties. If the courts were to accept too readily that the contractual relationship had ended in this way then access to employment protection would be severely threatened. As a result statute has intervened by providing that where an employee under notice gives the employer notice that s/he wishes to leave before the expiry of the employers's notice, the employee is deemed still to have been dismissed for unfair dismissal and redundancy purposes and not party to a early termination by mutual consent (EPCA ss. 55[3], 85[2]).

In general, the courts and tribunals have been reluctant to accept the argument that an employee has in reality agreed to give up his or her job and forego the possibility of an unfair dismissal or redundancy claim.

In *Igbo* v. *Johnson Matthey Chemicals Ltd* [1986] IRLR 215 the Court of Appeal had to consider the effect of an agreement by which an employee agrees that if the employee does not return to work from a period of extended leave by a specified time then the contract of employment will come to an end. In overruling the earlier decision in *British Leyland UK Ltd* v. *Ashraf* [1978] IRLR 330, the Court of Appeal held that these 'automatic termination' agreements were void under EPCA 1978, s. 140. This section makes void any provision in an agreement which purports to 'exclude or limit' any provision of EPCA 1978. By limiting Ms Igbo's right to claim unfair dismissal, the agreement offended s. 140 (1). Dismissals for overstaying leave, therefore, must be subject to the test of reasonableness and the ACAS advisory handbook, *Discipline At Work*, provides guidance on how such matters should be handled (see p. 42 of the handbook).

A factor which weighed heavily with the Court of Appeal in *Igbo* was that, if such 'automatic termination' were allowed, then there would be nothing to prevent an employer including a term in the contract that if the employee was more than five minutes late for work on any day, for whatever reason, the contract would automatically come to an end. In this way, the protections offered by the unfair dismissal legislation would be non-existent.

For similar policy reasons to those described above the courts have held that a resignation under threat of dismissal may constitute a dismissal (see *Sheffield* v. *Oxford Controls Ltd* [1979] IRLR 133). Whether a contract of employment is terminated by one party alone, or by mutual consent, is a question of fact for the industrial tribunal. In *Hellyer Bros Ltd* v. *Atkinson & Dickinson* [1992] IRLR 540, the EAT upheld a tribunal's decision that two trawlermen were dismissed even though the act which brought their contracts to an end was their own act of signing off the crew agreement. Since the company was decommissioning its fleet, the company's request to sign off amounted to a request for the crew's confirmation of an accomplished fact. This was the case even though the employer had not used threats or coercion to force the crew to sign off.

The distinction between a mutual termination on acceptable terms and a forced resignation was crucial to the EAT's decision in *Logan Salton* v. *Durham County Council* [1989] IRLR 99. Mr Logan Salton was employed by the local authority as a social worker. The local authority commenced disciplinary proceedings against him, based on a report from the director of social services which recommended that he should be summarily dismissed. With the assistance of NALGO he negotiated a severance payment which repaid an outstanding council car loan of £2,750 and he signed a written agreement with the local authority that his contract of employment would terminate by 'mutual agreement'. Mr Logan Salton then claimed that he had been unfairly dismissed and that the mutual agreement to terminate was either void as an agreement entered into under duress, or void because it contravened s. 140.

The EAT upheld the industrial tribunal's decision that there had been no dismissal in law. The present case was distinguishable on its facts from that of *Igbo* v. *Johnson Matthey Chemicals Ltd*, relied upon by the appellant. The agreement between the appellants and the respondents was not a contract of employment or a variation of an existing contract. It was a separate contract which was entered into willingly, without duress and after proper advice and for a financial inducement. Therefore the agreement was not caught by s. 140.

So it is not the case that an argument based upon termination by mutual consent can never succeed; for example, where a termination is willingly agreed to by the employee in return for financial compensation, as in *Salton* itself, or under an early retirement scheme, as in *University of Liverpool* v. *Humber* [1985] IRLR 165.

'Constructive Resignation?'

In a number of cases in the 1970s, the EAT was prepared to accept that certain acts of gross misconduct by an employee automatically terminated the contract without the need for the employer to dismiss. A good example of what was known as 'self-dismissal' or 'constructive resignation' is *Gannon* v. *J.C. Firth Ltd* [1976] IRLR 415 where employees 'downed tools' and walked out of the factory, leaving machinery in a dangerous state, and were held to have dismissed themselves by their actions.

Following the Court of Appeal's judgement in *London Transport Executive* v. *Clarke* [1981] IRLR 166 it is clear that self-dismissal arguments will no longer be successful. In this case, the majority of the Court of Appeal held that a contract of employment could not be 'automatically' terminated by a serious breach of contract on the part of the employee: the terminating event was the *dismissal* by the employer in response to that serious breach.

Wrongful Dismissal

At common law a contract of employment could be terminated by the giving of notice of a length which has been expressly agreed. In the absence of an expressed notice period, the law will imply a period of 'reasonable notice' whose length will depend on the circumstances of the employment. Moreover, the common law allowed an employer to dismiss an employee with no notice at all if the latter's conduct amounted to a repudiation of the contract of employment.

Until the introduction of the statutory right to claim unfair dismissal in 1971, the employer was left with an extremely wide managerial prerogative in the area of discipline given the largely obsolete and unjust legal principles which made up the action of wrongful dismissal. The major weaknesses in the action for wrongful dismissal may be summarised as follows:

- The low level of damages awarded to successful litigants, generally only compensating for the appropriate notice period (see *Addis* v. *Gramophone Co Ltd* [1909] AC 488 and *Bliss* v. *SE Thames RHA* [1985] IRLR 308).
- The inability of dismissed employees to regain their jobs because of the general rule against ordering specific performance of contracts of employment.

- The archaic nature of some of the principles of summary dismissal, reflecting 'almost an attitude of Tsar-serf' (Lord Justice Edmund Davies in *Wilson* v. *Racher* [1974] IRLR 114 CA).
- The lack of procedural protections for most employees, with only so-called office-holders entitled to natural justice and the remedies of public law (see *Ridge* v. *Baldwin* [1964] AC 40).

As stated above, the action for wrongful dismissal was perceived as largely irrelevant in practical terms. However, a number of recent developments have caused us to reassess the position and it may well be that wrongful dismissal cannot be consigned to employment law's lumber room.

As a result of these flaws in the framework of statutory protection, there has been a renewed interest in common law and public law remedies by employees seeking to prevent a dismissal taking place in breach of natural justice or because the power of dismissal has been exceeded.

This is a complex area which is still very much in a state of flux and it is important that you have a clear structure in mind for the presentation of the developments. The discussion of the area can be divided between (a) the public law remedies of judicial review; and (b) the private law remedies of injunctions and declarations.

Public Law Remedies

The holder of a public office has always received special protection over and above that of an employee so that the officer has the right to the protection of natural justice before dismissal. A good example of this position comes from *Ridge* v. *Baldwin* [1964] AC 40, where a chief constable who was dismissed without a proper opportunity to be heard in his own defence was granted a declaration that the decision to dismiss him was a nullity as it was in breach of natural justice.

However, there is immense difficulty in distinguishing a 'protected office' from 'mere employment'. In *Malloch* v. *Aberdeen Corporation* [1971] 2 All ER 1278, Lord Wilberforce was moved to comment that: 'A comparative list in which persons have been entitled to a hearing, or to observation of rules of natural justice looks illogical and even bizarre.'

In *Malloch*, a Scottish teacher whose employment was regulated by statute was held to be an office-holder and thereby entitled to a hearing. Lord Wilberforce offered a wide definition of the concept and stated that natural justice would only be excluded in those 'pure master and servant cases' where there was 'no element of public employment or service, no support by statute, nothing in the nature of an office or status which is capable of protection'. This statement opened up the possibility that many public sector workers possessed the status of office-holder and could challenge their employers' disciplinary actions by way of application for judicial review under Order 53 of the RSC (1977).

This potential alternative to unfair dismissal for large numbers of workers was severely restricted by the Court of Appeal in *R* v. *E Berkshire HA ex parte Walsh* [1984] IRLR 278. In this case the judge at first instance accepted the proposition that the employee, a hospital senior nursing officer, was entitled to judicial review of the health authority's decision to dismiss him on the grounds that it was ultra vires and in breach of natural justice. This view was firmly rejected by the Court of Appeal, holding that the relationship between the parties was one of pure master and servant and therefore a matter of private and not public law. According to Master of the Rolls Sir John Donaldson, the remedies of public law were only available to those individuals who were employed by a public authority under terms which were 'underpinned' by statute in one of two ways:

- by statute placing restrictions upon the authority's power to dismiss, or
- by statute requiring the authority to contract with employees on specified terms.

It was not enough, as Mr Justice Hodgson had held at first instance, for the employee to show that he was employed in a senior position by a public authority for public purposes, and that the public had an interest in seeing that public servants were treated lawfully and fairly.

Thus our survey of developments in the public law field offer little in the way of alternative or additional protection to the vast majority of employees. Indeed it is the very existence of the right to claim unfair dismissal which is one of the reasons why the courts have taken the view that most workers do not require the additional protection of public law. What of the recent developments in the private law sphere?

Private Law Remedies

We have seen that the courts were traditionally reluctant to force an employer to take an employee back. As regards employees this rule is now enshrined in TULR(C)A 1992, s. 207, which provides that 'no court shall issue an order compelling any employee to do any work or attend any place of work'.

Recent developments in the common law have opened up the possibility of alternative (and perhaps more potent) remedies than those provided by the statutory regime of unfair dismissal.

The decision in *Irani* v. *South West Hampshire Health Authority* [1985] ICR 590 is a good example of this development. The plaintiff was an ophthalmologist who was employed part-time in an out-patient eye clinic. He was dismissed with six weeks' notice because of irreconcilable differences with the consultant in charge of the clinic. No criticism at all was made of his competence or conduct. In dismissing him the employers were in breach of the disciplinary procedure established by the Whitley Council and incorporated into his contract of employment. He sought an injunction to prevent the employers from dismissing him without first following the appropriate disciplinary procedure. The employers argued that this would be contrary to the general rule that injunctions cannot be issued to keep a contract of employment alive. The plaintiff obtained his injunction.

The judge ruled that the case fell within the exception to the general rule for the following reasons. First, trust and confidence remained between employer and employee. The health authority retained complete faith in the honesty, integrity and loyalty of Mr Irani: any breakdown in confidence was between the consultant and Mr Irani, not Mr Irani and the authority. Second, damages would not be an adequate remedy since Mr Irani would become virtually unemployable throughout the National Health Service and would lose the right to use NHS facilities to treat his private patients.

A major landmark is provided by the Court of Appeal's decision in *Powell* v. *LB Brent* [1987] IRLR 466, in which an interlocutory injunction for specific performance was obtained. Part of the rationale for the general rule that there cannot be specific performance of a contract of employment is that mutual confidence is necessary for the satisfactory working and that this has often been destroyed.

The Powell case, in which the plaintiff claimed that she had been given promotion which the council subsequently purported to rescind, is authority for the proposition that the courts will consider granting an injunction to require an employer to let an employee continue in employment if, on the evidence, the employer still retains sufficient confidence in the employee's ability and other necessary attributes for it to be reasonable to make an order. *Powell* was an exceptional case in that dismissal was not an issue and the employee had been working in the new job for some time when the application was heard. As it was not disputed that the plaintiff had done the job satisfactorily and without complaint for over four months, there was no rational ground for the employers to lack confidence in her competence to do the job. Nor was there any basis for supposing that there was any defect in the relationship between her and any other person with whom she worked or with whom she might be expected to have worked.

This decision was applied in the subsequent case of *Hughes* v. *LB Southwark* [1988] IRLR 42. In this case, the plaintiff social workers successfully obtained an order restraining the council from enforcing an instruction, allegedly in breach of contract, which required them to cease their normal work during part of the week and carry out other work on those days. The mere fact that there was a dispute did not indicate an absence of mutual trust and confidence and there was no question of the employers not having confidence in the employees. On that basis, the judge went on to adopt the approach set out in the American Cyanamid case (see p. 363 below) and held that there was a serious issue to be tried as to the allegation of breach of contract since the instruction was 'arguably unreasonable'; that the plaintiffs, unlike the employers, could not be adequately compensated by damages since they would suffer loss of job satisfaction; and that the balance of convenience was in favour of granting the injunction.

Both these cases suggest a more liberal approach to the granting of orders to restrain breaches of contract, especially concerning the question of continuing trust and confidence. That is not to say that such applications will always succeed. In *Ali* v. *LB Southwark* [1988] IRLR 100, a care assistant was subjected to disciplinary charges following an independent inquiry on grounds of alleged ill-treatment of patients in an old persons' home. An injunction was refused despite claims that the contractual disciplinary procedure was not being adhered to. The employers had lost confidence in the ability of the employee to carry out the job and, pending the findings of the disciplinary hearing, they had lost confidence on reasonable grounds.

It should also be stressed that injunctive relief will be refused if there is evidence that the employee has accepted the employer's breach as terminating the contract. This acceptance might be implied in the electing to claim damages for wrongful dismissal, or in the making of an application for unfair dismissal. In *Dietman* v. *LB Brent* [1987] IRLR 299, the Court of Appeal held that the council was not entitled to dismiss the plaintiff social worker summarily without first affording her a hearing under the contractual disciplinary procedure and that, in any event, on a proper construction of her contract, 'gross negligence' did not constitute 'gross misconduct' as defined by the contract which would justify summary dismissal. The decision emphasises the importance of carefully drafted disciplinary procedures (as well as the importance of following such disciplinary procedures as have been drafted). The contract defined 'gross misconduct' as 'misconduct of such a nature that the authority is justified in no longer tolerating the continued presence at the place of work of the employee who commits' the offence. Examples were then listed, all of which involved an element of intention on the part of the guilty employee and involved conduct which was either dishonest or disruptive. The message here is that if employers wish to have the contractual right to be able to dismiss summarily for 'gross negligence', this should be explicitly set out in the disciplinary rules.

Mrs Dietman was accordingly awarded damages compensating her for the loss of pay she would have received had the proper disciplinary procedure been followed and had she been given proper notice. Her claim for an injunction, however, failed, because by that stage she had by then 'accepted' her employer's repudiation of the contract – she had accepted employment with another authority – with the result that her employment had already come to an end.

In *Wishart* v. *National Association of Citizen's Advice Bureaux* [1990] IRLR 393, the Court of Appeal refused to extend the principle applied in *Powell* v. *LB Brent* to require an employer, by injunction, to take a person into its employment and to keep him in that employment until full trial, when the employer clearly lacked confidence in the prospective employee in the light of unfavourable references.

Mr Wishart had been employed in the CAB since 1986, when he applied for the position of information officer. He was offered the post, and this offer was confirmed in writing 'subject to receipt of satisfactory written references'. The employer received a reference which, although favourable in other respects, mentioned that the employee had taken 23 days sick leave in the previous year. Worried about this level of absences, the employer sought and obtained a detailed breakdown of absences for the previous three years, commenced discussion with Mr Wishart about the nature of the problem, sought advice from the Occupational Health Service, and finally decided that the level of past absenteeism was unacceptable and that the job offer should be withdrawn.

Mr Wishart sought an interlocutory injunction restraining the CAB from readvertising the post. He also sought an order requiring the National Association of Citizens' Advice Bureaux (NACAB) to provide him with employment in his capacity of information officer until trial. Injunctions were granted by the High Court but the employer appealed.

Allowing the appeal, the court felt that the judge was wrong in treating the case as substantially similar to *Powell* and therefore not within the general rule against specific performance of contracts of service. There was no evidence in the present case that the defendants had or had not expressed confidence in the plaintiff. Unlike *Powell*, there was no established employment relationship. The plaintiff had never worked for the defendants and they did not wish to employ him.[1]

A significant development in the area of employee injunctions is seen in *Robb v. L B Hammersmith & Fulham* [1991] IRLR 72. Mr Robb was the borough's director of finance. In May 1990, when capital market transactions and interest rate swaps carried out when he was financial controller were declared unlawful, the council invoked the disciplinary procedure relating to capability set out in para. 41 of the Conditions of Service for Chief Officers of Local Authorities. This provides in the first instance for a preliminary investigation to determine whether there is an issue of substance. While this investigation was being conducted, the chief executive instructed Mr Robb to take special leave with pay. Meanwhile there were negotiations as to the possible terms of the termination of the contract. On 5 July, the chief executive wrote to Mr Robb stating that 'in view of your impending termination of service', there was no useful purpose in carrying on with the preliminary investigation and the disciplinary procedure would not be continued.

The negotiations were not successful and on 26 July Mr Robb was summarily dismissed for lack of capability. Mr Robb sought an injunction restraining the employers from giving effect to the purported dismissal until the contractual procedures had been complied with.

The High Court granted an injunction, notwithstanding that the employers had lost trust and confidence in Mr Robb's capacity to do the job. If an injunction is sought to reinstate employees dismissed in breach of contract, so that on reinstatement they can actually carry out the jobs for which they are employed, trust and confidence are highly relevant since, without the employer's trust and confidence the employees' position would be unworkable. In the present case, however, the plaintiff did not seek reinstatement so that he could actually perform his duties and responsibilities. He sought an Order to restore the position as it was before the defendant unilaterally aborted the disciplinary procedure and unlawfully terminated his contract. In such circumstances, the defendant's lack of trust and confidence in the plaintiff's ability to do his job had no relevance to the workability of the disciplinary procedure if ordered by the court. Without the injunction, Mr Robb would lose the opportunity of ventilating his case and justifying himself at the hearings under the procedure. In this sense, damages would not be an adequate remedy.[2]

Damages

Claims of up to £50,000 are heard in the county court, larger actions being heard in the Queen's Bench Division of the High Court. The jurisdiction of industrial tribunals to consider claims arising from breach of contract has not been extended, although provision for such an extension is provided for by EPCA 1978 s. 131 and in 1989 the government announced its intention to bring about the change in the near future. Section 38 of TURERA gives the minister more scope in terms of transferring jurisdiction to the industrial tribunals, but the Ministerial Order will not apply to claims for personal injuries and it may put a limit on the amount of payment which may be ordered.

After a period of uncertainty and conflicting decisions by the EAT, the House of Lords has now ruled that jurisdiction for unpaid wages in lieu of notice does not lie with industrial tribunals under the Wages Act 1986.

'Wages' is defined in s. 7 of the Act as any sum payable to the worker by the employer in connection with the employment, including 'any fee, bonus, commission, holiday pay or other emolument referable to his employment, whether payable under the contract or otherwise'.

In *Delaney v. Staples (t/a De Montfort Recruitment)* [1991] IRLR 112, the employee had been dismissed without notice; she was given a cheque for £82, stated to be in lieu of notice, but this was later stopped. She sought to recover this also as an unauthorised deduction. On this part of her claim she was unsuccessful. Section.7(1) (a) of the Act provides that wages 'means any sum payable to the worker by his employer *in connection with his employment*' (emphasis added). The Court of Appeal held that where an employee is dismissed without notice due under the contract, a claim for pay in lieu of notice is in effect a claim for damages for wrongful dismissal and that sums payable by way of damages for wrongful dismissal do not fall within s. 7(1) (a) since they 'are payable in connection with the termination of a worker's employment, rather than in connection with the worker's employment' as such. This decision was subsequently endorsed by the House of Lords [1992] IRLR 191.

Calculation

The High Court and county court will normally award damages based on the employee's loss up to the time at which s/he might have been lawfully dismissed with notice under the contract of employment. Net wages for the period in question will form the basis of the calculation, to which will be added commission, bonus and the value of such benefits as company car, pensions, health insurance schemes, meals allowances, holiday pay and profit-sharing schemes. Damages will reflect the net sum the employee would have received after deductions for tax and national insurance.

Damages for distress or humiliation, however, are not available (see *Bliss v. SE Thames Regional Health Authority* [1985] IRLR 308).

If there be a dismissal without notice, the employee must pay an indemnity; but that indemnity cannot include compensation either for the injured feelings of the servant, or for the loss he may sustain from the fact that his having been dismissed of itself makes it more difficult for him to obtain fresh employment. (Lord Loreburn in *Addis v. Gramophone Co Ltd* [1909] AC 488 HL).

In *Addis*, an employee who was paid at a fixed salary plus commission was wrongfully dismissed and claimed damages under the following heads:

(i)   salary for the six-month notice period;
(ii) reasonable commission for a-six month period;
(iii) damages for the humiliating manner of his dismissal;
(iv) damages for loss of reputation leading to future difficulty in obtaining employment.

The House of Lords held by a majority that only heads (i) and (ii) were recoverable.

With the exception of apprentices and actors/actresses, damages done to future prospects will also not be recoverable.

In *Marbe v. George Edwards (Daly's Theatres) Ltd* [1928] 1 KB 269, an American actress wishing to establish her reputation in London contracted to play a particular part for the defendant, who undertook to give full publicity. When she was wrongfully denied the chance to play the part, the CA held that she should recover the salary due to her plus an amount representing her loss of reputation. In *Dunk v. George Waller Ltd* [1970] 2 All ER the plaintiff, an apprentice, was wrongfully dismissed during the four-year term and was held entitled to his net loss of wages for the rest of the term plus an amount representing loss of tuition and training and diminution of future prospects.

Recently it has been suggested that where the employer breaks the contract of employment by dismissing the employee with no or short notice, thereby depriving him or her of the right to claim unfair dismissal, the employee may be able to claim extra damages representing loss of statutory rights: *Stapp* v. *Shaftesbury Society* [1982] IRLR 326, CA.

Reduction of Damages

Any award will be reduced by payment already made by the employer, such as payment in lieu of notice or ex-gratia payments, but will not normally be affected by redundancy payments. Credit will also be given for early payment. This is because damages are supposed to reflect what would have been paid under a contract which may still have some years to run. If receipt of those wages is accelerated – via the payment of damages – then this should be reflected in the final award.

In *Hopkins* v. *Norcross plc* [1992] IRLR 304 QBD, the High Court decided that money received under occupational pension schemes as a result of the termination of employment should not be deducted from damages for wrongful dismissal, unless the pension scheme or the contract specifically said so. The court ruled that a retirement pension is analogous to insurance and is a form of deferred pay to which the employee is entitled in any event.

Compensation for unfair dismissal representing the notice period will be set off against any damages for wrongful dismissal. For an interesting exception to this general rule, see *O'Laoire* v. *Jackel International Ltd* [1991] IRLR 170. This case does not establish as a general rule that unfair dismissal compensation should not be set-off against wrongful dismissal damages, but it does suggest that such a set-off may be impracticable where the employee's loss is in excess of the statutory limit on unfair dismissal awards. An IT hearing of O'Laoire's unfair dismissal complaint assessed his actual loss arising out of his dismissal as £100,700. After the employers failed to comply with an order for reinstatement, O'Laoire received the then maximum compensation award of £8,000. The issue which arose in connection with O'Laoire's claim for damages for wrongful dismissal was whether, in assessing loss of earnings in respect of the contractual notice period, the High Court had correctly held that the unfair dismissal award of £8,000 fell to be deducted in accordance with the rule against double recovery. The Court of Appeal pointed out that it was for the defendant to prove a double recovery for the same loss in order to provide a basis for a set-off. On the facts, that could not be shown since it was impossible to allocate the £8,000 to any one of the particular elements which together made up a loss of over £100,000 – only part of which related to loss recoverable for wrongful dismissal. Thus the defendants could not prove that the £8,000 was attributable to loss of earnings during the notice period (as opposed to some other loss) and the Court of Appeal thought it both unjust and impracticable to make an apportionment. This problem will only arise in cases where the loss exceeds the statutory maximum, so that compensation must be scaled down. In the usual case of loss within the overall limit, the different heads of loss will be expressly allocated by the IT and the rule against double recovery will bar common law damages for loss of earnings during the notice period.

The employee is under a duty to mitigate loss. S/he must make efforts to find alternative employment. This will be particularly relevant in the case of a fixed-term contract with some years to run, but is generally applicable to all dismissals. Any moneys received, or moneys which might have been received had the employee tried to get a job, will be taken into account, as will statutory benefits received. While the employee is under a duty to act reasonably, this does not impose a requirement to accept work at a much reduced status or lower pay.

The Relationship between Wrongful Dismissal and Unfair Dismissal

These are quite distinct remedies. This is not always appreciated by the layperson and you often hear people using the terms interchangeably. They are quite different legal concepts, although it is quite possible for the same conduct by the employer to result in claims under both headings; for example dismissal may have taken place without notice, and therefore be in breach of contract while at the same time being unfair under EPCA. Which action to choose will vary according to individual circumstances. The wrongful dismissal claim is worth considering where:

- the employee is a high earner whose losses in terms of salary and fringe benefits far exceed the relatively low maximum compensation limits set for unfair dismissal;
- the employee is prevented from claiming unfair dismissal because s/he lacks sufficient continuity of service, is over retirement age or has failed to lodge a complaint within three months;
- the dismissal is in breach of contract and the employee wishes to keep the contract alive.

Note also that a contract may be terminated lawfully in that proper notice has been given, but unfairly in that there was no fair reason for the dismissal. In such cases, the only action will be unfair dismissal.

Conversely, a dismissal may be held to be fair, but wrongful because the appropriate contractual notice was not provided. In *Treganowan* v. *Robert Knee & Co Ltd* [1975] IRLR 247, an employee was dismissed without notice because of a personality clash between her and her colleagues – she had openly described her sexual exploits and then boasted of a relationship with a young man half her age, and this had created a tense atmosphere in the office which was affecting business. This was held to be a fair dismissal justified under 'some other substantial reason'. However, the IT decided that she should not have been dismissed summarily, but should instead have received six weeks' pay in lieu of notice, though it did not have jurisdiction to award this sum. The employee appealed, claiming that the IT did have jurisdiction since the lack of notice was capable of making the dismissal unfair. The EAT rejected this argument, holding that, while lack of notice could possibly be of evidential value in deciding some of the points necessary for an unfair dismissal action, it could not per se make a dismissal unfair that was otherwise fair. When EPCA, s. 131 is finally brought into force – allowing claims arising out of contracts of employment (including actions for wrongful dismissal, but excluding actions for personal injury) to be brought before an IT- then it will be possible for the IT will be able to make the award which was desired in the Treganowen case.

With wrongful dismissal, the fairness of the dismissal is irrelevant – the court's concern is only whether the contract has been broken.

Unfair Dismissal	*Wrongful Dismissal*
Time limit in which to lodge complaint is usually three months	Statute of Limitation – six years
Remedies – compensation, reinstatement or re-engagement	Damages are the main remedy
Limit on compensation	No limit on compensation
Forum – industrial tribunal (EAT on appeal)	Forum – county court or High Court (appeal to Court of Appeal or, in Scotland, to the Court of Session)
Proceedings relatively informal	Usual court rules and accompanying formality apply
Employee must have been employed for a qualifying period – currently two years – for the majority of dismissals	No qualification period
Employee must not have reached normal retiring age	No age limit
Compensation can be reduced by up to 100 per cent for contributory fault	No account is taken of employee's action in contributing to dismissal
Acts or omissions discovered after dismissal are not relevant to the fairness issue (though they could reduce compensation)	Acts or omissions discovered after the dismissal will be taken into account

Settlement of Claims

The parties to the contract can agree that the employee will not bring or pursue any claim for wrongful dismissal provided that this agreement is supported by 'valuable consideration' – some material benefit to the employee. Employees will usually be asked to sign a receipt which states that they accept the payment in settlement of all claims arising out of or in any way connected with the termination of their employment. Unless this declaration has been signed under duress, it will prevent the employee pursuing a claim for *wrongful* dismissal any further. However, until recently such a signed declaration would not prevent the employee from going on to make a complaint of *unfair* dismissal. This could only be prevented if a special form (COT3) is signed in the presence of an ACAS conciliation officer. TURERA amends the relevant provisions to allow the parties to reach a 'compromise agreement' without ACAS involvement. The agreement will have to be in writing and the employee will have had to have received 'independent legal advice from a qualified lawyer as to the term and effect of the proposed agreement' (s. 39).

Terminations Deemed to be Dismissals for the Purposes of Unfair Dismissal and Redundancy Payments

We have seen that statute has extended the concept of dismissal beyond termination by the employer with or without notice to cover the non-renewal of a fixed-term contract and cases of 'constructive dismissal'. We have already examined what constitutes a fixed-term contract and below we discuss some of the issues which have arisen in reaction to the two other forms of dismissal: direct and constructive dismissal.

Direct Dismissal (EPCA s. 55[2][a])

This is the clearest and most obvious form of dismissal and consequently the concept has not generated the same amount of case law as the other two statutory forms of dismissal. Nevertheless, the following issues have arisen:

'Resign or Be Sacked'
A resignation under threat of dismissal may constitute a dismissal (see *E Sussex CC* v. *Walker* (1972) 7 ITR 280 and *Sheffield* v. *Oxford Controls* [1979] IRLR 133). However, in order to succeed in this argument the employee must establish a certain and immediate threat (*Martin* v. *Glynwed Distribution Ltd* [1983] IRLR 198).

Ambiguous/unambiguous Words of Dismissal/resignation
One problem which occasionally arises is whether the words used by the employer amount to a dismissal or not – for instance, they may have been merely intended as a rebuke or uttered in the heat of the moment. The problem can

also arise in the reverse, where you the employee use words which the employer chooses to interpret as a resignation.

The legal principles in this area may be summarised as follows:

(a) If, taking into account the context in which they were uttered, the words unambiguously amount to a dismissal (or resignation) then this should be the finding of the tribunal. So where Mrs Southern, an office manager in a firm of solicitors, announced to the partners at the end of a partners' meeting, 'I am resigning,' the Court of Appeal held her to her unambiguous statement (*Southern* v. *Franks Charlesly & Co* [1981] IRLR 278).

In *Kwik-Fit* v. *Lineham* [1992] IRLR 156 EAT, the employee, a depot manager, was given a written warning for a relatively minor offence in a public and humiliating way. He threw his keys down on the counter and left. On his claim for unfair dismissal, the issue arose as to whether he had been dismissed or had resigned. Both the IT and EAT found that there was a dismissal and that it was unfair.

Mr Justice Wood stated:

> If words of resignation are unambiguous then prima facie an employer is entitled to treat them as such, but in the field of employment, personalities constitute an important consideration. Words may be spoken or actions expressed in temper or in the heat of the moment or under extreme pressure ('being jostled into a decision') and indeed the intellectual make-up of an employee may be relevant ... These we refer to as 'special circumstances'. Where 'special circumstances' arise it may be unreasonable for an employer to assume a resignation and accept it forthwith. A reasonable period of time should be allowed to lapse and if circumstances arise during that period which put the employer on notice that further enquiry is desirable to see whether the resignation was really intended and can properly be assumed then such enquiry is ignored at the employer's risk.

(b) Where, however, the words employed are ambiguous, perhaps because they were uttered in the heat of the moment, the effect of the statement is determined by an objective test, that is, whether any 'reasonable' employer or employee might have understood the words to be tantamount to a dismissal or resignation.

A rather colourful example is provided by *Futty* v. *D and D Brekkes Ltd* [1974] IRLR 130. Futty was a fish filleter on Hull dock. During an altercation with his foreman, Futty was told, 'If you do not like the job, fuck off.' Futty stated that he interpreted the foreman's words as words of dismissal; the company denied dismissing him. The IT heard evidence from other fish filleters as to the meaning they would give to the words used because it was important to interpret the words 'not in isolation – but against the background of the fishdock'. The fish filleters, who had witnessed the incident, did not consider that Futty had been dismissed, and the IT agreed, stating that 'once the question of dismissal becomes imminent bad language tends to disappear and an unexpected formality seems to descend on the parties.' Futty was held to have terminated his own employment.

(c)   A dismissal or resignation given in the heat of the moment may be withdrawn. However, it is probable that retraction must follow almost immediately. Once notice of resignation or dismissal is given, it cannot be retracted without the consent of the other party to the contract. It may be that one exception to this general rule is where the words of dismissal or resignation uttered in the heat of the moment can be withdrawn provided the retraction follows almost immediately: see *Martin* v. *Yeomen Aggregates Ltd* [1983] IRLR 49.

Constructive Dismissal (EPCA s. 55[2][c]

The problems surrounding this form of dismissal have generated a mass of case law over the years. By virtue of the concept of constructive dismissal, the law treats some resignations as dismissals and therefore extends statutory dismissal rights to those employees who are forced to resign because of their employer's conduct. This form of dismissal may be extremely important in the context of reorganisations where employers may be seeking to introduce changes in terms and conditions of employment.

Under the current definition, which applies to both unfair and redundancy dismissals, it does not matter whether the employee left with or without notice provided s/he was entitled to leave by reason of the employer's conduct.

In the mid 1970s there was a difference of opinion among the judiciary as to the criteria which should be used in order to determine whether a constructive dismissal had taken place. Specifically, a number of decisions suggested that constructive dismissal was not confined, as had been previously assumed, to fundamental breaches of contract, but applied to any case where the employer's behaviour was held to be unreasonable.

Following a period of confusion, the Court of Appeal in *Western Excavating (ECC) Ltd* v. *Sharp* [1978] IRLR 127 clarified matters, rejecting the reasonableness test and holding that a contractual approach was the right one.

The key elements of the concept are as follows:

*   Has the employer broken a term of the contract or made it clear that he or she does not intend to be bound by the contract?
*   If yes, is the term which has or will be broken an essential or fundamental term of the contract?
*   If yes, has the employee resigned with or without notice in response to the breach within a reasonable time?

What constitutes a breach of a fundamental term and how long is a reasonable time? The difficulty in knowing where the employer or employee stand on these and other issues has been compounded by a development which has been referred to earlier in this chapter. This is the recent tendency of the Court of Appeal to hold that many of the issues in unfair dismissal, most notably for the purposes of this discussion the question as to whether there has been a serious breach of contract, are issues of fact alone or mixed fact and law and therefore the findings of industrial tribunals are only reviewable following perverse decisions (*Pedersen* v. *Camden London Borough Council* [1981] ICR 74 and *Woods* v. *WM Car Services (Peterborough)* [1982] ICR 693).

In the midst of this uncertainty, however, it is possible to produce a two part categorisation of acts or omissions which have been held to repudiate the contract by the courts and tribunals:

- First, an employer may break a positive contractual obligation to the employee, for example withdrawal of free transport, or fail to pay wages.
- Second, the employer may insist that the employee agree to a change in existing working arrangements or terms and conditions of employment, for instance a change of shift, or insist that the employee perform duties which s/he is not obliged under the contract to carry out.

Following the adoption of the contractual test by the Court of Appeal in *Western*, a number of commentators argued that it would impose a great restriction on the scope of constructive dismissal claims relative to the more generous reasonableness test. This has not occurred because the EAT has been prepared to hold that contracts of employment generally are subject to an implied term that the employer must not destroy or seriously damage the relationship of trust and confidence between employer and employee. As a result the difference between the *Western* approach and the discredited 'reasonableness' test looks rather slight, as is illustrated by looking at just some of the situations where the implied obligation has been held to be broken:

- Failing to respond to an employee's complaints about the lack of adequate safety equipment (*British Aircraft Corporation* v. *Austin* [1978] IRLR 332).
- Undermining the authority of senior staff over subordinates (*Courtaulds Northern Textiles Ltd* v. *Andrew* [1979] IRLR 84).
- Failure to provide an employee with reasonable support to enable him to carry out his job without disruption and harassment from fellow employees (*Wigan Borough Council* v. *Davies* [1979] IRLR 127).
- A failure properly to investigate allegations of sexual harassment or to treat the complaint with sufficient seriousness (*Bracebridge Engineering Ltd* v. *Darby* [1990] IRLR 3).
- Foul language by employer (*Palmanor Ltd* v. *Cedron* [1978] IRLR 303).

- Imposing a disciplinary penalty grossly out of proportion to the offence (*BBC* v. *Beckett* [1983] IRLR 43).
- A series of minor incidents of harassment over a period of time which cumulatively amount to repudiation: the so-called last straw doctrine (*Woods* v. *WM Car Services (Peterborough)* [see above]).

The potency of the implied obligation of trust and confidence can be seen in the case of *United Bank Ltd* v. *Akhtar* [1989] IRLR 507, which suggests that even where the contract contains a wide mobility clause employers must still operate the clause in a reasonable manner. Should they fail to do so, it may constitute a breach of contract and entitle the employee to claim constructive dismissal.

Mr Akhtar was a junior ranking and low-paid worker who had been employed by the bank since 1978 in Leeds. A clause in his contract provided:

> The Bank may from time to time require an employee to be transferred temporarily or permanently to any place of business which the Bank may have in the UK for which a location or other allowance may be payable at the discretion of the Bank.

The EAT held that the employee was entitled to treat himself as constructively dismissed by reason of the employer's conduct in requiring him to transfer his place of employment from Leeds to Birmingham at short notice (six days) and with no financial assistance, even if it could be held within the terms of the express mobility clause in the employee's contract of employment. This is because the general implied contractual duty set out in *Woods* v. *WM Car Services (Peterborough)* that employers will not, without reasonable and proper cause, conduct themselves in a manner calculated or likely to destroy the relationship of trust and confidence between employer and employee is an overriding obligation independent of and in addition to the literal terms of the contract.

While the EAT in *White* v. *Reflecting Roadstuds Ltd* [1991] IRLR 331 vigorously insisted that there is no general implied term that the employer must act reasonably, in practice the existence of the implied obligation to maintain trust and confidence will allow industrial tribunals to intervene in an appropriate fashion to override the unreasonable exercise of an express contractual power.

Fairness and Constructive Dismissal

A constructive dismissal is not necessarily an unfair dismissal. Tribunals having first determined whether the elements of constructive dismissal are present will then go on to consider the fairness question under EPCA s. 57 (3). In many cases this will not alter their conclusion, but there may be cases, such as those concerned with business reorganisations, where, although the employee was entitled to resign, the employer's action which prompted the resignation is held to be fair and reasonable in the circumstances.

In *Savoia* v. *Chiltern Herb Farms Ltd* [1982] IRLR 166, the employers embarked on a reorganisation of duties after the death of one of their foremen. They decided to move Mr Savoia from his role as supervisor in the packing department, following complaints about his performance, and to offer him the dead man's former position: that of foreman in charge of the production department.

Despite the offer of a higher salary, Mr Savoia refused to move to the new post because he was concerned that he would be exposed to conjunctivitis as a result of the heat and smoke in the production department. He refused the employers' offer of a medical examination so that they could judge whether his concerns were well founded.

Both the IT and EAT found that he had been constructively dismissed, but that the dismissal was for 'some other substantial reason' and fair. The Court of Appeal upheld the decision on the basis that 'the reorganisation of the business was imperative', and Mr Savoia's 'refusal to be medically examined when he protested that production work was unsuitable for him created a situation which was a substantial reason' for the dismissal and fair.

CHAPTER 14

Unfair Dismissal

The right to claim unfair dismissal has been part of the framework of labour law since February 1972, when it was introduced as part of the now repealed Industrial Relations Act. It was put on the statute book because the common law did not provide adequate protection against arbitrary terminations of employment and also in an attempt to reduce the number of strikes over dismissals.

The Weakness of Protection against Dismissal under Common Law

Under the common law, a contract of employment can be lawfully terminated simply by giving notice of a length which has been expressly agreed. In the absence of an expressed notice period, the common law merely implies a period of 'reasonable notice' whose length will depend on the status of the employee. Moreover, the common law allows an employer to dismiss an employee with no notice at all if the latter's conduct amounted to a serious breach of the contract.

Until the introduction of the statutory right to claim unfair dismissal, the employer wielded immense power in the area of discipline given the largely obsolete and unjust legal principles which constituted the action of wrongful dismissal. The major weaknesses, from the employee's point of view, in the action for wrongful dismissal can be summarised as follows:

- The general failure of the common law action to question the fairness of the employer's decision to terminate the contract: allowing an employer to dismiss for any reason – however arbitrary – provided the correct period of notice was given.
- The low level of damages awarded to successful litigants, generally only compensating for the appropriate notice period which should have been given.[1]
- The inability of the dismissed employee to regain his or her job because of the traditional reluctance of the courts to order reinstatement of the employee.

- The outdated nature of some of the principles of summary dismissal reflecting 'almost an attitude of Tsar-serf', as Lord Justice Edmund Davies observed in *Wilson* v. *M. Racher* [1974] IRLR 114 CA.
- The lack of procedural protections for most employees, with only an ill-defined group of so-called office-holders being entitled to natural justice, including the right to state their case before dismissal.[2]

When 'unfair dismissal' was introduced, the common law action was perceived as largely irrelevant in practical terms. After all, the statutory remedy *was* concerned with the overall merits of the employer's decision to dismiss and the determination of the fairness of the dismissal also involved a review of the procedure adopted by the employer in taking disciplinary action. Moreover, it did provide for reinstatement or re-engagement as remedies. Wrongful dismissal was seen only to retain a relevance for high-salary earners, particularly if they were employed on fixed-term contracts or had long notice periods.

The Impact of the Right to Claim Unfair Dismissal

The right to claim unfair dismissal is undoubtedly the most significant of the employment rights which were introduced during the 1970s. In quantitative terms, unfair dismissal claims dominate the work of industrial tribunals, accounting for the majority of their workload.[3] In addition, the introduction of the claim produced significant changes in employment relations practices during the 1970s, encouraging the reform or formalisation of procedures adopted by employers in taking disciplinary action.

The significance of this particular employment right is further enhanced because it is popularly presented as a powerful, perhaps too powerful, constraint on managerial prerogative. Indeed, there is a potent mythology among sections of British managers that holds that the law relating to unfair dismissal makes it almost impossible to dismiss even the most deserving case. This view persists in the face of judicial decisions, research and statistics which raise serious questions concerning the extent to which the legislative code on unfair dismissal does effectively control management's power of discipline.[4]

By the 1980s commentators had identified the following shortcomings in the action for unfair dismissal:[5]

(a) The generally low success rate of complainants. In 1990/1, 19,554 cases were disposed of (this figure represents a steady decline in unfair dismissal applications over recent years). Of these 13,133 (66 per cent) were settled without a hearing, either by ACAS conciliated settlement (7,326) or by some other form of withdrawal (5,807). Of the 6,066 cases actually heard by ITs, 3,536 were dismissed and 2,530 were upheld, a success rate for employee applicants of 41.7 per cent. (In 1981 this had reached a low of 23 per cent.)

(b) The few cases in which the reinstatement remedy is awarded. In 1990/1, of the cases upheld, only 63 ended in an order for reinstatement and re-engagement (1 per cent of cases heard; 0.3 per cent of cases disposed of).

(c) The low level of compensation. In 1990/1, of the cases upheld by industrial tribunals which resulted in compensation, the median award was £1,773 – an actual fall on the previous year's median award of £1,786.

(d) The devaluation between 1979–87 of the importance of adhering to fair procedures in unfair dismissal as a result of the application of the test laid down in *British Labour Pump Co Ltd* v. *Byrne* [1979] IRLR 94 (now no longer good law as a result of the Law Lords' decision in *Polkey* v. *AE Dayton Services Ltd* [1987] IRLR 503).

The Resurrection of the Common Law Remedies

Given these flaws in the framework of statutory protection, recently there has been a renewed interest in common law remedies by employees who are seeking to prevent a dismissal from taking place in breach of a contractually binding disciplinary procedure or to restrain some other breach of contract by the employer. The courts have responded by showing a greater willingness to grant court orders to prevent such breaches taking place.[6] Fortunately, the House of Lords reassertion of the importance of procedural fairness in *Polkey* has now restored a degree of potency to unfair dismissal action which had been sadly lacking for some time.

Creeping Legalism

In the decade or so since the introduction of the right to claim unfair dismissal, the amount of case law has multiplied and so has its complexity. As early as 1975 the first president of the EAT, Mr Justice Phillips, was moved to remark: 'The expression unfair dismissal is in no sense a common sense expression capable of being understood by the man in the street' (*Devis* v. *Atkins* [1976] IRLR 16).

The industrial tribunals and the procedure under which they operate were designed to provide a speedy, cheap and informal mechanism for the resolution of disputes over dismissal but the law they have to apply is often of great complexity. It is therefore not surprising that just over one-third of applicants and more than half of respondent employers are legally represented at tribunal hearings.[7] The obvious imbalance in representation between employers and employees which these statistics show underlines the urgent need for the state Legal Aid system to be extended to cover legal representation for workers at such hearings.

This tendency towards excessive legalism has been recognised by the Court of Appeal and it has attempted to reduce the number of cases coming through on appeal from industrial tribunals to the Employment Appeal Tribunal. First, it has ruled that many issues in employment law are ultimately questions of fact and not questions of law. Given that appeal to the Employment Appeal Tribunal (EAT) is generally restricted to claims that the tribunal has got the law wrong, this is clearly an attempt to return decision-making to the tribunals.[8]

Second, the Court of Appeal has rejected the EAT's practice of laying down guidelines for tribunals to follow when confronted with major problem areas of unfair dismissal law; for example, redundancy procedure, suspected dishonesty, long-term sickness absence. The court felt that too many cases were being appealed on the basis that the tribunal had not followed this guidance and the EAT was being asked to intervene and overturn a tribunal's conclusions on the facts of the case.[9]

There is no doubt that the law of unfair dismissal has become excessively technical, but it may be that the result of the Court of Appeal's attacks on legalism and the proliferation of appeals may be uncertainty and inconsistency. In the absence of established guidelines and precedent, it becomes extremely difficult for lawyers or trade union officials to offer advice to workers on the likely outcome of any particular case and there is every prospect that industrial tribunals in different parts of the country can come to diametrically opposed conclusions in cases involving identical facts and with little of no prospect of the EAT resolving the matter on appeal.

Where to Find the Law relating to Unfair Dismissal

Over the last 18 years or so, the legislation governing unfair dismissal has remained largely unaltered – the major amendments being concerned with dismissal for non-union membership. The other significant change concerned the qualification period necessary to claim, which was raised from 26 weeks in 1979 to the current level of two years in 1985.

In 1978 an attempt was made to consolidate the legislation in the Employment Protection (Consolidation) Act and ss. 54–80 still contain the relevant provisions. Since 1978, however, a number of amendments have been made via a succession of Employment Acts, the Sex Discrimination Act 1986, the Trade Union Reform and Employment Act 1993 and a number of pieces of subordinate legislation.

We can analyse the law of unfair dismissal in four stages (see figure 14.1):

- Stage one: has a dismissal taken place?
- Stage two: is the applicant qualified to make a claim?
- Stage three: is the dismissal fair or unfair?
- Stage four: what remedies are available?

Stage One: Has a Dismissal Taken Place?

This is discussed in the previous chapter.

Stage Two: Is the Applicant Qualified to Make a Claim?

The applicant must satisfy the industrial tribunal on the following three broad issues:

(1) That the applicant is an 'employee' (the vagaries surrounding the definition of employment status were discussed in Chapter 2 above).
(2) That applicant's employment does not fall within an excluded category and has the requisite continuity of service (see p. 191 and chapter 2).
(3) That the applicant has presented the claim in time.

Figure 14.1: Workers Who are Entitled to Bring a Claim for Unfair Dismissal and/or Redundancy Payments

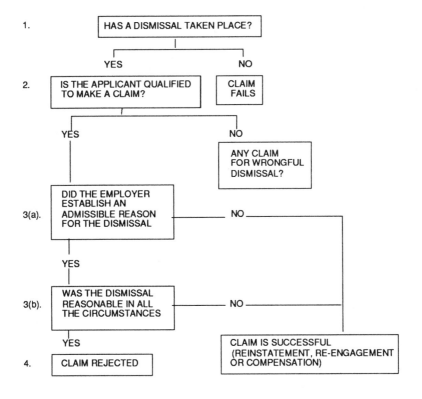

Figure 14.2: Excluded Employees

Workers who fail to satisfy the status of 'employee' (see ch. 2)

Employees who do not work 16 hours a week for a continuous period of two years – unless the dismissal was on grounds of trade union, sex or racial discrimination where no length of service is required (EPCA s. 64 [1] [a])

Employees who have worked for 8 hours or more per week for at least 5 years [unless alleging trade union, sex or racial discrimination]

Those who ordinarily work outside Great Britain (EPCA s. 141). The answer to this question depends on whether the worker's 'base' is outside the UK (see *Wilson* v. *Maynard Shipbuilding Consultants AB* [1977] IRLR 491 CA; *Janata Bank Ltd* v. *Ahmed* [1981] IRLR 457 CA

Share fishermen (EPCA s. 144 [2])

The police and prison officers (EPCA s. 146 [2]); *Home Office* v. *Robinson* [1982] ICR 31)

Members of the armed forces (EPCA s. 138 [3])

Crown employees where the relevant minister has issued an excepting certificate on grounds of national security (see EPCA s. 138 [4]); *Council of Civil Service Unions* v. *Minister for the Civil Service* [1985] ICR 14)

Workers on fixed-term contracts who have waived in writing their right to claim if the contract is not renewed (EPCA s. 142 [1])

Employees reaching retirement age: to claim employees must not have passed the "normal retiring age" for employees in that position; or, where there is no normal retirement age, must not have passed their 65th birthday (EPCA s. 64 [1] [b]). It has been held that where a contract specifies a retirement age then it can be presumed to be the " normal retiring age" (see *Nothman* v. *Barnet London Borough Council* [1979] IRLR 35 HL). But this presumption can be rebutted by evidence that the contractural age has been abandoned in practice. The test of whether this has happened is to ascertain what would be the reasonable expectation or understanding of employees holding that position at the relevant time (*Waite* v. *Government Communications Headquarters* [1983] ICR 653 HL). *Hughes* v. *Department of Health & Social Security* [1985] AC 776, concerned the question whether employers can effectively alter a normal retirement age established by practice by a simple announcement to that effect. The House of Lords held that this was possible, since an announcement would vary the expectations of the employees affected. (See also *Brooks* v. *British Telecommunications plc* [1992] IRLR 66 CA.)

Workers, who at the time of their dismissal, are taking industrial action or are locked out and there has been no selective dismissal or re-engagement of those taking the action. Unofficial strikers may be selectively dismissed or re-engaged (TULR[C] Act 1992, ss. 237, 238)

Those employees covered by a disciplinary procedure, voluntarily agreed between employers and independent trade union, where the Secretary of State has designated it to apply instead of the statutory scheme. The designation will be granted only if the voluntary scheme is at least as beneficial to employees as statutory protection. Only one such scheme – between the Electrical Contractors Association and the EETPU – is in operation (EPCA s. 65)

Illegal contracts: a contract of employment to do an act which is unlawful is unenforceable. The position is different, however, if the contract is capable of being performed lawfully, and was initially intended to be so performed, but which has in fact been performed by unlawful means. In this situation, the contract will be unenforceable only if the employee was a knowing and willing party to the illegality and stood to benefit – see *Hewcastle Catering Ltd* v. *Ahmed and Elkamah* [1991] IRLR 473 CA.

Where a settlement of the claim has been agreed with the involvement of an ACAS Conciliation Officer and the employee has agreed to withdraw his/her complaint (EPCA s. 140 [2] [d] [e])

Claim in Time

In common with the enforcement of other employment protection rights, an applicant must present a claim (using an IT1 form) to the Regional office of Industrial Tribunals within three months of the effective date of termination (see chapter 22 below). This time limit is fairly rigorously applied, although tribunals have the discretion to allow a claim to be presented within a reasonable time outside the three-month period where it considers that it was not reasonably practicable for the complaint to be presented in time. The leading cases in this area establish the following:

- The test to be applied in determining whether a late claim should be considered is not confined to whether the applicant knew of the right to claim but extends to a consideration as to whether s/he should have known.[10] In other words, ignorance of rights is not an excuse, unless it appears that the applicant could not reasonably be expected to be aware of them.
- A late claim will not be accepted even though the worker's failure to claim in time was due to a mistake of a 'skilled adviser' such as a lawyer, trade union official or CAB worker.[11]
- It will probably *not* be regarded as reasonable for the applicant to delay making a claim until the outcome of an internal appeal is known. The balance of authority would now suggest that this would not be a reason for admitting a late claim.[12]

So what excuses are the tribunals to accept as valid reasons for delay? The case law suggests the following list:

- physical incapacity
- absence abroad
- a postal strike
- a worker's failure to discover a fundamental fact until more than three months after the date of dismissal. For example, in *Churchill* v. *Yeates & Son Ltd* [1983] IRLR 187 the applicant, who did not discover evidence that his dismissal purportedly for redundancy may have been a sham until after the three-month deadline, had his claim admitted.[13]

The Effective Date of Termination (EDT)

At various stages in this chapter, this phrase has been referred to. The identity of the date of termination will determine whether a claim is made in time, whether the applicant possessed the requisite continuity of employment at the date of dismissal, whether the retirement age exclusion is to operate in any particular case and, if the claim is successful, from when to calculate compensation.

EPCA provides a definition of the date of termination for both unfair dismissal and redundancy payment claims and, although for unfair dismissal purposes it is called the 'effective date of termination' and for redundancy payments 'the relevant date', the definition is largely the same in both cases.[14]

(a) Where the contract of employment is terminated by notice, whether by employer or employee, the date of termination is the date on which the notice expires. Where notice is given orally on a day when work is carried out, the notice period does not begin to run until the following day (*West v. Kneels Ltd* [1986] IRLR 430). If an employee is dismissed *with notice* but is given a payment in lieu of working out that notice, the EDT is the date when the notice expires (*Adams v. GKN Sankey* [1980] IRLR 416). As will be seen below, a fine distinction is drawn between the latter situation and one where the employee is dismissed *with no notice* with the payment being made in lieu of notice.

(b) Where the contract of employment is terminated without notice, the date of termination is the date on which the termination takes effect. Two useful cases in this area are *Robert Cort & Sons* v. *Charman* [1981] IRLR 437 and *Stapp* v. *The Shaftesbury Society* [1982] IRLR 326, which both uphold the view that the effective date of termination is the actual date of termination regardless of whether the employment was lawfully or unlawfully terminated. So where, as in Cort's case, an employee is immediately dismissed with wages in lieu of notice, the effective date of termination is the actual date on which the employee is told of dismissal and not the date on which notice would expire.[15]

The only exception to this rule is provided by s. 55 (5), which artificially extends the EDT, either where summary dismissal has occurred despite a period of statutory minimum notice being due under s. 49, or where the statutory notice required to be given is longer than the actual notice given. In either case the date of the ending of the s. 49 notice period is treated as the EDT.

(c) Where the employee is employed under a contract for a fixed term, the date of termination is the date on which the term expires.

Internal Appeals and the Effective Date of Termination

Where the dismissed employee exercises a right of appeal, the question may arise as to the EDT. Does the EDT become the date of the determination of the appeal, or does the original date of dismissal still stand as the EDT?

The leading case on this question is the Court of Appeal's decision in *J. Sainsbury Ltd* v. *Savage* [1981] ICR 1, where it was held that if the dismissed employee invokes an internal appeal which is subsequently rejected, the EDT is the date of the original dismissal, unless the contract provides to the contrary. This approach was expressly approved by the House of Lords in the important case of *West Midlands Co-operative Society* v. *Tipton* [1986] IRLR 112, which is discussed in more detail later in this chapter.

Stage Three: Is the Dismissal Fair or Unfair?

This involves the resolution of two issues:

(i) has a potentially fair reason for the dismissal been established; *and*
(ii) whether, in the circumstances, the employer acted reasonably in treating that reason as a sufficient reason for dismissing the employee.

Potentially Fair Dismissals

It is for the employer to establish that there was a potentially facie reason for dismissal. These are as follows:

* capability or qualifications;
* conduct;
* redundancy;
* that the employee could not continue to work without contravention of a statute;
* some other substantial reason.

This stage in the process of justifying the dismissal will generally not be difficult for the employer to satisfy, since it does not involve any consideration of fairness and all that must be proved is the employer's subjective motivation for dismissal.

An employer will only be allowed to rely upon facts known at the time of dismissal to establish what was the reason for the dismissal. Facts which come to light after the dismissal cannot be relied on to justify the dismissal – though they may persuade a tribunal to reduce your compensation. This was the conclusion of the House of Lords in the important case of *W. Devis & Sons Ltd v. Atkins* [1977] AC 931.

The Right to Receive Written Reasons for the Dismissal
EPCA s. 53 provides that an employee who is under notice or who been dismissed has the right, on request to the employer, to be provided within 14 days with a written statement of reasons for the dismissal. The Employment Act 1989 s. 15 increased the period of continuous employment necessary for ex-employees to exercise this right from six months to two years. The significance of s. 53 is that a written statement provided under the section is expressly made admissible in subsequent proceedings. Any basic inconsistency between the contents of the statement and the reason actually put forward before the tribunal could seriously undermine the employer's case.

If an employer unreasonably refuses to comply with the request or provides particulars which are 'inadequate or untrue', the employee may present a complaint to an IT, which may declare what it finds the reasons for dismissal are and also make an award of two weeks' wages to the employee.

The statement provided by the employer must at least contain a simple statement of the essential reasons for the dismissal, but no particular form is required. Indeed, it has been held that it is acceptable for a written statement to refer the employee to earlier correspondence which contain the reasons for dismissal: attaching a copy of that correspondence (*Kent County Council* v. *Gilham and Others* [1985] IRLR 16).

It does not matter whether the reason put forward by the employer is 'intrinsically a good, bad or indifferent one'; at this stage the IT is only concerned about identifying the genuine reason for the dismissal. So, in *Harvard Securities plc* v. *Younghusband* [1990] IRLR 17, where the employers stated that they had dismissed the employee for divulging confidential information to a third party, whether the employers were correct in describing that information as 'confidential' was irrelevant to the identification of their reason for dismissal.

Pressure on an Employer to Dismiss

EPCA s. 63 states that, in determining the reason for the dismissal and its fairness, no account shall be taken of any industrial pressure (official or unofficial) exerted on the employer to dismiss the employee. It follows that if an employer cannot advance any reason other than the industrial pressure the dismissal will be held to be unfair.

Nevertheless, a trade union or union official who has exerted pressure to force the employer to dismiss a non-union member may be joined in subsequent unfair dismissal proceedings and be ordered to pay all or part of any compensation awarded (EPCA s. 76[a]).

Dismissals which are Deemed to be Unfair

Certain reasons for dismissal are regarded as automatically unfair. These are as follows:

- Dismissal for trade union membership and activity, or because of refusal to join a trade union or particular trade union (TULR[C]A, 1992, s. 152).
- Dismissal of a woman because she is pregnant or for a reason connected with her pregnancy (s. 60 EPCA). At present the law provides that it is automatically unfair to dismiss an employee if the reason for her dismissal is pregnancy or any other reason connected with her pregnancy. There are two exceptions to this general rule: where the employee is incapable of performing her job because of her pregnancy; or where her continuing work would contravene some statutory restriction. However, if the employers are to be able to rely on one or other of these exceptions, they must show that they offered a pregnant employee suitable alternative employment or that no suitable alternative employment was available.

In *Brown* v. *Stockton-on-Tees Borough Council* [1988] IRLR 263, the House of Lords decided that selection for redundancy on grounds of pregnancy is dismissal for a 'reason connected with her pregnancy' within the meaning of s. 60 of EPCA.

Currently protection under EPCA s. 60 is only available to women with two years' continuous service. If a woman does not have the necessary qualifying service, however, she can still challenge a pregnancy dismissal by way of the sex discrimination legislation (see our discussion of these issues in chapter 11).

In line with the recently adopted EC Directive (92/85) on pregnant workers, TURERA completely redrafts the existing provisions relating to the right of maternity leave and protection against pregnancy-related dismissals. The Act provides for all employees, irrespective of their length of service, a right not to be dismissed on grounds of pregnancy or childbirth. (For a discussion of these and other changes see chapter 8 above.)

- Dismissal because of a conviction which is 'spent' under the terms of the Rehabilitation of Offenders Act, 1974 (see s. 4[3][b] and p. 33 above).
- Dismissal connected with the transfer of an undertaking, unless there are economic, technical or organisational reasons entailing changes in the workforce (see the Transfer of Undertakings Regulations 1981, reg. 8).
- Unfair redundancy selection. The dismissal of an employee on the ground of redundancy will be unfair if the circumstances constituting the redundancy applied equally to one or more employees in the same undertaking who held posts similar to that held by the dismissed employee and who have not been dismissed by the employer, and either:

  (i) the reason (or, if more than one, the principal reason) for which s/he was selected was union-related (TULR(C)A s. 153); or

  (ii) the employee was selected for dismissal in contravention of a customary arrangement or agreed procedure relating to redundancy and there were no special reasons justifying a departure from that arrangement or procedure in the circumstances of the case (EPCA s. 59).

- Dismissal on grounds of assertion of a statutory right. Under TURERA, it is now automatically unfair to dismiss an employee, regardless of his/her length of service or hours of work, if the reason or principal reason for the dismissal was that the employee brought proceedings to enforce certain statutory rights, or alleged in good faith that his/her employer had infringed one of those rights. The relevant statutory rights are: any right under EPCA, or the Wages Act where the remedy is a complaint to an IT; minimum notice rights under EPCA; right to require an employer to stop deducting union subscriptions, contributions to a union's political fund; the right to complain of action short of dismissal on grounds related to union membership activities; and the right to time off for trade union duties and activities.

No Right to Claim for Those Taking Industrial Action

An important exclusion concerns dismissal for taking part in a strike or other industrial action where all strikers have been dismissed and there has been no selective re-engagement of those dismissed within a three-month period. In this situation statute prevents an industrial tribunal from hearing an unfair dismissal claim (TULR(C)A s. 238).

Unofficial strikers lose all unfair dismissal protections *whether or not* there are selective dismissals or selective re-engagements (TULR(C)A s. 237).

More about these pernicious provisions in chapter 20 below.

Did the Employer Act Reasonably?

Prior to 1980, the burden of proof in unfair dismissal claims at this stage was on the employer. The Employment Act 1980 amended s. 57 (3) of EPCA primarily by removing the requirement that employers *shall* satisfy the industrial tribunal as to the reasonableness of their actions and so rendered the burden of proof 'neutral'. A further amendment required tribunals to have regard to the size and administrative resources of an employer's undertaking in assessing the reasonableness of the dismissal. The specific reference to size and administrative resources is an encouragement to tribunals to be less exacting in their examination of the disciplinary standards and procedures of small employers.

In assessing the test of reasonableness, the question is what a reasonable employer would have done in the circumstances and not what a particular tribunal would have thought right. As such, the reasonableness test is viewed by a number of commentators as not unduly challenging managerial prerogatives in the matter of discipline and as a factor contributing to the low success rate of unfair dismissal applications. In its current formulation, the test is whether the dismissal fell within 'the band of reasonable responses to the employee's conduct within which one employer might take one view, another quite reasonably another' (*Iceland Frozen Foods* v. *Jones* [1982] IRLR 439 at 432).

Provided the industrial tribunal follows the 'band of reasonable responses' test and does not substitute its own view, it will have considerable discretion in reaching its decision and it will only be in rare cases that its decision will be overturned on appeal. This is because the fairness of the dismissal is essentially a question of fact, and so long as the industrial tribunal has properly directed itself as to the law then its decision will only be overturned if it was perverse – that is, if no reasonable tribunal could possibly have come to that decision on the particular facts.

In reaching a conclusion on the reasonableness of the dismissal, the tribunal may have regard to two broad questions: the substantive merits and procedural fairness.

Substantive Merits

The substantive merits may involve the tribunal taking into account mitigating factors such as the employee's length of service, previous disciplinary record and any explanation or excuse. It is also important to maintain consistency in the application of disciplinary rules so that employees who behave in much the same way should have meted out to them much the same punishment. In *The Post Office* v. *Fennell* [1981] IRLR 221, the employee was instantly dismissed following an assault on a fellow worker in the works canteen. The Court of Appeal upheld a finding of unfair dismissal on the grounds that there was evidence that other workers had been guilty of similar offences but these had not been met by dismissal.

The principle of consistency, however, should not be interpreted so as to force the employer merely to adopt a 'tariff' approach to misconduct and apply rules in an inflexible manner: the mitigating factors in each individual case should be fully considered before deciding whether the circumstances are truly parallel (*Hadjioannou* v. *Coral Casinos Ltd* [1981] IRLR 352 EAT).

Inconsistency of treatment in relation to those fighting at work was again in issue in *Cain* v. *Leeds Western Health Authority* [1990] IRLR 168. The applicant, a hospital laundry worker, was dismissed on the grounds of misconduct for fighting with another employee while on duty. Mr Cain claimed that his dismissal was unfair because in the past other employees guilty of acts of gross misconduct, including fighting, had not been dismissed. The IT, in dismissing his complaint, disregarded the inconsistencies in treatment on the grounds that the relevant decision in the various cases were taken by different members of management. This view was overturned by the EAT who held that it is inconsistency of treatment by the *employer* rather than by individual line managers that is the crucial question:

> Because an employer is acting in one case through his servants A and B, and the other case through his servant C and D, it is no answer to a complaint of unfair dismissal to say that there were different employees considering the seriousness of the two alleged cases of misconduct. The consistency must be consistency as between all the employees of the employer.

Procedural Fairness

The second element of the test of fairness relates to the question of the fairness of the procedures adopted by the employer in the events leading up to the dismissal. The concept of procedural fairness is not expressly articulated in the legislation but its development was influenced by the codes of practice which were introduced to accompany the legislation. The provisions relevant to discipline and dismissal are presently contained in the ACAS Code of Practice no.1, 'Disciplinary Practices & Procedures in Employment'. The Code's guidelines do not carry the force of law, but any of its provisions which appear to a court or tribunal to be relevant to a question arising in the proceedings must be taken into account in reaching a decision (see s. 6[11] EPA 1975).

In 1987 ACAS produced an updated and enlarged draft code of practice for the consideration of Lord Young, the then secretary of state for employment. The draft code offered advice on the handling of dismissals in general, together with more detailed consideration of common types of disciplinary problems such as absenteeism, sub-standard work and dishonesty. This guidance was based on the principles which had emerged from 15 years of unfair dismissal case law. Unfortunately, the draft code was rejected by Lord Young because he thought it over-lengthy and too detailed, 'aimed primarily at lawyers and personnel managers in larger firms', and incapable of application by a small employer. Following rejection of the draft code, ACAS published much of the material it contained in the form of an advisory handbook entitled *Discipline at Work*. Though the handbook has no statutory force, given that it concisely summarises the views of the leading cases on what constitutes good disciplinary practice it is well worthy of careful study and may well be influential in industrial tribunal adjudications.

Essential Features of Disciplinary Procedures – the ACAS Code

First, the ACAS Code emphasises that disciplinary procedures should not be viewed primarily as a means of imposing sanctions; they should also be designed to emphasise and encourage improvements in individual conduct.

Paragraph 10 of the Code recommends that the procedure should:

(a) Be in writing.
(b) Specify to whom it applies.
(c) Provide for matters to be dealt with quickly.
(d) Indicate the disciplinary actions which may be taken.
(e) Specify the levels of management which have the authority to take the various forms of disciplinary action, ensuring that immediate superiors do not normally have the power to dismiss without reference to senior management.
(f) Provide for individuals to be informed of the complaints against them and to be given an opportunity to state their case before decisions are reached.
(g) Give individuals the right to be accompanied by a trade union representative or by a fellow employee of their choice.
(h) Ensure that except for gross misconduct, no employees are dismissed for a first breach of discipline.
(i) Ensure that disciplinary action is not taken until the case has been carefully investigated.
(j) Ensure that individuals are given an explanation for any penalty imposed.
(k) Provide a right of appeal and specify the procedure to be followed.

Second, on warnings, the Code recommends that in the case of minor offences there should be a formal oral warning (stage 1), followed by a written warning (stage 2), and then a final written warning (stage 3) which should make it clear that any recurrence will result in dismissal. However, as the ACAS advisory handbook makes clear, this does not mean that three warnings must always be given before dismissal action is taken. On occasion, the seriousness of the offence may make it appropriate to enter the procedure at stage 2 or stage 3. As we shall see below, there are also occasions when dismissal without notice is applicable.

Paragraph 18 places emphasis on writing and retaining detailed personnel records by the employer who must be able if necessary to provide documentary proof of previous warnings. As a result a number of employers now adopt the practice of even giving written confirmation of an 'oral warning' and of requiring the employee's signature to acknowledge receipt.

The employer's system should include some time limit on warnings, so that after a set period they lapse; for example, warnings for minor offences may be valid for up to six months, while final warnings may remain active for 12 months or more. The life of a warning may also depend on the employee's previous disciplinary record. In rare cases, where there is serious misconduct, the employer may be held to be justified in refusing to set a time limit on the warning. Where this occurs, it should be made very clear to the employee that the final written warning can never be removed and that any recurrence will lead to dismissal.

A warning should be reasonably specific, identifying the precise ground of complaint by the employer. Commentators have suggested that one consequence of this is that a warning on ground A (such as bad language) should not be used as a step in the procedure to dismiss on ground B (such as bad timekeeping). This may mean that one employee may be subject to more than one series of warnings at the same time. Of course, there may come a point when the cumulative effect of a number of warnings on different matters provides reasonable grounds to dismiss on the grounds of generally unacceptable behaviour.

In *Auguste Noel Ltd* v. *Curtis* [1990] IRLR 326, however, we see the EAT taking a different approach in relation to previous warnings concerned with unrelated misconduct. Mr Curtis, a 'multi-drop' driver, was dismissed on 18 March 1988 for an act of misconduct involving mishandling company property. In deciding to dismiss him for that offence, the employer took into account two previous written warnings, one dated 16 October 1987 concerning his relationship with other employees and the other, dated 25 February 1988, referring to unsatisfactory documentation and absenteeism.

The EAT held that the IT had been wrong to find that the dismissal for mishandling company property was unfair because, in deciding to dismiss for that reason, the employers had taken into account two final written warnings for different offences.

Mr Justice Wood stated:

it can very rarely be said, if ever, that warnings are irrelevant to the consideration of an employer who is considering dismissal. The mere fact that the conduct was of a different kind on those occasions when warnings were given does not seem to us to render them irrelevant. It is essentially a matter of balance, of doing what is fair and reasonable in the circumstances and the employer is entitled to consider the existence of warnings. He is entitled to look at the substance of the complaint on each of those occasions, how many warnings there have been, the dates and the periods of time between those warnings and indeed all the circumstances of the case.

A third essential feature of disciplinary procedures concerns cases of gross misconduct. The ACAS Code of Practice advises that dismissal for a first breach of discipline should be restricted to cases of 'gross misconduct'. This phrase has no statutory definition, nor is it defined by the Code of Practice itself, but it is generally regarded as misconduct serious enough to destroy the relationship of trust and confidence between the employer and the employee. This would include:

- theft
- dishonesty
- violence at work
- serious incapability through drink or drugs
- deliberate damage to the employer's property
- serious acts of disobedience to lawful and reasonable orders
- gross negligence causing (or creating the risk of) significant economic loss, damage to property or personal injury

In other cases, what constitutes gross misconduct may depend on the circumstances and the employer's own disciplinary rules. Employers may codify the orders and requirements for their employees in a series of disciplinary rules. Indeed, EPCA s. 1(4) requires that the written statement of terms of employment must include 'any disciplinary rules applicable to the employee'. However, the Employment Act 1989 s. 13 removes the statutory requirement to provide a note of disciplinary rules and appeals procedure where the number of employees of the employer and any associated employer is less than 20. This amendment is yet a further example of the government's policy of deregulation in the name of encouraging the growth of small businesses. However, given that a factor which will be influential in many dismissal cases is whether the employer adequately brought the existence of a particular disciplinary rule to the attention of an employee, small employers might be well advised not to take advantage of this exemption.

Disciplinary rules may be regarded as preliminary warnings to employees that the employer regards certain types of offence with particular gravity and that these will be likely to result in instant dismissal. However, while it is important that employees should be given a clear indication of the likely sanction consequent upon certain types of misconduct, imposition of that sanction should not be seen as following inexorably once the offence is committed. In other words, there is no such thing as an 'automatic' dismissal rule and employers must be prepared to exercise a discretion, having allowed the employee to state his or her case and having considered such matters as the seriousness of the infringement of the rule, the employee's length of service and previous disciplinary record.

An illustration is provided by *Ladbroke Racing* v. *Arnott* [1983] IRLR 154. The applicants were employed in a betting shop. The employer's disciplinary rules specifically provided that employees were not permitted to place bets or to allow other staff to do so. Two of the applicants had placed such bets, one for her brother on one occasion and the other occasionally for old-age pensioners; the third, the office manager, had condoned these actions. All three employees were dismissed and an IT found the dismissals to be unfair. This decision was upheld by the EAT and the Court of Session on the basis that rules framed in mandatory terms did not leave the employer free from the obligation to act reasonably and to take into account the relatively minor nature of the offences in this particular case.

A final question concerns the situation where an employer summarily dismisses an employee for an offence which is not expressly set out in the disciplinary rules. The answer to this depends on fact and degree: the more serious the misconduct, the more likely the tribunal will find it reasonable for the employee to have anticipated the employer's reaction.

In *CA Parsons Ltd* v. *McLoughlin* [1978] IRLR 65, the dismissal of a shop steward for fighting was upheld although it was not included in the company's disciplinary rules as gross misconduct. Mr Justice Kilner Brown expressed the view that 'it ought not to be necessary for anybody, let alone a shop steward, to have in black and white in the form of a rule that a fight is going to be something that is to be regarded very gravely by management'.

Similarly, in *Ulsterbus* v. *Henderson* [1989] IRLR 253, the Northern Ireland Court of Appeal rejected a tribunal finding that it was unreasonable to dismiss a bus conductor for failure to give tickets in return for payment in circumstances where it was not made clear in the disciplinary procedure that offences of this nature would merit the ultimate sanction of dismissal. The court was of the view that it would be obvious to any employee that failure to give tickets in return for payment was a most serious offence which was likely to lead to dismissal.

Conversely, for offences whose gravity is not so immediately obvious there will be a requirement for the offence and likely sanction to be clearly expressed in the disciplinary rules - for example, consuming alcohol during working hours (*Dairy Produce Packers Ltd* v. *Beverstock* [1981] IRLR 265), or overstaying leave (*Hoover* v. *Forde* [1980] ICR 239).

While it is clear that the employer does not need to list every offence which could lead to dismissal, the offences which *are* listed will be taken as an indication of the character and class of offence which the employer views as gross misconduct. Therefore a dismissal for an offence of a less serious class or entirely different character than those set out in the disciplinary rules is likely to be regarded as unfair (see *Dietman* v. *London Borough of Brent* [1987] IRLR 299).

Hearings constitute a fourth key element of procedural fairness. Paragraph 11 of the ACAS Code states:

> Before a decision is made or a penalty imposed the individual should be interviewed and given the opportunity to state his or her case and should be advised of any rights under the procedure including the right to be represented.

Employees have the right to expect the following procedural guarantees when subject to disciplinary action:

(a) that they be informed of the nature of the allegations made against them;
(b) that they should be allowed to state their case;
(c) that those conducting the hearing should be free from bias.

However, the courts and tribunals have held that it is not necessary for the conduct of a fair hearing for the employee to be given the opportunity to cross-examine witnesses (*Ulsterbus* v. *Henderson* [1989] IRLR 251).

It is a general principle that a person who holds an inquiry must be seen to be impartial, that justice must not only be done but be seen to be done, and that if a reasonable observer with full knowledge of the facts would conclude that the hearing might not be impartial that is enough.

An illustration of an application of these principles is to be found in the decision of the EAT in *Moyes* v. *Hylton Castle Working Men's Social Club and Institute* [1986] IRLR 483, where two witnesses to an alleged act of sexual harassment by a club steward towards a barmaid were also members of the committee which dismissed the steward. The EAT held the dismissal to be unfair on the ground that it was a breach of natural justice for an apparently biased committee to decide the disciplinary matter. While the general rule is that if a person has been a witness s/he should not conduct the inquiry, the EAT did identify certain exceptions – for example, a firm which is owned and run by one person.

As for appeals, both the Code of Practice and advisory handbook lay great emphasis on the availability of an appeal against an initial decision to dismiss and tribunals have held dismissals to be unfair if such a procedure does not exist.

The handbook advises that an appeals procedure should:

- Specify any time limit within which the appeal should be lodged.
- Provide for appeals to be dealt with speedily, particularly those involving suspension without pay or dismissal.
- Wherever possible, provide for the appeal to be heard by an authority higher than that taking the disciplinary action.
- Spell out the action which may be taken by those hearing the appeal.
- Provide that the employee, or a representative if the employee so wishes, has an opportunity to comment on any new evidence arising during the appeal before any decision is taken.

The handbook recognises that in small organisations there may be no authority higher than the individual who took the original disciplinary action and that it is inevitable that they will hear the appeal. In such circumstances the handbook's advice is that the appeal hearing 'should be seen as an opportunity to review the original decision in an objective manner and at a quieter time. This can more readily be achieved if some time is allowed to lapse before the appeal hearing' (p. 33).

The importance of according the employee a right of appeal was underlined by the House of Lords in *W Midlands Cooperative Society* v. *Tipton* [1986] IRLR 112, where it was held that a dismissal will be unfair if:

(1) the employer unreasonably treated his or her real reason as a sufficient reason to dismiss the employee – either at the time the original decision to dismiss was made or at the conclusion of an internal appeal;

(2) the employer refused to entertain an appeal to which the employee was contractually entitled and thereby denied him or her the opportunity to show that, in all the circumstances, the real reason for dismissal could not reasonably be treated as sufficient.

Renewed Emphasis on Procedural Rectitude

In the early 1970s, the courts and tribunals laid much emphasis on the importance of employers adhering strictly to the basic procedural requirements of fairness, taking the Code as their guide. In one of the earliest cases, Sir John Donaldson thought that the only exception to the need for the employee to be allowed to state his or her case was 'where there can be no explanation which could cause the employer to refrain from dismissing the employee'(see *Earl* v. *Slater Wheeler (Airlyne) Ltd* [1972] IRLR 115). So it had to be almost inconceivable that the hearing could have made any difference. This test was, however, replaced by more lenient standards.

While the earlier approach could result in a dismissal being found to be unfair on procedural failings alone, the contemporary position is to view procedural matters as just one of a number of factors to be taken into account (see *Bailey* v. *BP Oil (Kent Refinery) Ltd*, cited above).

The high point of this dilution of procedural requirements is to be found in the test laid down by the Employment Appeal Tribunal in *British Labour Pump Co Ltd* v. *Byrne* [1979] IRLR. This test allowed the employer to argue that an element of procedural unfairness (such as a failure to give a proper hearing) may be 'forgiven' if the employer can show that, on the balance of probabilities, even if a proper procedure had been complied with the employee would still have been dismissed and the dismissal would then have been fair.

This decision received considerable academic and judicial criticism but was specifically approved of by the Court of Appeal in *Wass* v. *Binns* [1982] ICR 347. The major criticism of the *Labour Pump* principle was that it was irreconcilable with the ruling of the House of Lords in *W. Devis & Sons Ltd* v. *Atkin* [1977] AC 931, which held that the employer was not entitled to rely on evidence acquired after dismissal and that fairness must be judged in the light of facts known to the employer at the time of the dismissal.

This forceful criticism of the logic of *Labour Pump* was accepted by the House of Lords in *Polkey* v. *AE Dayton Services* (1987) IRLR 503 and the principle was overruled. This decision is perhaps the most important unfair dismissal decision of the last decade and in the judgements we find a re-emphasis on the importance of following a fair procedure. In the view of Lord Bridge:

> an employer having prima facie grounds to dismiss ... will in the great majority of cases not act reasonably in treating the reason as a sufficient reason for the dismissal unless he has taken steps, conveniently classified in most authorities as 'procedural', which are necessary in the circumstances of the case to justify that course of action.

Lord Mackay was of the view that what must be considered is what a reasonable employer would have had in mind at the time he decided to dismiss:

> If the employer could reasonably have concluded in the light of circumstances known to him at the time of dismissal that consultation or warning would be utterly useless he might well act reasonably even if he did not observe the provisions of the Code.

It has been argued that there is a significant practical difference between asking whether at the time of the dismissal the employer had reasonable grounds for believing that a fair procedure would have been 'utterly useless' (the new test) and asking whether, in retrospect, it would have made any difference to the outcome (the old test). As a result it is likely that failure to follow a fair procedure may well lead to a finding of unfair dismissal in a much increased proportion of cases.[16]

For those who recognise the value of natural justice in discipline the decision will be welcomed along with an earlier ruling of the House of Lords in *W Midlands Cooperative Society* v. *Tipton* [1986] IRLR 112, discussed earlier.

Representation

The ACAS Code recommends that employees should have the right to be accompanied by a trade union representative or fellow employee of their choice. Employees should be informed of this right on being invited to attend the disciplinary interview, and a refusal to allow representation may well result in a finding of unfair dismissal (*Rank Xerox (UK) Ltd* v. *Goodchild* [1976] IRLR 185).

The case law would tend to suggest that there is no *general* right to legal representation at internal disciplinary hearings (*Sharma* v. *British Gas Corporation* 27.7.83 EAT 495/82). However, there may be situations which require that a solicitor be present; for instance, where criminal proceedings are pending.

Given the potential damage to industrial relations where management propose to discipline a trade union official, the Code recommends that no action beyond an oral warning should be taken until the case has been discussed with a senior trade union representative or full-time official.

Some Common Disciplinary Issues

In this section, we discuss the scope of the five categories of potentially fair reasons for dismissal: capability/qualifications; conduct; redundancy; continued employment involving breach of the law; and some other substantial reason. In the course of this discussion we shall focus on the approaches adopted by the courts and tribunals in relation to a number of frequently recurring dismissal issues. These are as follows: sub-standard performance; absence (long-term illness, persistent absenteeism); dishonesty; and business reorganisation dismissals.

Capability/Qualifications

Under this head the employer has to show that the reason (or, if there was more than one, the principal reason) for the dismissal 'related to the capability or qualifications of the employee for performing work of the kind which he was employed to do' (EPCA s. 57 [2][a]). 'Capability' is defined in s. 57 (4) as 'capability assessed by reference to skill, aptitude, health or any other physical or mental quality' and 'qualifications' as 'any degree, diploma or other academic, technical or professional qualification relevant to the position which the employee held.' 'Qualifications' has to be construed in the light of the particular position which the employee held. Therefore, in certain circumstances, failure to pass a required aptitude test can be a reason for dismissal relating to qualification to do the job (*Blackman* v. *The Post Office* [1974] IRLR 46 NIRC). However, a mere licence, permit or authorisation is not a qualification unless it is substantially concerned with the employee's aptitude or ability to do the job (*Blue Star Ship Management Ltd* v. *Williams* [1979] IRLR 16 EAT).

Sub-Standard Work

Sub-standard work may occur for a variety of reasons. It has been suggested that it is only when the employee is inherently incapable of reasonable standards of work that the dismissal is related to 'capability' within EPCA s. 57 (2) (a). Where the employee has the capacity to do the job but produces poor performance because of carelessness or lack of motivation, then the matter is probably better dealt with as misconduct (*Sutton and Gates (Luton) Ltd* v. *Bloxall* [1978] IRLR 486).

Evidence of Incompetence

> Wherever a man is dismissed for incapacity or incompetence it is sufficient that the employer honestly believes on reasonable grounds that the man is incapable or incompetent. It is not necessary for the employer to prove that he is in fact incapable or incompetent.
>
> (Lord Denning in *Alidair Ltd* v. *Taylor* [1978] IRLR 82)

Therefore, the test is not purely subjective and the requirement of reasonable grounds dictates that the employer should have carried out a proper and full investigation into the question. However, as the above quote from Lord Denning suggests, the employer is not required to *prove* that the employee was in fact incompetent. In this sense, the test resembles the approach adopted in relation to suspected misconduct, discussed later in this chapter.

In the application of the test, the courts and tribunals have shown themselves prepared to give considerable weight to the employer's opinions and views concerning incapacity. In *Cook* v. *Thomas Linnell & Sons Ltd* [1977] IRLR 132, for example, the EAT expressed the view that although employers must act reasonably when removing from a particular post an employee whom they consider to be unsatisfactory, it was important that the unfair dismissal legislation did not impede employers unreasonably in the efficient management of their business. The tribunal went on to state: 'When responsible employers have genuinely come to the conclusion over a reasonable period of time that a manager is incompetent we think that it is some evidence that he is incompetent.'

The ACAS advisory handbook offers the following guidance on how alleged poor performance cases should be approached:

- The employee should be asked for an explanation and the explanation checked
- where the reason is the lack of the required skills, the employee should, wherever practicable, be assisted through training and given reasonable time to reach the required standard of performance
- where despite encouragement and assistance the employee is unable to reach the required standard of performance, consideration should be given to finding suitable alternative work
- where alternative work is not available, the position should be explained to the employee before dismissal action is taken
- an employee should not normally be dismissed because of poor performance unless warnings and a chance to improve have been given
- if the main cause of poor performance is the changing nature of the job, employers should consider whether the situation may properly be treated as redundancy rather than a capability issue.

While in most cases of poor performance a system of warnings should be operated, there are rare occasions where the employee commits a single mistake and the actual or potential consequences of that mistake are so serious that to warn would not be appropriate. This class of case was discussed by the Court of Appeal in *Taylor* v. *Alidair* [1978] IRLR 82, where it was stated that there are activities in which the degree of professional skill which must be required is so high, and the potential consequences of the smallest departure from that high standard are so serious, that one failure to perform in accordance with those standards is enough to justify dismissal. Examples might be the passenger-carrying airline pilot, the scientist operating the nuclear reactor, the chemist in charge of research into the possible effect of thalidomide, the driver of the Manchester to London express, the driver of an articulated lorry full of sulphuric acid.

Long-term Sickness Absence

One of the most common and difficult problems facing employers and trade union representatives in the realm of disciplinary practice and procedure is employee absence through sickness or injury. In these situations the employer will frequently have to resolve a conflict between economic considerations and the employee's claim for job security and fair treatment where s/he is absent through no fault of his/her own. Likewise, trade union representatives must protect those members who, in addition to shouldering the burden of ill-health, face the prospect of unemployment.

In cases of exceptionally severe and incapacitating illness where it is highly unlikely that the employee will ever be fit to return to work, the contract may be regarded as 'frustrated' and, therefore, terminated by operation of law rather than dismissal. The rules governing the doctrine of frustration and its relationship to long-term sickness absence and imprisonment were discussed in the previous chapter.

Given that the frustration doctrine offers employers a convenient way in which to avoid the unfair dismissal provisions, the courts are generally reluctant to apply it to contracts which are terminable by notice. Therefore, in less drastic cases of long-term sickness absence a body of case law has developed on the question of the fairness of a dismissal in such circumstances.

Two broad tests have been used by industrial tribunals in determining fairness: the substantive and the procedural. The substantive aspect of the tribunal's inquiry revolves around the question of whether it was reasonable of the employer to dismiss in the particular circumstances of the case. In *Spencer* v. *Paragon Wallpapers Ltd* [1976] IRLR 373, Mr Justice Phillips set out the relevant consideration as follows:

> the nature of the illness, the likely length of the continuing absence, the need for the employers to have done the work which the employee was employed to do ... The basic question which has to be determined in every case is whether, in all the circumstances, the employer can be expected to wait any longer and, if so, how much longer? Every case will be different, depending on the circumstances.

Therefore a balance has to be struck between job security and the interests of the business (see para. 40 of the Industrial Relations Code of Practice, 1972). Where the absent employee holds a position which cannot be filled easily on a temporary basis and his/her continued absence is inconsistent with the operation efficiency of the undertaking, tribunals have held dismissals to be fair (see *Tan* v. *Berry Bros and Rudd Ltd* [1974] IRLR 244; *Coulson* v. *Felixstowe Docks and Railway Co* [1975] IRLR 11; *McPhee* v. *George H. Wright* [1975] IRLR 132).

The question of the time the employee must be away from work before it may be reasonable for an employer to dismiss him or her depends, as was stated in *Spencer*, on the circumstances of each case. A significant factor may be the size of the employer's undertaking. In a large firm, the disruption caused by sickness absence may be minimal, but in a small business such absences may be extremely serious.

Where an employee is covered by a contractual sick-pay scheme, can the employer dismiss before the sick-pay entitlement elapses? It may be assumed that if an employer has contracted to provide a certain period of sick pay it would not normally be reasonable to dismiss before this time span has elapsed. However, this does not mean that it will always be unfair to dismiss during the currency of a sick pay period. In *Coulson* v. *Felixstowe Docks Co* [1975] IRLR 11, the company dismissed an employee whose lengthy absence over the previous two years had caused inconvenience from time to time when, because of a labour shortage, a replacement could not be found. He sought to argue before the industrial tribunal, inter alia, that he should not have been dismissed before his sick pay entitlement was exhausted. This contention was rejected by the tribunal, which found that the sick-pay scheme was 'a financial provision and not a provision which in any event indicates the amount of absence to which an employee is entitled, if he is sick'. In line with this approach, merely because the absent employee has exhausted his/her sick-pay entitlement does not mean that an employer can automatically dismiss the employee even where the contract so provides (see *Hardwick* v. *Leeds Area Health Authority* [1975] IRLR 319).

The second aspect of the reasonableness test involves a consideration of the adequacy of the procedures the employer has adopted in coming to the conclusion that the dismissal was necessary. An employer will be expected to make a reasonable effort to inform himself of the true medical position and this will normally entail consulting the employee and seeking, with the employee's consent, a medical opinion. A model letter of enquiry to an employee's general practitioner, approved by the BMA, is included as Appendix 4 (vii) to the ACAS advisory handbook.

The Access to Medical Reports Act 1988, which came into force on 1 January 1989, now regulates the supply of medical reports on employees to employers. The Act obliges an employer to inform an employee of the intention to ask the employee's doctor for a medical report and to obtain the employee's consent. There is also a requirement that the employee be informed of the following rights under the Act: the right to refuse consent; the right of access to the report both before and after it is supplied to the employer; the right to refuse consent to the report being supplied to the employer; the right to amend the report where it is considered by the employee to be 'incorrect and misleading'. The right to amend is qualified by the fact that the Act allows the doctor to accept or reject the amendments. However, where the doctor does not accept the patient's amendments, s/he must attach a statement of the patient's views to the report (s. 5 [2] [b]).

If an employee does refuse to give consent to allow the employer to approach his/her GP, this may be taken by the tribunal to confirm the employer's doubts that the employee is fit to carry out his/her duties – see *Leeves* v. *Edward Hope Ltd* COIT 19464/77 July 1977.

Many employers now make it a term of employment that the employee agrees, if and when requested, to undergo a medical examination by the organisation's own occupational health practitioner or by an independent doctor to be nominated by the employer. The provisions of the Access to Medical Reports Act only apply to reports requested from the employee's *own* doctor.

The decision whether to dismiss is a managerial one rather than a medical question and, therefore, the medical opinion which the employer seeks must be sufficiently detailed to allow him/her to make a rational and informed decision (*East Lindsey District Council* v. *Daubney*). In the event of a conflict of opinion, some tribunal decisions have favoured the opinion of the employer's medical officer over that of the employee's own GP on the basis that the former is more aware of the demands of the job (see *Jeffries* v. *BP Tanker Co Ltd* [1974] IRLR 260; *Ford Motor Co Ltd* v. *Nawaz* [1987] IRLR 163; compare *Liverpool Area Health Authority* v. *Edwards* [1977] IRLR 471).

The need for consultation with the employee was stressed in *Spencer* v. *Paragon Wallpapers Ltd* and strongly affirmed by the EAT's decision in *E Lindsey District Council* v. *Daubney* [1977] IRLR 181. On the other hand, consultation has not always been required by industrial tribunals. In *Taylorplan Catering (Scotland) Ltd* v. *McInally* [1980] IRLR 53 it was suggested that where a tribunal finds that the circumstances were such that a consultation would have made no difference to the result, lack of consultation could be justified. In this case, the EAT was of the view that the guidelines in *British Labour Pump* could be applied in cases involving ill-health. With the rejection of those guidelines by the House of Lords in *Polkey* it is likely that consultation will be required in the vast majority of cases.[17]

Assuming that the industrial tribunal is satisfied that the employer could not be expected to wait any longer before replacing the sick employee and that he or she has made reasonable efforts to establish the true medical position, the employer may find that there is one further requirement to comply with before it is possible successfully to defend a claim of unfair dismissal: an obligation to look for alternative work for the sick employee within the organisation. Where there is a suitable job in existence which the employee is capable of performing, a failure to offer it to the employee may well cast doubt upon the fairness of the dismissal.

Therefore, if there is an existing job, even if it is lower paid, the employer should offer the alternative work to the employee. If the employee refuses any such offers, then it seems reasonable for the employer to dismiss the employee. This statement requires some qualification in the sense that the employer is only required to consider the employee's ability to perform existing jobs: there is no duty on the employer to create a new job (see *Merseyside and North Wales Electricity Board* v. *Taylor* [1975] IRLR 60). However, the employer may be expected to go to reasonable lengths to modify a particular job in order to meet the employee's needs (see *Carricks [Caterers] Ltd* v. *Nolan* [1980] IRLR 259).

For a checklist on handling long-term sickness absence see p. 42 of the ACAS advisory handbook, *Discipline at Work*.

Persistent Absenteeism

While long-term absence is treated as a matter of incapability it is clear that persistent absenteeism should be regarded as a matter of misconduct and can be dealt with under the ordinary disciplinary procedure (see *International Sports Ltd* v. *Thomson* [1980] IRLR 340; *Rolls Royce* v. *Walpole* [1980] IRLR 343).

The following extract from the ACAS handbook, *Discipline at Work*, provides a checklist of what the courts and tribunals expect from employers in handling cases of frequent and persistent short-term absence:

- Absences should be investigated promptly and the employee asked to give an explanation.
- Where there is no medical advice to support frequent self-certificated medical absences, the employee should be asked to consult a doctor to establish whether medical treatment is necessary and whether the underlying reason for absence is work-related.
- If after investigation it appears that there were no good reasons for the absences, the matter should be dealt with under the disciplinary procedure.
- Where absences arise from temporary domestic problems, the employer in deciding appropriate action should consider whether an improvement in attendance is likely.
- In all cases the employee should be told what improvement in attendance is expected and warned of the likely consequence if this does not happen.
- If there is no improvement, the employee's age, length of service, performance, the likelihood of a change in attendance, the availability of suitable alternative work and the effect of past and future absences on the business should all be taken into account in deciding appropriate action.

The Malingering Employee

Where the employer suspects that the absent employee is malingering, the issue should be treated as a matter of misconduct and normal disciplinary procedures followed. In *Hutchinson* v. *Enfield Rolling Mills Ltd* [1981] IRLR 318, it was held that a doctor's medical certificate was not conclusive proof of genuine sickness absence if the employer had other evidence that the employee was fit enough to attend work. This principle would, of course, apply with even more force where the employee has self-certificated absence.

Conduct

Dismissal for a reason related to the conduct of the employer covers a multitude of sins, encompassing those capable of amounting to gross misconduct (violence, theft, a serious act of disobedience, gross negligence) and also less serious infringements of discipline such as minor acts of insubordination, bad language and bad timekeeping. As we have seen, except in cases of dismissal for a single act of gross misconduct, the courts and tribunals expect employers to adopt the system of warnings discussed earlier.

Dishonesty and Other Criminal Offences

The courts and tribunals maintain a distinction between offences committed at work and those outside. Whether the commission of a criminal offence outside work merits an employee's dismissal depends above all on its relevance to the individual's duties as an employee. Tribunals take into account the following matters: the status of the employee; the nature of the offence; the employee's past record; the employee's access to cash (in cases of dishonesty); and proximity to members of the public (in cases of offences of violence).

In *P* v. *Nottinghamshire County Council* [1992] IRLR 362, the Court of Appeal stated that:

> in an appropriate case and where the size and administrative resources of the employer's undertaking permit, it may be unfair to dismiss an employee without the employer first considering whether the employee can be offered some other job, notwithstanding that it may be clear that he cannot be allowed to continue in his original job. (Lord Justice Balcombe)

Furthermore, where the alleged offence is committed outside employment, the Code of Practice advises that employees should not be dismissed 'solely because a charge against them is pending or because they are absent through having been remanded in custody' (para. 15[c]). Nevertheless, there may be cases where the period of absence on remand is lengthy and the employer may be held to be justified, in the interests of the business, in seeking a permanent replacement (see *Kingston* v. *British Railways Board* [1984] IRLR 146 CA). Indeed, a lengthy period in custody on remand or a sentence of imprisonment on conviction may result in a finding that the employment contract has been 'frustrated', as discussed in the previous chapter.

An employee may be fairly dismissed where s/he conceals from his/her employer a criminal conviction imposed before the employment began and which is not a 'spent' conviction under the Rehabilitation of Offenders Act, 1974. Whether or not a conviction is spent and the individual is a 'rehabilitated person' under the Act depends upon the severity of the sentence and the time which has elapsed since it was imposed. (See chapter 3 above for the rehabilitation periods.)

Section 4 (3) of the Act makes it automatically unfair to dismiss someone on the grounds of a conviction which is spent or because of failure to disclose it (see *Property Guards Ltd* v. *Taylor and Kershaw* [1982] IRLR 175). The scope of this provision is limited by subsequent regulations which exclude certain professions and employments from the Act. Exempted groups include: medical practitioners, lawyers, accountants, veterinary surgeons, dentists, nurses, opticians, pharmaceutical chemists, judicial appointments, justices' clerks, probation officers, those employed by local authorities in connection with the provision of social services, those offices and employments concerned with the provisions of services, schooling, training and so on to persons under the age of 18 where the holder will have access to young persons (or employment on premises used for providing such services) – see the Rehabilitation of Offenders Act 1974 (Exceptions) Order 1975 (SI 1975 no. 1023) as amended by the Rehabilitation of Offenders Act 1974 (Exceptions) (Amendment) Orders 1986 (SI 1986 no. 1249 and SI 1986 no. 2268).

An employer, when recruiting to an exempted occupation, should inform candidates in writing that spent convictions must be disclosed. If a person is then employed having failed to disclose a conviction, the employer may be held to have acted fairly if it dismisses on subsequent discovery of the conviction (see *Torr* v. *British Railways Board* [1977] ICR 785).

Suspected Dishonesty within Employment

As in all cases of misconduct, employers should not dismiss for dishonesty unless and until they have formed a genuine and reasonable belief in the guilt of the employee. The authoritative guidance on this issue is *BHS* v. *Burchell* [1978] IRLR 379 (approved by the Court of Appeal in *W. Weddel & Co Ltd* v. *Tepper* [1980] IRLR 96 CA). The test formulated by the EAT in *Burchell* is whether the employer:

(a)   entertained a reasonable belief in the guilt of the employee;
(b)   had reasonable grounds for that belief; and
(c)   had carried out as much investigation into the matter as was reasonable.

What if the criminal court subsequently acquits a dismissed person? Remember that the employers are judged on the reasonableness of their actions *at the time of the dismissal* and not on the basis of what happens afterwards. Therefore, as long as the *Burchell* tests are satisfied then such a dismissal will be likely to be held to be fair. The standard of proof required in an unfair dismissal case (on the balance of probabilities) is not as onerous as in a criminal case (beyond all reasonable doubt).

A Reasonable Investigation

What constitutes reasonable investigation will very much depend on the circumstances of the particular case. At one extreme there is the employee who is caught red-handed, while at the other the guilt of the employee may be a matter of pure inference. The closer the case is to the latter end of the continuum, the more exacting the standard of inquiry and investigation required.

In cases where the position is less than clear-cut, it is clearly advisable for the employer to carry out an investigation *before* putting the accusation to the employee. This is because an accusation without reasonable foundation could entitle the recipient employee to resign and claim constructive dismissal (see *Robinson* v. *Crompton Parkinson Ltd* [1978] ICR 401).

Where an employee, having been charged with or convicted of a criminal offence, refuses to co-operate with the employer's investigation, it has been held that this should not prevent the employer from proceeding. In *Carr* v. *Alexander Russell Ltd* [1976] IRLR 220 it was suggested that it would be improper, after an employee has been arrested and charged with a criminal offence alleged to have been committed in the course of employment, for the employer to seek to question the employee. However, this approach was rejected in *Harris (Ipswich) Ltd* v. *Harrison* [1978] IRLR 382, where the view was expressed that there was nothing to prevent an employer in such circumstances from discussing the matter with the employee or his/her representative. What needs to be discussed is not so much the alleged offence as the action the employer is proposing to take and whether there are any mitigating circumstances, such as a lengthy and previously unblemished service record.

Therefore, where an employee – perhaps after having taken legal advice – chooses to remain silent, s/he should be given written warning that, unless s/he does provide further information, a disciplinary decision will be taken on the basis of the information that is available and could result in dismissal (see *Harris and Shepherd* v. *Courage (Eastern) Ltd* [1981] IRLR 153).

The ACAS Handbook, *Discipline at Work*, advises that where the police are involved they should not be asked to conduct the investigation on behalf of the employer nor should they be present at any disciplinary hearing or interview (see p. 37 of the handbook). Similarly, the employer cannot simply leave the disciplinary decision to the criminal justice system – deciding not to carry out an internal investigation but to dismiss the employee automatically if s/he is found guilty at trial (see *McLaren* v. *National Coal Board* [1988] IRLR 215).

'Blanket' Dismissals

The general rule is that employers may only dismiss for misconduct if they entertain a genuine and reasonable belief in the employee's guilt (see *BHS* v. *Burchell*, cited above). This rule was modified in cases where, despite all reasonable investigations, the employer is unable to identify the culprit but knows it must be one of two employees. In such a case the Court of Appeal has held that it is reasonable to dismiss both (see *Monie* v. *Coral Racing Ltd* [1981] ICR 109).

This principle concerning blanket dismissals has recently been extended by the EAT to cases of conduct or capability not involving dishonesty (see *Whitbread & Co* v. *Thomas* [1988] IRLR 43). According to this case, an employer who cannot identify which member of a group was responsible for an act can fairly dismiss the whole group, even where it is probable that not all were guilty of the act – provided three conditions are satisfied. First, the act in question must be such that, if committed by an identified individual, it would justify dismissal of that individual; second, the tribunal must be satisfied that the act was committed by one or more of the group, all of whom can be shown to be individually capable of having committed the act complained of; third, the tribunal must be satisfied that there has been a proper investigation by the employer to identify the person or persons responsible for the act.

This principle has been most recently applied by the EAT in *Parr* v. *Whitbread plc* [1990] IRLR 39. Mr Parr was employed as a branch manager of one of the respondent's off-licence shops. He was dismissed along with three other employees when the sum of £4,600 was stolen from the shop in circumstances which indicated that it was an inside job. Each of the four had equal opportunity of committing the theft and the employers found it impossible to ascertain which of them was actually guilty. The EAT upheld the IT's finding of a fair dismissal.

Unfair Redundancy Dismissals

As we have seen, redundancy is a prima facie fair ground for dismissal. It is important to note, however, that the statutory presumption that a dismissal is for redundancy under EPCA s. 91 (2), which applies when the claim is for a redundancy payment, does not apply in relation to an unfair dismissal claim. Therefore it is up to the employer to prove that redundancy was the reason for dismissal.

Even where the employer has succeeded in this task, the dismissal for redundancy may still be attacked as unfair on one of three grounds:

(i)   Selection for redundancy for a reason 'specified in TULR(C)A s. 152 (1)', meaning trade union membership or activity or non-membership (TULR(C)A s. 153). Under TURERA, complaints of unfair dismissal on trade union grounds is no longer subject to a qualifying period of service. This closes an inconsistency in the law where protection against trade union related dismissals under s. 512(1) is extended to all employees, but protection against selection for redundancy for those same reasons was limited to those with two years' service.

(ii) Selection for redundancy in contravention of a customary arrangement or agreed procedure relating to redundancy and where there were no 'special reasons' justifying departure from that arrangement or procedure in the circumstances of the particular case (EPCA s. 59). This provision, as with TULR(C)A s. 153, is subject to the proviso that another employee holding a similar position to the one selected for redundancy has been retained, although the circumstances constituting redundancy applied equally to that employee. The most common basis for selection under a redundancy agreement is 'Last in, first out' (LIFO), but it may also allow other criteria to be taken into account, such as skill, competence, attendance and disciplinary records.

(iii) Unreasonable redundancy under s. 57 (3). While it is an automatically unfair dismissal not to comply with a redundancy agreement or arrangement, it does not follow that it is necessarily fair to follow it. Under s. 57 (3), the industrial tribunal still has to decide whether an employer's selection of a particular employee for redundancy was reasonable (see *Watling* v. *Richardson* [1978] IRLR 255). Also certain types of selection agreements, such as 'part-timers first', may amount to indirect sex discrimination (see *Clarke and Powell* v. *Eley [IMI] Kynoch Ltd* [1982] IRLR 131 and compare with *Kidd* v. *DRG Ltd [UK]* [1985] IRLR 190).

Whether or not there is a redundancy agreement, the employee may challenge the fairness of the redundancy dismissal under s. 57 (3) (this was decided by the CA in *Bessenden Properties Ltd* v. *Corness* [1977] ICR 821).

The leading case in this area is *Williams* v. *Compair Maxam Ltd* [1982] IRLR 83, where the EAT laid down five principles of 'good industrial relations practice' which should generally be followed in redundancies where the employees are represented by an independent and recognised trade union. These guidelines were as follows:

(i) to give as much warning as possible;
(ii) to consult with the union, particularly relating to the criteria to be applied in selection for redundancy. (Principles [i] and [ii] find an echo in what is now TULR[C]A, ss. 188–98, which oblige employers to consult recognised unions 'at the earliest opportunity'. If the employer is proposing to dismiss 100 or more employees at one establishment over a 90-day period, consultations must commence not less 90 days before the first dismissal. If it is proposed to dismiss 10 or more over a 30-day period, consultations should take place not less than 30 days before the first dismissal takes effect. There is no minimum period where the employer proposes to dismiss less than 10 employees. An employee who suffers loss by the lack of consultation may receive a compensation in the form of a 'protective award'.)
(iii) to adopt objective rather than subjective criteria for selection; for example experience, length of service, attendance.
(iv) to select in accordance with the criteria, considering any representations made by the union regarding selection.
(v) to consider the possibility of redeployment rather than dismissal.

These guidelines have since been approved and applied by the Northern Ireland Court of Appeal in *Robinson* v. *Carrickfergus BC* [1983] IRLR 122, while in *Grundy (Teddington) Ltd* v. *Plummer* [1983] IRLR 98, the EAT emphasised that the guidelines should be applied flexibly, as one or more of the five points may not be appropriate in the particular circumstances of the case.

While the EAT in England has been in favour for a flexible but general application of the *Compair Maxam* guidelines, this approach has not found favour north of the border. In *A. Simpson & Son (Motors) Ltd* v. *Reid and Findlater* [1983] IRLR 401, Lord MacDermott felt that the principles had been misapplied by the tribunals and that they only had application in situations where there was an independent recognised trade union. He was of the view that the principles had no relevance in a situation, such as that before the court, of a small business faced with a selection of two out of three people where no trade union was involved. In *Meikle* v. *McPhail (Charleston Arms)* [1983] IRLR 351, Lord MacDonald, referring somewhat despairingly to the 'so-called principles' set out in *Compair Maxam* stated:

> These principles must primarily refer to large organisations in which a significant number of redundancies are contemplated. In our view they should be applied with caution to circumstances such as the present where the size and administrative resources of the employer are minimal. (See also *Buchanan* v. *Tilcon Ltd* [1983] IRLR 417.)

We have been awaiting a decision from the Court of Appeal as to whether it approves of the *Compair Maxam* principles or adopts the restrictive Scottish approach. If the latter view is adopted, then the law will return to a pre-*Compair Maxam* state of affairs which rarely challenged management's approach to redundancy.

Strong implicit support for the need for the *Compair Maxam* principles, however, may now be derived from the House of Lords decision in *Polkey* v. *AE Dayton Services Ltd* which was discussed earlier in this chapter. As you will recall, this decision rejected the so-called no-difference rule – the rule that an unfair procedure leading to a dismissal does not render the dismissal unfair if it made no difference to the outcome. In the course of his judgement, Lord Bridge, while not referring to *Compair Maxam* by name, stated:

> in the case of redundancy, the employer will not normally be acting reasonably unless he warns and consults any employees affected or their representative, adopts a fair basis on which to select for redundancy and takes such steps as may be reasonable to avoid or minimise redundancy by redeployment within his own organisation.

Lord Bridge felt that if an industrial tribunal felt it likely the employee would have been dismissed even if consultation had taken place, the compensation could be reduced by 'a percentage representing the chance that the employee would still have lost his employment'. This was a better approach than the 'all or nothing' decision which resulted from the application of the no-difference rule. Moreover, Lord Bridge was of the view that:

> In a case where an Industrial Tribunal held that dismissal on the ground of redundancy would have been inevitable at the time it took place, even if the appropriate procedural steps had been taken, I do not, as presently advised,

think this would necessarily preclude a discretionary order for re-engagement on suitable terms, if the altered circumstances considered by the Tribunal at the date of the hearing were thought to justify it.

For further discussion of redundancy dismissals see the following chapter.

Dismissal to Avoid Breach of a Statutory Duty or Restriction (EPCA s. 57 [2][d])

It is potentially fair for an employer to dismiss an employee because the employee 'could not continue to work in the position which he held without contravention (either on his part or on that of his employer) of a duty or restriction imposed by or under an enactment' (EPCA s. 57 [2][d]). Before proposing to act under this heading, the employee should seek legal advice as to whether the continued employment of the employee would involve a breach of the law. The courts and tribunals have taken a particularly strict view of the scope of the subsection and have held that it does not apply where the employer genuinely but mistakenly believes that continued employment would be unlawful (*Bouchaala* v. *Trusthouse Forte Hotels Ltd* [1980] IRLR 382).

The fact that the employer could not have lawfully continued to employ an employee without contravening the law does not inevitably lead to the conclusion that a dismissal falling within s. 57 (2) (d) is fair. In other words, the tribunal still has to be satisfied that the employer behaved reasonably within s. 57 (3) (*Sandhu* v. *1. Department of Education and Science 2. London Borough of Hillingdon* [1978] IRLR 208).

In practical terms, very few cases arise under this heading. The most common examples are cases where the individual employee is employed as a driver and then is disqualified from driving. In this sort of situation the employer should consider whether there is alternative work which can be offered to the disqualified driver before moving to dismissal (*Fearn* v. *Tayford Motor Company Ltd* [1975] IRLR 336).

Some Other Substantial Reason (s. 57[1][b])

This is a catch-all category, intended to cover situations not encompassed by the four explicit admissible reasons (*RS Components Ltd* v. *Irwin* [1973] IRLR 239). As with the other admissible reasons, the burden of proof is on the employer and if it cannot be shown that the reason which motivated the employer to dismiss was 'substantial', then the tribunal will find for the applicant.

Examples of dismissals which have been held to fall within this general residual category are given here.

Non-renewal of a Fixed-term Contract

This applies where it can be shown that there was a genuine need for fixed-term employment and the temporary nature of the employment was made known to the employee at the outset (see *Terry* v. *E Sussex County Council* [1976] IRLR 332; *N Yorkshire County Council* v. *Fay* [1985] IRLR 247).

Dismissal of Temporary Replacements

In two cases, statute provides that the dismissal of temporary replacement staff will constitute 'some other substantial reason'. The first is in respect of the dismissal of the replacement of an employee who has been on maternity leave (EPCA s. 61[1]) and the other concerns the dismissal of an individual employed to cover the absence of an employee who is suspended on medical grounds under EPCA s. 19 (EPCA s. 61 [2]). Such dismissals will be potentially justifiable, provided that the replacements have been informed in writing at the time of their engagement that their employment would be terminated on the return to work of the permanent employee. In addition, the tribunal must be satisfied that it was reasonable to dismiss and a relevant factor may be whether the employer has considered the availability of alternative work for the replacement employee.

Customer Pressure to Dismiss

Dismissal of an employee because an important customer of the employer was not willing to accept that employee doing the work has been held to constitute a substantial reason for dismissal (*Scott Packing & Warehousing Ltd* v. *Paterson* [1978] IRLR 166). However, if the employer wishes to rely on this ground for dismissal clear evidence must be produced that the valued customer had threatened to withdraw custom unless the employee was dismissed (*Grootcon [UK] Ltd* v. *Keld* [1984] IRLR 302).

In addition, before finally acceding to the demand, the employer should investigate the matter thoroughly in consultation with the customer and the employee, considering the possibility of deploying the employee on alternative work if it is available (*Dobie* v. *Burns International Security Services [UK] Ltd* [1984] IRLR 329).

Conflicts between Employees

Behaviour on the part of an employee which is causing disruption and discontent within the rest of the workforce has been held to constitute some other substantial reason for dismissal. For example, in *Treganowan* v. *Robert Knee & Co Ltd* [1975] IRLR 247, a female employee's frequent and open boasting about her sexual exploits had created tensions within the office which were affecting business. This behaviour was held to be some other substantial reason for dismissal and fair in the circumstances because she was completely insensitive to the effect she was having.

In such cases, however, dismissal must be viewed as a weapon of last resort and the employer must make sensible, practical and genuine efforts to see whether an improvement in relationships can be effected. The possibility of transferring the employee to another department should also be explored (*Turner v. Vestric Ltd* [1981] IRLR 23).

Finally, it should be borne in mind that pressure for the dismissal of an employee from the rest of the workforce which takes the form of industrial action will not help the employee justify the dismissal. As we saw earlier in this chapter, EPCA s. 63 specifically provides that, in determining the reason for the dismissal and its reasonableness, no account shall be taken of any industrial action threatened or taken against the employer.

Dismissal for Refusal to Accept Changes in Contractual Terms Resulting from a Business Reorganisation

One of the most controversial areas of unfair dismissal has concerned the correct approach to the situation where the employer wishes to reorganise the business in such a way that changes result in the employees' terms and condition of employment. These changes may not fall within the legal concept of redundancy because the work that the employee does is not diminished (see *Johnson v. Nottinghamshire Combined Police Authority* [1974] IRLR 20; *Lesney Products Ltd v. Nolan* [1977] IRLR 77).

The test of fairness is not inevitably controlled by the content of the contract of employment. As a result, the courts and tribunals have been prepared to hold as fair dismissals where the employee has refused to agree to a change in terms and conditions of employment in line with the employer's perception of business efficacy. Dismissals for refusal to agree to unilateral changes in job content, pay, location and hours of work have been held to be for some other substantial reason and fair (see, for example, *Ellis v. Brighton Cooperative Society* [1976] IRLR 419; *Hollister v. NFU* [1979] IRLR 23).

The tribunal will expect the employer to show evidence why it was felt to be necessary to impose the changes (*Banerjee v. City and E London AHA* [1979] IRLR 147) and it is also material for the tribunal to know whether the company was making profits or losses (*Ladbroke Courage Holidays Ltd v. Asten [1981]* IRLR 59.

On the other hand, the courts and tribunals have not imposed particularly strict criteria when judging the 'substantiality' of the decision to reorganise. In *Ellis* (above) it was suggested that the test was whether, if the changes were not implemented, the whole business would be brought to a standstill. A much less stringent test was formulated by Lord Denning in *Hollister* (above), where he felt that the principle should extend to situations 'where there was some sound, good business reason for the reorganisation'. In subsequent cases, the EAT has been prepared to dilute the test even further; in one case requiring only that the changes were considered as 'matters of importance' or to have 'discernible advantages to the organisation' (*Banerjee*, cited above) and in another demanding that the reorganisation be 'beneficial' (*Bowater Containers v. McCormack* [1980] IRLR 50).

Surveys of the case law on reorganisation or 'business efficacy' tend to show the adoption of a strong conception of managerial prerogative by the courts and tribunals.[18]

In *Evans* v. *Elementa Holdings* [1982] IRLR 143, a case involving the imposition of an obligation to work overtime, the EAT moved some way to redressing this imbalance in favour of managerial prerogative in holding that if it was unreasonable to expect an employee to accept the changes, it was unfair for the employer to dismiss. This view, however, was not accepted by a differently constituted EAT in *Chubb Fire Security Ltd* v. *Harper* [1983] IRLR 311. In its view the correct approach, in accordance with the decision of the Court of Appeal in *Hollister* v. *NFU* (above), is for the industrial tribunal to concentrate on whether it was reasonable for the employer to implement the reorganisation by terminating existing contracts and offering new ones.

> It may be perfectly reasonable for an employee to decline to work extra overtime, having regard to his family commitments. Yet from the employer's point of view, having regard to his business commitments, it may be perfectly reasonable to require an employee to work overtime.

For a recent application of the approach adopted in Chubb, see *St. John of God (Care Services) Ltd* v. *Brooks* [1992] IRLR 546 EAT.

Some form of consultation over the reorganisation has been expected in the past in order to maintain the fairness of the dismissal. The dilution of the importance of consultation in *Hollister* – where the Court of Appeal held that consultation is only one of the factors to be taken into account when judging reasonableness and lack of it would not necessarily render a dismissal unfair – should be reassessed following the decision of the House of Lords in *Polkey* v. *AE Dayton Services Ltd* (above). Having said that, there is no clear guidance on the form the consultation should take. In *Ellis* v. *Brighton Cooperative Society Ltd* (above), the EAT was satisfied that the requirement of consultation had been fulfilled by union agreement to the scheme even though Ellis, as a non-union member, had little chance in participating in the scheme. In *Martin* v. *Automobile Proprietary Ltd* [1979] IRLR 64, on the other hand, there are suggestions that non-union members should expect to be individually consulted.

Dismissal on a Transfer of Undertaking

As we saw earlier, reg. 8 of the Transfer of Undertakings (Protection of Employment) Regulations 1981 provides that a dismissal of an employee of the transferor or transferee which is connected with the transfer of the business is automatically unfair unless it is for an 'economic, technical or organisational reason entailing changes in the workforce' – known as ETO. By virtue of reg. 8 (2) such dismissals are deemed to be for a substantial reason for the purpose of EPCA 1978, s. 57 (1), and are fair provided they pass the statutory test of reasonableness. It is now clear that, if the employer does successfully establish the ETO defence, an employee can claim a redundancy payment if redundancy was the reason for the transfer dismissal (*Gorictree Ltd* v. *Jenkinson* [1984] IRLR 391).

The scope of the ETO defence was considered by the Court of Appeal in *Berriman* v. *Delabole Slate Ltd* [1985] IRLR 305. The court held that in order to come within reg. 8 (2), the employer must show that a change in the workforce is part of the economic, technical or organisational reason for dismissal. It must be an objective of the employer's plan to achieve changes in the workforce, not just a possible consequence of the plan. So where an employee resigned following a transfer because the transferee employer proposed to remove his guaranteed weekly wage so as to bring his pay into line with the transferee's existing workforce, the reason behind the plan was to produce uniform terms and conditions and was not in any way to reduce the numbers in the workforce.

In order to counter the effects of the decision in *Berriman*, there was a developing practice of purchasers of a business insisting that the vendor dismisses the workforce before the transfer takes place. In this way, the transferee sought to avoid any liability for unfair dismissal and/or redundancy pay in relation to the transferor's workforce. In *Anderson* v. *Dalkeith Engineering Ltd* [1985] ICR 66, the Scottish EAT held that a dismissal by the transferor at the behest of the transferee was an 'economic' reason and therefore fell within reg. 8 (2). The EAT was of the view that to get the best deal for the sale of the business, the vendor had to accede to the purchaser's demand and that was clearly an 'economic reason'. This approach was not adopted by the English EAT in *Wheeler* v. *Patel* [1987] ICR 631, where it thought that the word 'economic' should be given a more restricted meaning. It was felt that an 'economic reason' must relate to the conduct of the business. A desire to obtain an enhanced price for the business or to achieve a sale was not a reason which related to the conduct of the business and was therefore not an economic reason. The *Wheeler* approach was subsequently supported by the EAT in *Gateway Hotels Ltd* v. *Stewart and Others* [1988] IRLR 287.

It is clear from the decision of the House of Lords in *Litster* v. *Forth Dry Dock & Engineering Co Ltd* [1989] IRLR 161 – discussed in detail in chapter 15 below – that the mere insistence of the purchaser that the vendor dismiss as a condition of sale will not be regarded as an 'economic, technical or organisational reason entailing changes in the workforce'. As a result of the *Litster* decision, where an employee has been unfairly dismissed for a reason connected with the transfer, s/he is to be deemed to have been employed in the undertaking 'immediately before the transfer' and the employment is statutorily continued with the transferee.

Stage Four: Remedies for Unfair Dismissal

Once the tribunal is satisfied that an employee has been unfairly dismissed, it has to consider one of three forms of remedy:

- an order for reinstatement
- an order of re-engagement
- an award of compensation (see ss. 67–9 EPCA)

Although reinstatement and re-engagement are regarded as primary remedies by the statute, in practice compensation is the normal remedy for unfair dismissal, the first two orders only being made by tribunals in roughly 3 per cent of successful cases. As a result, the re-employment of dismissed workers has been described as 'the lost remedy'.[19] There may be many reasons for the low level of re-engagement/reinstatement orders. By the time the IT hearing is held – normally three to four months after the dismissal – the applicant may have found another job. Even if this is not the case, the passage of time and the adversarial nature of the proceedings may result in the relationship between the parties breaking down so severely that it would be unrealistic to expect them to resume a normal working relationship.[20]

The principles governing the normal remedies are set out below, together with the special rules and procedures concerning trade union related dismissals.

Reinstatement or Re-engagement

On finding the complaint well founded, the industrial tribunal must explain to the applicant the availability of the orders of reinstatement or re-engagement and ask whether s/he wishes the tribunal to make such an order. Assuming that the applicant wishes to be reinstated or re-engaged, the industrial tribunal must then take the following additional factors into account in exercising its discretion:

(a) whether it is practicable for an employer to comply with such an order; and

(b) whether the employee caused or contributed to his/her dismissal and, if so, whether it would be just and equitable to make the order.

An order for reinstatement is an order that the employer shall treat the applicant in all respects as if he or she had not been dismissed. An order for re-engagement is an order that the complainant be engaged by the employer, or by a successor of the employer or by an associated employer, in employment comparable to that from which he or she was dismissed, or to other suitable employment.

On making the order the tribunal shall specify:

(a) any amounts payable to the employee in respect of any benefit which the employee might have received but for the dismissal, including arrears of pay, for the period from the date of termination to the date of reinstatement, including any benefits which the employee might have enjoyed by way of improvements in terms and conditions but for the dismissal;

(b) any rights and privileges, including seniority and pension rights, which must be restored to the employee;

(c) the date by which the order must be complied with.

Is It Practicable to Reinstate or Re-engage?

Employers will not be able to argue that it is not practicable to reinstate/re-engage the employee because a replacement employee has been engaged unless they can show either:

*   that it was not practicable to arrange for the dismissed employee's work to be done without employing a permanent replacement; or
*   that the replacement was engaged after the lapse of a reasonable period of time, without having heard from the dismissed employee that s/he wished to be reinstated or re-engaged; it no longer being reasonable for the employer to have the dismissed employee's work carried out by anyone except a permanent replacement (EPCA s. 70[1]).

Partial or Total Failure to Comply with an Order for Reinstatement or Re-engagement

Where an order is made and the employee is taken back but the employer does not comply fully with its terms, the tribunal will make such an award of compensation as it thinks fit, having regard to the loss sustained by the complainant in consequence of the failure to comply fully with the order (EPCA s. 71[1]).

In the more frequent situation of a total failure to comply with the order, the tribunal will award compensation using the normal rules of computation plus an 'additional award' (see below). It is a defence to the granting of the additional award if the employer can show that it was not practicable to comply with the order.

Impracticability is therefore a possible defence at two stages in the process of IT decision-making. The following circumstances have been held to render a reinstatement/re-engagement impracticable:

*   Where it would inevitably lead to industrial unrest (*Coleman* v. *Magnet Joinery Ltd* [1974] IRLR 343.
*   Where there is no suitable vacancy. A re-engagement order does not place a duty on the employer to search for and find work for the dismissed employee irrespective of existing vacancies (*Freemans plc* v. *Flynn* [1984] IRLR 486).
*   Where the employee believes him/herself to be a victim of conspiracy by his employers, s/he is not likely to be a satisfactory employee in any circumstances if reinstated or re-engaged (*Nothman* v. *LB Barnet (No. 2)* [1980] IRLR 65).
*   Where there must exist a close personal relationship, reinstatement can only be appropriate in exceptional circumstances and to force it upon a reluctant employer is not a course which an industrial tribunal should pursue unless

persuaded by powerful evidence that it would succeed (*Enessy Co SA t/a The Tulchan Estate* v. *Minoprio and Minoprio* [1978] IRLR 489).

Compensation

The rules relating to the calculation of unfair dismissal compensation can be summarised as follows.

The Basic Award (EPCA s. 73)

An award of half, one or one and a half weeks' pay for each year of continuous service (depending on age), subject to a maximum of 20 years. A week's pay is calculated in accordance with EPCA 14 schedule and is based on gross pay. The maximum allowable for a week's pay is currently £205 (1993/4); this figure is reviewed each year and any changes made operate from the 1 June.

Table 14.1: Basic Award and Age

If aged	But less than	No. of weeks pay for each year
	22	$^1/_2$
22	41	1
41	65	$1^1/_2$

If aged 64, entitlement goes down by one-twelfth for each month after your 64th birthday. Therefore, in general, the maximum payment under this head of calculation in the year 1993/4 will be:

$$£205 \times 20 \times 1^1/_2 = £6,150$$

Compensatory Award

The tribunal may also make a compensatory award (EPCA s. 74): This is an amount which the tribunal considers 'just and equitable'. Both the basic and compensatory award may be reduced if the applicant contributed to his/her own dismissal or as a result of any conduct before dismissal. The maximum award under this head is currently £11,000 (1993/4).

The aim of the award is to reimburse the employee for any financial loss experienced: interim loss of net earnings between the date of the dismissal and the tribunal hearing, and future losses that s/he is likely to sustain, including wages, pensions and other fringe benefits.

The Additional Award

This award is made where an order for reinstatement of re-engagement is not complied with. If the original dismissal was for a reason other than sex or race discrimination, the award may be between 13 and 26 weeks' pay (maximum 26 x £205 = £5,330 currently). If the reason was for discrimination, then there is a discretion to award between 26 and 52 weeks' pay (maximum 52 x £205 = £10,660 currently).

The Special Award in Union-Related Dismissals

By virtue of amendments introduced by the Employment Act 1982, the amount of compensation to be awarded to employees who are unfairly dismissed (or selected for redundancy) on grounds of trade union membership and activities or non-membership is much higher than for other types of dismissal because a 'special award' is made in addition to the basic and compensatory elements (TULR[C]A 1992, ss. 155–67). Also, unlike other cases, where the dismissal is union-related there is a minimum basic award (£2,700 in 1993/4).

The special award can be made *only* where the applicant requests the industrial tribunal to make an order for reinstatement or re-engagement (TULR[C]A s. 157). Where reinstatement/re-engagement is sought by the dismissed employee, there are two different levels of compensation laid down depending on the following two circumstances:

(a) Where reinstatement/re-engagement is requested but no such order is made by the industrial tribunal under the discretionary powers vested in it by EPCA s. 69.

If this is the case, then the special award will comprise 104 week's pay subject to a minimum of £13,400 and a maximum of £26,800.

(b) Where reinstatement/re-engagement is ordered by the industrial tribunal but the order is not complied with.

In this instance, unless the employer can satisfy the tribunal that it was not practicable to comply with the order, the special award will be 156 week's pay subject to a minimum of £20,100 and no maximum figure.

Where the tribunal is satisfied that it was not practicable for the employer to comply with the original order, the compensation will be as under (a) above.

In common with the other compensation limits, the levels of the special award are reviewed annually by the secretary of state. Those given here are for 1993/4. Unlike the basic and compensatory awards, a week's pay for the purposes of the special award is not subject to any statutory limit.

The special award may be reduced by a tribunal where it feels that it is just and equitable to do so because of the employee's conduct before the dismissal or because the employee had in some way obstructed the employer's attempt to comply with the reinstatement/re-engagement order. However, TULR[C]A s. 155 makes it clear that the tribunals should disregard certain types of conduct by the employee when considering the level of the award. These are:

- any breach by the employee of an undertaking to become a member of a trade union or of a particular trade union; to cease to be a member of a trade union or of a particular trade union or not to take part in the activities of any trade union or of a particular trade union.
- any breach of an undertaking to make a payment in lieu of union membership, or any objection to the employer making a deduction from his/her wages to cover payments in lieu.

Union Liability for Compensation

Either the employer or the applicant may request that a trade union or other party be joined in the proceedings if it has exerted or threatened to exert industrial pressure on the employer to dismiss. If the tribunal finds the complaint of third-party pressure well founded, the industrial tribunal has the power to order that the trade union or other party to pay any or all of the compensation awarded.

Interim Relief in Respect of Trade Union-related Dismissals

An employee who alleges that s/he has been dismissed for union/non-union membership or trade union activities can apply to the tribunal for an order for interim relief (TULR[C]A s. 161).

The order for interim relief is intended to preserve the status quo until the full hearing of cases which by their very nature can be extremely damaging to the industrial relations in any organisation. Where relief is granted it will result in either the reinstatement/re-engagement of the employee pending a full hearing or, in some cases, a suspension of the employee on continued terms and conditions.

Three conditions must be satisfied before an order for interim relief will be made:

(i) The application must be presented to the tribunal before the end of the period of seven days immediately following the effective date of termination.

(ii) Where the allegation relates to dismissal for trade union membership or taking part in union activities, there must also be presented to the tribunal within the same seven-day period a certificate signed by an authorised official of the union concerned. This certificate should state that in the official's opinion there appear to be reasonable grounds for the allegation. Having received the application, supported by the certificate, the tribunal must hear the application 'as soon as practicable', though giving at least seven days' notice of hearing to the employer.

(iii) It must appear to the tribunal 'likely' that the complaint is likely to succeed at full hearing.

If these conditions are satisfied, the tribunal must ask the employer whether s/he is willing to reinstate or re-engage the employee. If the employer is not willing, then the tribunal must make an order for the continuation of the employee's contract of employment. This means that the contract of employment will continue in force until the full hearing as if it had not been terminated. During that period the pay or any other benefits derived from the employment, seniority, pension rights and so on, together with continuity of employment, will be preserved.

Non-Compliance with an Order for Interim Relief

Where the employer fails to comply with an order for reinstatement or re-engagement, the tribunal must:

(a) make an order for the continuation of the contract; and
(b) order the employer to pay the employee such compensation as the tribunal considers just and equitable having regard to the failure to comply and the loss suffered by the employee as a result.

If the employer fails to observe the terms of a continuation order then:

(a) if non-compliance consists of a failure to pay an amount specified in order, the tribunal shall determine the amount owed;
(b) in any other case of non-compliance, the tribunal shall order the employer to pay the employee such compensation as the tribunal considers just and equitable in all the circumstances.

The Law of Unfair Dismissal: A Critique

Critics of this legislation[21] argue that the law has been unsuccessful as an effective control upon managerial prerogative in relation to dismissals and that, far from acting as a constraint on power, the law actually legitimates managerial control. An explanation for the weakness of the law lies in the attitude of the appeal court judges to the legislation. The judges are not happy with the unfair dismissal provisions because they are perceived to be 'corporatist' in that they overstep the boundary between matters which are suitable for state intervention and those which are not. The judges feel unhappy about meddling in affairs they have always thought should be left to individuals to resolve. Consequently, the courts and tribunals are unwilling to substitute their own standards of fairness for management opinion and instead have the tendency to endorse the ordinary practices of employers. Once this occurs it is inevitable that the concept of fairness will tend to favour managerial control. Evidence of this approach can be seen in the following areas.

The Concept of the Reasonable Employer

Earlier in this chapter we saw that in assessing reasonableness, the question is what the reasonable employer would have done in the circumstances and not what the industrial tribunal would have thought. In this sense, the courts do not set the norms of behaviour but merely reflect existing managerial standards. A notorious example of this approach can be seen in *Saunders* v. *Scottish National Camps Association Ltd* [1980] IRLR 174. The employee was a maintenance worker at a children's camp. He was dismissed on the grounds of being a homosexual. The dismissal was held to be fair because a considerable proportion of employers would take the view that the employment of a homosexual should be restricted, particularly when required to work in close proximity to children. Instead of setting its own standards, the court in this case accepted the commonly held and highly prejudicial views of some employers.

Overriding Contractual Rights

As we have seen, a dismissal may be held to be fair even when it is the employer who breaks the contract. So the courts and tribunals have been prepared to hold as fair dismissals where the employee has refused to agree to a change in terms and conditions of employment in line with the employer's perception of business efficiency.

The Dilution of Procedural Fairness

An additional criticism of the approach of the judges was their increasing will-ingness to put less emphasis on the need to follow a fair procedure. Since the Polkey decision, however, it may well be that flouting procedures will result in a finding of unfair dismissal in a much increased proportion of cases. But employees in such cases may find that they have achieved a Pyrrhic victory because the tribunal may reduce their compensation to nil if it is found that they were in any way at fault for their dismissal.[22]

These illustrations tend to confirm the view that the judges are most reluctant to trespass too far into the area of managerial prerogative. If they do intervene it has been to regulate the procedure by which the decision to dismiss is effected rather to question the substance of decision. This attitude is vividly illustrated by the following statement by Mr Justice Phillips in *Cook* v. *Thomas Linnell & Sons Ltd* [1977] ICR 770: 'It is important that the operation of the legislation in relation to unfair dismissal should not impede employers unreasonably in the efficient management of their business, which must be in the interests of all.'

Reform

A number of reforms have been mooted by those who see the need to strengthen the present system, including amending the law so that a dismissal decision, if challenged, could not be implemented unless and until justified before an industrial tribunal (a similar approach already exists under the 'interim relief' procedures presently used for dismissals for union reasons; see EPCA 1978, ss. 77–9).

A more radical approach would be to remove unfair dismissal from the jurisdiction of industrial tribunals and introduce a system of private arbitration which, it is claimed, would be cheaper, quicker and generally much less formal and legalistic.[23]

CHAPTER 15

Redundancy and Insolvency Rights

Redundancy in Britain

One of the most significant features of the employment scene in Britain is the power of employers to dismiss workers for redundancy. 'Redundancy' means, basically, that an employee's services are no longer required by the business. The likeliest reasons for this are a workplace reorganisation, displacement as a result of the introduction of new technology, or the employer's business running into financial difficulties.

In this chapter we will be considering the exact extent of this power, and the rights of workers affected by its use. Consideration will also be given to employees' rights when employers are hit by insolvency, that is, going into liquidation, receivership, or administration. This will be dealt with under the following sections:

- Employers' use of 'redundancy'
- Challenging redundancy decisions
- Statutory rights
- Compensation
- Collective redundancies
- Rights on insolvency

Employers' Use of 'Redundancy'

Unfortunately, people made redundant may be given very little explanation of the reasons for it. Generally speaking, the redundancy decision-making process is, in legal and practical terms, completely within the employer's control. If the employer has clearly gone bust and there is no realistic possibility of further employment (either from the employer or from a new owner of the business), there is usually little alternative but to accept redundancy and try to get any compensation which is due. There may, however, be other situations where the position is not so clear-cut. In this case it may be worthwhile pressing for further information and considering if there might be other options to immediate redundancy.

Not surprisingly, perhaps, employers are not always going to co-operate in such a dialogue and may prefer to take the line that the problem is one over which they have no control. It is worth remembering, if you get into this situation, that while there are undoubtedly situations in which job cuts are unavoidable or have been forced on an employer (job cuts forced on local authorities and public sector bodies because of spending limits are an obvious example), redundancy, and particularly compulsory redundancy, can often be shown to be entirely unnecessary. In particular, the reasons given for a plant closure, 'reorganisation' or other organisational change leading to redundancies can be very controversial on purely business grounds. Nor is it unusual for large companies and multinationals to shut down even profitable operations if this is seen as necessary to their corporate strategy. Even if companies, or successful parts of them, could be sold off as going concerns it may be corporate policy not to do so – especially if they could be acquired by a competitor.[1] If redundancies *are* forced, managements often fail to take steps to avert job losses, or will refuse to give adequate consideration to alternatives to redundancy. This is because there are no effective legal obligations or other pressures on them to do so, and because redundancy offers an easy option to what are often just short-term problems.

Abuse of 'Redundancy' by Employers

There are many well-documented examples of employers blatantly abusing redundancy procedures. In particular redundancy can be engineered as a ground for sacking staff when no other legally justifiable reasons are to hand, thereby avoiding what could be a far more expensive unfair dismissal claim. Redundancy, or the threat of it, is also an important weapon routinely threatened or used by employers' in industrial disputes (see p. 342 below).

Challenging Redundancy Decisions

For these reasons it is always important to enquire critically into any explanation given to justify redundancies. Unfortunately the law does not require employers to explain their actions in any objective or meaningful way. Although directors of companies have a duty to have regard to employees' interests, as well as to companies' members interests (under the Companies Act 1985, s. 309), it does not require them to observe any specific duties, for example to try to maintain jobs as a priority. Even EC proposals for worker participation in the management of their employers' organisations will not change the basic priority of companies' managements, which is to run their companies for the benefit of shareholders.

Nevertheless, as discussed below, individuals and unions do have certain rights to be consulted. As part of the requirement to 'act fairly' there might be a right to be given information and to be considered for any alternative jobs elsewhere within the business. While these rights are only limited they should be used as effectively as possible. If you are not satisfied with the reasons given, or having heard the explanation given to you you do not accept that redundancy is necessary, management decisions should be challenged. This should be done by using any internal disputes or appeals procedures that are available. Industrial action may be appropriate, although it is important to note the risks of forfeiting compensation rights that may be involved (see p. 255 below).

One important reason for challenging redundancy decisions at this stage, and as a workplace issue, is that it may only be possible to raise the 'fairness' of a redundancy decision later in tribunal proceedings in very limited cases. Tribunals do not generally concern themselves with the business and managerial merits of redundancy dismissals, so it is important to note that the issue should always be contested from the earliest possible stages and before legal steps begin.

Court Action to Stop Threatened Redundancy

In some circumstances, although this will be rare, there may be scope for going to court to try to get orders to prevent a management from carrying out redundancy dismissals. This could be a possibility, for example, where giving redundancy notice would be a threatened breach of contractual rights, or a breach of procedures laid down in a collective agreement. Unfortunately, the grant of court orders is a matter for judges' discretion, and in practice they are reluctant to get involved in disputes at this stage.

Example
Members of the Transport and General Workers' Union working for Standard Telephones and Cables Ltd argued that they had rights under a collective redundancy agreement. This provided, among other things, that in the event of a compulsory redundancy selection for redundancy would be made on the basis of length of service with the company, that is to say that a 'last in first out' system (LIFO) was in operation. But when redundancies were made the company insisted that the main criterion for selection should be its needs for workers with the most suitable skills rather than a LIFO system. Although the members were initially successful in temporarily blocking the dismissals (because LIFO had not been complied with), they later failed to get an injunction requiring the employers to treat them as continuously employed. The court's objection was that such an injunction would effectively reinstate them and require the employment relationship to be reimposed on the employer. This it was not prepared to do, even if it would only have been a temporary measure until a proper trial of all the issues took place.[2]

Employees and unions in the public sector may be able to take advantage of the scope for bringing 'judicial review' proceedings to challenge the legality of what an employer which is a public body is doing, or proposing to do. Such proceedings may be brought if a public sector employer has not acted in accordance with its statutory duties, or incorrectly in procedural terms – for example by not consulting adequately with recognised unions before making redundancy decisions. The scope for such proceedings was demonstrated in the GCHQ case (*Council of Civil Service Unions* v. *Civil Service Minister* [1984] 3 All ER 935; [1985] IRLR 28, HL), when ministerial action removing union membership rights was 'reviewed'; and again at the end of 1992 when miners' unions successfully obtained a court order that British Coal's handling of the pits closure programme was unlawful.

The Redundancy System

Before considering redundancy in detail it is worth considering some of the background to the present legislation, and then identifying the key features of it. Redundancy law is largely contained in the Employment Protection (Consolidation) Act 1978 (the EPCA) which replaced the Redundancy Payments Act 1965. Although the 1965 Act introduced statutory compensation for redundancy for the first time, its principal objective was to promote job 'mobility' – that is, to make it easier to move workers between different areas of the economy in response to employers' changing demands for labour and skills. Unfortunately the levels of compensation required to be paid under the EPCA are so low (with no signs that they might be raised) that for most people they are hardly a realistic incentive to accept the loss of their job willingly.

Like other employment legislation of the 1960s and 1970s the redundancy regime, with its unnecessarily complex rules and procedures, has been seen as part of a policy of trying to remove industrial relations conflicts from the workplace by individualising and 'judicialising' them.[3] Despite its many elaborate provisions the legislation does not in fact do anything to give workers any greater job security, nor has it in any way really restricted managerial power in redundancy situations. These and other limitations in the present scheme were, in fact, quickly realised within a few years of the 1965 Act coming into operation.[4] Arguably the rules we now have simply institutionalise redundancy as an easy way of sacking unwanted workers.

Main Features of Redundancy

The main features of the present system are that:

- there is no such thing as a 'right' to your job – nor do you have a right to an alternative job if that job becomes redundant;
- if a 'redundancy' situation exists your employer can dismiss you, usually without any come-back in a tribunal or court if the right procedural steps are taken (see p. 237–8);

- procedural rights, for example to be given information, to be consulted, are generally limited, although the EC has imposed certain procedural requirements in relation to mass redundancies (see section on collective redundancies below);
- compensation is limited;
- collective action to fight redundancy can be punished by the withdrawal of compensation rights (see p. 255 below).

Although there are demands made from time to time for changes,[5] and the EC will legislate to introduce further procedural requirements on employers, it is likely that these features will remain in place for the foreseeable future.

Negotiating Enhanced Redundancy Rights

While the EPCA contains important minimum rights it should be remembered that *improved* rights can be negotiated and established. It obviously makes sense to do this at a time when you (or the union) are in a stronger bargaining position than to try to do it later when redundancy is threatened and the position is weaker.

Although such improved rights are worth pursuing, whether they are agreed collectively or individually, they are unlikely in themselves to guarantee job security and experience shows that they cannot be a substitute for effective collective organisation, or industrial action if this becomes necessary. Nevertheless they can require, among other things:

- regular provision by the employer of *information* on anything which might affect future job levels, such as profitability, plans for new technology and threats to the viability of the business;
- *consultation and other procedural rights* prior to redundancy decisions being made. If collectively agreed redundancy consultation obligations are reinforced by statutory consultation machinery (which is quite possible for public sector workers) it may be possible to go to court to enforce these in a 'judicial review'. This requires evidence of the employer's failure to consult properly to be shown.[6] Such legal action was successful in December 1992 when the High Court ruled that British Coal's pit closure programme was unlawful – principally because of non-consultation and the 'unreasonableness' of the closure plan.
- agreed *limits on redundancy dismissals*, that is, on the circumstances in which jobs can be declared redundant;[7]
- *enhanced compensation* above statutory levels. Recent developments have, unfortunately, restricted the amount of compensation local authorities can pay above the statutory minimum entitlements, given that authorities are legally limited by their statutory powers.

In legal terms enhanced compensation terms are rights which the courts will most readily enforce against an employer.

Statutory Rights[8]

Even if you do not have the benefit of such collectively agreed rights (or individual terms) there are a number of important statutory rights guaranteed by the EPCA. It is essential, though, to check whether you are eligible for these.

In particular, you must be an 'employee' *and* have completed the appropriate period of service with your employer. This has been discussed in chapter 2 above, where you will also be able to see whether you are barred from claiming for any other reason.

In most cases you will also need to show that you have been 'dismissed'. Again, this has already been discussed (pp. 168–70) when looking at unfair dismissal, and the principles are similar. For redundancy purposes you are 'dismissed' if:

- your contract is terminated with or without notice (pp. 163–4);
- your fixed-term contract is not renewed (pp. 167–8);
- you decide to leave (with or without notice) in a situation in which your employer's conduct entitles you to do so (see pp. 163, 183–6);
- your employer's business goes into receivership or liquidation, or he or she dies.

In most cases it should be clear whether you have been dismissed or not, but nevertheless there are some pitfalls to watch out for. Some of these have been discussed before in chapter 14, but in particular:

- avoid making agreements with your employer which might be interpreted later as leaving 'voluntarily' (pp. 169–70);
- if you volunteer for redundancy make sure your employer formally confirms it is a *redundancy* situation, even if you are responding to an invitation by the employer for 'volunteers';
- if you have arranged another job to go to do not jump the gun and leave before the redundancy is confirmed and you are *dismissed*, as this could also be regarded as leaving voluntarily.

When you are dismissed for redundancy you will normally be given notice. If you do not want to work out that notice (or all of it) do *not* just leave. If you do so you risk losing some or all of your redundancy pay. It may be possible to leave earlier, but only if you formally agree with your employer a leaving date, providing the minimum notice period to which you are entitled has actually started.

Excluding Your Claim

Employers may well want to 'contract out' of the redundancy system. In fact it is not possible to do this or to prevent you from claiming your redundancy rights – even where this is provided in your contract. An important exception, however, is where you are on a fixed-term contract of two years or more and have agreed in writing not to claim redundancy pay.

In addition, some collectively agreed schemes may, if approved by a minister, replace the statutory scheme, and in this case your entitlements will be as set out in that scheme. If you are a worker who is covered by such an approved scheme you will still be able to take any dispute you have to a tribunal.

Compensation

The EPCA provides for compensation in the form of a redundancy payment, but in order to qualify the claimant must have been dismissed for 'redundancy'. The Act states that this is where the dismissal is due 'wholly or mainly' to:

- the employer ceasing business; or
- the place of work being moved; or
- the requirements of the business for employees diminishing.

A payment may also be claimed:

- following a period of lay-off or short time; or
- on a transfer, in certain circumstances, of the employer's business.

If your employer refuses to make you a payment (or you think the payment is too small) you can contest that refusal by making a tribunal claim (see p. 256). In this event you would have the initial advantage of a legal presumption that the dismissal was for redundancy – but the claim could still be defeated if it can be shown that the dismissal was for some other reason.

Unfair Dismissal

Before considering redundancy payment claims, it is always necessary to consider any possibilities there may be for claiming unfair dismissal compensation.

This point is always important as compensation levels are generally higher than if the claim is limited to a redundancy payment – and there may also be scope for claiming both a redundancy payment *and* compensation for unfair dismissal. In some situations a dismissal can be deemed to be automatically unfair, for example where the reason is a transfer of the employer's business (see below). Unfair dismissal is discussed in chapter 14 (see specifically on redundancy pp. 216–18), but a redundancy may be unfair where:

(1) You are selected for redundancy because of your membership or proposed membership of an independent trade union; or because of participation in union activities at an 'appropriate time'; or because of reasons relating to non-membership of a union;[9] or

(2) your selection is in breach of a customary arrangement or agreed procedure, and there were no special reasons to justify this;[10] or

(3) your employer has not in the particular circumstances of your case acted reasonably in treating redundancy as a sufficient reason for sacking you. There are different ways in which this is possible, including unfair selection and a failure to follow good industrial relations practices.[11]

The onus of proving that a dismissal was for 'redundancy', and is therefore *prima facie* 'fair', is on the employer.

If you think any of the above possibilities apply you should refer to chapter 14 in this book.

If unfair dismissal does not apply, you are concerned with 'redundancy'. The central provision of the Act concerning redundancy states that a dismissed employee is to be taken as dismissed for redundancy if the dismissal is attributable 'wholly or mainly' to:

(a) the fact that the employer has ceased, or intends to cease, to carry on the business for the purposes of which the employee was employed, or has ceased, or intends to cease, to carry on that business in the place where the employee was so employed; *or*

(b) the fact that the requirements of that business for employees to carry out work of a particular kind, or for employees to carry out work of a particular kind in the place where they were so employed, have ceased or diminished or are expected to cease or diminish.

Employer's Business Ceasing

Closure of an employer's business (or the part of it where the dismissals take place) is a redundancy situation – even if the closure is only temporary. If the closure is due to the business becoming insolvent you should refer to pp. 259–60 here, as there may be problems in obtaining arrears of wages, redundancy pay and the like.

Employers sometimes try to resist paying redundancy pay where closure has followed the taking of industrial action, non-cooperation and so on because they do not think it should be payable in such circumstances. There is no legal justification for this, and if it happens you should promptly put in a claim to the tribunal.

Change of Workplace

If you are employed at a particular location and your employer's business there closes, or your work is no longer needed there, you will usually be entitled to redundancy compensation. If adequate consideration is not given to any scope there may be for employing you elsewhere, for example if there are other employment opportunities in the organisation and these are not adequately explored, there might also be a potential unfair dismissal claim.

Reference should be made to pp. 216–19 of this book, where this point, and other procedural aspects of handling redundancies, are considered further.

Problems also frequently arise where, instead of being made redundant, staff are asked to move to a different location. Such a move may well be unacceptable for a variety of reasons, such as the increased travel time and costs that would be involved, or changes to children's schools. Essentially the problem will centre on your *contractual* rights and obligations.

If the employer's insistence is not based on any contractual authority, for example a 'mobility' clause, there may be scope for a 'constructive dismissal' claim if an attempt is made to require you to move, and you could still be eligible for a redundancy payment. The other side of the coin, though, is that if there *is* such authority a refusal to move may justify your dismissal. The reason for this is that the phrase 'the place where the employee was so employed' in section 81 has been interpreted by the courts as meaning 'where under his/her contract s/he *could be required to work*'.

In one leading case that illustrates this the UK Atomic Energy Authority reserved the right to require its staff to work anywhere in the UK or overseas. One of its draughtsmen, who worked at Orfordness, refused to be transferred to Aldermaston. As under his contract his employment was not just at Orfordness, and because the Authority still had requirements for draughtspeople at its other establishments, it was held that he was not redundant and his claim failed.[12]

It is worth pointing out, though, that even if your employer does have the benefit of a mobility clause or other authority to move you to another location, such contractual rights must be used reasonably. In practice this depends on how the relevant parts of the contract are worded, but it could be held, for example, that the power to require you to move is subject to an implied duty to give you adequate notice and to pay you expenses to do so (see the *Akhtar* case referred to on p. 55).

Assuming that under your contract your employer has no authority to require you to move and the site at which you work closes (or you are no longer needed there), you will be eligible for a redundancy payment unless suitable alternative work at another location is offered and you unreasonably refuse it. Under rules which are explained below (p. 252–4), the tribunal would have to consider any objections you raised to the proposed move before deciding that point.

Diminishing Requirements for Employees

This is the most difficult aspect of the redundancy formula, and in practical terms the most important, and it is concerned with situations where the business has not closed down but where the requirements for labour have, for whatever reason, been reduced or altered. This might occur in a variety of ways, and could range from straight job cut-backs caused by a reduction in the amount of work coming in to the business to rather more complex (and technically contentious) situations – for example, where new technology or changes in work patterns have been introduced.

In some cases a management will readily accept the existence of a 'redundancy' situation on the 'diminished requirements' basis, and pay the appropriate compensation. In other cases it may seek to resist redundancy claims brought under this head – for instance in order to defend the dismissal against an unfair dismissal claim. In this case you will need to make a claim to the tribunal.

What Must be Shown?

Whatever the background to the claim, it will generally be necessary to demonstrate that there has been a clear reduction in the need for the person to undertake work of the particular kind which s/he is employed to do. Redundancy on this basis can generally be established whatever the reasons for the 'diminution', and it can be maintained even if dismissal was anticipated when the employment began, for example where the employment is on a temporary contract.[13] A possibility also exists, under this head of redundancy, for it to be shown that the job has changed so significantly that it could be said to have 'gone'.

The clearest scenario in which redundancy might occur is where a reduction in the amount of work required to be done, or in the number of workers required to perform the work which is available, has prompted an employer to sack workers who could otherwise have been expected to do such work. But *is* there a 'redundancy', or is there some other explanation which could be put forward for the dismissal? As we have already seen when considering constructive dismissal claims (chapter 14) the courts can be extremely sympathetic to employers faced with such claims – for example if they can establish a defence based on 'some other substantial reason', such as the need for a workplace reorganisation (p. 58 above).

Changing the Work Requirements: What Does the Contract Say?

An important consideration in deciding whether there is a diminished need for the kind of work a claimant for redundancy does – and therefore deciding whether a 'redundancy' situation exists – is to look at what the contract says s/he can be required to do.

As we have already seen (pp. 59–61), it can be a particularly difficult situation when your employer requires you to accept a change from what you normally do to other duties. If you go along with imposed changes you may be accepting a substantial deterioration in your conditions. If you do not you risk dismissal if the contract does, in fact, allow the employer to impose such changes.

In the context of redundancy a similar approach to contract principles operates. On one interpretation the introduction of changes by an employer could be regarded as a 'redundancy', as this may well amount to a diminution in the work you would normally be doing. However, the courts will look at the sort of work which under your contract your employer *could* require you to do, even if you would not normally be asked to do such work. The following case illustrates this approach in operation:

Example
Mr Pink was employed at a shoe factory as a making and finishing room operative, but in practice he spent most of his time specifically as a sole layer/pre-sole fitter. While he had been away a trainee had been brought in to carry out sole laying work, and when redundancies were declared Mr Pink was selected rather than that person. His claim for unfair dismissal was rejected, and it was held that he was 'redundant'. The tribunal reached this conclusion on the basis of his formal employment as a making and finishing room operative, and on that basis there had been a diminution in the employers' requirements for such staff. The EAT upheld the decision, saying it was irrelevant that there had been no diminution in the requirements for the sort of work Mr Pink was actually doing.[14]

As we have seen, the courts' approach in applying contractual provisions is now of considerable importance to the whole question of the use of management power. There is clearly now a need for a review of the whole question of employers' power to dictate the terms on which people are employed. Even where there are strong collective bargaining arrangements in operation, the evidence suggests that since the leading redundancy cases established the 'contract' approach employers have become increasingly careful to introduce 'flexibility' requirements into their workers' contracts, thereby putting themselves in a much stronger position to resist redundancy and constructive dismissal claims.

Changing Skill Requirements
When changing skill requirements prompt employers to sack unwanted staff, statutory redundancy pay is rarely an adequate recompense for the inherent unfairness which is often involved. This is particularly so in the case of people with long service, or when workers are forced out to make way for people with different skills.

In one leading case, which illustrates important aspects of the 'diminishing requirements' concept, the employer was trying to establish that the dismissal was due to 'redundancy' and the employee was claiming it was an 'unfair dismissal':

Example
Mr Murphy was a resident plumber at a college and his work included attending to and maintaining the heating system, and assisting with general plumbing work. Changes were made to the heating system, and he was not

technically qualified to deal with all the problems that might arise. He wrote to the employer saying he would refuse to undertake work not undertaken by a plumber, except under certain conditions. These included close supervision and the prior receipt of instructions detailing what was required.[15]

The college's response was to appoint a 'heating engineer' and that person was also expected to do general plumbing work. Mr Murphy was thereupon sacked. The court held that this was not unfair dismissal but a 'redundancy' situation, despite obvious doubts as to how, exactly, a 'diminution' could be said to have occurred. Nevertheless the Court of Appeal has in this case made it clear that tribunals dealing with similar circumstances in the future can, depending on the effects this has on the employer's overall employment requirements, conclude that such a reorganisation or 're-allocation of functions' amounts to a 'redundancy'.

The most negative aspect on redundancy rights which cases like *Murphy* illustrate is how the law allows employers, as part of so-called modernisation programmes, to bring in new staff – over the heads of the existing staff – without having to account for the obvious unfairness which could be caused to the 'redundant' person. It also gives employers the green light to take this easier course rather than, for example, retraining the existing workers or taking other, less convenient, options. There is also an incentive for them to do this if there are savings on wages (and other on-costs) to be made – for example by not having to upgrade, or pay more to, existing staff for the different type of work involved.

Workplace Changes – 'Diminution' or 'Reorganisation'?
The points referred to in the last section beg the question of whether all workplace changes and reorganisations do necessarily amount to 'redundancy'. In fact there is not always such a ready acceptance by the courts of this, particularly when carried out on a collective scale (rather than in individual cases like Mr Murphy's). The central point remains whether there has been either a clear diminution in the work required; or that the job, as it has been reorganised, is different to the point that it can be said that the existing job has been replaced.

The issue has arisen in earlier decisions, and it has frequently appeared that for policy reasons – and in particular a desire not to inhibit management's 'right to manage' – the courts remain extremely reluctant to burden employers with the trouble and expense of meeting redundancy claims in these situations, and thus inhibit change. One, in particular, has remained a bench-mark for this important area of redundancy rights:

Example
Employees were machine maintenance setters who worked in a toy factory where a three-shift system of day, evening and night work was in operation. To cut operating costs the night shift was ended for both the direct workers and the setters. The latter, instead of working a day shift with long overtime

and a night shift, were asked to work a double-day shift on alternate weeks. Among other things this reduced their opportunities to earn overtime pay, which was not fully recompensed despite payment of a shift premium. Some of them were sacked for refusing to accept the changes, and a number of them argued that the changes amounted to a 'redundancy'. The employers were able to show that the amount of work being done since the changes remained the same and it was held by the Court of Appeal, who rejected their claim, that their dismissal was not 'wholly or mainly' due to a diminution in the requirements of the business. A reorganisation of hours did not, in itself, amount to 'redundancy'.[16]

Lord Denning referred to a key passage in an earlier leading case (*Johnson* v. *Nottinghamshire Combined Police Authority* [1974] ICR 170 at 176) when it was said that:

> An employer is entitled to reorganise his business so as to improve its efficiency and, in so doing, to propose to his staff a change in the terms and conditions of their employment: and to dispense with their services if they do not agree. Such a change does not automatically give the staff a right to redundancy payments. It only does so if there is a redundancy situation.

While an *unfair dismissal* claim might sometimes be appropriate in cases of imposed changes, the scope for this will depend on the extent to which the changes impinge on your pay and other contractual rights (see chapters 7 and 14).

Although there are occasional examples of where changes to collective work arrangements have been held to amount to a 'redundancy' on a diminished requirements basis, these are exceptional and can be explained by their special circumstances. This could include, for example, differences in the type of work the change involves.

Example
Macfisheries Ltd decided to end night-shift working and asked Mrs Findlay and other workers to switch to days. However they wanted to work nights for domestic reasons, and it was an accepted point in the case that under their contracts they could not be required to make the change. The IT's decision that night shift work was 'work of a particular kind' and that it had ceased or diminished, thus making her redundant, was upheld by the EAT.[17]

Displacement
If you are replaced by 'contractors' (see pp. 18–21 for the meaning of this) you will normally be able to claim redundancy compensation on the ground that your employer's need for 'employees' has diminished.

Example
Two decorators were dismissed when their employer decided it was cheaper to employ 'self-employed' workers. The employer said this was not a

redundancy situation as the business was actually expanding and the work increasing. Nevertheless it was held that there had been a reduction in the need for 'employees' and they were therefore entitled to redundancy payments.[18]

Displacement by another worker from *within* the organisation whose job has become redundant – a process sometimes called 'bumping' – will, again, entitle you to redundancy pay. But although this has been recognised by the courts, in order to qualify you must still be able to show that the dismissal was the result of a diminution in the employer's work requirements.

Example

Mrs Fay was a teacher who had been employed on four successive short-term contracts, and each time this was to fill a temporary shortfall in the staffing requirements of the department where she had worked. She was dismissed when the last contract was not renewed and claimed both unfair dismissal and a redundancy payment. The redundancy claim was based partly on the fact that another teacher had been brought in from another school where there had been 'overstaffing'. The IT held that the dismissal had *not* been due to redundancy, but was for 'some other substantial reason' (see p. 195, 219–20 above), namely the expiry of her contract. The Court of Appeal, while upholding the 'bumping' principle, decided that she had not lost her job directly as a result of the other teacher's employment, nor on the evidence had it been shown that there had been a diminution in either the school's or the authority's requirements for teachers.[19]

Lay-off/Short-time

The EPCA allows you to claim a redundancy payment if you have been laid off or kept on short time for either four or more consecutive weeks *or* for a series of six or more weeks (of which not more than three are consecutive) within a period of 13 weeks.[20]

To claim you should take the following steps:

- at the end of the periods referred to, and no later than four weeks from then, write to your employer stating you wish to claim a redundancy payment;
- terminate the job by serving at least one week's notice, or, if the notice you are required to give by your contract is longer than that, by giving that longer period of notice;
- your claim can be blocked if it can reasonably be shown that within four weeks of your notice to claim you would be able to work for at least 13 weeks without being laid off or put on short time again;
- in order to do this, however, the employer must have served a written notice on you to contest the claim.

The big problem will often be, of course, in deciding whether to cut your losses and resign or to stay in the hope that things will pick up and you will be able to return to normal working. Serving a notice of claim may help if this prompts your employer to discuss the prospects realistically – and it might also be a useful lever in negotiating financial assistance while the lay-off or short-time continues. No particular form of words is required as long as you make your intention to resign clear.

Transfer of an Employer's Business

Recent years have seen a massive increase in the number and scale of business transfers. For the workers involved this usually means not only a change of employer and management but significant changes in working conditions and enforced redundancies.[21] The EC has said it intends to do more to protect workers' interests in these situations.[22] In the meantime the present rules, including legislation which is supposed to implement current EC measures, can often leave workers in an extremely vulnerable position.

There are three aspects to consider:

- 'continuity' of employment when there is a change of employer
- rules on transfers
- rights on a transfer

Continuity

As already discussed (in chapter 2) a period of continuous employment must be shown before redundancy, unfair dismissal and other rights can be claimed. Normally if your job finishes any rights you have will be exercisable against your employer at that time. Your continuity of service will be broken on termination, and before you can assert rights against any new employer you would normally have to start accruing the appropriate service all over again.

However the EPCA[23] preserves continuity in certain situations, so that any past service will count in the new employment. This will apply:

(a) on trustees or personal representatives taking over from an employer who has died;

(b) on a change of partners if you are employed by a partnership;

(c) on a transfer of your employment to an 'associated employer' (for example another company within a group);

(d) on a change of employer under an Act of Parliament (for example as a result of a privatisation Act);

(e) on a transfer of a trade, business or undertaking from one person to another.

If there is a transfer of the ownership of the business and the new owner offers to renew your contract (or offers a new one), provisions in the EPCA[24] have the effect that, despite your employment ending, you will only be entitled to a redundancy payment if you refuse that offer *and* your refusal is 'reasonable' (see pp. 252–4 below). If you accept the offer point (e) will apply and your continuity of service will be maintained.

Another situation where a redundancy claim is possible (because your employment terminates without continuity being maintained) is where, instead of the entire ownership of the business being sold, the part of the business you are working in is the subject of a so-called 'assets' sale. Here the position is that your contract is treated as terminating, even if you are re-employed at that time.

Example
Mrs Crompton worked at a childrens' clothing factory which, because business was slack, was sold off to another business. However, the company carried on making clothes at other factories. She was immediately re-employed on the same terms by the new owners of the factory. As there had not been a transfer of the business her continuity of service had been broken and she was eligible for redundancy pay.[25]

Since these rules in the EPCA came in the Transfer of Undertakings (Protection of Employment) Regulations 1981 (which were supposed to implement EEC rules to protect workers) have come into operation. These will generally now apply to most transfers, although the rules in the EPCA will still be relevant if the regulations do not apply. As originally enacted the regulations only applied to 'commercial' organisations or businesses. This had the potential effect of excluding workers in non-commercial parts of the economy – government, local government, and so on – from protection when their organisations were transferred or sold off. Non-commercial undertakings are now covered following amendments by the Trade Union Reform and Employment Rights Act 1993 s. 33(2). This change was needed in order to comply with the EC position and the consistently broad interpretation of the Acquired Rights Directive (EEC/77/187) given by the EC Commission and ECJ in deciding whether a 'transfer of an undertaking' has taken place.[26] The point was also illustrated by an important ECJ decision in a Dutch case,[27] when it was held that the withdrawal of a local government subsidy to a drugs rehabilitation organisation, and its reallocation to another organisation, could amount to a 'transfer', thus bringing some of the staff who had been made redundant within the directive's protection.

Whether or not the regulations apply will also depend on the *type* of transaction by which the business is transferred (discussed further below). If they do not apply then workers will not have the protection which they give.

A 'transfer' may, for the regulations to apply, include a transfer of an undertaking effected by a series of transactions, and it is not dependent on property being transferred.[28]

The Rules on Transfers

If the regulations do apply to the transfer they do more than just preserve continuity. Their effect is, once the transfer is completed, to put the transferee employer in the same position as the original employer for most employment purposes.[29] Although it is not possible to set out all the effects of the regulations, the main consequences are, as made clear by the key provision (reg. 5, as amended by TURERA s. 33(4)), that with effect from the transfer:

- except where the employee/s object, employment contracts with the old employer do not terminate at the time of the transfer, but will instead be treated as if they had been originally made with the new employer;
- all the old employer's 'rights, powers, duties and liabilities under or relating to any such contract' are transferred to the new employer;
- anything done in relation to the contract by the old employer before the transfer (including for example breaches of contract or statutory obligations) is to be treated as if done by the new employer.

If an employee does object, the transfer will operate to terminate his/her employment with the transferor, but this will not constitute a 'dismissal'.

Union consultation rights are given in transfer situations and these are strengthened by the Trade Union Reform and Employment Rights Act 1993, s. 33 – although it is not clear that this will fully comply with EC requirements.

Scope of the Regulations

The rights given by the regulations will apply whether the transfer of the undertaking is carried out by a sale of the business, or by any other form of 'disposition'. They extend to a potentially wide range of situations where changes are brought about by governmental action, such as the withdrawal of financial support or subsidies. They will also apply if the transfer occurred by 'operation of law' (which would cover, for example, situations where businesses are transferred under an Act of Parliament).

They also apply to workers:

- in a business which might be regulated by another legal system than the UK's – for instance if the sale was of a UK business to a US company in accordance with US law. Whatever the terms of the sale were the regulations would apply to the UK workers;
- who work for the business but who do not ordinarily work in the UK.

Unfortunately, though, the courts have limited the scope of the regulations and removed workers from their protection in several important ways. In particular, they do not apply where there is just a transfer of 'assets'. There must be a transfer of the business itself, or part of it, as opposed to just a transfer of part of the assets. In a leading case on this point[30] it was said that the former involved a transfer of the business as a going concern 'so that the business remains the same business but in different hands'. The regulations also do not apply to changes in ownership effected by just a share transfer.

Court Action to Prevent Transfers

As an employer's action in transferring a contract to another employer is, on the face of it, a repudiation of the employer's obligations under the contract, could an employee or union get a court order to stop it? This issue arose in 1992 when British Airways hived off part of the company to a subsidiary and simply notified staff of the changes. The TGWU and an employee tried unsuccessfully to get an injunction pending court action where the issue could be considered. The Court of Appeal ruled[31] that the effect of regulation 5 of the regulations overrode any rights an employee might have had at common law and provided for a statutory change of employers. Nor, on the evidence, had any proposals relating to the transfer shown a breach of the implied duty of good faith by British Airways which could, in some circumstances, be restrained by injunction.

Which Employer is Liable – the Transferor or Transferee?

In theory this question ought not to raise any problem, as the policy objective of the legislation was to try to maintain the rights of any workers who have been employed by a transferor as a result of a transfer. In practice, however, the issue has been turned into yet another limitation on the operation of the regulations, and a potential pitfall for workers caught up in transfer situations.

The problem, put simply, is at what point in time before the transfer actually takes place must the employees be in the transferor's employment before they can come within the transfer rules in regulation 5 referred to above?

The language in regulation 5 (3) suggests that this is, in fact, limited to anyone who is 'employed immediately before the transfer' – and if the transfer is carried out in stages, for example if there is more than one transaction involved, it will apply to anyone who was employed immediately before any of those stages.

At first sight, then, this restriction seems to exclude any workers who are employed earlier than the point which is 'immediately before' the precise moment of transfer.

Of course this interpretation would clearly be a licence to evade the rules – for instance where an insolvent employer arranges with the transferee to sack the workers before the transfer takes place, thus removing any responsibilities on the transferee and leaving the workers with a worthless claim against the insolvent employer.

In an earlier case this was exactly the interpretation that was adopted, with the Court of Appeal saying that the regulations could *only* apply to people employed at the exact moment of transfer.

Fortunately the full impact of this decision has now been averted by a 1989 judgement of the House of Lords in *Litster and Others* v. *Forth Dry Dock & Engineering Co Ltd* – a case which illustrates the threat that transfers and related corporate transactions can pose to workers' rights.

The case concerned 12 shipworkers employed by Forth Dry Dock (FDC), who were summarily sacked when the company went into receivership and who were thereupon told that no funds could be 'made available' for wages, outstanding holiday pay or pay in lieu of notice. A few hours later on the same day the company's assets were acquired by Forth Estuary (FE), a new company set up by people previously involved in the running of FDC, which immediately started recruiting workers (but not the dismissed workers).

As pointed out later by one of the judges in the Lords (at p. 167) FE very soon had a workforce the size of FDC, employed on similar trades but at lower rates of pay. The same judge also referred to 'one of the less creditable aspects of the matter'. When the shop steward had tried to get information about the transfer he was told by a director of FDC (who was also, by then, involved in FE) that he knew nothing about a new company taking over, and by a representative of the receivers that 'he knew nothing about a company called Forth Estuary Engineering' (ibid). This was described by the judge as a 'calculated disregard' of the workers' rights to information and to be consulted under regulation 10 of the regulations.

At the industrial tribunal the shipworkers claimed they had been unfairly dismissed, but FE denied they were liable as the workers were not employed 'immediately' before the transfer. Any responsibility for them, they argued, remained with FDC. The tribunal ruled against FE on this point and then went on to decide that:

- the dismissals had been automatically unfair (see the section on rights on a transfer below) as they had obviously been connected with the transfer;
- even had the dismissals been for 'economic, technical or organisational' reasons (which could have given the employers a way out under reg. 8 (2)), the dismissals had still been unfair because they had been carried out unfairly.

The issue then went to three further stages of appeal, culminating in the House of Lords ruling.

The EAT said that the IT was wrong to say that the dismissal was not for an 'economic, technical or organisational' reason. As it was caused by FDC's closure it was 'economic'. Nevertheless, the EAT agreed that the dismissal was unfair in terms of s. 57 (3) – the 'reasonableness' requirement – as it had been unnecessary to sack the workers for redundancy.

The Scottish Court of Session reversed this, saying there had not been a 'transfer' as the employees had not been employed at the moment of transfer (applying *Spence*), and therefore FE should not have been held responsible.

The House of Lords overturned this and, in doing so, has now established the ground rules which will apply to transfers of this kind. These are that:

- if workers are dismissed by the transferor employer prior to the transfer for a reason which is connected with the transfer, they must be treated as if they were still employed at the time of transfer;
- the regulations are therefore to be applied to any worker who was *either* employed immediately before the transfer *or* who would have been employed at that time had s/he not been unfairly dismissed for a reason connected with the transfer;
- transferees will be responsible for unfair dismissals unless they can be shown to be for an 'economic, technical or organisational' reason entailing a change in the workforce;
- the *Spence* principle will, in future, only apply if the reason for the dismissal is unconnected with the transfer, and in such cases liability will remain with the transferor up until the moment of transfer.

In the *Litster* case itself the Lords concluded that there had been no legitimate 'economic, technical or organisational' reasons for the dismissals, and the workers had not been 'redundant'. FE therefore was liable for the unfair dismissals.

Unfortunately it is unlikely that the *Litster* decision will be the end of the story. There are still significant divergences between UK law and EC law. For example EC law appears to treat workers as continuing in employment, despite a dismissal in *Litster*-type situations, thereby protecting their employment unless and until the transferee properly terminates it.[32]

Rights on a Transfer

(a) *Contractual rights.* If the regulations apply it follows from regulation 5 that all rights you have under any contract you have had with the transferor business will become enforceable against the new business. Similarly, the new business could enforce any obligations you owed under that contract against you.

> *Example*
> You are employed under a five-year 'service agreement' (see p. 42) and at the time of the transfer you still have three years of it left to run. If it is terminated after the transfer, for example because you are 'no longer required', you would be able to sue the transferee employer for damages for loss of the earnings, entitlements and so on that you would have received had the contract continued (as well possibly being entitled to redundancy payment compensation and compensation for infringement of other statutory rights).

As well as the transferee being liable for its own actions after the transfer the transferee can also be responsible for actions of the business *prior* to the transfer (reg. 5 [2] [b]).

(b) *'Unfair' dismissals.* If the regulations apply to the transfer, a dismissal (including a 'constructive' dismissal where, for example changes are forced on you) will be automatically unfair if the transfer – or a reason connected with it – is the principal reason for it (reg. 8 [1]). A practical example of this was seen in the *Litster* case discussed in the section above.

Employers can, however, take advantage of an exemption which drives a coach and horses through this right, namely if they can show that the dismissal was for an 'economic, technical or organisational reason entailing changes in the workforce of either the transferor or the transferee before or after a relevant transfer ...' (reg. 8 [2]).

As long as the employer can bring the reorganisation, changes and so on within the terms of this exemption and has otherwise acted 'reasonably', particularly in relation to the 'fairness' requirement (s. 57 [3] – see p. 000) an unfair dismissal claim can be blocked.

(c) *Redundancy compensation.* Even if the employer can successfully avoid an unfair dismissal claim a redundancy payment may still be payable as long as the conditions for obtaining this, as already considered, are met.

> *Example*
> Mr Jenkinson worked as a mechanic for Feastcroft Ltd (F Ltd), and the owners were a couple who also owned Gorictree Ltd (G Ltd). F Ltd was then sold to one of the couple. Six days later G Ltd started to trade and offered Mr Jenkinson a contract on a 'self-employed' basis. Although his dismissal was treated as being for an 'economic, technical or organisational' reason entailing a change in the workforce, and was not unfair, he was still held to be entitled to a redundancy payment on the basis that there had been a diminution in the requirements for employees.[33]

Disqualification and Offers of Alternative Employment

All the rules on disqualification (as discussed below) apply to 'transfer' redundancies. In particular the rules where offers of suitable employment are made will be relevant. This is because the new employer may well make such offers as part of a reorganisation within a short time of taking over the firm's management. If new working arrangements or different terms are required by the new employer there will be an opportunity for a statutory trial period (see below).

In the transfer context an important priority for the new employer will often be to 'standardise' working conditions and other arrangements between existing staff and the new workers who have been 'transferred in'. In this situation there is obviously considerable scope for disagreement if the new terms and conditions, or other arrangements, are worse or different than those that previously operated.

An important defect in the existing legislation is that it does not guarantee that the conditions of the workers being brought in to the business will, necessarily, be brought into line with conditions of workers doing comparable work in the transferee business (or vice versa). In many cases significant differences can remain long after the transfer has taken place. The present rules effectively allow employers to decide whether, and to what extent, assimilation in those conditions is to take place.[34] There are also due to be EC proposals on this and on supranational collective agreements affecting workers in different parts of an enterprise.

Disqualification from Entitlement

There are several ways in which entitlement to redundancy compensation may be lost, and each of these must be considered.

Offers of Renewal of Contract: Re-engagement

You could be disqualified from receiving compensation if your employer, before your employment is due to end, offers to renew your contract or engage you on new terms – and that employment would begin either immediately on the ending of the existing contract, or within four weeks.[35] For this bar to operate, however, the new job offered must either be on the same terms as you already have or, if they are different, the new job must be suitable. In this context 'suitable' means suitable in respect of the specific terms on which it is offered *and* in relation to any other personal considerations which are relevant. This is what is meant in the Act by 'suitable in relation to the employee'.

An unreasonable refusal of such an offer, whether it is made by your employer, by an associated employer (such as another company in the same group of companies) or from a new owner of the business, will normally disqualify you.

Although such offers are not required to be in writing it is always safer to ask the employer to confirm all the relevant details in writing. This will serve as a record in case of any arguments over what was actually offered. It can, in fact, work to an employer's disadvantage not to co-operate over this as a tribunal could take into account any uncertainties you had about the offer in deciding if refusal was unreasonable.

If the offer is to keep you on the *same* terms it will usually be very difficult to justify a refusal without good reasons. Another important consideration is that it is not usually possible to argue that the new job would involve changes which you would find difficult to adapt to if what is proposed is something which could have been required under your existing contract.

A proposal to re-engage on *different* terms obviously puts you into a stronger position to reject the offer or to negotiate better terms. The difficulty with this, though, is that tribunals are given a considerable amount of discretion in deciding whether the job offer amounted to suitable alternative employment, and whether the refusal was otherwise reasonable in the circumstances. Unfortunately it is not possible to lay down any hard and fast rules as to what sort of changes you might rely on to justify refusal, although significant changes to things like job responsibility and status, earnings and the opportunity to enhance basic earnings, and more demanding travelling requirements, have been held to constitute good reasons.

Example

Gloucestershire County Council, as part of a cost-cutting exercise, reduced the number of its school cleaners and cut the hours of the remaining staff. This, it was accepted, meant reduced standards of cleanliness, and some of the remaining workers (who had been offered new terms) said they could not do a satisfactory job given the reduction in staff. The Court of Appeal held that this was something an IT could take into account in considering their refusal. It added that although there were usually two issues which ITs had to consider, which could be categorised under the headings of suitability of the job offered in relation to the employee and the reasonableness of the employee in refusing the offer – a distinction developed in earlier cases – there is not always such a rigid distinction between the two questions in practice, and some objections which people raised could be relevant to both questions.[36]

Trial Period

If you are offered renewed employment, or a new contract, on different terms you have a statutory right to a trial period of four calendar weeks in that new job.[37] If the statutory period is 'refused' or not properly confirmed when the new job is offered there may be scope for an unfair dismissal claim.[38] A longer period for retraining purposes may be agreed if a contract is agreed before work begins.

During the trial period you (or your employer, for reasons relating to the contract) may decide to terminate the employment. If this does happen – or notice is given which leads to eventual termination – you will generally be regarded as having been dismissed on the date your previous contract ended and for the reasons for which you were dismissed (or would have been dismissed) at that time;[39] note that there may be an *additional* 'reasonable period' added prior to the statutory period if you have been constructively dismissed.[40] If you are later adjudged by a tribunal to have terminated the trial period 'unreasonably' the penalty is that you can lose your redundancy pay.

If the employer terminates unjustifiably, or forces you to leave, the reason for which you were originally dismissed (or would have been dismissed) – that is, redundancy, 'some other substantive reason', or similar – does not automatically operate. The way is therefore clear in this event to claim unfair dismissal. For example in one case[41] the employer claimed the employee had to be dismissed because of 'unsuitability'. It was held that an unfair dismissal claim for unfairness was possible.

Dismissal for Misconduct: Industrial Action

Obviously if employers can dismiss for misconduct rather than for redundancy they may try to do so, as this will avoid having to pay redundancy pay. The position is, however, affected by the EPCA,[42] where redundancy is in the offing or has already been formally notified. The exact position will depend on whether you are sacked *before* the obligatory statutory period of redundancy notice has begun or *during* that period.

If the dismissal takes place before the notice period has begun the employer, in order to take advantage of the disentitlement provisions, must dismiss without notice or by reduced notice. If notice is to be 'worked out' a written statement explaining that you *could* have been dismissed without notice must be provided.

Dismissal during the obligatory period may result in disqualification of all, or just some, of the payment depending on what a tribunal decides is 'just and equitable'. It could decide that the dismissal was justified but that only a partial reduction should be made. For example it was held in one case[43] that 40 per cent of the compensation which would otherwise have been due should be withheld for stealing the employer's property after notice was given.

Strikes are treated in employment law as a form of 'misconduct' by the workers involved. This means that a strike prior to notice of dismissal being given will usually entitle the employer to dismiss and redundancy payments will therefore be immediately forfeited.[44]

If you are sacked for striking *after* notice of dismissal for redundancy has been given the right to a redundancy payment is preserved[45] – although the employer would be able to terminate the contract immediately. There are also provisions[46] whereby an employer can recoup any lost time due to the action taken. This involves serving a 'notice of extension' demanding an additional period to be worked to make up for time lost, and warning that the redundancy entitlement will be contested if it is not complied with. Non-compliance would result in either disqualification or a reduced award.

Fighting Redundancy by Industrial Action

There are obvious pitfalls in taking industrial action amounting to a strike before any notice of redundancy/ies has been issued, for example when a management's decision is known and in an attempt to exert pressure to get that decision reversed. This was, no doubt, deliberately included in the legislation, and it creates a dilemma for many workers. Do you fight a decision before it is formally notified (and thereby risk forfeiture)? Or do you abandon what may be the only effective response to the threatened redundancy there may be?

After Redundancy Notice is Given – the Steps to Take

Time Off

Once you have been given notice of redundancy you should take advantage of your right to take reasonable time off to look for other work and for retraining.[47]

You are entitled to be paid for this at the 'appropriate rate', but as long as you are paid your normal pay while you are off this will satisfy the employer's obligations. The exact amount of time you can get is a matter for agreement, although this is something which may already be dealt with in your contract or in a collective agreement. The only sanction if time off is refused or you are not paid is to go to the IT, which can award up to two days pay.

Making a Claim for Redundancy Pay

Eligibility to make a claim has already been referred to above, and here we outline the steps to be taken to present the claim. You should, of course, ask for the advice and support of your union, or obtain advice from a CAB, law centre or solicitor if you are in any doubt about eligibility, what your claim is worth, or other aspects of a claim.

The key section of the EPCA is s. 101 and this says that within six months of the 'relevant date'[48] you *must* have either:

(a) agreed and been paid a redundancy payment; *or*
(b) claimed a payment from the employer in writing; *or*
(c) made a claim to the IT which either relates to your eligibility or the amount you think you are entitled to ; *or*
(d) made an unfair dismissal complaint to the IT. In this case the IT can deal with the complaint and your claim for a payment at the same time.

An extension of up to six months may be allowed, but this is exceptional and depends on how good your reason is for missing the deadline.

Claims should be made against the receiver or liquidator if the business has become insolvent. If the business has been transferred to a new employer a claim should normally be made against that employer rather than your former employer. If in any doubt about who to make a claim against you should claim against both and let the tribunal decide which is appropriate. If 'all reasonable steps' have been taken to recover payment from the employer but it has not been paid, or if the employer is insolvent and it remains unpaid, an application can be made for payment out of the government's National Insurance Fund.[49]

Filling in Form IT1 (the form used to present industrial tribunal claims) is discussed in chapter 22 below, and in redundancy cases you can obtain further advice from your local ACAS office.

Calculating the Payment

Information about the rules governing redundancy payments and their calculation can be obtained from Department of Employment offices, and is contained in the Department's booklet[50] available on request.

Basically, the payment is calculated by reference to the 'week's pay' formula in schedule 14 to the EPCA. The exact payment will then depend on how much that week's pay amounts to (up to a maximum limit which in 1993/4 is £205 but which is reviewed by the secretary of state each year), and on the employee's age. For each year of service that you were aged between 41 and 64 you receive one and a half week's pay; for each year you were aged between 22 and 40 you receive one week's pay; for each year you were aged between 18 and 21 you receive half a week's pay.

In calculating the payment you can include overtime pay if this is something the employer must provide under your contract. Any 'remuneration' paid under your contract can be included in the calculation, that is you can include other payments such as bonuses as long as these are entitlements. Expenses, and 'perks' such as the value of a car are not included.

The employer is required to provide a written statement of how the payment has been calculated; advice should be obtained if potential items have been excluded, or if there are doubts about the method of computation used. In practice, the statutory redundancy scheme's limitations are ridiculously low, and this has prompted employers to negotiate improved arrangements in collective agreements and to pay enhanced benefits to workers dismissed for redundancy.

Collective Redundancies

As a result of EC legislation in the mid-1970s, the Employment Protection Act 1975,[51] gave unions rights to be consulted when employers propose to make redundancies. The procedures, are now in TULR(C)A, ss. 188–98, as amended by TURERA, s. 34. They only apply if a union is recognised by an employer (as to 'recognition' see chapter 19 below).

The key provision is s. 188. This states that an employer proposing to dismiss as redundant 'an employee of a description in respect of which an independent trade union is recognised by him', shall consult with that union's representatives. Consultation must begin at the earliest opportunity, and in any event begin:

- at least 90 days before the first dismissal takes effect if 100 or more employees are to be made redundant at one establishment;
- at least 30 days before the first dismissals take place where it is proposed to dismiss 10 or more employees at one establishment.

No specific timetable is set for dismissals of less than 10 staff.

An employer must disclose in writing details including the reasons for the proposals, the numbers of staff proposed for dismissal, and the method of calculating redundancy compensation:

- the total number of any such employees of any such description employed at the establishment in question;

- the proposed method of selecting employees for dismissal;
- the proposed method of carrying out the dismissals, with due regard to any agreed procedure, including the period over which the dismissals are to take effect.

Consultation must, among other things, cover ways of avoiding dismissals, reducing the numbers of staff affected, and mitigating the consequences. It must be undertaken with a view to reaching agreement.

The employer is required to consider the union's representations and must reply to them. If they are rejected reasons must be given. There is a possible defence, if the consultation requirements are not met, if the employer can show that compliance was not 'reasonably practicable'. An example of this would be a company suddenly going into receivership.

There are some important problems in the practical operation of these procedures, not least of which is the uncertainty about *when* an employer is required to tell the union that the redundancies are proposed. Arguably this is not until the employer has decided that redundancies will definitely be necessary and has determined a timetable for dismissals. In this case consultation may be too late to have much effect on the process. Nor is it clear how much notice an employer needs to take of representations, to satisfy the rules. As several EAT decisions have made clear, the policy considerations on which redundancy decisions are based, and the decisions themselves, remain a management responsibility despite the consultation requirements. On the other hand cases have also made it clear that the consultation process should not be a 'sham' as, for example, where redundancy notices were issued shortly after representatives were formally notified of the redundancies.[52]

Failure to Consult

A failure to consult, or consult properly, entitles the union to make a complaint to an industrial tribunal. The tribunal can make a 'protective award' (ss. 189–92), that is, an award of remuneration for the employees affected for a 'protected' period. The claim must normally be made before the proposed dismissal takes effect, or within three months of the dismissal taking effect. The award can be for a maximum of 90 days' pay (in the case of redundancies of 100 or more employees); 30 days' pay (for 10 or more redundancies); and 28 days' pay in any other case. Individual employees can take enforcement action to recover the pay if it is not paid.

Although non-consultation with the union may be a relevant factor if you are claiming unfair dismissal, in formal terms the main consequence is a claim for a protective award (s. 188[8]). In practice, though, the issue of an employer's conduct may well be considered by the tribunal in the general context of procedural fairness.

Rights on Insolvency

There are a number of ways in which a company can be put out of business or affected by insolvency. Broadly speaking, insolvency means either that a company is going into liquidation (either voluntarily or compulsorily); or that a 'receiver' has been appointed; or that an 'administration' order has been made under which an administrator has taken over the running of the company for the time being. It can also mean an 'arrangement' has been made, for example to satisfy the company's creditors. In the case of individuals running a company the equivalent of corporate insolvency is bankruptcy (or in Scotland, 'sequestration').

Most insolvency procedures are bad news for employees. In the first place employees have little or no rights in the insolvency process, unlike shareholders and creditors. Apart from being wrong in principle, as employees have usually made an important contribution to a company, this treatment is inconsistent given that they are a form of 'creditor' with rights in respect of matters like outstanding pay, pension rights and possibly a variety of other claims on the company. To some extent this is recognised by giving employees 'preferential creditor' status (ranking with, for example, the tax and VAT authorities and ahead of unsecured creditors). But despite this employees are still in a vulnerable position and claims are often not settled until after long delays. As far as employment is concerned, there may be scope for continued or alternative employment depending on what course the insolvency takes and whether the business continues in some form or other, or is purchased by a new owner. In general terms it is a period of great uncertainty and insecurity for employees.

If during the course of the insolvency procedure you are made redundant, a redundancy claim can be made against the liquidator, receiver or equivalent. If there are problems in obtaining payment a claim can be made on the National Insurance Fund as previously discussed. There might, however, be other claims for debts which might not have been settled.

The EPCA, ss. 122–7, establishes minimum rights and enables claims to be made on the National Insurance Fund for certain debts. These include:

- arrears of pay up to a statutory weekly limit and in respect of a maximum period of eight weeks. This includes such things as overtime pay owed, any commission earned and guarantee payments (relevant if you were previously on short-time working);
- holiday pay up to a limit of six weeks and subject to a maximum limit;
- compensation for not getting the proper statutory notice;
- unpaid 'basic award' made by a tribunal for unfair dismissal.

If an insolvent employer has not paid contributions into an occupational pension scheme, the Department of Employment may make up shortfalls to cover the unpaid amounts.[53] Scheme administrators will usually be responsible for ensuring scheme funds are maintained in this way.

Claiming Debts

Claims for arrears of pay or other debts should be made to the receiver, liquidator, trustee or eqivalent, and this should be done on Forms IP1 and IP2. It is then usually necessary, before payment is made, to sign a statement agreeing to transfer any rights you have to the secretary of state for employment. If payment is refused or is insufficient, a complaint can be made to an industrial tribunal.

Further information can be obtained from Department of Employment Redundancy Payments Offices, and guidance is in 'Employees' Rights on Insolvency of Employer' (DE booklet PL 718).

PART FIVE

Health and Safety

CHAPTER 16

Health, Safety and the Work Environment

The right to a working environment which is safe and free from risks to health is one of the most important aspects of modern employment rights. In this chapter we consider the specific ways in which the law deals with health and safety issues.

As with most other areas of employment, the establishment and maintenance of good standards of health and safety in the workplace are more readily achieved where there is a joint approach between employer and staff. In the modern context this means using any recognised trade union arrangements and by means of the safety representative and safety committees system which is provided for in the legislation.

Historically, health and safety issues have always been a key element in the role of trades unions, both at a workplace level and as an issue on which unions have campaigned for more legislation.[1] Unfortunately, health and safety has been an area which has suffered as part of the general weakening of union organisation, and also as a result of changes in employment patterns, leaving groups like temporary, part-time and 'self-employed' workers particularly vulnerable.

The Health and Safety at Work Act 1974 ('HSAWA')

The mid-1970s saw significant policy and legislative changes. In particular, the Health and Safety at Work Act 1974 laid down a series of minimum requirements for employers and provided an 'enabling' scheme whereby more detailed regulations on specific processes could be progressively introduced. Not all employers took kindly to the new legal regime, in particular those aspects which they saw as impinging on managerial prerogative – for example, being told to produce policy statements detailing their management structures, and the arrangements for implementing their legal responsibilities. Nor did they like other features of the Act, such as the new Health and Safety Executive (HSE) inspectors' powers to issue 'improvement' and 'prohibition' notices. Both these developments, and the other measures in the legislation, signalled important improvements in health and safety law. On the other hand the system introduced in 1974 contained (and still contains) important weaknesses. Many of the duties on employers are limited by the proviso 'so far as is reasonably practicable'. In effect, this can provide a let out for employers who can argue that the trouble, time and possibly costs, involved in dealing with a problem are not justified given the scale of the risk involved. Such an approach, involving, as it does, taking a 'cost-benefit' yardstick to safety measures, pre-dated the Act.[2] Also, in many areas of risk detailed requirements have not been put into legislation, in the Act or in regulations, but have been dealt with, if at all, in official 'guidance' or in codes of practice. This is made worse by the courts' reluctance to see the Act's 'general duties' used as a spring-board to extend employers' responsibilities.

Other difficulties have been due, not to the legislation itself, but to failures of enforcement. It had always been clear from the outset that to tackle health and safety issues effectively would require government commitment to provide adequate resources to enforcement agencies and in particular to increase the staffing levels of the HSE and its inspectorate. This has never happened on the scale that has been needed. This has been due, in part, to a combination of cost-saving policies and a preference for 'self-regulation' rather than official enforcement activity. In this way health and safety has become a casualty of the 'deregulation' process discussed in chapter 1 above.

The 1980s was clearly a stand-still period, both in terms of the failure to extend the scope and intensity of legislative requirements in areas where this has clearly been required, and in official unwillingness to take enforcement action against companies breaking the rules. This policy was facilitated by deregulatory measures signalled in a series of White Papers and Department of Employment documents.[3] One aspect of that policy was to single out small companies, that is, workplaces of 20 or less people, and remove requirements such as the duty to produce company health and safety statements. Yet it is often in such small organisations that the worst standards are to be found. The effects of government action in this period can be seen from the worsening statistics on fatal accidents and injuries, particularly in high-risk areas like construction work, North Sea Oil operations, and agricultural work.[4] As far as general accident statistics are concerned the director-general of the HSE admitted to the House of Commons Employment Select Committee that the number of workplace accidents had reached a 'disturbing and stubborn plateau'. Recession had, he said, led to an erosion of the safety infrastructure with employers cutting corners and not investing in safety.[5]

EC Policies

EC initiatives in the health and safety field have already resulted in a number of important changes and new policy directions for the 1990s. The pivotal legislation is the 'Framework' Directive[6] setting out in general terms employers' responsibilities, including the planning, organisational and monitoring requirements which are seen as essential prerequisites to raising workplace safety standards. More detailed aspects are discussed below.

The rights of UK workers have, however, suffered a potentially major setback as a result of the UK's opt out from the Maastricht Treaty on political union (discussed in chapter 1). The Social Chapter, which is part of the treaty, extends the scope of qualified majority voting (QMV) to facilitate legislation in a much wider area of employment rights. These include health and safety, and the working environment. The UK government's refusal to co-operate in agreeing even watered-down proposals resulted in the position that from 1 January 1993 the other member states will be able to legislate on health and safety using the new procedures. Legislation made in this way will not, however, be binding on the UK and UK employers.

The UK will, though, be required to implement existing legislation including health and safety rules made under the Social Action Programme. Although the position is uncertain because of threatened court action by the UK government, the UK will also be bound, despite Maastricht, by legislation made under existing QMV procedures that apply to a more limited range of health and safety issues that can be made under art. 118a of the Rome Treaty.

Employers' Contractual Duties

As a matter of contract an employer may have both express and implied duties in relation to the working environment. Express responsibilities can, and do, frequently derive from collective arrangements negotiated with unions; examples being the provision of rest periods for staff using visual display units (VDUs), safety training, or the supply of protective wear. Depending on the nature of the work and any special risks involved, it may also be possible to argue successfully that there are implied obligations to be performed by the employer, or that there are limitations on what you should be asked to do. Excessive demands for overtime working, or requiring long hours doing stressful work, could fall into this category.

Example
Junior hospital doctors' contracts required them to work 40 hours a week and to be 'available' for a further 48 hours a week on average. A doctor sued the employer, a health authority, on the basis that it was not taking reasonable care for his safety and well-being. In particular it was requiring him to work intolerably long hours and this was causing him stress and depression. He also argued the contract was void as being contrary to 'public policy', that is, it was not in the public interest.

The Court of Appeal held that, although the contract did allow the authority to require such overtime the power to do so had to be exercised in a way that did not injure its employees. In other words, the express contractual powers of an employer must be read subject to implied limitations on how those powers can be used. If the facts of a case showed an employment contract was *not* being operated fairly then the employer would be in breach of that duty. The court refused, however, to entertain the other part of the claim as issues like inadequate funding of the health service were more appropriate for Parliament rather than the courts to consider.

In the course of the judgement it was said that the duty in this case was no different from the duty owed to a factory worker not to expose him/her to noxious fumes. The exact scope of the employer's duty could vary depending on the particular employee's physical strength or weakness. The authority's lawyer argued that it could not be expected to treat its staff differently 'according to their physical stamina'. The court disagreed. The duty employers owe *is* a 'personal' one. Giving the example of back problems it observed that: 'If employers know, or ought to know, that a workman has a vulnerable back they are in breach of duty in requiring him to lift and move weights which are likely to cause him injury even if a normal man can carry them without risk.'[7]

In earlier cases it has been established that employers are not entitled, as a matter of contract, to require you to do things which can jeopardise your health and safety, for example by instructing you to go to a country where your personal safety is at risk.[8] It is also arguable that employees have an implied contractual right not to be subject to smoke from other employees' smoking. Employers are increasingly introducing smoking bans and restrictions; as long as this is done fairly, disciplinary and dismissal action can be taken against people who ignore these. In one case a constructive dismissal claim failed when an employee unsuccessfully argued that he had an implied 'right to smoke'.[9]

Employers' Other Duties

The health and safety system makes employers responsible in other ways and makes them potentially liable to criminal, administrative and civil sanctions.

The starting point is that employers are legally responsible for what happens on their premises, for deficiencies in the workplace environment and for failures in their organisational and management systems. Although workers must co-operate in carrying out statutory requirements and must take reasonable care of themselves and others at the workplace,[10] the employer is given and cannot transfer responsibility for (or otherwise get out of) the key general duty by HSAWA, which is: 'to ensure, so far as is reasonably practicable, the health, safety and welfare at work of all his employees.'[11]

HSAWA duties are reinforced by legislation *deeming* the employer to be liable in certain situations, for example where workers are injured because of defective equipment, and the defect was the supplier's fault (Employers' Liability [Defective Equipment] Act 1969).

Employers are responsible at several levels for maintaining a safe working environment. If standards are below what is required, or an accident occurs, they will be subject to criminal or enforcement action by the HSE, local authority, or possibly other enforcement agencies (for example HM Pollution Inspectorate if an incident involves a wider threat to the environment). In addition, a worker can claim compensation in a civil action on the basis of the employer's civil duties (in particular for failure to provide a safe place of work or systems of work),[12] or for breach of a statutory duty where compensation is appropriate.

Employers are required by law to take out insurance to cover their liability for personal injury to their staff. They are criminally liable if they fail to do so (Employers' Liability [Compulsory Insurance] Act 1969). This is an important requirement and provides workers with a safety net against workplace injuries when an employer may not be able to afford compensation. On the other hand courts have criticised the inadequacy and limitations of policies, and it is worth checking the exact scope of workplace policies and insisting on improvements if they are inadequate.

Although insurance has to some extent helped, adequate compensation for accidents or occupational illness may depend on establishing fault on the employer's part. The difficulties and delays in doing this have been much criticised and the position was not helped when the Pearson Commission on civil liability and personal injuries compensation failed to recommend any significant changes.[13]

Overview

A summary of health and safety responsibilities is illustrated in Fig. 16.1 overleaf. This shows an employer's duties on the left, and the legal sanction/remedy on the right.

In the rest of this chapter we will consider in more detail the two most important areas of health and safety, namely HSAWA duties and rights; and employers' duty of care and compensation.

Employers' responsibilities in relation to fire hazards are generally set out in the Fire Precautions Act 1971 and related legislation and regulations (although HSAWA general duties to ensure employees' health and safety will still apply). Most workplaces will be subject to local fire authority inspection and certification.

HSAWA Duties and Rights

When Parliament passed the Health and Safety at Work Act in 1974 the intention was to get rid of much of the existing factories and other legislation. In particular

Figure 16.1: Health and Safety Responsibilities

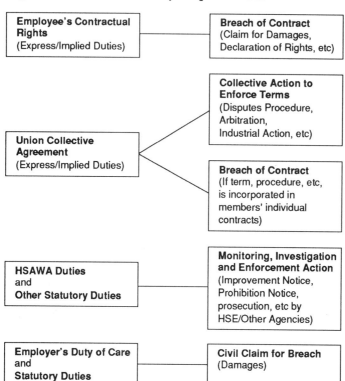

the Factories Act 1961, containing important legislation affecting employers' duties as occupiers of workplaces, fencing and guarding of dangerous machinery and so on, which has been a basis of compensation claims for breach of statutory duty, is being progressively repealed.[14] Regulations made under the HSAWA set out more specific standards to supplement the general legal requirements that HSAWA lays down. Those regulations deal with particular processes and workplace health and safety problems.[15] Codes of Practice containing 'practical guidance' can be issued and although a breach of them will not in itself render an employer liable, it could be important in establishing a contravention of the Act or Regulations (HSAWA, s. 17).

Enforcement and Civil Liability

A breach of the Act's general duties (as summarised below), and in most cases the regulations, will be a criminal offence, enforceable by the HSE or local authority. A breach of the regulations, but *not* the general duties in the Act, may also be grounds for *civil* proceedings for compensation if injury and damage are caused (HSAWA, s. 47 [1], [2]). Civil claims for damages if an employer breaches the 'duty of care' are also still a possibility (see below).

HSAWA: General Duties

Part I (ss. 1–9) of the Act is the most important part of the Act. Among other things it makes it clear that the scope of an employer's duties can go beyond employees and apply to other people. This will include workers on the site (such as visiting contractors) and people in the local community – for example by not exposing them to risks as a result of the way the undertaking is conducted (HSAWA, s. 3).[16]

The key requirement in s. 2 is the duty of: 'every employer to ensure, so far as is reasonably practicable, the health, safety and welfare at work of all his employees.' The section then goes on to specify the particular matters to which that duty extends. These include in particular:

(a) the provision and maintenance of plant and systems of work that are, so far as is reasonably practicable, safe and without risks to health;
(b) arrangements for ensuring, so far as is reasonably practicable, safety and absence of risks to health in connection with the use, handling, storage and transport of articles and substances;
(c) the provision of such information, instruction, training and supervision as is necessary to ensure, so far as is reasonably practicable, the health and safety at work of the employees;
(d) so far as is reasonably practicable as regards any place of work under the employer's control, the maintenance of it in a condition that is safe and without risks to health, and the provision and maintenance of means of access to and egress from it that are safe and without such risks;
(e) the provision and maintenance of a working environment for employees that is, so far as is reasonably practicable, safe, without risks to health, and adequate as regards facilities and arrangements for their welfare at work.

By way of comment on s. 2, General Duties, it must be said that their scope and enforcement largely depends on the extent to which enforcement agencies are prepared to use them in particular situations, and for particular purposes. In the absence of detailed regulations on specific matters, the ability to use the general duties flexibly and in response to the needs of particular workplace situations will be crucial to the Act's success. This point is recognised as important in the promotion of proactive workplace health and safety policies.[17] The Act's effectiveness will also depend on how far the courts and tribunals will allow them to be used, for example, in relation to workplace environment issues like smoking or employee behaviour and violence. Employees' rights to a safe working environment, for instance protective measures against violent fellow workers, might, in some circumstances, be recognised through the operation of implied contractual duties, or the 'duty of care' employers owe staff (see below). But there has, however, been judicial reluctance on several occasions to recognise that HSAWA, s. 2, can be used to impose duties on employers to protect staff from the risk of violence.[18] In the light of medical evidence about the effects of 'passive smoking' it is also arguable that s. 2 ought to be the basis for action by employers to ban smoking in the workplace.[19]

Other key duties, also in s. 2, are:

- To prepare and revise as appropriate a written statement of general policy with respect to employees' health and safety and the organisation and arrangements for carrying out that policy (and to bring the policy to employees' notice).
- To establish safety representative arrangements for the purposes of consultation (in accordance with regulations).[20] Employers have a duty to consult the representatives 'with a view to the making and maintenance of arrangements which will enable him and his employees to co-operate effectively in promoting and developing measures ... and in checking the effectiveness of such measures'.
- If the safety representatives request this, to set up a safety committee to review the measure taken and to carry out any other functions prescribed by the regulations.

The safety representatives and safety committee system gives workers an important say in monitoring workplace hazards and in ensuring that employers implement health and safety requirements. The regulations make it clear, though, that the employer remains legally responsible – *not* the representatives or committee. Representatives are entitled to:

- training they might need;
- carry out inspections, and investigate accidents, dangerous occurrences and complaints;
- access to health and safety information held by the employer;
- make representations on health and safety issues;
- paid time off for union duties and activities.

The regulations require the employer to provide 'facilities and assistance' that are responsibly required.[21] The role of safety representatives and committees will become increasingly important as EC rules require much greater worker involvement in risk assessment, workplace design and the like (see section on EC legislation below). In addition, workers have a right not to have action taken against them for stopping work in dangerous situations, particularly if there is a serious and imminent risk which cannot be averted. This is now provided for in the TURERA, s. 28 and schedule 5, which will, among other things, create a right not to be dismissed or subjected to any detriment for exercising this right.

As far as employees are concerned the 1974 Act underpins the implied contractual duty of 'co-operation' by imposing duties to:

- take reasonable care of him/herself and 'other persons who may be affected' by acts or omissions;
- co-operate in enabling duties and requirements imposed on employers to be performed or complied with.

These requirements (in s. 7) permit enforcement action to be taken by the HSE (and other enforcement agencies) and they strengthen the employer's hand in taking disciplinary or dismissal action, for example if you refuse to attend a safety training course.

Detailed Requirements – Regulations

The detailed requirements that apply to particular kinds of operations, workplaces and operations are in regulations and codes of practice. The HSE also publishes guidance notes and booklets on most workplace activities involving hazards. Once you have identified the relevant regulations covering a particular process or activity, explanatory information can be obtained from the HSE's guidance series (HS[G]), or regulations booklets (HS[R]). As well as HSE advice (see note 15 on p. 414) help can also be obtained on detailed health and safety points from your union, and from health and safety organisations. The Labour Research Department provides advice for affiliated individuals and organisations and there are local resource centres who may be able to assist (see appendix 1).

Among the more important regulations, which will be relevant in most workplaces, and their key requirements, are:

Control of Substances Hazardous to Health Regulations 1988 (COSHH)

Employers must:

- carry out 'assessments' of risks from any substances hazardous to health in the workplace;
- detail the health and safety measures to be taken (which must be adequate and acceptable to enforcement inspectors) and implement those measures;
- monitor the measures taken.

Electricity at Work Regulations 1989

- All systems to be constructed and maintained so as to prevent danger.

- Work activities on or near systems to be carried out so as not to give rise to danger.
- Work environment, lighting arrangements, and so on near electrical systems must be suitable.
- Employees must be properly trained and supervised.
- Activities involving electricity must be assessed for suitability, design and siting.

Reporting of Injuries, Diseases and Dangerous Occurrences Regulations 1985 (RIDDOR)

- Serious and certain prescribed accidents, injuries and dangerous occurrences must be recorded and reported to the HSE and enforcement bodies to facilitate official action.
- Work-related diseases must, as prescribed, be reported.

Health and Safety (First Aid) Regulations 1981

- Employers must provide appropriate first-aid materials and equipment.
- Sufficient trained first-aiders must be on site (the exact number depends on the workplace, size and hazards involved).

Noise at Work Regulations 1989

- Employers must assess noise hazards if 'action' levels are being exceeded (the first level over 85 dB(A)).
- Employers must reduce noise at *source* 'so far as reasonably practicable' in some cases (usually if 90 dB(A) is exceeded), rather than just relying on individual ear protection.
- Ear protection must be provided, and ear protection zones established as necessary.
- Information, training and instruction must be provided.

EC Legislation

The EC has now become the most important source of new health and safety legislation and workers' rights. Progress in implementing the 1988 Third Action Programme on health and safety has been good, and has been responsible for a variety of new UK implementing regulations and proposals for new action.[22] Prior to 1988, the Treaty of Rome allowed the Commission to make legislation on health and safety as part of the process of 'harmonising' member states' standards, but it was not until the Single Europe Act that specific powers were given. A new art. 118A in the treaty now enables legislation to be made by the Council of Ministers by qualified majority.

The Framework Directive (EC Directive 89/391) sets new standards for employers and requires, among other things:

- increased instruction and training, information and supervision for workers.
- formal risk assessments and appropriate health and safety measures.
- implementation of a right to stop work in a dangerous situation, or to take 'appropriate steps' to protect yourself or others from danger (at present in the UK an employer could fairly dismiss staff doing this, unless procedural requirements are not followed).[23]
- risk evaluation and avoidance policies which deal with risks at source.
- 'design' of working practices, work-stations, and the general workplace environment.
- close involvement of workers' representatives (unions and safety representatives) in health and safety issues and measures.

There are a variety of directives springing from these that have been progressively implemented by HSC regulations in the UK. Detailed information on each of these important directives and UK regulations which implement them are now available from the HSE (see the address in appendix I). In outline, they deal with the following matters:

- The Workplace Directive (setting new standards on buildings, equipment maintenance, fire-fighting arrangements, lighting, ventilation, sanitary and welfare facilities. Among other things facilities for pregnant women are required).
- The VDU Directive (providing, among other things, for minimum equipment standards, rest periods, proper training and education, regular eye-tests and suitable eye-wear, and the design of work-stations. Arrangements should deal with physical and mental stress factors, including problems caused by software).[24]
- The Manual Handling Directive (requiring the avoidance of manual handling if possible, and where it is necessary laying down risk-avoidance requirements. Operations must be properly assessed and work requirements must be adapted to the worker's abilities and limitations).
- The Work Equipment and Personal Protective Equipment directives (setting minimum standards in relation to the selection and use of equipment, and making the employer responsible for training, instruction and use).

Other directives are directed at more specific problem areas, for example the Carcinogens, Asbestos and Biological Agents directives. Legislation is also being introduced in 'high-risk' industries such as construction and civil engineering, mining and offshore oil and gas production. On wider environmental issues, the

EC Commission's legislation on company environmental audits is expected to include requirements on employee participation, particularly where these involve the integration of workplace health and safety problems and general environmental issues.

Civil Claims and Compensation

An injured employee, and the relatives of a worker killed at work,[25] may need to take legal action to get compensation.[26] This is because, as mentioned earlier in this chapter, the basis of the right to compensation is still 'fault' by the employer. Employers are usually covered by insurance, as required by law, but claims are contested if liability is not clear. For example, there may well be arguments over possible 'contributory negligence' by the worker, whether the worker was acting in the 'course of his/her employment' when the accident happened, whether there was 'third party' involvement, and other possible points that could be disputed. The outcome can be uncertain and compensation is often delayed.

The basis of liability to pay compensation for injury is twofold, that is it involves the employer's duty of care; and/or breach of statutory duty.

In practice claims are often made under both heads. In both cases the claim will be made in respect of injuries suffered by the claimant.[27]

Employer's Duty of Care

There is no automatic liability on employers. The standard required is a 'reasonable' one and is measured by reference to factors which may be difficult to establish, such as foreseeability of an accident happening in the particular circumstances. This aspect may well require a consideration of the state of knowledge and awareness of the particular risk among employers at the time of the accident. The duty is balanced by a requirement on workers to take care of themselves, and by the courts setting a standard which simply requires an employer to take steps which are 'reasonably practicable' and which would have been taken by a notional, reasonable and 'prudent' employer.[28] The employer is liable for the acts and omissions of other workers, so that the duty of care cannot be delegated or passed on to others.

There is extensive case law, and numerous precedents, in relation to particular types of accidents. There is a considerable overlap between different grounds for liability, but responsibilities can be grouped under the following headings.

Safe Systems and Place of Work
This covers the employer's site, the physical layout of the workplace and the area where the accident occurred, and the systems operated by the employer

(including quality of training and supervision). The particular requirements of the worker concerned should have been met; for example, should specific types of personal protection have been provided to do the job?

If you suspect that a particular aspect of your work is affecting your health, or could injure you, it is important that you notify your employer and ask for action to be taken. If you do not do this it is possible that any later claim for compensation may fail.

As a general rule it is not enough to supply protective equipment, even if that equipment is suitable. There must be proper warnings given about any risks involved, and proper supervision given in safe ways of carrying out the job.[29] The measures taken should be in line with any COSHH measures taken following the employer's assessment, and with the requirements of any relevant regulations, for example on personal equipment (see above).

Employers are deemed to be responsible for defective equipment supplied by third parties (Employers' Liability [Defective Equipment] Act 1969).

Safe Plant, Appliances and Equipment

The test is, again, whether the employer has met the standards required of a 'reasonable' employer. There are numerous examples of employers failing to meet this requirement, including cases where they failed to keep abreast of knowledge and developments in the field of accident prevention and occupational health. An important area is noise, where employers' potential liability in the 1990s is enormous. The key considerations concern the adequacy of risk assessment, inadequate control measures and unsuitable equipment. If the employer *knows* there is a potential problem, action should be taken.[30] This point will become increasingly important in relation to claims relating to VDU use and in particular to word-processor operation, where employers should by now be aware of the risk of repetitive strain injury and other hazards caused by badly designed workstations.

Competent Staff

Accidents are often caused by other workers, either through their lack of training or supervision, or because the employer has not taken action despite knowing the risk they may represent. The basis of the employer's liability under this head is knowledge of a risk, and a failure to take preventative action.

Defences and Limitations

Even if, at first sight, it looks as if you could bring a claim under one or more of these headings, there may be a defence to the claim (or a limitation on how much compensation is payable).

Defences and limitations include:

* Employee's own fault/absence of 'negligence'.
* Contributory negligence by the employee.

- Claim is 'out of time' (normally three years from when the right to claim arises, or from when you are aware of the problem and a possible claim).

Breach of Statutory Duty

In order to bring a claim there must be a statutory duty on the employer, that is a duty in an Act or regulations. There must have been a breach of that duty. This could be, but does not have to be, evidenced by a previous prosecution and conviction. The breach must have been the cause of injury for which compensation could be claimed.

PART SIX

Collective Rights

CHAPTER 17

Trade Unions, the Judges and the Law

In this part of the book we examine the law relating to trade unions, namely political involvement; trade union membership and government; and the provisions relating to collective bargaining such as disclosure of bargaining information, consultation over redundancies and transfers of undertaking and the legal effects of collective agreements. However, the most important, complex and controversial part of collective labour law is the law relating to industrial conflict. As a result, it is this area which is given particular emphasis in this section.

The following quote from a member of the judiciary gives a fascinating insight:

> The habits you are trained in, the people with whom you mix, lead to your having a certain class of ideas of such a nature that, when you have to deal with other ideas, you do not give as sound and accurate judgements as you would wish. This is one of the great difficulties at present with Labour. Labour says 'Where are your impartial judges? They all move in the same circle as the employers, and they are all educated and nursed in the same ideas as the employers. How can a labour man or a trade unionist get impartial justice?' It is very difficult sometimes to be sure that you have put yourself into a thoroughly impartial position between two disputants, one of your own class and one not of your class.[1]

The Importance of a Historical Perspective

A study of the law relating to trade unions should begin by an examination of the historical background to labour law in Britain. This is necessary in order to understand its unique character; most importantly, the fact that the law does not provide a positive right to engage in collective bargaining or to take industrial action. Instead of a positive right to strike, the law operates a system of negative 'immunities' from civil or criminal liability.

In addition, an historical analysis of the interplay between the legislation on industrial action and the judges' decisions helps to explain the British trade union movement's traditional suspicion of legal intervention in industrial relations. As one group of labour lawyers have observed:

> Any account of the law cannot ignore the fact that its present shape has been a result of cat and mouse, played between the courts and legislature for more

than a century, in which Parliament has consistently tried to maximise and the courts almost as consistently to minimise the extent to which the taking of industrial action attracts legal sanctions.[2]

Why Immunities Instead of Rights?

Wedderburn finds the major reason for this in the nature of the labour movement in the formative period of our labour law. That period lies between 1867 (the year of the first royal commission on trade unions) and 1906 (when the Trade Disputes Act was passed):

> The central feature of that period was a labour movement which was relatively strong but which was a wholly industrial movement. Unlike its European counterparts it had as yet no ideological political wing. The Labour Party was not born until 1906. It was, therefore a movement which made pragmatic not ideological demands. And those demands registered upon bourgeois parties in Parliament as they encountered a gradual extension of the franchise in 1867 and 1884 – although the universal franchise did not come until the end of this formative period.[3]

Wedderburn observes that from its inception the modern labour movement in countries such as France and Italy was accustomed, in both its industrial and political wings, to talk in terms of political ideology and rights. The industrial and political wings grew up together – but this was not the case in Britain.

The system of immunities from civil or criminal liability reflected the tradition of legal abstention in British industrial relations: the courts were to be excluded from matters that were deemed to be the private concerns of workers, unions and employers.

Development of British Law on Trade Unions to 1979

The unique British approach to the freedom to strike, however, can be vulnerable to judicial intervention where judges develop the common law in ways unforeseen by those who drafted the statutory immunities. Indeed a number of writers have characterised British labour law as a pendulum that has swung between judge-made law and Parliament's enactments. The major developments in the law relating to trade unions can be set out in the following way:

The Trade Union Act 1871

This removed the doctrine of 'restraint of trade' which rendered trade unions unlawful associations at common law: see *Hornby* v. *Close* [1867] LR 2 QB 153.

The Conspiracy and Protection of Property Act 1875

This Act offered an immunity against the crime of 'simple conspiracy' which had been used against strikers in *R* v. *Bunn* [1872] 12 Cox CC 316. In this case, the organisers of a strike aimed at securing the reinstatement of a dismissed fellow worker were held guilty of the crime of conspiracy. The sole element of illegality was the combination itself, because it amounted to an 'unjustifiable annoyance and interference with the masters in the conduct of their business'. The legislation provided that an agreement by one or more persons to commit an act in contemplation or furtherance of a trade dispute should not be a criminal conspiracy unless the act itself was punishable as a crime. Notice that the statute did not abolish the crime of conspiracy to injure; it offered an immunity provided that the action was taken 'in contemplation or furtherance of a trade dispute'. This phrase, often described as the 'golden formula', became the foundation stone of subsequent immunities.

The Trades Disputes Act 1906

This important statute overturned four judicial decisions which posed serious threats to the freedom to strike. This judicial onslaught of the 1890s should be seen in the context of the rapid unionisation of semi-skilled and unskilled labour and widespread trade union militancy during this period.

Section 1 provided that an act committed in pursuance of an agreement by two or more persons in contemplation or furtherance of a trade dispute should not be actionable unless the act would amount to a civil wrong if committed without combination. In other words, the provision was intended to overrule the decision in *Quinn* v. *Leathem* [1901] AC 495 which had developed the tort of conspiracy to injure.

Section 2 provided an enlarged definition of what constituted lawful picketing and was designed to overcome the highly restrictive effects of the decision in *Lyons* v. *Wilkins* [1896] 1 Ch 811. The 1875 Act had legalised peaceful picketing but its wording was such that it only referred to the act of peacefully communicating information and not acts of peaceful persuasion. In *Lyons*, the pickets had sought to persuade workers not to work for the employer in dispute and that was held to be an illegal 'watching and besetting' and a common law nuisance.

Section 3 provided immunity for a person who, in contemplation or furtherance of a trade dispute, induced another to break a contract of employment. This provided a limited immunity from the tort established in *Lumley* v. *Gye* [1853] 2 E&B 216. In this case, it had been held that a theatre owner had committed a tort when he gave financial inducements to an actress to break a contract with a rival in order that she might appear in his production. A perfectly acceptable decision on the facts of the particular case, perhaps, but when applied to industrial relations the tort threatens to undermine the freedom to strike. This is because virtually all forms of industrial action involve workers acting in breach of their contracts of employment and so any organiser of the industrial action is an easy target for attack by the *Lumley* v. *Gye* tort. Hence the need for the immunity.

Section 4 stated that no action in tort could be brought against a trade union and its funds for acts by its members or officials even though carried out on its behalf. In other words, the House of Lords' decision in *Taff Vale Railway Co* v. *Amalgamated Society of Railway Servants* [1901] AC 426 was overturned and trade unions as such were provided with a complete immunity in tort and could not be sued for damages.

The Trade Union Act 1913

This statute was enacted in order to restore the right of unions to spend money on political objects following the decision of the House of Lords in *Amalgamated Society of Railway Servants* v. *Osborne* [1910] AC 87. Since its formation in 1900 the Labour Party had been financed almost exclusively by the affiliated trade unions and an MP at this time did not receive a salary from the state. The *Osborne* decision held that it was unlawful for a union to impose on its members a compulsory levy for the purposes of creating a parliamentary fund to promote Labour MPs. While the Act allowed the trade unions the right to maintain a political fund, it imposed a series of restrictive conditions on their ability to incur expenditure in respect of certain specified political objects. The union was required to ballot its members in order to approve the adoption of political objects; payment in furtherance of such objects had to be made out of a separate political fund; individual members were allowed to 'contract out' and were safeguarded against discrimination arising from their failure to contribute to the fund. As we shall see, two major changes made to this system by the Trade Union Act 1984 relate to the introduction of ballots held at 10-yearly intervals in order to test continued support for the political objects of the union and an enlarged definition of those items of expenditure which must be met out of the political, as opposed to general, funds.

The Trade Disputes Act 1965

This measure extended immunity to the tort of intimidation. This was necessary because in *Rookes* v. *Barnard* [1964] AC 1129, the House of Lords had expanded this tort to include threats to break a contract as well as threats of violence.

The Trade Union and Labour Relations Act 1974

At the same time as repealing the interventionist Industrial Relations Act 1971, this legislation sought to deal with some of the new tortious liabilities developed by the judiciary during the 1960s – most notably extending trade dispute immunity to liability for inducing breaches of commercial contracts (*Stratford* v. *Lindley* [1965] AC 269) and for interference with contractual relations short of breach (*Torquay Hotel Co Ltd* v. *Cousins* [1969] 2 Ch 106).

The Judiciary and the Trade Union Movement

Those commentators who thought that TULRA's extension of the scope of the immunities had severely restricted further interventions by the judiciary had badly underestimated the judicial creativity of Lord Denning. In *Meade* v. *Haringey LBC* [1979] ICR 494, the then Master of the Rolls and Lord Justice Eveleigh both expressed the opinion that it was tortious to induce a breach of statutory duty, for example to cause a local education authority to break its statutory duty to provide education. This potential head of liability has particular relevance for public sector industrial relations and is not encompassed by the framework of immunities set out in TULRA.[4]

In addition, the late 1970s saw Lord Denning and the Court of Appeal seeking to undermine the scope of the immunities by putting a narrow construction on the phrase 'in contemplation or furtherance of a trade dispute'. In a series of cases the Court of Appeal held that a union official could not claim immunity for certain types of sympathy action because it found, using an objective test, that it was not capable of furthering the primary dispute, being too remote from it.[5] This particular attempt to control 'sympathetic' industrial action was rather regretfully rejected by the House of Lords, with Lord Diplock observing that the scope of the statutory immunities provided to trade unions 'not surprisingly, have tended to stick in judicial gorges' (*Express Newspapers Ltd* v. *McShane* [1980] ICR 42 at p. 57). As we shall see, the Employment Act 1980 subsequently returned matters to much the same position as that reached by the Court of Appeal.

This catalogue of developments helps to explain the British trade union movement's deep distrust of the courts and its firm commitment to a policy of legal abstention in relation to industrial conflict.

The reasons for the degree of tension between the trade union movement and the judiciary are complex. In part it may derive from the common law's emphasis on the importance of individual property and contractual rights, and the inability of judges trained in the common law tradition to give sufficient recognition to the rights of collectivities. A number of writers would also point to the narrow social base from which judges are recruited and the inevitable effect that this background has on the frame of reference they adopt.

The judges define the public interest, inevitably, from the viewpoint of their own class. And the public interest, so defined, is by a natural, not an artificial, coincidence, the interest of others in authority, whether in government, in the City or in the church. It includes the maintenance of order, the protection of private property, the promotion of certain economic aims, the containment of the trade union movement, and the continuance of governments which conduct their business largely in private and on the advice of others of what I have called the governing group.[6]

If this view is correct, then the following observation from Wedderburn should not surprise us:

> it is of significance that the eras of judicial 'creativity' of new doctrines hostile to trade union interests, have been largely, though not entirely, coterminous with the periods of British social history in which trade unions have been perceived by middle-class opinion as a threat to the established social order.[7]

A Positive Right to Strike?

The perceived problems with the immunities approach as a means of protecting the freedom to strike have produced calls from a number of quarters for the enactment of a positive right to strike, perhaps adjudicated by a specialised labour court.[8]

The problem with a right to strike, perhaps enshrined in a Bill of Rights along with other protections for workers and their trade unions, is that it will still be up to courts to interpret the scope of such a right. An example of the dangers can be derived from the way the judiciary have gone about interpreting the so-called right to picket. This is the one activity that is defined in positive terms, that is, 'it shall be lawful ...' Yet, as we shall see, the judiciary have interpreted the rights of a picket to be as limited as that of a hitch-hiker seeking to persuade a car or lorry to stop. The lessons of our own history, together with a whole catalogue of restrictive judicial interpretations in countries where a positive right to strike exists, suggest that it would be highly dangerous for the trade union movement to contemplate transferring this degree of power to the courts.[9]

In a number of writings, Lord Wedderburn has advanced the argument that the question of rights versus immunities is not of practical relevance, the major issue being the type of forum and procedure for the adjudication of industrial disputes. He advocates the establishment of a system of autonomous labour courts staffed by lay experts in industrial relations and lawyers of both genders and drawn from differing ethnic and class backgrounds.[10] This proposition may seem to offer a way forward although, as Roger Welch has observed: 'It is debatable whether a country such as Britain ever could give birth to a legal profession free from sexism, racism and class bias. Patently, such a profession does not exist in the here and now.'[11]

Breaking the Mould: The New Policies of Restriction[12]

With the exception of wartime and the brief interlude of the Industrial Relations Act 1971, the non-interventionist model established by the 1906 Act was maintained until the Conservative government came to power in 1979. At this point the pattern described above changed and we see Parliament adopting the traditional judicial role of restricting the scope of the immunities.

The Employment Act 1980 marked the first step towards the fulfilment of the Conservative Party manifesto pledge of 'striking a balance between the rights and duties of the trade union movement'. This piece of legislation was designed to restrict two forms of industrial action which had come to the forefront of public debate during the so-called winter of discontent in 1978/9; namely, secondary picketing and certain types of 'sympathetic' industrial action. The Act also sought to limit the effectiveness of the closed shop by enlarging those situations in which dismissal for failure to join a particular union was unfair and allowing the employer to reclaim any compensation from the union itself if its action had contributed to the dismissal. Individuals were given a right to complain of unreasonable exclusion or expulsion from a union in a closed shop.

Unlike the Heath Government's attempts, via the Industrial Relations Act, to accomplish fundamental industrial relations law reform 'at a stroke', the Thatcher/Major administrations have adopted a much more subtle and incremental approach. Following the legislation of 1980, the Employment Act of 1982 narrowed further the parameters of lawful industrial action and, for the first time since 1906, exposed trade union funds to damages claims. The 1982 Act added further to the restrictions on the closed-shop, rendering it unfair to dismiss a worker for non-membership unless the closed-shop arrangement had received a specified level of support by the workers affected in a ballot conducted within five years of the dismissal.

Two years later, the Trade Union Act contained provisions which sought to limit the autonomy of trade unions in three areas. First, it required that unions ballot their members every 10 years as to whether they wished to maintain a political fund. Second, all voting members of a trade union's principal executive committee henceforth had to be elected by ballot at least every five years. Finally, the Act removed immunity in tort where a trade union authorised or endorsed industrial action without first calling a ballot which meets the criteria laid down by the Act. This legislation did not mark the completion of the government's industrial relations law reform strategy.

The Employment Act 1988 extended the rights of individual trade union members where the existing framework was thought by the government to be deficient and also strengthened aspects of the law in the light of experience during the miners' strike of 1984/5. The Act's major provisions are summarised below:

- Union members gained the right to apply for a court order to end industrial action which has not been authorised or endorsed by a union without the support of a ballot. Under the Trade Union Act 1984, the cause of action was restricted to employers.
- Where those likely to take part in industrial action have different places of work, the union must either hold separate ballots at each workplace or ballot only complete bargaining units.
- Members gained a right not to be denied access to the courts in respect of matters which have been considered for six months in proceedings under the union's rules.
- Members gained a right not to be unjustifiably disciplined. Discipline is to be treated as unjustifiable, inter alia, if the reason for it is that the member has refused to take part in industrial action.
- Further curbs on the closed shop. Without making the closed shop illegal, the Act made the post-entry closed shop virtually impossible to enforce.
- Workplace ballots for the purposes of union elections and political funds were replaced by postal ballots.
- The requirement for members of a union's principal executive committee to hold their position by virtue of an election was extended to non-voting members of that committee and the president and the general secretary.
- A post of Commissioner for the Rights of Trade Union members (CROTUM) was created. The Commissioner's function is to assist union members who wish to bring proceedings to enforce certain of their statutory rights against the union.

More recent, and the fifth piece of legislation since 1979, is the Employment Act 1990. Its contents reflect the proposals set out in two 1989 Green Papers: 'Removing Barriers to Employment' and 'Unofficial Action and the Law'. Commenting on the Bill, the (then) secretary of state for employment, Norman Fowler, stated: 'This Bill will strengthen the rights of people at work and help to protect the community as a whole against irresponsible industrial action. It tackles three long-standing problems: the closed shop, secondary action and unofficial strikes.'

Summary of the Main Provisions of the Employment Act 1990

The Closed Shop

- It is now unlawful to refuse to employ someone because s/he is, or is not, a trade union member, or because s/he refuses to become or cease to be a member. This provision seeks to outlaw so-called pre-entry closed shops.
- It is also unlawful for an employment agency to refuse any of its services to someone on those grounds.

- Complaints that the above rights have been infringed may be taken to an industrial tribunal.

Industrial Action

- The statutory immunity for industrial action taken in 'contemplation or furtherance of a trade dispute' will not apply in cases where there has been 'secondary action' except in the case of peaceful and lawful picketing.
- Trade unions are made liable in tort for the acts of all their officials (including shop stewards) and committees, unless the union effectively repudiates the action in accordance with the Act's requirements.
- Section 62 of the EPCA 1978, which removes the unfair dismissal jurisdiction of an industrial tribunal where the applicant was taking part in industrial action at the time of the dismissal, and all other 'relevant' employees were treated the same, is amended. There is now no right to claim unfair dismissal if an employee is dismissed while taking 'unofficial industrial action', regardless of how other employees are dealt with.
- There is now no statutory 'immunity' for any industrial action taken in support of a worker dismissed in the above circumstances.

In a clear and perceptive analysis of the 1990 Act, Hazel Carty concludes:

Overall, the Act lacks justification. At the heart of the provision is the attempt to prevent effective trade union pressure. Even those who seek to keep within the rules for taking lawful industrial action will find it difficult to apply those rules. It is hard not to agree with Tony Blair, the Opposition spokesman, that it is a leftover from the old agenda of the industrial cold war. No doubt the severe reduction in the ability to take industrial action will fuel the need for guaranteed rights to take industrial action. The Employment Act 1990 leaves industrial action immunities in tatters.[13]

The Position in the Early 1990s

In 1991 the government published plans for yet further changes to trade union law. Under the proposals contained in a Green Paper, 'Industrial Relations in the 'Nineties':

- unions will have to give seven days notice of industrial action following a ballot;
- workers will be given the right to join a union of their choice, thus undermining the TUC's so-called Bridlington Principles which prevent affiliated unions from poaching each other's members;
- it will not be possible to deduct union dues without the written consent of the individual worker;

- members of the public will have new rights to seek an injunction to halt unlawful industrial action that disrupts public services;
- unions will be obliged to conduct independently scrutinised postal ballots before strikes;
- collective agreements are to be legally binding unless they include a provision making them unenforceable.

All of the proposals, with the exception of the one concerned with making collective agreements legally enforceable, are given statutory force by the Trade Union Reform and Employment Rights Act 1993.

At first sight there would appear to be a contradiction between the neo-liberal philosophy of the Conservative administration, which essentially believes in keeping the business of the state and the business of government to a minimum, and the highly interventionist policy adopted in relation to trade union reform. There is no contradiction. For the free marketeer, the market is the mechanism by which individual wants and desires can be controlled. The only valid function of government is to protect this mechanism from interference. According to this philosophy trade unions not only distort the market, but also infringe the political liberty that the free market offers. The basis of trade union power is seen to be coercion resting on legal privileges: 'No salvation for Britain until the special privileges granted to trade unions three-quarters of a century ago are revoked.'[14]

Given this philosophy, it is perhaps not surprising that the UK has been found to be in breach of International Labour Organisation (ILO) Conventions which the country had ratified. The banning of union membership at Government Communications Headquarters in 1984 was found by the ILO's Committee on Freedom of Association to be in breach of Convention no. 87 which guarantees the basic right of workers to form and join organisations of their own choosing. The second of the three major complaints to the ILO related to the Teachers' Pay and Conditions Act 1987 which effectively abolished collective bargaining for teachers. This time the government was held to be in breach of Convention no. 98 which provides, among other things,

> that machinery appropriate to national conditions shall be taken, where necessary, to encourage and promote the full development and utilisation of machinery for voluntary negotiation between employers or employers' organisations and workers' organisations with a view to the regulation of terms and conditions of employment by means of collective agreements.

The most recent complaint from Britain to the ILO was made in 1988 by the TUC and the NUM relating to various aspects of the Conservative employment legislation. The ILO's Committee of Experts concluded that Britain's labour law had fallen below the acceptable standards set by Convention no. 87 on no less than six different grounds. These were as follows:[15]

- The GCHQ dismissals of those who refused to relinquish trade union membership. The Committee of Experts, like the Committee on Freedom of Association before them, found that the government's action was in breach of art. 2 of Convention no. 87.
- The Committee of Experts was of the view that s. 3 of the Employment Act 1988 (now TULR[C]A, s. 64), was in conflict with art. 3 of Convention no. 87. The particular concern revolved around the fact that s. 3 made it unlawful for trade unions to discipline members who refuse to participate in industrial action. In the view of the Committee art. 3 requires that 'union members should be permitted, when drawing up their constitutions and rules, to determine whether or not it should be possible to discipline members who refuse to participate in lawful strikes and other industrial action.' Section 3 should be amended accordingly.
- The Committee found that s. 8 of the Employment Act 1988 (now TULR[C]A, s. 15), which made it unlawful for the property of any trade union to be applied so as to indemnify any individual against any criminal sanction or contempt of court, was in breach of Convention no. 87:

> The Committee has consistently taken the view that legislative provisions which are intended to ensure sound administration and the honest and efficient management of union funds and other funds and assets are not incompatible with the Convention. However, such provisions should not be such a character as to deprive unions of the right to draw up their constitutions or rules and to organise their administration and activities free of interference by the public authorities – nor should they deny trade unions the right to utilise their funds as they wish for normal and lawful trade union purposes. Section 8 of the 1988 Act appears to do both of these things, and as such is not compatible with the guarantees provided by Article 3 and should be amended.

The Committee expressed the view that the narrowing of the definition of a trade dispute in 1982 and restrictions on secondary action introduced in s. 17 of the Employment Act 1980 unduly restricted workers' legitimate right to strike in protection of their own economic and social interests, as guaranteed by articles 3, 8 and 10 of the Convention.
- The Committee considered that it was inconsistent with the right to strike as guaranteed by articles 3, 8 and 10 of the Convention for an employer to be permitted to refuse to reinstate some or all of its employees at the conclusion of a strike, lock-out or other industrial action without those employees having the right to challenge the fairness of that dismissal before an independent court or tribunal. This is exactly the freedom given to employers under EPCA 1978 (now TULR[C]A, s.238).
- Finally, the Committee expressed its concern at the volume and complexity of legislative change since 1980:

Whilst it is true that most of the legislative measures under consideration are not incompatible with the requirements of the Convention, there is a point at which the cumulative effect of legislative changes which are themselves consistent with the principles of freedom of association may nevertheless by virtue of their complexity and extent, constitute an incursion upon the rights guaranteed by the Convention.

The complexity and uncertainty of the law may inhibit industrial action. Concern was also expressed that while giving so much emphasis to individual 'rights' the government has demonstrated lesser concern for the 'rights' of individual trade unionists. The Committee considered that a more positive statement of these rights would be 'of advantage'.

The government has done nothing to meet any of the ILO's concerns. Indeed, as we have seen, since the ILO observation was published in 1989 the Conservative administration has introduced yet more legislation, which has further weakened job protection for strikers and has almost completely outlawed sympathy action. In terms of the complexity of the legislation, the government has made a very limited response by consolidating collective labour law and all the changes made during the 1980s and the early 1990s into one statute: the Trade Union and Labour Relations (Consolidation) Act 1992. Even then, the new provisions contained in TURERA further complicate matters.

The response (or lack of it) by the government to the ILO's findings exposes the lack of effective sanctions to deal with those who violate ILO standards but it also pinpoints major hypocrisy on the government's part. As Keith Ewing observes:

The government will, of course, do nothing to comply with any of the obligations. This is despite the fact that one of the Thatcher government's great concerns since 1979 has been to introduce what it has called the 'rule of law' to industrial relations. But when called upon to comply with legal obligations – this time arising in the international arena – it is very reluctant to do so. The government, apparently, is prepared to impose obligations on others but to pick and choose which of its own legal duties to comply with. In short, the administration is prepared to act above the law while condemning others who, it claims, do the same. It is a strange example to set for trade unions in this country who are in dispute with the courts. And it is a depressing message to send to the rest of the world.[16]

CHAPTER 18

Trade Unions and their Members

The Legal Definitions

There are two parts to the legal definition of a trade union. First, it must be an organisation (permanent or temporary) that consists wholly or mainly of workers of one or more descriptions. Second, its 'principal purposes' must include 'the regulation of relations between workers of that description or those descriptions and employers or employers' associations'.

A federation, or similar organisation, may also be a 'trade union' if:

(1) it consists of constituent or affiliated organisations that are themselves trade unions (or their representatives); and
(2) its principal purposes include the regulation of relations between workers and employer or employers' associations, or the regulation of relations between its constituent or affiliated organisation. (This phrase would probably encompass the TUC.) Such bodies as the International Transport Workers' Federation are clearly within the definition. (TULR[C] Act 1992, s. 1).

'Regulation of Relations'

This phrase was considered in *Midland Cold Storage Ltd* v. *Turner* [1972] ICR 773 NIRC.

The plaintiffs sought to prevent a joint shop stewards' committee from taking industrial action. The action was brought to restrain the commission of certain 'unfair industrial practices' created by the Industrial Relations Act. It was necessary to establish that the committee was an 'organisation of workers', a term defined by s. 61 of the Act in substantially the same words as s. 1 (TULR[C]A above).

The committee was held not to qualify within the definition because

its most apparent activity seems to consist of recommending the taking or abandonment of industrial action in the London Docks and organising any such action which may be decided upon. Thereafter, it does not seem to enter into negotiations with the employers, but leaves this task to the established union machinery.

Listing

Before 1971, the Registrar of Friendly Societies had the responsibility of maintaining a register of trade unions and most unions complied because there were tax advantages. The Industrial Relations Act 1971 introduced the office of Registrar of Trade Unions and made registration the precondition for any benefits to be gained under the Act. Since it also involved many interventions in the internal affairs of unions and control of the rule book, only a few registered. Any unions that did register were expelled from the TUC.

TULRA 1974 reverted to the substance of pre-1971 approach and the law is now set out in TULR(C)A 1992, ss. 2, 3, 4. By s. 2 the certification officer is charged with the duty of keeping a voluntary list of trade unions and employers' associations. The certification officer grants a listing if he or she is satisfied that the organisation comes within the appropriate definition.

Inclusion in the list is evidence that the organisation is a trade union. Unions on the list receive tax relief in respect of sums paid as 'provident benefits' (Income and Corporation Taxes Act 1988, s. 467) and listing is a precondition for a certificate from the certification officer that the union is 'independent'. Such status is an important attribute in relation to the following rights of unions' officials and members: to take part in trade union activities; to gain information for collective bargaining; to secure consultation over redundancies; to insist on time off for union duties and activities and to appoint health and safety representatives.

Certificate of Independence

Employers who wish to prevent trade unions recruiting their workforce may engage in two forms of 'peaceful competition'. They may ensure that the terms and conditions of their workforce are better than the negotiated rates, or they can encourage the formation of a staff association which does not pose an effective challenge to management's power. Such organisations are termed 'sweetheart unions'. The certificate of independence is the means by which the law seeks to ensure that such groupings do not receive the rights accorded to independent trade unions.

An independent trade union is defined by TULR(C)A, s. 5 as:

a trade union which:

(a) is not under the domination and control of an employer or a group of employers or of one or more employers' associations; and
(b) is not liable to interference by an employer or any such group or association (arising out of the provisions of financial or material support or by any means whatsoever) tending towards such control.

Item (b) of the test has caused the greatest difficulties in interpretation, requiring as it does a degree of speculation on the question as to whether the union is 'liable to interference'. In *Squibb UK Staff Association* v. *Certification Officer* [1980] IRLR 431, the Court of Appeal supported the certification officer's narrow interpretation of this phrase and held that 'liable to interference' means 'vulnerable to interference': being dependent on the employer for facilities and in a weak financial position. According to Lord Denning, the test was not satisfied merely because such interference was unlikely to occur in practice:

> One has to envisage the possibility that there may be a difference of opinion in the future between the employers and the staff association. It does not matter whether it is likely or not — it may be completely unlikely — but one has to envisage the possibility of a difference of opinion ... But when it arises, the questions have to be asked. What is the strength of the employers? What pressures could they bring to bear against the staff association? What facilities could they withdraw?

Criteria against Which Independence is to be Judged

These were set in *Blue Circle Staff Association* v. *Certification Officer* [1977] IRLR 20, EAT and are as follows:

1. Finance: If there is any evidence that a union is getting a direct subsidy from an employer, it is immediately ruled out.
2. Other Assistance: The Certification Officer's inspectors see what material support, such as free premises, time off work for officials, or office facilities a union is getting from an employer, and attempt to cost them out.
3. Employer Interference: If a union is very small, and weak, and gets a good deal of help, then on the face of it its independence must be in danger and liable to interference.
4. History: The recent history of a union, important in the case of the Blue Circle Staff Association which before February 1976 was dominated by the employers, is considered. It was not unusual for a staff association to start as a 'creature of management and grow into something independent'. The staff association had started on this road but still had a way to travel.
5. Rules: The applicant union's rule book is scrutinised to see if the employer can interfere with, or control it, and if there are any restrictions on membership. If a union is run by people near the top of a company it could be detrimental to the rank and file members.
6. Single Company Unions: Whilst they were not debarred from getting certificates, because such a rule could exclude unions like those of the miners and railwaymen, they were more liable to employer interference. Broadly based multi-company unions were more difficult to influence.

7. Organisation: The Certification Officer's inspectors then examine the applicant union in detail, its size and recruiting ability, whether it is run by competent and experienced officers, the state of its finance, and its branch and committee structure. Again, if the union was run by senior men in a company, employer interference was a greater risk.

8. Attitude: Once the other factors had been assessed, inspectors looked for a 'robust attitude in negotiation' as a sign of genuine independence, backed up by a good negotiating record ...

In coming to a decision, the certification officer is free to make such enquiries as he or she thinks fit and 'shall take into account any relevant information submitted to him [sic] by any person'. If an applicant union is refused a certificate, an appeal on fact or law may be made to the EAT. The right to appeal in TULR(C)A, s. 9 (2) is so worded that no other competing union can appeal against the certification officer's decision to grant a certificate: *General and Municipal Workers' Union v. Certification Officer* [1977] ICR 183.

The Legal Status of a Trade Union

A trade union has a strange status in law. A trade union is not a body corporate, that is, a separate legal entity, existing independently of its members. It is an unincorporated association and its property must rest in the hands of trustees. When unions first received recognition under law, they were allowed, but not obliged, to register under the Trade Union Act 1871. Whether or not they were registered, unions remained unincorporated associations, and it was therefore assumed that it was impossible to sue them in their own name.

However, the notorious House of Lords decision in *Taff Vale Railway Co v. Amalgamated Society of Railway Servants* [1901] AC 426, held that a trade union registered under the 1871 Act could be sued in tort, as registered unions had a rather peculiar quasi-corporate status. The later House of Lords decision in *Bonsor v. Musicians Union* [1956] AC 104 confirmed this position.

The IRA 1971 then incorporated registered trade unions. TULRA 1974 essentially restored the pre-1971 position, except that no distinction was now drawn between listed and non-listed trade unions and their status was put on a more satisfactory legal footing.

The current position is that, with the exception of special registered bodies, no union, whether listed or not, is to be, or is to be treated as it were, a body corporate, except as specifically provided by the Act itself (TULR[C]A, s.10[2]).

Although the legal form is different from corporate entities, the underlying reality is not, since TULR[C]A, s.10[1] confers on unions many of the characteristics of legal corporate status, as indeed did the pre-1971 Acts. So:

(a) a trade union is capable of making contracts in its own name;

(b) all property belonging to a trade union shall be vested in trustees in trust for the union;

(c) it shall be capable of suing or being sued in its own name;

(d) proceedings may be brought against a trade union for a criminal offence;

(e) a trade union is liable for the enforcement of judgements as if it were a body corporate.

There are, however, some residual consequences of unincorporated status. Thus a trade union does not have the necessary legal personality to suffer injury to its reputation and so cannot sue for libel (*EETPU* v. *Times Newspapers* [1980] 1 All ER 1097).

Liability in Tort

Both employers' associations and trade unions used to have immunity from actions in tort for acts alleged or threatened, whether in their own name or by way of representative action. The immunity stemmed from the Trades Dispute Act 1906, passed in response to the *Taff Vale* decision (above).

Section 4 TDA 1906 stated that no action in tort was to be allowed against a trade union (whether in its registered name or through a representative action) 'in respect of any tortious act alleged to have been committed by or on behalf of a trade union'. The minor exception to this comprehensive immunity provided for tort actions against the trustees concerning a union's registered property outside trade disputes. Further, the union remained liable in contract; and individuals, officials and others remained liable in tort.

This blanket immunity was latched on to by critics of the unions – 'This is a Bill for legalising tyranny' (Lord Halsbury). Section 14 TULRA re-enacted this immunity but in a rather more restricted form. Actions in tort brought outside trade disputes for negligence, nuisance or other torts causing personal injury or connected with use of property were allowed.

This position was radically changed by the Employment Act 1982, which made unions liable in tort, made them vicariously liable for the unlawful actions of its officials and set out a scale of maximum damages depending on the size of the union. This scale applies unless the liability arises from personal injury caused by negligence, nuisance or other breach of duty, or a breach of duty which has arisen in connection with ownership, occupation, control or use of property, real or personal (TULR[C]A, s. 22).

Restraint of Trade

TULR(C)A, s. 11, provides immunity from the restraint of trade doctrine. This immunity is fundamental if unions are to operate lawfully. Where a union is empowered to take strike action or to impose various other forms of pressure on an employer, at common law these would be regarded as restraint of trade. Consequently, a union would be perceived to be an organisation pursuing purposes in a manner contrary to public policy, and as such would be unable to enforce its rules or protect its funds.

The vulnerability of the unions to the doctrine of restraint of trade was vividly illustrated in *Hornby* v. *Close* (1867) LR 2 QB 153. The United Order of Boilermakers, which had registered under the Friendly Societies Act 1855, wanted the help of the courts to prosecute an official who had embezzled its funds. It was refused: 'I do not say the objects of this society are criminal. I do not say they are not. But I am clearly of the opinion that the rules referred to are illegal in the sense that they cannot be enforced' (Mr Justice Blackburn).

Consequently, it was recognised by the framers of the Trade Union Act 1871 that if unions were to be made lawful they would need to be granted immunity from this doctrine. TULR(C)A, s. 11, retains this immunity but expands it slightly.

The provision declares that the purposes of a trade union are not, by reason only that they are in restraint of trade, to be regarded as unlawful so as:

(a)   to make any union member liable to criminal proceedings for conspiracy or otherwise; or

(b)   to make any agreement or trust void or voidable.

This protection is also provided for *rules* (in addition to purposes) which are not to be regarded as unlawful or enforceable by reason only that they are in restraint of trade. This extension to the immunity of rules was necessary because of the restrictive interpretation placed on 'purposes' by the Court of Appeal in *Edwards* v. *SOGAT* [1971] 3 All ER 689.

The plaintiff was expelled from the defendant trade union of which he had been classed a temporary member. His expulsion was carried out under rule 18 (4) (h), which provided for automatic termination of membership for arrears of subscription. The defendant conceded that the expulsion for this reason was unlawful because it was based on a misunderstanding about payment of his dues. However, the union argued that his damages should be nominal, since he could have been validly expelled under another rule, rule 18 (4) (j), which, it was argued, gave the union an unfettered right to terminate the membership of temporary members.

Lord Justice Sachs rejected this argument and found such an all empowering rule an unreasonable restraint of trade: 'It cannot be said that a rule that enabled such capricious and despotic action is proper to the purposes of this or indeed of any trade union.' This approach is now no longer possible given the extended s. 11. However, the reasoning adopted by another judge in the case, Lord Denning, was based on general public policy and a 'right to work' not tied to the doctrine of restraint of trade: if this approach is correct, then s. 11 would not offer immunity in such circumstances.

Political Funds and Objects

The Trade Union Act 1913 was enacted in order to restore the right of unions to spend money on political objects following the decision of the House of Lords in *Amalgamated Society of Railway Servants* v. *Osborne* [1910] AC 87 which held that it was unlawful for a union to impose on its members a compulsory levy for the purposes of creating a parliamentary fund to promote Labour MPs. However, whilst the Act allowed trade unions the right to maintain a political fund, it imposed a series of restrictive conditions on their ability to incur expenditure in respect of certain specified political objects. The union was required to ballot its members in order to approve the adoption of political objects – payments in furtherance of such objects had to be made out of a separate political fund, individual members were allowed to 'contract out' and were safeguarded against discrimination arising from their failure to contribute to the fund.

The two major changes introduced into this system by the Trade Union Act 1984 relate to the introduction of periodic ballots to test continued support for the political objects of the union and a new definition of 'political objects'. The law is now contained in the Trade Union and Labour Relations (Consolidation) Act 1992.

The Act provides that trade unions which maintain political funds must ballot their members at least every 10 years to determine the continued operation of such funds. The Act stipulates rules regarding the conduct of political fund ballots which have to be approved by the certification officer. Most notably the ballot must be a fully postal ballot, with the papers sent out and returned by post. (The other ballot requirements are listed in our section on Union Elections and Ballots below.)

The second major change concerns the enlarged definition of those objects of expenditure which must be met out of the political fund. Political objects will now include expenditure:

(a) on any contributions to the funds of, or payment of any expenses incurred directly or indirectly by, a political party;

(b) on the provision of any service or property for use by or on behalf of any political party;[1]

(c) in connection with the registration of electors, the candidature of any person, the selection of any candidate or the holding of any ballot by the union in connection with any election to a political office;

(d) on the maintenance of any holder of political office;[2]

(e) on the holding of any conference or meeting by, or on behalf of, a political party or any other meeting the main purpose of which is the transaction of business in connection with a political party; and

(f) on the production, publication or distribution of any literature, document, film, sound recording or advertisement, the main purpose of which is to persuade people to vote for a political party or candidate or to persuade them not to vote for a political party or candidate (TULR[C]A, s. 72).

Perhaps the most far-reaching change concerns paragraph (f). First, it is much wider than the previous definition, covering not only literature and documents but other forms of publicity such as TV, radio and advertisements. Second, because the provision encompasses any publication whose main purpose is to persuade persons to vote or not to vote for a particular party or candidate, unions, particularly those operating in the public sector, will need to exercise care about the material they publish which is not paid for out of the political fund (see *Paul v. NALGO* [1987] IRLR 413). Publicity campaigns against privatisation or trade union legislation, for example, will need a thorough vetting if they are to be financed from the general fund. It is important to bear in mind that these changes affect all unions, whether or not they possess a political fund, since they limit the ways in which general funds can be spent.

Sections 89–91 of the 1992 Act deal with the case of a union which has a political fund but which fails to renew its resolution either by failing to get a majority in favour of renewal or by failing to call a ballot within a 10-year period.

In such situations, the trade union must ensure that the collection of contributions to the political fund is discontinued 'as soon as is reasonably practicable'. Any contributions which are received after a political resolution has lapsed may be paid into any of its other funds, subject to the individual member's right to claim a refund.

Where a union has held a ballot but fails to secure a majority for renewal, the union is allowed a period of six months during which it may continue to spend on political objects. Unions which fail to call a ballot within the 10-year period are penalised by not being allowed this 'breathing space'. Trade unions which do not run down their political funds in such situations may transfer the money into their non-political funds. Alternatively, the political fund is frozen until such time as the union can secure a majority in favour of renewal in a subsequent ballot.

Any member who claims that a union has failed to comply with the political fund ballot rules may apply to the High Court (Court of Session in Scotland) or the certification officer for a declaration to that effect. The High Court may, in addition, make an enforcement order specifying the steps the union must take and the time-scale within which they must be taken. The court order may be enforced by any individual who was a member both at the time the original order was made and when enforcement proceedings commenced. The right of enforcement is, therefore, not confined to the original litigant.

Contracting out and the Check-off

Despite the fact that the Conservative government initially had proposed substituting contracting in for contracting out, ultimately it did not change the present system. Instead, discussions between the Department of Employment and the TUC resulted in the latter's Statement of Guidance to its affiliates. The secretary of state for employment, however, made it clear that the government would legislate if it believed that the TUC voluntary code was not working satisfactorily.

The Statement of Guidance advises unions to draw up an information sheet containing information, inter alia, on how to contract out, on the right not to be discriminated against for non-contribution and on the amount of the levy as a proportion of the normal subscription. The information sheet should be supplied to new members, existing members on request and all union members after any ballot concerning the establishment or continuation of the political fund.[3]

In relation to contracting out procedures, the statement advises that no obstacles should be placed in the way of members wishing to contract out and, in particular, that forms of exemption should be available through workplace representatives, union branches and the union's head office; that receipt of completed notices should be acknowledged; that exemption should be put into effect speedily,[4] and that unions should ensure that members who do not wish to pay the levy do not do so inadvertently (for instance, under check-off arrangements).[5]

Indeed, in order to safeguard against the latter eventuality, the 1992 Act itself makes it unlawful for employers operating the check-off system to deduct the political levy from the pay of an employee who has given notification that he/she has contracted out. Employees must certify to their employer in writing that they have contracted out and the employer must ensure as soon as is reasonably practicable that the political levy is not deducted from the employee's pay (s. 86).

Employers are often unwilling to deduct different amounts from employees' wages, according to whether or not they pay the political levy. As a result, unions have adopted the practice of periodically refunding to exempt members such amounts deducted by their employer as represents the political levy. This practice, held to be lawful by the EAT in *Reeves* v. *TGWU* [1980] ICR 728, is now outlawed by s. 86 (3) of the 1992 Act. Employers are now faced with the choice between the administrative burden of operating a check-off system which deducts variable amounts from pay, depending on whether the employee does or does not contribute to the political fund, or completely abandoning the check-off system.

Employees who wish to challenge their employer's actions in this area may apply to the county court for a declaration and an order requiring the employer to take remedial action. As to IT complaints concerning unauthorised deductions of union dues, see chapter 17.

Regulation of Trade Unions

The last two decades have witnessed an increasing tendency to subject internal union affairs to legal regulation. Although the Donovan Commission (1968), para. 622, found it 'unlikely that abuse of power by trade unions is widespread', it still recommended that the chief registrar of trade unions be given a supervisory role over the content of union rules and that an independent review body should be created to deal with arbitrary exclusion and expulsions. Section 65 IRA 1971 laid down a number of 'guiding principles' for trade union rules which forbid, inter alia, arbitrary or unreasonable exclusions from membership and unfair or unreasonable disciplinary action. In the 1980s, we witnessed considerable statutory intervention in this field. Moreover, judicial intervention via the common law has also played a major role in the trend towards intervention in internal union affairs.

The Residual Importance of the Common Law

Statutory protection for individuals has increased markedly since 1980, with the enactment of the right not to be unreasonably excluded or expelled from union membership where there is a closed shop in operation (Employment Act 1980 s. 4) and the right not to be disciplined for certain listed reasons (Employment Act 1988, s. 3). TURERA tightens the screw even further by exacting a general right not to be excluded and expanding the scope of unjustifiable discipline. However, as I.T. Smith and J.T. Wood point out, these statutes have not replaced the common law because:

> there may be situations where the statutory actions are available, but some tactical advantage may be gained by bringing common law proceedings instead; such proceedings may be brought for speed, or in order to obtain declaratory or injunctive relief, particulary where what is at stake is not just the position of one individual member, but rather the government of the Union itself.[6]

The Rule Book

The Rule Book and the Courts

The starting point for judicial involvement has traditionally been the contract of membership. The professed function of the law in this area is to strike a balance between the conflicting notions of union autonomy on the one hand and the rights of the individual member on the other.

In readily intervening to protect the individual, it may be that – as with strike law – the courts have shown little understanding of the needs for collective solidarity within trade unions.

Means of Intervention

The foundation of the court's jurisdiction is contract, and the courts may regularly review affairs on that basis. But contract law has its limitations. In particular, members can sign away their rights and freedom of contract means that a union cannot be compelled to let an applicant join the group. The courts have therefore found new ways of intervening in the internal affairs of trade unions where contract fails to provide a satisfactory solution.

First, and most importantly, they have said that union committees and tribunals must observe the rules of natural justice in determining the rights of members. Second, they have developed the principle of the right to work. It is said that the common law recognises that every worker has a right to work, a right not to be arbitrarily and unreasonably prevented from earning his/her living as s/he wills. Third, on occasion, they have argued that the authority of the rule book derives from some other source other than the contract of membership and that certain actions were ultra vires (beyond the powers of) the union. An early and notorious example of this was the so-called *Osborne Judgement* in 1915 (*Amalgamated Society of Railway Servants* v. *Osborne* [1910] AC 87), where the House of Lords held that a trade union had no power to sponsor a member of Parliament. The Law Lords held that a union, whether registered or unregistered, had only the powers conferred on it by the Trade Union Acts 1871–6. That did not include the power to spend money on political objects. Rules allowing such expenditure were ultra vires the statute. The decision was reversed by the Trade Union Act 1913, which made it clear that a trade union could have other objects besides its 'statutory objects' of conducting industrial relations. That is the basis of the present law, as we saw from the definition in TULR(C)A, s. 1. The 1913 Act specifically enacted that a trade union had the power to apply its funds for any lawful object for any lawful purpose or object authorised by its constitution. Therefore, ever since 1913 it has been impossible to claim that any union rule was ultra vires the statute.

However, more recently it has been suggested that a union rule can be invalidated as 'ultra vires at common law'. The basis of the argument – the main proponent of which was Lord Denning – is that the rule book is not a contract at all, but akin to a legislative code of bye-laws. It this is correct, then the court has the power to intervene, as in administrative law, if the rule is unreasonable. Having said that, Lord Denning's approach attracted little or no support from other judges and was unequivocally rejected by the House of Lords in *Faramus* v. *Film Artistes Association* [1964] AC 925.

Admission to a Union at Common Law

The lack of contractual relationship between the union and the applicant for membership has made it difficult for the courts to find a theoretical basis for review in exclusion cases. Indeed, in two decisions the House of Lords construed the fact that the plaintiffs had been admitted wrongly into membership as meaning that they had never been members of the relevant unions.

In *Faramus* v. *Film Artistes Association* [1964] 1 All ER 25 HL,[7] rule 4 (2) of the defendant association provided that: 'No person who has been convicted in a court of law of a criminal offence (other than a motoring offence not punishable by imprisonment) shall be eligible for, or retain membership of the association.' When he signed the application forms for membership, the appellant denied that he had been convicted of any offence, though he had twice been convicted of minor offences in Jersey several years earlier. After he had been in the union for eight years, his previous convictions were discovered and the union claimed that he was not, and had never been, a member. He sought a declaration that he was a member and an injunction restraining the union from excluding him from membership.

The House of Lords held:

(1) That Faramus had never in fact been validly elected a member.
(2) The membership contract, including the relevant rule, was validated as regards restraint of trade by s. 3 Trade Union Act 1871 (see now TULR[C]A, s. 11).
(3) The rules prescribing qualifications for entry into a union cannot be invalidated on the grounds of 'unreasonableness' or being contrary to natural justice.

The concept of the 'right to work', however, provided the most radical means of attack for the judges in their attempt to review decisions on admission. This was a development carried out almost single-handedly by Lord Denning. Although first discussed in 1952 (*Lee* v. *Showmen's Guild* [1952] 2 QB 329 CA), it was used for the first time in *Nagle* v. *Feilden* [1966] 2 QB 633 CA.

The stewards of the Jockey Club refused Mrs Nagle a licence to train racehorses in pursuance of their unwritten policy of refusing a licence to a woman. Mrs Nagle sued for an injunction and a declaration that the practice was against public policy, but her statement of claim was struck out as disclosing no cause of action. She appealed against this decision. The Court of Appeal granted an interlocutory injunction on the basis that she had an arguable case.

Lord Denning stated:

> The common law of England has for centuries recognised that a man has a right to work at his trade or profession without being unjustly excluded from it. He is not to be shut out from it at the whim of those having the governance of it. If they make a rule which enables them to reject his application arbitrarily or capriciously, not reasonably, that rule is bad. It is against public policy. The court will not give effect to it.

The interlocutory injunction enabled the parties to reach a settlement. Hence the case did not come to court for final judgement.

Edwards v. *SOGAT* (1971) Ch 354 CA, constituted the most radical application of the doctrine. The union's decision not to readmit Edwards into membership meant loss of employment. In such circumstances, Lord Denning offered the following opinion:

> I do not think the defendant union, or any other trade union, can give itself by its rules an unfettered discretion to expel a man or to withdraw his membership. The reason lies in the man's right to work. This is now fully recognised by law. It is a right which is of especial importance when a trade union operates a 'closed shop' or '100 per cent membership', for that means that no man can become employed or remain in employment with a firm unless he is a member of the union. If his union card is withdrawn, he has to leave the employment. He is deprived of his livelihood. The courts of this country will not allow so great a power to be exercised arbitrarily or capriciously or with unfair discrimination, neither in the making of rules, nor in the enforcement of them.

Prima facie the *Nagle* v. *Feilden* doctrine would seem equally applicable to those unions operating a closed shop. However, there is a fundamental difficulty. It is not clear that the concept of the right to work is anything more than the doctrine of restraint of trade reinterpreted from the standpoint of the individual. Whenever a union by its rules or policies arbitrarily or unreasonably restrains trade, it necessarily arbitrarily or unreasonably interferes with the right to work. This point is addressed in neither *Nagle* or *Edwards*.

Discipline and Expulsion at Common Law

Two principal methods of judicial control of trade union disciplinary action are that:

(1) A union should comply strictly with its rules on a contract.
(2) Union rules and procedures must comply with the rules of natural justice.

Strict Compliance with Rules

Union rules can broadly be classified into two kinds:

(a) those which permit disciplinary sanctions to be imposed for some specific offence such as disobedience to instructions issued by the union executive; and

(b) those which leave the particular actions unspecified – for example, rules permitting sanctions to be imposed for such offences as conduct detrimental to the union, or prejudicial to its interests. Sometimes these rules are phrased subjectively, such as those that prohibit conduct which *in the opinion* of the executive committee might be detrimental to union interests.

The courts have construed both kinds of rules strictly, and they will resolve any ambiguity in favour of the member.

The following two cases illustrate the principles which the courts will adopt where the rules are general and inherently ambiguous.

In *Lee* v. *Showmen's Guild of GB* [1952] 1 All ER 1175 CA, the plaintiff was charged with 'unfair competition' under a union rule. An area committee of the union fined him for breaking the rule. Failure to pay the fine was, under the rules, to result in expulsion. The plaintiff did not pay the fine and was expelled. He sought an injunction to prevent the union from enforcing his expulsion. The Court of Appeal held that the courts will examine the decisions of domestic tribunals to see that the tribunal has observed the law, including the correct interpretation of the rules, which form the contract between the members. 'The true construction of the contract is to be decided by the courts and by no one else' (per Lord Justice Denning, at p. 344).

On the evidence in this case, the plaintiff could not properly have been found guilty of unfair competition and the committee was, therefore, acting without jurisdiction.

The basis for the intervention was described by Lord Justice Denning thus:

the question whether the committee has acted within its jurisdiction depends, in my opinion, on whether the facts adduced before them were reasonably capable of being held to be a breach of the rules. If they were, then the proper inference is that the committee correctly construed the rules and have acted within their jurisdiction. If, however, the facts were not reasonably capable of being held to be in breach and yet the committee held them in breach, then the only inference is that the committee have misconstrued the rules and exceeded their jurisdiction.

That is, it had come to a conclusion which no reasonable tribunal would have reached. Hence any purported expulsion was invalid. The effect of this decision, therefore, was to allow the courts to substitute their own view of the meaning of a blanket offence for that of the union.

The manner in which the courts have extended contractual principles to deal with blanket offence cases is most vividly illustrated by the case law on unions' powers to discipline members who have failed to participate in industrial action.

In *Esterman* v. *NALGO* [1974] ICR 625 ChD, there was a pay dispute and NALGO held a ballot on the question of selective strike action but only 49 per cent of the vote was cast in favour. Subsequently the union instructed its members not to assist in administering local elections. Esterman defied this instruction and, in consequence, was to be disciplined by the union on the basis that she was guilty of conduct rendering her unfit for membership. The relevant rule read: 'Any member who disregards any regulation issued by the branch, or is guilty of conduct which, in the opinion of the executive committee, renders him unfit for membership, shall be liable to expulsion.'

Esterman sought an injunction against the union to restrain it from taking disciplinary action against her. An injunction was granted on the basis that in the circumstances no reasonable tribunal could bona fide come to the conclusion that disobedience of the order to strike demonstrated any unfitness to be a member of NALGO.

The Lee and Esterman cases are important because they emphasise that the courts' jurisdiction between unions and members is based on contract, that questions of interpretation are reserved to the courts; and because it indicates the way in which the courts will control general blanket disciplinary provisions. Esterman's case shows that the mere fact that the provision is in subjective terms – 'in the opinion of' the disciplinary body – is unlikely to make a difference to the willingness of the courts to intervene.

Natural Justice

When exercising disciplinary functions, the trade union is taken to operate as a quasi-judicial body: 'although the jurisdiction of a domestic tribunal is founded on contract, express or implied, nevertheless the parties are not free to make any contract they like.' (*Breen* v. *AEU* [1971] 2 QB 175). It is thus impossible to exclude, even by an express and unambiguous rule, the right of members to be heard in their own defence before disciplinary action is taken against them. This means that the rules of natural justice require two things:

(1) A disciplined member must have a proper notice of the complaint and an opportunity to be heard by the appropriate committee.

(2) The tribunal must act in an unbiased manner and reach an honest decision.

An example of a 'notice' is found in *Annamunthodo* v. *Oilfield Workers' Trade Union* [1961] 3 All ER 621. The appellant was charged in writing with four specific offences under a named union rule. None of the offences gave rise to the possibility of expulsion from the union. The initial hearing attended by the appellant was adjourned and he did not attend the remainder of the hearing. He was subsequently informed that he had been convicted on all four charges but had been expelled under a blanket rule with which he had not been charged. It was held by the Privy Council that he should have been given notice of the new charge and a fair opportunity of meeting it. The order for expulsion was set aside.

The other requirement of natural justice is for an unbiased tribunal to adjudicate on the merits of the case. Clearly, the disciplinary proceedings of trade unions are controlled by lay people and the law cannot demand the same level of impartiality that would be required of a judge or arbitrator. Instead their task is to have 'a will to reach an honest conclusion after hearing what was argued on either side and a resolve not to make their minds up beforehand' (per Viscount Simon in *White* v. *Kuzych* [1951] AC 585, Privy Council).

But this tolerance does not excuse the intervention of those with particular interests over and above those inevitable in such situations. *Roebuck* v. *NUM (Yorkshire Area) (No. 2)* [1978] ICR 676 arose after the union area president (Arthur Scargill), acting on behalf of the union, had successfully sued a newspaper for libel. In the action two union members had given evidence for the newspaper. At the instigation of Mr Scargill, the area executive resolved to charge those members with conduct detrimental to the interests of the union. The executive found the charges proved and this was confirmed by the area council which had originally referred the matter to the executive. Mr Scargill was president of both bodies and participated in their proceedings, questioning the plaintiffs and taking part in the deliberations. However, he did not vote on the resolution to suspend one of the plaintiffs from office as branch chairman and declare the other ineligible for office in the union for two years.

The judge found that it was irrelevant to consider whether Scargill's presence and conduct had an influence on the result. The real issue concerned the fact that his presence at all stages of the disciplinary procedure gave the impression that the dice were loaded against Roebuck. The decision to discipline Roebuck, therefore, could not stand since justice had to be seen to be done.

Excluding the Jurisdiction of the Court at Common Law

A union rule which seeks to bar the member from pursuing legal redress is void and unenforceable as against public policy.[8]

Less clear-cut is the validity of a rule that the union's internal disciplinary procedures must be exhausted before a member can apply to the court. Courts recognise that there are many advantages in internal resolution of the dispute. Thus in *Leigh* v. *NUR* [1970] Ch 326, Mr Justice Goff stated:

[Wh]ere there is an express provision in the rules that the plaintiff must first exhaust his domestic remedies, the court is not absolutely bound by that because its jurisdiction cannot be ousted, but the plaintiff will have to show cause why it should interfere with the contractual position ...

[In] the absence of such a provision the court can readily, or at all events more readily, grant relief without prior recourse to the domestic remedies, but may require the plaintiff to resort first to those remedies.

Exhaustion of internal procedures would not be required if the domestic proceedings were irretrievably biased; if they involve a serious point of law or fraud is at issue; or if the internal procedures would involve excessive delay.

In *Esterman* the court went further to hold that a plaintiff may bring an action to stop *impending* disciplinary action if s/he can show that there is no lawful basis for it.

Access to the Courts

The Employment Act 1988, s. 2, provided a new right for union members not to be denied access to the court to pursue a grievance against their union. The relevant provisions are now to be found in TULR(C)A 1992. Where court proceedings relate to a grievance which a member began to pursue against his/her union more than six months before applying to the court, the court must not: (a) dismiss; (b) stay or resist; or (c) adjourn the proceedings on the ground that further internal procedures for resolving the grievance are available under the union rules. (TULR[C]A, s. 63).

However, TULR(C)A, s. 63 (6), states that this six-month rule is without prejudice to any rule of law by which a court could ignore any such union rule already – so the principles discussed in *Leigh* above are still relevant.

Refusals to Admit and Expulsions in the Interests of Inter-union Relations

The TUC has drawn up a set of 'Principles Governing Relations between Unions' – the so-called Bridlington Principles. They require every affiliated union to ask all applicants for membership if they are or have recently been a union member. The new union must then ask the old union whether the member has resigned, has any subscription arrears, is 'under discipline or penalty', or if there are any other reasons why s/he should not be accepted. If the old union objects, the dispute may be resolved by the TUC Disputes Committee. Most affiliated unions have a provision in their rule books providing for the automatic termination of membership, following a period of notice, in order to comply with the decision of the Disputes Committee. The courts have upheld the validity of such rules, provided that the power is exercised following a *valid* decision of the Disputes Committee itself.[9]

In *Cheall* v. *APEX* [1983] 2 AC 180, the House of Lords held that an individual trade unionist had no right to be heard by the TUC Disputes Committee before it made its determination. Furthermore, there was

no existing rule of public policy that would prevent trade unions from entering into arrangements with one another which they consider to be in the interests of their members in promoting order in industrial relations and enhancing their members' bargaining power with their employers.

In its 1991 Green Paper, 'Industrial Relations in the 1990s' (Cm. 1602), the government expressed the view that the law should be amended so as to guarantee freedom of choice where more than one trade union can genuinely claim to be able to represent an employee's interests.

In the government's opinion, a union should not be obliged to accept someone into membership if it does not represent employees of a similar skill or occupation. Nor should it be obliged to accept an applicant who has been an unsatisfactory member of another union because, for example, of a record of refusing to pay subscriptions. However, a union should not be at liberty to refuse to accept an individual into membership simply because s/he was previously a member of another union, which gives that union sole recruitment rights in a particular company or sector. TURERA s. 14 contains provisions designed to implement these views.

The remedy for an infringement of this new right will be by way of a complaint to an IT for a declaration and compensation. The remedies will operate in a very similar way to those which already apply to unreasonable exclusion or expulsion from a trade union, and to unjustifiable discipline by a trade union (see below).

Statutory Controls over Admissions and Expulsions

Pre-1980 Law

As we have seen, in 1968 the Donovan Commission suggested that a review body should be created to hear complaints concerning arbitrary exclusions or expulsions. No such body was ever created by statute, although s. 65 IRA 1971 did contain provisions prohibiting arbitrary or unreasonable discrimination against applicants as members. A similar provision contained in s. 5 TULRA 1974 was repealed by TULR(A)A 1976. In response, the TUC established its own Independent Review Committee in April 1976 to provide a voluntary forum for hearing cases alleging unreasonable exclusion or expulsion from unions operating a closed shop.

The IRC's awards were not legally binding but the affiliates agreed to be bound by them. The remedy was a recommendation that a union admit or readmit the complainant into membership; it had no authority to award compensation. The major weakness was that an IRC recommendation could not be enforced against an employer – that is, even if the union reinstated a worker, there was nothing to force the employer to take that employee back if dismissed – though, of course, there is now the unfair dismissal remedy in such cases.

Once the government introduced legislation covering the area of admissions and expulsions in unions operating the closed shop, the voluntary machinery, in the words of the TUC, 'faded away'.

The Employment Act 1980

The Conservative government was not satisfied with the TUC's self-regulation and enacted s. 4 of EA 1980. This reverted the position to broadly that of the period of the IRA 1971, except s. 4 *only* applied where the employer operated a union membership agreement. This law is now set out in TULR(C)A, s. 174. This right remains alongside the more recent and general provisions on unjustifiable discipline by trade unions, which apply in all cases whether inside or outside closed shops (see below). Finally, as we saw in chapter 17, pre-entry closed shops experienced yet a further legal onslaught as a result of the Employment Act 1990 which made it unlawful to refuse a person employment because s/he is not or does not wish to become a union member. (See now TULR[C]A, s. 137.)

Under the current statutory regime, an individual seeking a job where a closed shop – or 'union membership agreement' – operates has a right: (a) not to have his/her membership application unreasonably refused; and (b) not to be unreasonably expelled from the union (TULR[C]A ss. 174–7).

TURERA s. 14 replaces these provisions with new ss. 174–7 which provide a general right for workers not to be excluded or expelled from any union unless the exclusion or expulsion is for a statutory 'permitted' reason. The permitted exceptions are:

- The individual fails to satisfy an 'enforceable membership requirement' contained in the rules of the union. A requirement is 'enforceable' if it restricts membership solely by reference to one or more of the following criteria: employment in a specified trade, industry or profession; occupational description (including grade, level or category of employment); or possession of specified trade, industrial or professional qualifications or work experience.
- The individual does not qualify by reason of the union operating only in particular parts of Great Britain.
- The exclusion or expulsion is entirely attributable to the individual's conduct. But 'conduct' does not include ceasing to be, or having ceased to be, a member of another trade union or an employee of a particular employer or at a particular place. The definition also excludes any conduct to which TULR(C)A s. 65 – the right not to be unjustifiably disciplined by a trade union – applies (see below).

Remedies

These are complex. A person who has obtained a declaration from a tribunal that he or she was unreasonably excluded or expelled may claim compensation. The level will depend on whether the union has in fact admitted or readmitted him or her pursuant to the declaration.

Where the applicant has been admitted or readmitted, the basis of the award is to compensate for the loss sustained by the union's earlier refusal, subject to the obligation of the applicant to mitigate his/her damage, and to a reduction where the refusal to admit or the expulsion was to any extent caused or contributed to by the action of the applicant. The maximum compensation is 30 times the maximum amount of a week's pay allowable in computing the basic award for unfair dismissal cases plus the maximum compensatory award for time being in force in respect of unfair dismissal (s. 176[4]).

So, from 1 June 1993 this is 30 x £205 + £11,000 = £17,150.

If the union refuses to abide by the tribunal's initial declaration, having been given four weeks to do so, the sanction becomes more draconian. The complainant may now go straight to the EAT, within six months of the declaration. The EAT may then award a sum which it 'considers just and equitable in all the circumstances' (s. 176[5]). The size of the award will probably reflect, among other things, the estimated loss of future earnings caused by the employee not being able to work in 'closed shop employment'.

The maximum award is calculated in three parts:

(a)   30 times the maximum calculable weeks' pay (30 x £205 = £6,150)
(b)   maximum compensatory award (£11,000)
(c)   52 times the maximum weeks pay calculable when assessing the additional award in unfair dismissal (52 x £205 = £10,660)

Therefore the maximum is £27,810 (from 1 June 1993).

The minimum award before the EAT is £2,700; there is no minimum award before an IT. The rules of mitigation and contributory fault apply to the action before the EAT. The maximum or minimum is to be applied before any deduction on account of failure to mitigate, contributory fault or compensation already paid.

In *Howard* v. *NGA* [1985] ICR 101, the EAT reduced the award by 15 per cent because the applicant had contributed to the refusal of membership by the union when he took a job with a company which he knew subscribed to the closed shop agreement, while his application for union membership was still under consideration.

Other Relevant Provisions

Four other statutes are relevant to this area. RRA 1976 and SDA 1975 make it unlawful to discriminate on grounds of gender or race against an applicant for trade union membership. The Trade Union and Labour Relations (Consolidation) Act, s. 82 (c), states that where the union operates a political fund, it must not make contribution to the fund a condition of admission or discriminate against a non-contributor. Union rule books are required to contain a rule to this effect. Finally, as we see below, the EA 1988 provides a general prohibition on unjustifiable discipline of trade union members.

Unjustifiable Discipline

The Employment Act 1988, s. 3, provides that a union member may not be unjustifiably disciplined by his or her union. The law is now set out in TULR(C)A, s. 64.

This is a controversial provision, widely regarded by critics as a 'scab's charter'. The provision means that a union is prohibited from disciplining a member for not taking part in industrial action notwithstanding that a majority of that member's fellow workers voted in favour of the action in a properly held ballot. As such, s. 64 is understandably seen by the union movement as an attack on the fundamental concepts of union solidarity and collectivism.

Ewan McKendrick has argued:

> By prohibiting the exercise of disciplinary sanctions by unions, [s. 64] stacks all the disciplinary powers on the side of the employer. In sum [s. 64] is an objectionable intervention in union affairs, it is a possible violation of our international obligations and it elevates the individual interest of a union member to a point where it unacceptably undermines the collective strength of the union and represents an unwarranted intrusion into internal union affairs.[10]

It is deemed to be unjustifiable to discipline a trade union member for the following types of conduct:

(a) failure to participate in or support a strike or industrial action by members of his or her own trade union or any other or indicate opposition to the industrial action;

(b) failure to breach a contract of employment or any other agreement between the member and 'a person for whom he normally works' (this is a broader concept than 'employee and employer' and is likely to cover workers who are classified as self-employed);

(c) the making of an assertion (in legal proceedings or otherwise) that the union, or any official, representative or trustee, has contravened or is proposing to contravene a requirement imposed by the unions rules;

(d) encouraging or assisting a worker to perform his/her contractual duty or encouraging or assisting him/her to make or attempt to vindicate an allegation covered by (c) above;

(e) consulting the commissioner for the rights of trade union members or certification officer or asking them to provide advice or assistance;

(f) failing to comply with any requirement imposed as a result of unjustifiable disciplinary action, whether taken against the complainant or another, for example, refusing to comply with a ruling that a particular member should be fined or expelled;

(g) proposing to do any of the above, or doing acts which are preparatory or incidental to them.

TURERA extends the list of conduct for which it is unjustifiable for a trade union to discipline a member to include the following:

(h) failing to agree, or withdrawing agreement, to a check-off agreement;
(i) resigning, or proposing to resign, from the union, joining or proposing to join another union, or refusing to join another union;
(j) working with, or proposing to work with, individuals who are not members of another union; or
(k) working for, or proposing to work for, an employer who employs or who has employed non-members of the union, or non-members of another union
(l) requiring the union to do an act which the union is, by virtue of TURERA, required to do on the requisition of a member (see s. 16).

Discipline is widely defined by TULR(C)A, s. 64 (2), and includes expulsion from a union or a branch of a union; fines; loss of any benefits, facilities or services; that another trade union, or a branch or section of another trade union, should be encouraged or advised not to accept that individual as a member; or that the individual should be subjected to any other detriment.

Procedure

A claim must be made to the IT within three months of the imposition of the disciplinary sanction. There is power to extend the period if the IT is satisfied:

(a) that it was not reasonably practicable for the complaint to have been presented within the three-month limit; and

(b) that any delay in making the complaint is wholly or partly attributable to any reasonable attempt to appeal internally against the determination to which the complaint relates.

Remedies

Where the IT find that the complainant has been unjustifiably disciplined, it will make a declaration to that effect. The complainant may then make a further application to the IT for compensation not earlier than four weeks but not later than six months after the date of the initial declaration.

What happens next depends on the trade union's response. If the union has revoked its disciplinary decision and taken all necessary steps to put that decision into effect, the further application is to the IT. If, on the other hand, the union fails to revoke its decision, the further application is to the EAT.

The amount of compensation to be awarded will be such as is considered to be just and equitable in all the circumstances of the case, subject to the usual rules relating to mitigation of loss and contributory fault.

Where the application is to the IT the maximum award is 30 times a week's pay (that is, for 1993/4, 30 x £205 = £6,150) together with the maximum compensatory award currently available (that is £11,000) – a grand total of £17,150.

Where the application is to the EAT, the same maximum figure applies, but there is a fixed minimum award which currently stands at £2,700 (s. 67[8]).

Trade Union Democracy

Rule Book as Contract and Constitution

At common law, the government and administration of a union must be carried out in accordance with the terms of the contract of membership which are contained primarily in the rule book. A failure to do this will normally constitute a breach of contract, and the courts may well declare it ultra vires (beyond the powers of) the union.

The potential for challenging the action taken by a union in breach of its rules was repeatedly illustrated in the cases raised by working miners against various areas of the NUM during the miners' strike of 1984–5. In these cases, the judges relied on a strict construction of the NUM's rule book to establish the requirement for conducting ballots before authorising industrial action. In *Taylor* v. *NUM (Derbyshire Area) (No. 1)* [1984] IRLR 440, it was held that the local area was required by its rules to obtain 55 per cent support in a ballot for strike action before such action could be official; in *Taylor* v. *NUM (Yorkshire Area)* [1984] IRLR 445, it was held that an area ballot held some two and a half years previously was too remote to be capable of justifying a lawful call for strike action under the rules. In both cases the judges accepted that the strike in reality constituted national action, which was also unlawful in the absence of a national ballot.

Once the strike was called in breach of the rules, injunctions were granted preventing the issuing of instructions to the membership not to work or to cross picket lines *(Taylor* v. *NUM [Derbyshire Area] [No.1]).* A second consequence of the holding that the action was beyond the rules was that the use of union funds to support the strike could be restrained. In *Taylor* v. *NUM (Derbyshire Area)(No. 3)* [1985] IRLR 99, the judge held that it was ultra vires for the union to authorise expenditure on strike action which had been called in breach of the area's rules. Further, the officials who had misapplied union monies in this way were in breach of the fiduciary duty which they owed to the members, and could be personally liable for such unauthorised expenditure. The miners' cases demonstrated the readiness of the judges to issue interlocutory injunctions to restrain the alleged unlawful behaviour and, as we shall see, the potential for using 'scab' workers to mount legal challenges against a striking union was not lost on the government when it framed the Employment Act 1988.[11]

Union Accounts

TULR(C)A lays down detailed rules for the carrying on of a union's financial affairs. The union must make annual returns to the certification officer (s. 32), including a profit and loss account, a balance sheet, an auditor's report and any other documents that may be required. All must be approved by auditors, who should be independent and professionally qualified. The overriding obligation is to present accounts which give a 'true and fair view' of the matters to which they relate (s. 32[3]).

Failure either to submit an annual return or to maintain proper accounts and accounting controls is a criminal offence (s. 45[1]). It is also an offence to falsify the accounts (s. 45[4]).

Annual returns are open to public inspection at the offices of the certification officer (s. 32[6]). The union itself must also provide a copy of its latest annual return to anyone who asks (s. 32[5]). It may make a reasonable charge.

The 1991 Green Paper, 'Industrial Relations in the 1990s', contained a number of proposals for strengthening the law as it affects the responsibility of trade union leaders for union finances. In the government's view, the Lightman Inquiry into allegations of serious misconduct by senior officials of the NUM in the management of the union's finances indicated that the rights of union members in this area need further support.[12]

Consequently, TURERA contains provisions:

- providing the certification officer (CO) with wider powers to direct a trade union to produce documents relating to its financial affairs and to appoint inspectors to investigate the financial affairs of a trade union where it appears to the CO that there is impropriety in the conduct of those affairs. It requires reports of investigations to be published. Reports will be admissible in legal proceedings.

- creating new offences in connection with the CO's proposed powers of inspection and investigation. It will be an offence to: contravene any duty or requirement imposed by the CO or inspectors relating to the production of documents and so on; destroy, mutilate or falsify a document relating to the financial affairs of the union (unless there was no intention to conceal information or defeat the law); fraudulently part with, alter or delete anything in such a document; or provide or make an explanation or statement, either knowingly or recklessly, which is false.

- increasing the maximum penalty for an offence relating to the duty to keep accounting records or the duties as to annual returns, auditors or members' superannuation schemes from a fine not exceeding level 3 on the standard scale to a fine not exceeding level 5 (£2,000 in 1992/3). The new offence of failing to comply with any requirements by the CO or inspectors relating to the production of financial documents and the like will attract a similar penalty.

- providing that certain offences relating to falsification, destruction, alteration or mutilation of financial documents may result in imprisonment for up to six months, a fine of up to £5,000, or both.

- that instead of a six-month limit, proceedings under the Act should be possible at any time within three years of the relevant offence, provided that the information is laid before the court within six months of the discovery of the offence.

- providing that persons convicted of offences in connection with the financial affairs of trade unions are disqualified from being a member of a union's executive or from being president or general secretary of a union. The disqualification periods are five years or 10 years, depending on the gravity of the offence.

- a new statutory duty for a trade union to provide each of its members, on an annual basis, with a written summary of its financial affairs. The statement is to include an indication of what the member may do if s/he suspects an irregularity in the conduct of the union's affairs.

- annual returns to the CO to identify the salary or other remuneration (including loans and benefits in kind) provided out of union funds to each member of the union's principal executive committee, president and general secretary and to include a statement of the number of names on the union's register of members and how many are not accompanied by an address. (TURERA ss. 8, 9, 10, 11, 12)

Members' Right of Access to a Trade Union's Accounts

Prior to 1988 an ordinary member did not possess a statutory right to inspect the union's accounts, though s/he may have been given that right under the rule book. If there was such a right under the rules, then the member also had the right to be accompanied by an accountant or other agent when inspecting the accounts – see *Norey* v. *Keep* [1909] 1 Ch 561 and *Taylor* v. *NUM (Derbyshire Area)* [1985] IRLR 65.

The first *statutory* provision giving rights of access to union records, whether or not there is an express rule, was provided by the Employment Act 1988. The relevant provisions are now contained in TULR(C)A. Unions must:

(a) make their accounting records available for inspection by members for six years beginning with 1 January following the end of the period to which the records relate (s. 29);
(b) give members (but only members) the right to inspect such records on request (s. 30[1]);
(c) allow members the right to inspect the records in the company of an accountant (s. 30[2][b]);
(d) supply members with copies or extracts from any such records as they may require (s. 30[2][c]).

The union may exact a charge to cover reasonable administrative expenses.

Where it is claimed that a union has failed to comply with a request within 28 days, a member may apply to the court for an order requiring inspection and so forth. It is also a criminal offence to fail to keep accounting records available for inspection (s. 31).

Indemnification by Unions of Officials

Prior to 1988 it was not clear as to what extent (if any) a trade union might use its funds to indemnify members for criminal sanctions imposed upon them for activities such as illegal picketing, or for being held in contempt of court.

The issue was first raised in *Drake* v. *Morgan* [1978] ICR 56. During the journalists' strike in 1977, a number of members of the NUJ were charged with offences in connection with picketing and fined. The union's national executive committee passed a resolution that it would indemnify members in respect of these offences, with the exception of cases involving physical violence. The judge refused the application for an injunction to restrain the union from implementing this resolution, on the basis that the resolution had been passed *after* the offences had been committed and therefore there was not a general indemnity for members who might commit offences. He thought that different considerations might apply if continued resolutions authorising expenditure from funds might lead to an expectation that a union would indemnify its members against the consequences of future offences (see also *Thomas* v. *NUM [S Wales Area]* [1985] IRLR 136).

The government was of the view that the common law position was unsatisfactory. It was anxious to ensure that union officials should take the full legal consequences of unlawful acts, and that they should not rely upon indemnification by their unions.

The EA 1988 banned all forms of indemnity, retrospective or prospective. Once again the law is now set out in TULR(C)A. Section 15 makes it unlawful for a union's property to be applied for the purposes of indemnifying individuals for any penalty imposed by a court for:

(a) contempt of court; or
(b) a relevant criminal offence as set out in an order.

As McKendrick wryly observes: 'Thus, even the payment of an individual's parking fine by the union will be caught, unless it is exempted by order.'[13]

Remedy

If the property of the union is applied in a manner caught by s. 15, the union may recover its value from the individual indemnified (s. 15[2]).

Any member who claims that the union is *unreasonably* refusing to take steps towards recovery may apply to the court for authority to take such proceedings on behalf of the union – at the union's expense (s. 15[3]). This special provision overcomes the procedural difficulties which might otherwise be created by the rule in *Foss* v. *Harbottle* (1843) 2 Hare 461,[14] often applied to unions, which provides that where a wrong has been done to a corporate body, a minority of the members will be bound by a decision of the majority to take no legal action to remedy the wrong, if none of the members in the minority has personally suffered any harm.

Section 15 is without prejudice to any other enactment, trade union rule or provision which would otherwise make it unlawful for trade union property to be used in a particular way (s. 15[6]). Thus the expenditure of money may be restricted to lawful objects or objects other than industrial action in the union rule book.

McKendrick observes:

> As was pointed out in the Green Paper ['Trade Unions and Their Members'], the incorporation of contempt of court opens up considerable 'scope for willing martyrdom' where individual members of the union are named by the plaintiff in the proceedings. In the NUM dispute martyrdom for Mr Scargill was avoided by an anonymous donor paying Mr Scargill's fine but, presumably, were such a fine to be paid in such a way in the future, union members would be able to exercise their right to inspect the union accounts to ensure that the fine was not paid by their union. It is rather surprising that the Government has seen fit to include a provision which increases, rather than decreases, the prospect of martyrdom when they have consistently sought to ensure that remedies are enforceable against union property rather than individual union members.[15]

Control of Union Trustees

It will be remembered that the property of a trade union is vested in trustees in trust for the union (TULR(C)A s. 12[1]). This arises because a union is an unincorporated association and so, not being a legal person, it cannot hold property in its own name.

Union officials in general owe a fiduciary duty to their union. In *Taylor* v. *NUM (Derbyshire Area) (No. 3)* [1985] IRLR 99, Mr Justice Vinelott held that union officers who sanctioned payments to unofficial strikers, where such payments were in breach of union rules, were liable to reimburse the trade union.

The role of union trustees came into sharp focus during the miners' strike when there were allegations that the trustees – Scargill, McGahey and Heathfield – were in breach of their fiduciary position through repeatedly being in contempt of court. In November 1984 a receiver was appointed on the grounds that the trustees were 'not fit and proper people to be in charge of other people's money'.

The Employment Act 1988 gave members new powers against trustees of the union's property in respect of the unlawful application of its assets, or in cases where the trustees comply with any unlawful direction given to them under the rules of the union. A claim may be brought where the trustees are proposing or have already acted in this way, but to bring a claim in the latter case the claimant must have been a member at the time when the property was applied or the unlawful direction complied with (see now TULR(C)A, s. 16).

Commenting on the section, Bowers and Auerbach observe that it is:

> Another measure designed to give members powerful and effective controls over the use of the union's property and funds, thought to be particularly needed in the context of a later dispute which the union may be waging in the face of the law and the courts. Once again, the litigation of the miners' strike has helped to focus minds on the problem and to suggest a solution. That litigation demonstrated that the courts will not hesitate to respond to individual member actions brought where the union or its officials are thought to be ignoring the rule book or otherwise behaving unlawfully. However, as the Green Paper (*Trade Unions and Their Members*, Paragraph 3.9) pointed out, a right for members to restrain union officials from sponsoring unlawful industrial action, or behaving in an unlawful way, might in practice prove ineffectual, if the situation has been reached where those officials are committed to defying the courts in any event. S.9 therefore adopts a different strategy which might prove more effective: that of aiming at the union's trustees, who are the legal holders and controllers of its property. The powers to remove trustees and to appoint a receiver can thus be used to take the assets completely out of reach and control of officials.[16]

The Orders Which Can Be Made

The court can make such orders as it considers appropriate including:

(a) a requirement that the trustees take all steps specified to protect or recover the union's property;

(b) a power to appoint a receiver;

(c) a power to remove the trustees (s. 16[3]).

Where the property of the union has been applied, or the trustees are proposing to apply the union's property:

(a) in contravention of the order of any court; or

(b) in compliance with any direction given in contravention of a court order

then the court must remove all trustees except any trustee who satisfies the court that there are good reasons for being allowed to remain as a trustee.[17]

Union Elections and Ballots

Imposition of balloting requirements has been a central feature of Conservative governments' industrial relations policy, although views on the efficacy of ballots have varied over time. The Donovan Commission in 1968 rejected compulsory strike ballots on the ground that North American experience showed that they are seen as 'tests of solidarity' and nearly always favour industrial action.

The IRA 1971 contained compulsory balloting procedures but they were only employed on one occasion, the railwayworkers' dispute of 1972, when the subsequent vote was 5-to-1 in favour of strike action.

The 1979 Conservative government again tried to encourage trade union ballots, providing subsidies from public funds under EA 1980. The Trade Union Act went further and required ballots before industrial action, for the principal executive committee and on retaining the political fund. The EA 1988 refined and modified these requirements and also introduced the office of commissioner for the rights of trade union members.

State Funds for Union Postal Ballots
This measure was enacted to encourage unions to hold secret ballots in the hope that 'responsible' union leaders would be elected. It enables the secretary of state to create a scheme for the refund of certain expenses incurred in conducting secret ballots. The scheme is contained in the Funds for Trade Union Ballots Regulations, s. 1 1984 no. 1654. This scheme is narrower than might have been envisaged by the enabling section, since it applies only to postal ballots and not to non-postal or workplace ballots (see reg. 7 of the scheme).

Under the Act money is available for secret ballots on the following issues:

(a) obtaining a decision or ascertaining the view of members of a trade union as to the calling or ending of a strike or other industrial action;

(b) carrying out an election[18] provided by the rules of a trade union or elections to the national executive as required by the TULR(C)A;

(c) elections of workplace representatives (the scheme itself still *does not* apply to such ballots);

(d) amendments to trade union rules;

(e) trade union amalgamations or transfer of engagements;

(f) the *continuation* of a political fund under the Trade Union Act 1913, as amended by the Trade Union Act 1984 – but *not* a ballot to seek to *establish* a political fund;

(g) any such other purposes as the secretary of state may by order specify (TULR[C]A, s. 115).

(h) obtaining a decision or ascertaining the views of members of a trade union as to the acceptance or rejection of a proposal made by an employer which relates in whole or in part to remuneration (whether in money or money's worth), hours of work, level of performance, holiday or pensions.

Application for payments is made to the certification officer – application must be made within six months of the date of the ballot in question. The certification officer will not make payments unless s/he considers that adequate assurances have been given regarding the conditions under which the ballot was held: viz.

all those entitled to vote allowed to vote, provided with a convenient opportunity to vote by post, ballot votes fairly and accurately counted.

If the requirements are satisfied the union may claim to be reimbursed for reasonable costs of stationery and printing for ballot papers, envelopes, explanatory material and the postal costs of sending them out and their return. Applications for payment must be made to the certification officer, itemising all expenditure, but the union cannot receive the money until six weeks after the result of the ballot becomes known. This period provides an opportunity for the making of objections that the appropriate conditions have not been met.

Most TUC unions at first refused to accept government funds as part of their overall policy of non-co-operation with the government's employment legislation. The exceptions were the Electrical, Electronic, Telecommunications, Plumbing Union (EETPU) and the AUEW, who were threatened with TUC discipline for doing so. This policy was subsequently reviewed and the decision whether or not to claim was left to individual unions. By the late 1980s many unions were claiming under the 1980 Act. In 1991, 78 unions made applications in respect of 716 ballots; the certification officer made payments during that year of £4 million. This contrasts with applications in respect of 30 ballots and payments amounting to £72,498 in 1984.

At the end of 1992 the employment secretary, Gillian Shepherd, announced plans to phase the scheme out over the next three years. In her view: 'the scheme now operates largely as a public subsidy for ballots which unions are required to carry out to meet their obligations under the law.'[19]

In 1993/4, public funds will meet only 75 per cent of each qualifying claim. This level of support is to be reduced to 50 per cent of each claim in 1994/5 and 25 per cent in 1995/6. The scheme will cease to operate from 1 April 1996 (TURERA, s. 7(4)).

Executive Elections

By the Trade Union Act 1984 every voting member of the principal executive committee of a trade union had to be elected every five years by all members of the union. The Act overrode anything provided in the rule book of the union, and the union could face an enforcement order in the High Court. The Act also overrode any provision to the contrary in a contract of employment of any executive committee member relating to the tenure.

The 1984 Act related only to a voting member of the executive. But in certain unions the president or general secretary does not have a vote. Even if they had a vote, there was nothing to stop unions changing their rules by constitutional means – to remove the right to vote and therefore avoid the application of the Act. Indeed, such a rule change was carried out by the NUM in 1985 to remove its president's vote.

This was seen by the government to be a weakness in its legislative framework and the law was considerably heightened by what Smith and Wood[20] describe as the 'We'll Get Scargill This Time' amendments in the Employment Act 1988 (see now TULR(C)A, s. 46).

The EA 1988 extended the provisions for the periodic re-election of the members of the principal executive committee of each trade union to:

(a) non-voting members of the principal executive committee who attend and speak at some or all of its meetings;
(b) a union's president and general secretary or any equivalent position.

The provisions *do not* apply to persons who attend the principal executive committee merely to provide:

(a) factual information (such as a research officer)
(b) technical or professional advice (such as union solicitors or accountants). (TULR[C]A, s. 46[2][3])

The Conduct of the Ballot

The Trade Union Act 1984 stipulated a postal ballot as the norm, but went on to allow a trade union to opt for a semi or full workplace ballot if the union was satisfied that there were no reasonable grounds to believe that this would not result in a free election as required by the Act. The 1987 Green Paper, however, pointed to 'concern over ... the non-postal ballot held in 1984 for the election of the Transport and General Workers Union's General Secretary and more recent Civil and Public Services Association elections for General Secretary', as a 'justification for examining this issue more closely'. In the government's view, postal ballots offered less scope for manipulation in the context of executive elections and political fund ballots. This is despite the fact that the most infamous example of union election malpractice, the Electrical Trade Union (ETU) case, involved a postal ballot. EA 1988 ensured that such ballots are to be held by postal voting only. Ballot papers must now both be sent out and returned by post.

Election Addresses

The aim of this provision of the Employment Act 1988 is to allow all candidates an equal opportunity to set out their 'manifesto'. The relevant rule is now set out in TULR(C)A, s. 48. Under this section:

(a) the union must give every candidate in the election the right to have an election address in his or her own words distributed to members entitled to vote;
(b) the union must secure so far as is reasonably practicable that a copy of each election address is distributed by post to each voter at his or her proper address;
(c) none of the candidates should be required to bear the expense of producing those copies;
(d) no modification of any election address must be made by the union save:
(i) at the request of or with the consent of the candidate;

(ii) where the modification is necessarily incidental to the method adopted for producing that copy.

The same method of producing copies must be applied to each election address and no facility or information should be given to one candidate but not to others in respect of:

(a) the method by which copies of the election addresses are produced (by photocopying or printing); or
(b) the modifications which are necessarily incidental to that method.

So far as is reasonably practicable, the union should also secure the same facilities and restrictions for all candidates in relation to:

(a) preparation of election addresses;
(b) submission of election addresses;
(c) length of election addresses;
(d) modification of election addresses;
(e) the incorporation of a photograph or any other matter not in words.

A union may impose restrictions, provided they are applied equally to all candidates, in respect of:

(a) the length of the address, subject to a minimum of 100 words; and
(b) photographs and any other matter not in words.

Moreover,

(a) a deadline for the submission of election addresses must not be earlier than the latest time at which a person may become a candidate at that election;
(b) no person other than the candidate him/herself shall be subject to civil or criminal liability in respect of any publication of a candidate's election address.

Independent Scrutiny of Ballots

Under TULR(C)A, s. 49, both political fund and principal executive committee ballots must be independently scrutinised. TURERA extends this requirement to industrial action ballots and a failure to subject the ballot to independent scrutiny will render any subsequent industrial action unlawful (see s. 20).

The independent scrutineer must satisfy conditions set down in an order made by the secretary of state (s. 49[2]). Under this order, the following may be scrutineers:

(a) solicitors or accountants qualified to be an auditor;
(b) the Electoral Reform Society, the Industrial Society or Unity Security Services Ltd (TU Ballots and Elections Independent Scrutineers Qualifications) Order 1988 (SI 1988 no. 2117).

Section 49 (4) sets out the following duties for the scrutineers:

(a) supervision of production and distribution of all voting papers;
(b) to be the person to whom the voting papers are returned;
(c) to retain custody of all voting papers:

    (i) for one year after the announcement of the ballot result; and
    (ii) if any application is made under s. 54 (complaint of failure to comply with election techniques) or s. 79 (complaint of failure to comply with political fund ballot rules), for a period extending beyond the year until the certification officer or the High Court orders disposal of the papers;

(d) as soon as is reasonably practicable after the last date for return of voting papers, to make a report to the union.

The scrutineer's report must state:

(a) the number of voting papers distributed;
(b) the number of voting papers returned;
(c) the number of votes cast for each proposition or candidate, as the case may be;
(d) the number of spoiled or otherwise invalid voting papers returned.

The scrutineer must also state whether s/he is satisfied that:

(a) there was no reasonable grounds for believing that there was any contravention of a requirement imposed by statute;
(b) reasonable practicable steps were taken with regard to the security arrangements for the production, storage, distribution, return or other handling of the voting papers so as to minimise the risk of any unfairness or malpractice which might occur;
(c) the scrutineer has been able to carry out his/her functions without interference (s. 52[1][2]).

The trade union must *not* publish the result of the election/ballot until this report is received. A copy of the report must also be sent by the trade union to every member of the union within three months of its receipt of the report. Alternatively, the union must take such other steps for notifying members of the contents of the report as is its practice when matters of general interest to all members need to be brought to their attention (s. 52[4]). Where the union does not send a copy of the report to each member, it must include a statement that the union will on request supply any member with a copy of the report either free of charge or on payment of a reasonable fee.

Enforcement of Rules on Elections and Ballots

• Complaint to the certification officer or High Court for a declaration.

- In complaints concerning improperly held elections, the complainant must have been a member at the date of the election *and* when the application is made to the court.
- If the complaint is that the election has not been held, the complainant must be a member on the date of the application.
- Action must be taken within one year from the default.
- The court (but only the court) has the power to make an enforcement order. Such an order will require the union to hold an election, to take such other steps to remedy the declared failure within a specified time, or to abstain from certain acts in the future. Failure to comply with the order amounts to a contempt of court.

Ballots before Industrial Action

Part II of the Trade Union Act 1984 withdrew certain of the immunities contained in s. 13 TULRA in respect of industrial action not approved by a ballot. So, under the original formulation it was the employers who were seen to be the potential plaintiffs: it did *not* provide a cause of action to trade union members themselves.

At common law the members' rights are very restricted. The member may apply to the High Court for an interlocutory mandatory injunction requiring the union to hold a ballot in accordance with its rules, but such an action requires that there is a positive obligation under union rules to hold a ballot and, even in such a case, an interlocutory injunction may be refused because it is a 'very exceptional form of relief' (see *Taylor* v. *NUM [Yorkshire Area]* [1984] IRLR 445. The Green Paper, 'Trade Unions and Their Members', pointed out (para. 2.5) that in the miners' strike (1984/5) there were 19 common law actions brought against the NUM under the rule book for failing to hold a ballot.

The Employment Act 1988 changed the position in line with the proposals contained in the Green Paper and provided a cause of action to members themselves. The complex rules surrounding ballots before industrial action are discussed in detail in chapter 20.

The Role of the CROTUM

The Employment Act 1988 created the role of the commissioner of the rights of trade union members. The first and current commissioner is Mrs Gill Rowlands and her address is to be found in appendix I.

The remit of the CROTUM is now set out in TULR(C)A, part VIII.

An individual who is an actual or prospective party to certain proceedings may apply to the commissioner for the costs of legal assistance.

The proceedings covered by the commissioner's remit are:

(a) right of a trade union member to require a ballot before industrial action (s. 62);

(b) right of a union member to inspect accounts (s. 31);

(c) the unlawful use by trustees of union property (s. 16);

(d) failure to comply with the rules relating to political fund ballots (s. 81);

(e) applications to the court for recovery of trade union property used to indemnify unlawful conduct (s. 15[3]);

(f) applications to the court which concern the failure to hold proper ballots for trade union elections (s. 56);

(g) proceedings which relate to the unlawful application of union funds for political purposes (s. 71).

The secretary of state may make an order adding other categories to this list, and the EA 1990 has extended the Commissioner's potential involvement to include proceedings arising out of an alleged or threatened breach of the rules of a trade union or one of its branches or sections relating to:

(a) the appointment or election of a person to, or removal of a person from, any office

(b) disciplinary proceedings by the union, including expulsion

(c) the authorising or endorsing of industrial action

(d) the balloting of members

(e) the application of the union's funds or property

(f) the imposition, collection or distribution of any levy for the purposes of industrial action

(g) the constitution or proceedings of any committee, conference or other body (see now TULR[C]A, s. 109[2]).

However, the commissioner cannot grant an application for assistance under s. 109 (2) unless it appears that the breach affects (or may affect) other members, or that similar breaches have been committed in relation to other members (TULR[C]A, s. 110[4]).

The commissioner may provide the following forms of assistance:

(a) paying for any legal advice or representation

(b) making arrangements for legal advice or representation

(c) arranging for or paying the costs incurred in arriving at or giving effect to a compromise of proceedings

In exercising her discretion, the commissioner will have regard to, among other things:

(a) whether the case raises a matter of principle

(b) whether the complexity of the case makes it unreasonable to expect the applicant to proceed without assistance

(c) whether the cases involves a matter of substantial public interest (s. 110[2]).

Assistance is mandatory where the proposed proceedings relate to the same matter as a declaration already made against the union by the certification officer about a union election, membership register or political fund ballot, provided that it appears to the commissioner that there is a reasonable prospect of success in obtaining the court order under s. 54 or s. 79 (TULR[C]A, s. 110[3]).

Conclusions on the Recent Legislation on Trade Unions and their Members

The Trade Union Act 1984, the Employment Act 1988, and the Trade Union Reform and Employment Rights Act 1993 extended far-reaching controls over the internal affairs of trade unions. In the name of 'giving the unions back to their members', the legislation attempts to dissipate the strength of organised labour. Nowhere is this better highlighted than in the dual standard adopted by the law in relation to striking workers and those who, in the face of majority vote in favour, refuse to take strike action. Striking union members can be dismissed by the employer with virtual impunity, but if a union disciplines members who have undermined the solidarity of a strike by remaining at work, the prospect of 'pools win' compensation levels looms into sight.

CHAPTER 19

Collective Bargaining

As we have already seen in Chapter 4, collective agreements are a key means by which contracts of employment are formed. The central role which the collective bargaining process occupies can be seen at every stage of employment, from recruitment through to termination.

As well as dealing with a wide range of issues affecting employees collectively and individually, these agreements are crucially important to unions in organisational terms. This is because agreements also deal with essential requirements in the collective bargaining process, such as recognition, rights to information and consultation, and workplace organisational rights. For this reason they can be a key factor in the success or failure of a union as a representative organisation which can promote and defend its members' interests.

Development of Collective Bargaining in the UK

Collective bargaining as a means of agreeing workplace terms and conditions has been established in the UK since the eighteenth century. Unfortunately unions' organisational rights have not always been so well established and recognised.[1] The process received official encouragement after World War I, when joint industrial councils representing 'both sides' of industry were formed to negotiate, agree and periodically revise industry-wide agreements. This important development came at a time when there was intense debate between trade unionists about what the industrial role of unions should be, and how, and to what extent, they should be involved in fixing workers' terms and conditions.[2] The attraction of such national arrangements for employers, as with workplace collective agreements, was that they offered 'stability' in setting terms and maintaining labour costs in the industries they covered.

The system that has developed since then includes bargaining arrangements at national, intermediate and local levels. In some cases national agreements are fairly comprehensive, dealing with both procedural issues (such as the machinery for settling disputes, and redundancy selection) and more central issues like pay, hours and entitlements. In other cases national agreements may do little more than set minimum conditions, leaving it to local negotiations and agreements (or management discretion in some cases) to adapt those conditions according to particular requirements and conditions at a workplace level.

Depending on the particular economic climate at the time, employers and unions have see-sawed between preferences for national and more 'localised' bargaining arrangements, and the picture can vary greatly between different industries and types of employment. This will also depend on the industry concerned and the relative strengths and weaknesses of the unions involved.[3]

Soon after the Donovan Commission reported in 1968, the collective bargaining system came under considerable political scrutiny. Worsening industrial relations problems were put down to a mixture of causes, but principally the uncertainty and unenforceability of collective agreements. Excessive union power in workplaces was also identified by some sections of management and politicians on the right as a factor in undermining the stability of the collective agreement system. These conclusions had not been reached by Donovan, although the Commission did criticise the problems that can occur when workplace bargaining displaces, or overlaps with, agreements negotiated at a sectoral or national level. Nevertheless, the result was new legislation in the form of the Industrial Relations Act 1971, which included a provision that collective agreements were to be presumed to be legally enforceable. There were also elaborate arrangements made for making it an 'unfair industrial practice' to take industrial action which broke agreements (with punishing sanctions for unions and those concerned). The position was changed by the incoming Labour government in 1974, when agreements were, once again, deemed in most cases not to be legally enforceable and this has remained the position to date (see below for details).

Legislative Policies

Government policies towards collective bargaining have been contradictory under both Labour and Conservative. Labour has, at various times, tried to introduce greater elements of compulsion into the process, as seen when the Wilson government made proposals that were completely unacceptable to the labour movement.[4] But at the same time Labour legislation did try to develop collective bargaining, for example by establishing statutory rights to recognition and giving unions legal rights to information for bargaining purposes. As has been observed, there was in the 1960s and 1970s a broad consensus on the desirability of state support for collective bargaining.[5]

Conservative policy has been tolerant of the collective bargaining system itself, offering as it does a disciplined framework within which corporate managements can operate. At the same time, however, the thrust of industrial relations legislation has been directed against unions organisationally. Nor has there been any attempt to develop or maintain procedures which give unions the ability to function effectively. In particular the prerequisites for bargaining, which exist in other countries, are lacking, or missing altogether, in the UK context. These include legal rights to recognition, union membership and organisational rights, and effective rights to information and consultation. Moreover, there is no duty on UK employers to negotiate if they are unwilling to do so, or any requirement for them to negotiate in good faith (unlike other comparable countries). Despite these formidable limitations, the bargaining process and the collective agreement system itself, continues. As ACAS has noted, this is notwithstanding significant changes in patterns of employment and a decline in union membership. 'Collective bargaining', it has said, 'remains the dominant determinant, either directly or indirectly, of the terms and conditions of the majority of employees'.[6] In addition, there is evidence that the role and scope of collective agreements is being widened, for example to accommodate arrangements for meeting production quality standards and to extend 'employee participation' policies along European lines.[7] Intensification of ownership and control of companies, and the speed at which merger activity takes place, has also required collective employment arrangements which can adjust quickly. Collective agreements have a pivotal role in relation to changes in corporate ownership and control. These can frequently involve transfers of large numbers of employees between employers.

EC Policies

These developments have been taken on board by EC employment policies, legislation which has pre-empted 'Europeanisation' of bargaining systems, and Europe-wide bargaining structures to reflect the increasing number of 'cross-border' mergers.[8] As well as formally establishing the right of employers' and workers' organisations to negotiate and conclude collective agreements (something UK legislation has never comprehensively done), art. 12 of the EC Charter of the Fundamental Social Rights of Workers (adopted by EC heads of state and government, 10 December 1989) states that 'the dialogue between the two sides of industry at European level which must be developed, may, if the parties deem it desirable, result in contractual relations, in particular at inter-occupational and sectoral level.'

European norms in relation to collective bargaining, although generally better than in the UK, can be criticised in important respects. A legal duty on employers to bargain with recognised unions is not yet established throughout the European Community,[9] and the Action Programme for implementing the Social Charter is, unfortunately, unlikely to deal with this problem.[10] In addition, some EC countries impose restraints on workplace bargaining that many UK trade unionists would find unacceptable.

Collective Agreements: Legal Status and Effects

Although a collective agreement may have the characteristics of a contract – that is, there may be two parties (or 'sides') to it, and it contains rights and obligations – it is *not* in most cases a contract. Typically, agreements contain two types of provisions. The first are what are sometimes called 'substantive' or 'normative' terms dealing with issues like pay, overtime, hours and holidays. Second, it will often set out procedures for dealing with industrial relations issues and problems, for example representation on works councils and procedures for dealing with individual and collective disputes.[11]

Agreements can be lengthy and very detailed documents, or they may amount to little more than locally agreed understandings, for instance between a personnel manager and workplace shop stewards.

There is no prescribed format for such agreements, nor are there any legal requirements governing their content or how they are made. How they are expressed, and their intended scope, purposes and so on, will be relevant, though, if there is any argument about incorporation into the individual contract of employment and the legal enforceability of its terms, as discussed in the next section.

Legal Enforceability

A collective agreement generally operates on two levels. In the first place it is an agreement between the union(s) and employer(s) who made it. Second, as the agreement may have been made for *other* parties, that is, the workers and employers it covers, it may be the basis of more extensive rights and obligations. In particular, all or some of its contents may be 'incorporated' into the individual contracts of employment between the workers and employers expressly within its scope. In some cases it may also be incorporated into *other* workers' contracts, for example those of any non-union members whose individual contracts state that agreements made between the union and the employer will apply to them; or of workers in organisations where the employer has decided to adopt the agreement.

Employer(s) and Union(s)

The courts have generally not treated collective agreements as legally binding between the parties who make them. This has largely been due to the difficulties of interpreting and enforcing them, and also because there is no tradition in industry of treating them as enforceable. It is also a recognition that employers and unions have preferred the use of industrial relations procedures to using the courts.[12] Following a brief period between 1971 and 1974 when there was a legal presumption in the Industrial Relations Act 1971 that agreements *were* enforceable, the position is now back to where it was. Specifically, the Trade Union and Labour Relations (Consolidation) Act 1992, s. 179, says that collective agreements are to be conclusively presumed *not* to have been intended to be legally enforceable unless they are in writing and clearly provide that they are to be legally enforceable.[13]

The practical effect of this position (which was under review prior to the 1992 general election)[14] is that employers cannot sue unions (nor can they themselves be sued) to enforce the terms of a collective agreement.

Change of Employer
In the event of a transfer of the employer's business any relevant collective agreement has effect as if it had been made with the transferee employer, and it must therefore be observed by the new employer.[15] Although the union that made the agreement is not able to enforce individual employees of the new employer will be able to do so if any terms of the agreement have been incorporated into their individual contracts.

'Incorporation' into Employment Contracts

The system by which collective agreements, or parts of them, become part of an individual's contract of employment has already been described in chapter 4 above. That process may have been assisted by TURERA requirements that collective agreement terms which directly affect individuals' employment must be included in their written statement (see chapter 4). From the union's point of view it will have a continuing interest, after a collective agreement has been made or revised, in ensuring that its terms are being properly observed. In practice most breaches and non-implementation are dealt with at an industrial relations level, either by the operation of 'disputes' procedures or through negotiations. Ultimately the union, or its members, may take industrial action if the point in issue is sufficiently serious. Conciliation, mediation and arbitration may be possible to break a deadlock or to end a dispute, with arbitration providing a means of reaching a definitive and binding settlement of the point of difference. If the agreement itself does not contain disputes procedures, ACAS can provide conciliation, mediation and arbitration services, and can refer issues to the Central Arbitration Committee.[16]

Taking Legal Action
For a variety of reasons, though, there may be no alternative to legal action, particularly if one side will not accept arbitration or other procedures, or because it is determined to pursue a particular course of action. It is not unusual for agreements (or important parts of them) to be terminated unilaterally, or simply to be ignored. In this case the scope for legal action will depend on whether individual members who have rights under the collective agreement can take action. As we have seen, the union itself cannot do so. In this sense members may be acting as the union's 'proxy'. Although the union may provide financial support and encouragement, a member does not need the union's formal support to take action.

There are many situations in which legal action will not be possible because the rights, which may be very important ones for both the union and its members, are not regarded as 'suitable' for incorporation. The courts may also decide that the rights in the collective agreement are rights of the union but not of its members. This artificial distinction can mean that the withdrawal of important collective rights like recognition of the union, organisational rights for its workplace representatives, consultation and participation procedures, and many other collective entitlements, can be undertaken without any legal means of prevention. The only way in which such action might be blocked is on the basis that the employer's action also infringes a *personal* entitlement which has become incorporated into an individual's contract. An example might be where a collective agreement gives a workplace representative rights to time off in lieu for approved industrial relations work that s/he does; or, possibly, personal facilities like accommodation expenses for union responsibilities.

In practical terms, though, such rights can be very hard to enforce in the courts.

Example

Following an industrial occupation at a hospital that was due to be closed, a shop steward was suspended from his job and barred from the building. He was successful, at first, in getting an injunction to lift the health authority's action. The Court of Appeal then reversed this decision. Even if the collective agreement gave a shop steward representational rights, and these operated on a personal level, the right depended on the normal continuation of the employment relationship between the employer and the person concerned. This was not the position following the suspension.[17]

'Implied' Rights

The absence of any formal statement in the member's individual contract, that is to say in the statutory written statement, letter of appointment or the like, expressly incorporating the relevant part of the collective agreement is not nec-essarily fatal to the member's (and union's) position. It may be possible, as discussed in chapter 4 above, to demonstrate that particular parts of a collective agreement are *implied* as incorporated. The difficulties of doing this, though, can be seen in cases where the courts have refused to accept that agreed redundancy procedures operate as a contractual 'right' when it actually comes to deciding how workers are to be selected for redundancy. (See, for example, the *Standard Telephones and Cables* case, discussed in chapter 15 above). Other 'procedural' rights, such as disputes procedures, have also been held not to be incorporated.[18]

The Effects of Incorporation

Assuming the terms of a collective agreement have been effectively incorpor-ated into members' contracts, there are a variety of practical consequences for both the union and members. Collectively, the position is strengthened because there will be scope to take court action to prevent breaches of members' rights taking place. In one case, for example, it was held that a guarantee payment scheme for dockworkers could not be terminated, as the scheme formed an integral part of their terms and conditions.[19] Individual members can obviously sue for entitlements given to them in the agreement, if necessary in a test case on behalf of other workers also covered by its terms. The terms of an agreement may also be the central issue in dismissal and constructive dismissal cases. Management's powers under an agreement to move workers between jobs and work locations are frequently tested in the context of such cases. Although there are examples of where collectively-agreed 'mobility' arrangements are incorporated, and therefore do give a management the power it claims,[20] there is no hard and fast rule on the point. The outcome will depend – as in all incorporation issues – on the term in question, the intentions of the parties making the collective agreement (and the individual contract), and the particular circumstances in each case.

Collective Bargaining and Union Organisation

For collective bargaining to work effectively, and for employees' interests to be properly represented in the process, unions must have the ability to function properly at a national and local level. Restrictions on trade unions are discussed elsewhere, in particular in relation to trade union government (chapter 18), and industrial action (chapter 20). In relation to collective bargaining, consideration must be given to certification, recognition, time off and facilities for union representatives and for union activities, and disclosure of information.

Certification

If a union is on the list kept by the certification officer[21] it is entitled to a certificate that it is 'independent'. Basically, this requires it to be free from domination or control of an employer or employers' organisation, and it should not run the risk of interference as a result of financial or other powers an employer might have. Not all organisations can meet these requirements, particularly smaller employer-financed staff associations.[22]

Certification is important for collective bargaining purposes because it is the key to significant bargaining rights, particularly if these have not already been agreed with the employer (and in many cases they have not been). 'Independence' is a legal precondition for such rights. In most cases it must also be shown that the union is recognised by the employer (as discussed below). The most important rights are:

- time off for employees to take part in union activities (see chapter 8 above);

- information needed by union representatives for collective bargaining purposes (see below);
- information and consultation when there is a transfer of the employer's business (see below);
- government financial assistance for holding ballots (including ballots on the employer's premises) concerned with strike action, elections of representatives and other union purposes;
- details and supplementary information about pensions and employers' occupational pension scheme arrangements;
- time off for representatives to have industrial relations training (see chapter 8);
- notification and consultation rights when collective redundancies are proposed by the employer (see chapter 15).

Recognition

Recognition by the employer of a union's right to negotiate terms and conditions on behalf of its members is an essential requirement in the collective bargaining process. Apart from establishing the employer's formal support, it also opens the door to statutory rights which are of fundamental importance. These invariably depend on recognition, as discussed in the last section. In formal terms 'recognition' simply means that an employer has agreed to discuss terms that will cover that employer's employees, either on all workplace issues or for more limited purposes. It can be formally recorded, for example in correspondence or an agreement, or, more problematically, it can be implicit from previous dealings between the employer and union.

Recognition can take place at different levels. An employer can operate through an employers' association, and with other employers recognise a union (or unions) for the purposes of agreeing industry-wide arrangements. Recognition, however, may be more 'localised'. In the 1980s there was a tendency, particularly among some large employers, to break away from industry-wide arrangements. There have also been other important trends that have affected the position. In particular, there has been a movement away from multi-union representation in favour of the establishment of single-union and other bargaining structures. In some cases deals are accompanied by severe restraints on a union's abilities to take industrial action. Recognition may also depend on union commitment to restrictive arbitration procedures.

This process has to some extent been inevitable, and has been dictated by the preferences of some employers for operating within more rational or simplified industrial relations structures. On the other hand, employers have not been slow to exploit the absence of legal requirements to recognise and to impose tough conditions on recognition arrangements. Ultimately an employer can unilaterally change recognition arrangements or simply walk away from recognition commitments altogether. This has been made easier by a combination of circumstances, not least of which is legislation restricting unions' organisational rights. The weakening of the closed shop,[23] which has been a cornerstone in promoting and defending collective entitlements, and essential in maintaining recognition and representation rights, has been a major factor. Another problem has been the legitimation by TURERA, s. 13, of 'action short of dismissal' against union members by employers, for example, to persuade them to relinquish union membership, or to change to 'personal contracts' or to other collective bargaining arrangements.

In the face of such pressures the TUC published a consultative document in 1991 outlining possible means of attaining recognition rights, including new arrangements reinforced by law. The extent of an employer's obligations would depend, among other things, on the proportion of union membership among staff at the workplace and on the claims of any other unions claiming rights. The issue is, however, very complex and there have been considerable problems in the legal enforcement of recognition, under both Conservative legislation and Labour's Employment Protection Act 1975 (when ACAS had the job of dealing with recognition claims and disputes).[24] Other suggestions have revolved around ways of reinforcing recognition through an emphasis on individual workers' rights to representation, and on legal curbs on employers' ability to derecognise.[25]

Legal Procedures
Recognition can be provided for in an agreement setting out in detail the rights of the union and its representatives. Agreements commonly deal with such matters as collection of union dues on behalf of the union, arrangements for holding union meetings, the timing and conduct of negotiating meetings and other organisational arrangements. Practice varies greatly, however, and some agreements are expressed in reciprocal terms, for example requiring unions to try to ensure that agreed procedures are maintained, and ensuring that arrangements for avoiding disputes are followed. Managements are sometimes prepared to agree to assist in encouraging staff to belong to the union, although in practice employers are less willing to take active steps to do this since the Employment Act 1990.

In the absence of a formalised recognition arrangement, the issue of whether a union has been recognised will depend on previous evidence of its dealings with the employer. If consultation practices, routine representation at disciplinary and grievance proceedings, and involvement in other normal industrial relations can be shown, it will usually be possible to demonstrate recognition has been established (even if the employer denies it).[26] More recently, however, the courts have made such implied recognition more difficult.

Example
Five polytechnic lecturers were members of the Association of Polytechnic Lecturers (APL). Their employers, Cleveland County Council, had repeatedly refused to recognise the association, and continued to recognise other estab-

lished lecturers' organisations. The council did, however, answer queries on working conditions and there was some dialogue on matters like health and safety. The secretary of state later indicated that he thought APT should attend Burnham Committee negotiations on pay.

Nevertheless, the council still refused to recognise the union. APT thereupon appointed safety representatives and then successfully persuaded an industrial tribunal to order that the representatives had formal rights (including time off and so on), on the basis that APT had been 'recognised'. The decision was overturned on appeal. The EAT held that the secretary of state's actions and the other possible factors involved did *not* amount to 'recognition'. In particular, it said, recognition could not be foisted on unwilling employers as a result of actions over which they had no control (in this case the secretary of state's views).[27]

Obtaining Employer Recognition

Without a statutory framework setting out the requirements for obtaining (and retaining) recognition rights, the present system has produced some very strange results. Companies in which there may be a large proportion of union members may resolutely refuse recognition rights or, worse still, withdraw them, as occurred in a succession of major disputes in the 1980s. On the other hand companies can, and do, maintain extensive collective bargaining arrangements where membership has fallen to minimal levels – a situation which is obviously very advantageous to the employer.

Until 1993, ACAS had a duty 'of encouraging the extension of collective bargaining and the development and, where necessary, the reform of collective bargaining machinery'[28] and the union organisation that sustained it. Its advice to date has been cast in fairly low-key terms. The ACAS *Employment Handbook* (1990) states:

There is no statutory obligation to recognise a trade union but if a company receives such a request all the circumstances should be considered. These would include the appropriateness of the union and, in particular, the strength of support from employees. One way of finding out the views of employees is to hold a secret ballot, preferably conducted by ACAS or some other independent organisation. In some cases, it may be agreed that there is insufficient support to justify full recognition at that time, but that representation rights, which entitle members to be represented by their union individually (e.g. in disciplinary cases or if the employee has a grievance), would be more appropriate.[29]

It remains to be seen, with the removal of ACAS' duty by the Trade Union Reform and Employment Rights Act, whether recognition advice by ACAS will appear in future publications and guidance, or whether it will continue in some other form.

In some areas of public sector employment there may be statutory duties on employers (such as government departments or nationalised industries) to consult unions on pay and conditions, and even to set up bargaining arrangements. Such legislation has not given unions anything significant in the way of collective bargaining rights and it has not prevented the derecognition and the erosion of unions' rights in many public sector areas. An example has been derecognition of teachers' unions by governors of schools that have opted out of local education authority control.

Other government action, notably the Trade Union and Labour Relations (Consolidation) Act 1992, ss. 144, 145, has ended provisions in commercial contracts, for instance between councils and suppliers, which required companies to recognise unions. This also extends to tendering arrangements which might otherwise exclude anti-union employers from entering into contracts.

Business Transfers

If an employer's business is transferred, that is, a new employer takes over, the Transfer of Undertaking (Employment Protection) Regulations 1981 require any recognition arrangements to be maintained. In practice, however, there is nothing to stop such rights being curtailed or withdrawn.

Time Off and Facilities for Union Representatives and Union Activities

The time-off rights of shop stewards and other union officials working for an employer, and of employees, have been described in chapter 8 above. In the case of representatives' time off for collective bargaining itself, in other words attendance at meetings with an employer, this is clearly covered by the Trade Union and Labour Relations (Consolidation) Act 1992, s. 168. Problems usually arise, though, over activities which may by *related* to negotiating but for which an employer is less willing to provide time off. These include training courses and time spent on communicating information to members, meetings with full-time officials and so forth. The ACAS Code of Practice 'Time off for Trade Union Duties and Activities' (no. 3) does, however, specifically list the activities which require paid time off. They include 'informing constituents about negotiations or consultations with management' and 'meetings with other lay officials or with full-time union officers on matters which are concerned with industrial relations between his or her employer and any associated employer and their employees'. These are provided as illustrative examples of what is usually needed. As far as facilities are concerned, managements should 'make available to officials the facilities necessary for them to perform their duties efficiently and to communicate with members fellow lay officials and full-time officers' (para. 24).

Ideally, the needs of representatives should be dealt with in detail in written arrangements agreed with the employer. Among other matters, these should provide people with sufficient time to carry out the specific responsibilities for which they have been elected, and this will obviously depend on the extent to which they have to be involved in collective bargaining issues. Arrangements should be designed to avoid problems in relations with immediate supervisors, particularly if absence means work commitments could be affected. Workplace representatives who take on union responsibilities should not have to accept worse working conditions or career disadvantages.[30]

If disputes do arise industrial tribunals have the basic task of deciding whether or not a refusal of time off is 'reasonable' in the particular circumstances.[31] As far as other members are concerned the ACAS Code states that 'to operate effectively and democratically trade unions need the active participation of members in certain union activities'. As well as time off for workplace meetings and ballots, it refers to attendance at union policymaking bodies and external bodies.

Disclosure of Information

The Trade Union and Labour Relations (Consolidation) Act 1992, s. 181, imposes a duty on employers to disclose information at all stages of collective bargaining relating to their undertakings, without which union representatives involved in collective bargaining would be 'to a material extent' impeded. If the employer does not recognise the union (or decides not to recognise it for the specific purpose for which the information is claimed) the duty does not apply.

There are limitations on what the employer is required to produce (ss. 181, 182). The information must be relevant and it must be sufficiently important to the negotiations, claim and so on in respect of which it is claimed. Disclosure is required if it would be in accordance with 'good industrial relations practice', and in some cases disclosure has been refused on the basis that it would not be in line with normal practice. In addition, disclosure can be specifically refused (s. 182) in certain cases if these concern:

- national security interests;
- data held subject to legal and 'confidentiality' requirements;
- information held on individuals (like personnel data) unless consent to disclose it has been given;
- information which, if disclosed, would cause 'substantial injury' to the employer's undertaking (but only for reasons other than the effect on collective bargaining);
- information obtained by the employer for legal proceedings.

Complaints of non-disclosure can be taken under s. 183 to the Central Arbitration Committee (CAC) and if ACAS cannot settle the claim, the CAC can make a ruling. The CAC's powers extend to requiring an employer to observe the terms and conditions specified in the claim that the union has made or 'other terms which the Committee consider appropriate'. The effect of this is to give the employees covered contractual entitlements pending a later collective agreement or improved terms.[32].

On information requirements relating to redundancy and transfers of the employer's business, see chapter 15 above.

CHAPTER 20

Industrial Conflict I: Industrial Action

As we saw in an earlier chapter, there is no positive right to strike. Instead there is merely a system of immunities from liability which offer a limited shield of protection to trade unions and strike organisers. This shield, always vulnerable to attack by an unsympathetic judiciary, has been weakened still further by the changes introduced by the government since 1980. Moreover, those workers who take strike or other industrial action may have some or all of their pay 'docked' and may incur the risk of dismissal with no right to challenge its fairness before an industrial tribunal.[1]

In this chapter, we will start by examining the scope of the employer's power lawfully to sack its striking workforce or make deductions from wages. In the second part of the chapter, we will look at the liability of trade unions and strike organisers for unlawful industrial action. Finally, we will identify those groups of workers who are denied the right to withdraw their labour and examine recent proposals to control industrial action in public services.

The changes to collective labour law introduced during the 1980s have now been put together in one Act of Parliament: the Trade Union and Labour Relations (Consolidation) Act 1992, or TULR(C)A. The relevant provisions of this Act are referred to in the text.

Sanctions against Individual Strikers

Dismissal: No Right to Claim Unfair Dismissal for Those Taking Industrial Action

Where dismissal is for taking part in a strike or other industrial action, where all those still on strike have been dismissed and there has been no selective re-engagement of those dismissed within a three-month period, the law prevents an industrial tribunal from hearing an unfair dismissal claim (TULR[C])A 1992 s. 238).

'Other industrial action' is not defined by the Act but it is now clear that it can cover forms of action which do not constitute a breach of the contract of employment. In *Faust* v. *Power Packing Casemakers Ltd* [1983] IRLR 117, three employees refused to work overtime because of a dispute over wages. The IT found the dismissals unfair on the grounds that there was no contractual obligation to work overtime. Both the EAT and the Court of Appeal rejected this view, stating that any action taken against employers during the course of a dispute which was designed to extract some benefit from them constituted 'other industrial action' – whether or not it was in breach of contract.

In determining whether there has been a selective dismissal or re-engagement of strikers, the tribunal must have regard to the 'relevant employee.' These are defined as those employees at the establishment who were taking part in the industrial action at the date of the complainant's dismissal. In other words, those who have been on strike but who have returned to work before that date are not included and the fact that they are not dismissed does not entitle the dismissed employees to present a claim.

The time at which it must be shown that one or more relevant employees who took part in a strike were not dismissed, for the purposes of deciding whether an IT has jurisdiction to hear the unfair dismissal claim, is the conclusion of the relevant hearing at which the tribunal determines whether it has jurisdiction (*P&O European Ferries (Dover) Ltd* v. *Byrne* [1989] IRLR 254). This is an extremely favourable interpretation for employers because if the identities of those strikers which the employer has, by mistake, failed to dismiss are revealed during the proceedings, then the employer can escape liability by dismissing them before the conclusion of those proceedings.

Whether a particular employee is taking part in a strike within the meaning of s. 238 is a question of fact for the industrial tribunal to decide. In *Coates* v. *Modem Methods and Materials Ltd* [1982] IRLR 318, however, the majority of the Court of Appeal expressed the view that the matter should be judged by what the employee does and not by what s/he thinks or why s/he does it. Reasons or motives are irrelevant. Therefore, an employee who does not support a strike but who does not cross a picket line because of fear of abuse could reasonably be regarded as taking part in the strike.

The Employment Act 1990 tightened the law even further. The effect of this amendment is that, henceforth, no employee can complain of unfair dismissal if at the time of the dismissal s/he was taking part in unofficial industrial action. In such a situation the employer may selectively dismiss or re-engage any participating employee without risking unfair dismissal liability (see now TULR[C]A 1992, s. 237).

An employee's action will be unofficial unless:

- s/he is a member of a trade union and the action is authorised and endorsed by that union; or
- s/he is not a trade union member, but members of a union which has authorised or endorsed the action also take part; or
- no trade union members are taking part in the industrial action.

It is interesting to note that this provision, although substantially strengthened by the Tories in 1982 and 1990, owes its origins to the last Labour government.

The policy underlying it is that the courts and tribunals are not appropriate places in which to decide the rights and wrongs of industrial disputes. As such, the provision is very much in line with the earlier abstentionist tradition in British industrial relations.

The fact that the employer has the legal freedom to sack those taking industrial action, even if the action has been sanctioned by a properly conducted ballot, may come as surprise to many trade unionists. Indeed, research conducted by Roger Welch in 1987 established that almost 45 per cent of his sample of active trade unionists believed that employers could not dismiss strikers. This proportion increased to 70 per cent if the industrial action involved was short of a strike, such as an overtime ban.[2] This misconception is entirely understandable. After all, how can we talk of a right or freedom to strike unless it is possible for workers to withdraw their labour, in whole or in part, without fearing lawful dismissal? Those workers to whom the existence of this legal prop to managerial prerogative will come as no surprise are the News International printers and the P&O seafarers who during the 1980s fell victim to its use in defeating strikes.

Possible Loss of Redundancy Payments

Strikes and other types of industrial action have often been called as a defensive response to an employer's announcement of impending redundancies. It is also the case that employers will often threaten redundancies during a strike: on occasions these threats may be genuine; at other times they may merely form part of the employer's bargaining strategy. We have examined the legal position in some detail in our chapter above on redundancy but, given the importance of issue for strikers, it is worthwhile summarising the possible outcomes here:

Scenario One
Employees at Capital plc take strike or other industrial action in breach of their contracts either before they are given their redundancy notices, or after receipt but before the obligatory period of notice (the minimum contractual and/or statutory notice to which each employee is entitled). In this situation, Capital plc dismisses the strikers without incurring liability for redundancy payments.

Scenario Two
Employees at Capital plc take strike action after having received the obligatory period of notice. If they are then dismissed for taking part in the strike, they are entitled to a full redundancy payment. This entitlement is subject to the employer's statutory right to serve a written notice of extension on the striking employees requiring them to work extra days after the expiry of the redundancy notice, equivalent to the number of days lost during the strike. If the employees

fail without reasonable cause to comply with the notice, they will lose their right to claim all or any part of the redundancy payment.

Scenario Three

Employees at Capital plc take industrial action short of a strike involving a breach of their contracts after having received the obligatory period of notice. If Capital's response is dismissal, the employees may apply to an industrial tribunal, which has discretion to award some or all of the redundancy payment.

Suing for Breach of Contract

As we shall see below, most forms of industrial action will involve a breach of the worker's contract of employment. Consequently, the employer has the option to sue the worker for damages. Employers rarely do this because the amount of damages recoverable is likely to be extremely small. The employer is limited to claiming the loss caused by the individual contract-breaker – normally the cost of employing a substitute. In order to recover something approaching actual loss, the employer would have to sue each and every striker individually: hardly a realistic proposition. A far more effective sanction is to deduct the whole or part of the worker's pay.

Deductions from Wages of Those Taking Industrial Action

As we saw in chapter 7 above, the Wages Act 1986 allows employers to make deductions from a worker's pay provided written 'consent' has been given by the worker. But deductions from the wages of those taking industrial action are exempt from the requirements of the Act (see s. 1 [5] [c]). Whether the employer can make deductions from the wages of any employee who is engaged in industrial action remains a question governed by the common law: hence the importance of *Miles* v. *Wakefield Metropolitan District Council* [1987] IRLR 193.

The central question in this case was: if an employee, entitled to a weekly wage for a defined number of hours, refuses to work the whole or part of a week, is the employer entitled, without terminating the contract and without relying on damages for breach of contract, to withhold the whole or a proportion of a week's pay?

The House of Lords upheld the principle of 'no work, no pay' as the basis for the mutual obligations between employer and employee. This principle was described by Lord Templeman as follows: 'In a contract of employment wages and work go together ... In an action by a worker to recover his pay he must allege and be ready to prove that he is ready and willing to work.' Therefore in Miles' case the employer was entitled to withhold wages for the Saturday mornings on which the superintendent registrar of births, marriages and deaths, in furtherance of industrial action, had refused to carry out marriage ceremonies as part of his normal contractual duties.

In disputes where the action being taken does not involve clearly defined periods where work is not being done the legal position has never been clear. An example would be where normal hours were being worked but selective aspects of the job, such as providing cover for absent colleagues, or answering correspondence, are withdrawn. In this case the employer's main options have generally been either to sack staff or to carry on paying wages. Another local authority case has, however, widened the employer's options.

Example
Housing Department officials took industrial action by refusing to deal with certain telephone enquiries. Although this was a minor part of the job the council told staff they would not be needed at work unless they worked properly, and if they did come to work and carry on the action they would not be paid. One of the staff got a court order that normal wages should continue to be paid, as there had been substantial performance. This was reversed by the Court of Appeal. As the employer had confirmed that it would not pay for incomplete performance, it was entitled to withhold pay for the period of the dispute.[3]

The Effect of a Strike Or A Lock-Out on an Employee's Continuity of Employment [4]

In chapter 2 we saw that, in order to qualify for most employment protection rights, it was necessary for employees to show that they had been continuously employed for the appropriate length of time, such as two years in the case of unfair dismissal or redundancy payment claims. It was also noted that certain events could break continuous service.

Strikes
If an employee is on strike during the whole or part of any week, that week does not count in aggregating the period of time the employee has been employed (EPCA 1978, sched.13, para. 15 (1). However, continuity of employment is not broken by a strike (para. 15 [2]).

It is often the case that an employer will dismiss its striking workers and then re-engage them on settlement of the dispute. Does the dismissal break continuity? No, according to the decision in *Bloomfield* v. *Springfield Hosiery Finishing Co Ltd* [1972] 1 All ER 609, the rules made no distinction between strikes where there are dismissals and those where there are not. Moreover, an employer cannot re-engage a striker on the basis that service prior to the dismissal will not count for continuity purposes (*Hamson* v. *Fashion Industries [Hartlepool] Ltd* [1980] IRLR 393).

Lock-outs

It is also the case that continuity is not broken when an employee is absent from work because of a lock-out. However, whether the period during which the employee is locked-out counts for aggregation purposes is not specifically dealt with in the legislation. It would appear that, so long as the employer does not dismiss those who have been locked-out, the employee will be able to include the period in the total period of continuous service.

Guarantee Payments

In chapter 6 we saw that EPCA provides a very limited right to a guaranteed payment to workers who are laid off through no fault of their own. However, the employee loses the right where the lay-off is in consequence of a strike, lock-out or other industrial action involving any employee of his/her employer or of an associated employer (EPCA 1978, s. 13 [3], as amended by the Employment Protection Act 1982, sched. 3, para. 5). Although the disqualification only involves disputes 'internal' to the company or group for which the employee works, it can produce some rather surprising and unjust results. This is illustrated in *Garvey v. J. and J. Maybank (Oldham) Ltd* [1979] IRLR 408:

> Maybanks were paper merchants. Paper supplies to their works were made using their own fleet of lorries and those of haulage contractors. As a result of a road haulage strike, Maybanks could only rely on their own drivers to make deliveries but they refused to cross the picket lines set up by the road haulage drivers. Consequently, no supplies were delivered and approximately 50 workers were laid off by Maybanks. It was held that there these workers had no entitlement to guarantee payments because they were laid off in consequence of a dispute between Maybanks and its own lorry drivers.

Strikers and Social Security

Workers who are involved in industrial action are denied entitlement to unemployment benefit and income support during the currency of the dispute. The rationale for this disqualification is the same one which underlies the exclusion of unfair dismissal claims from strikers – the perceived need to maintain state neutrality in industrial disputes. Both exclusions, however, totally ignore the inequality of economic power between employers and workers and further weaken the ability of workers to defend their interests.

Unemployment Benefit Disqualification

This will apply where the loss of employment arises out of a 'trade dispute' at the claimant's place of work. A trade dispute is defined as:

any dispute between employers and employees or between employees, which is connected with the employment or non-employment or the terms of employment or the conditions of employment of any persons, whether employees in the employment of the employer with whom the dispute arises, or not. (Social Security Act 1975, s. 19 [2] [b])

This definition is based on that contained in the Trade Disputes Act 1906. You will see later in this chapter that this definition is wider than the current definition of trade dispute used for determining immunity from tort liability for trade unions and strike organisers. It is a bitter irony that a wide definition, beneficial to strikers in the context of immunity from tort liability, has major disadvantages when applied to unemployment benefit claims because it increases the scope for disqualification.

Disqualification is generally maintained throughout the duration of the dispute but it can cease before the end of the stoppage in the following situations:

- If the employee can show that s/he had become 'bona fide employed elsewhere', s/he will again be eligible for benefit if the new employment then terminates.
- If the employee's contract has been terminated by redundancy. This provision was inserted by the Social Security Act 1986 in order to counteract the harshness of the Court of Appeal's decision in *Cartlidge* v. *Chief Adjudication Officer* [1986] IRLR 182. Cartlidge was a miner who was already under notice of redundancy when the miners' strike of 1984/5 commenced. As a result, he was unable to work during his notice period. The court determined that he was not only prevented from claiming unemployment during his notice period but was, in addition, precluded from benefit for the duration of the strike.
- If the employee can establish that s/he bona fide resumed employment with his/her employer but then left for genuine reasons other than the dispute, eligibility will return.
- If the employee can establish that s/he was not 'directly interested' in the dispute eligibility is restored. This phrase was given a wide definition by the House of Lords in *Presho* v. *DHSS (Insurance Officer)* [1984] IRLR 74. Employees, who were members of the AUEW, took strike action in support of a pay rise. The claimant, a member of USDAW, was laid off as a result and claimed benefit. The insurance officer refused her claim on the basis that she and the other USDAW members were directly interested in the dispute, since there was evidence of a custom and practice that USDAW members would automatically get the same pay rise if they asked for it. This decision was upheld by the Law Lords.

Disqualification from Income Support

Strikers are also ineligible for income support – though strikers with families are able to claim income support for them but not for the striker's own needs.

Even this very limited financial cushion against hardship proved unacceptable to many in the Conservative Party who maintained that the state was subsidising strike activity. Therefore, in the 1980s, strikers – particularly the miners in 1984/5 – found the financial screw turned even tighter and in the following ways:[5]

- A sum (£23.50 in 1993/4, though subject to periodic review) is deducted from the striker's family's weekly entitlement to income support as representing deemed strike pay. This sum will be deducted whether or not the union pays strike pay.[6]
- As a result of changes to the tax regime in the early years of the Thatcher government, the payment of tax rebates to a person on strike is prohibited.[7]

Legal Action against the Trade Union and Strike Organisers

Attempting to Demystify the Law

The incremental approach to strike law 'reform' adopted by the government has obviously proved a successful political strategy, but it has meant that an already complex area of law has become even more difficult to unravel. Of course, the sheer complexity of the legislative framework is in itself a powerful weapon against trade unions and their members. It will often be the case that the legality of the proposed action cannot be determined with any certainty and this may encourage trade unions to adopt a 'safety-first' attitude so as not to put union funds at risk.[8]

In trying to make sense of the law relating to industrial action it is important that you adopt a structured approach. We suggest that you adopt the following three-stage framework of analysis:[9]

- Stage one. Does the industrial action give rise to civil liability at common law?
- Stage two. If so, is there an immunity from liability provided by what was s. 13 of TULRA, 1974 (now TULR(C)A 1992, s. 219)?
- Stage three. If so, has that immunity now been removed by virtue of the changes introduced by the Employment Acts 1980, 1982, 1988, 1990 and the Trade Union Act,1984?

Let us try and add a little detail to our analytical framework.

Stage One: Civil Liabilities for Industrial Action

Industrial Action and How it Affects Your Contract of Employment

Your contract of employment is not suspended during a strike. The traditionally accepted view is that a strike is a breach of contract: it is a breach of the
obligation on the part of the employee to be ready and willing to work. This is
so even if strike notice has been given: this is merely construed as notice of
impending breach.

Most other forms of industrial action short of a strike also amount to contractual breaches. If workers boycott (refuse to carry out) certain work then they
are in breach for refusing to comply with a reasonable order. A go-slow or work-
to-rule probably breaks an implied term not to frustrate the commercial objectives
of the business. This last point is illustrated by a case which arose under the now-
repealed Industrial Relations Act 1971, *Secretary of State for Employment* v. *ASLEF
(No. 2)* [1972] 2 QB 455.[10]

> The railwayworkers embarked on a work-to-rule and the question arose
> whether there was a breach of contract (under the law as it then was, if the
> action amounted to a breach of contract, a 'cooling-off' period could be ordered,
> followed by a ballot). The Court of Appeal found that there was a breach
> because, although the workers claimed to be strictly working to the terms of
> their contracts, what in fact they were doing was giving their contracts a wholly
> unreasonable interpretation and working on the basis of that interpretation.
> (A cooling-off period and ballot were ordered and the ballot secured a massive
> majority in favour of industrial action. The procedure was never used again.)

An overtime ban will also certainly amount to breach of contract if the
employer is entitled under the contract to demand overtime, but not if overtime
is voluntary on the part of the employee. However, as you saw earlier in this
chapter, a ban on voluntary overtime was classed as 'industrial action' for the
purposes of s. 62 of EPCA in *Faust* v. *Power Packing Casemakers Ltd* [1983] ICR
292, with the somewhat surprising result that the IT had no jurisdiction to hear
the workers' unfair dismissal claims.

As we have seen, where the industrial action does constitute breach, the
employer may summarily dismiss or also sue for damages. But, in relation to strike
organisers, the true significance of a finding of breach is that it constitutes the
'unlawful means' element necessary for certain of the economic torts to which
we will now turn our attention.

The Economic Torts

It is possible to place the torts relevant to industrial action under four broad
headings:

(a) Inducement of breach of contract
(b) Interference with contract, trade or business
(c) Intimidation
(d) Conspiracy

Inducement of Breach of Contract

This is the main economic tort and derives from *Lumley* v. *Gye* [1853] 2 E&B 216, discussed in chapter 17 above. In this case it was established that it was a tort to induce a person to break a contract to which s/he was a party. Since, as we have seen, virtually all industrial action involves a breach of contract you can readily appreciate that anyone who calls on workers to take industrial action commits the tort. The inducement may take one of two forms: direct and indirect.

Direct inducement occurs where the defendant induces a third party to break an existing contract which that third party has with the plaintiff who thereby suffers loss. It may help you conceptualise this and other torts if you express the position in diagram form:

```
Inducement                 Breach of contract of employment
Ann——————————————>Brenda————————————>Capital plc
(union official)           (employee)              (employer)
```

In this example Brenda is employed by Capital plc. Ann, a trade union officer, instructs her to strike. Ann is directly inducing Brenda to break her contract with Capital and is therefore committing a tort.

The necessary elements of this form of the tort are:

(a) Knowledge of the contract
(b) Intention to cause its breach
(c) Evidence of an inducement
(d) Actual breach

Note also that this form of the tort can also be committed where a union directly puts pressure on one of the employer's suppliers to cease delivery of vital supplies, thereby inducing a breach of a commercial contract. However, boycotting the employer in dispute usually arises in the second form of the tort, that is, indirect inducement.

Indirect inducement occurs where the unlawful means are used to render performance of the contract by one of the parties impossible.

```
              Breach of         Breach of
Ann————>Brenda————————>Capital————————>Delta
              employment        commercial
              contract          contract
```

In this example, Delta plc's workers are in dispute with their employer. Capital plc is a supplier of Delta. Brenda is employed by Capital as a lorry driver. Ann, a union official, persuades Brenda not to make deliveries to Delta. Not only has Ann directly induced Brenda to break her contract of employment with Capital, she has also used unlawful means through which she has indirectly induced a breach of commercial contract between Capital and Delta.

Interference with Contract, Trade or Business

In contrast to the well-established inducement to breach of contract, this tort is of more recent vintage. In several cases, Master of the Rolls Lord Denning expressed his view that 'if one party interferes with the trade or business of another, and does so by unlawful means, then he is acting unlawfully, even though he does not procure or induce any actual breach of contract'.[11] Therefore it will be unlawful to interfere with a contract short of breach, for example, by preventing performance in cases where the contract contains a *force majeure* clause, exempting a party in breach from liability to pay damages. (For an interesting application of this tort, see the county court judgement in *Falconer* v. *ASLEF and NUR* [1986] IRLR, where a commuter succeeded in claiming damages for the expenditure and inconvenience caused to him by a rail strike.)

More recently, it would appear that this head of liability is even broader in scope, encompassing any intentional use of unlawful means aimed at interfering with the plaintiff's trade or business. The existence of this 'super tort', as Smith and Wood aptly describe it,[12] was recognised by Lord Diplock in *Merkur Island Shipping Corporation* v. *Laughton* [1983] 2 All ER 189.

Intimidation

The tort of intimidation may take the form of compelling a person, by threats of unlawful action, to do some act which causes him or her loss; or of intimidating other persons, by threats of unlawful action, with the intention and effect of causing loss to a third party. Prior to 1964 it was assumed that the tort was confined to threats of physical violence, but in that year the House of Lords held that threats to break a contract were encompassed by the tort (*Rookes* v. *Barnard* [1964] AC 1129).

Conspiracy

This tort may take two forms:

(i) Conspiracy to commit an unlawful act. A conspiracy to commit a crime or tort is clearly included in this category.

(ii) Conspiracy to injure by lawful means. It is, however, the second form of conspiracy which is most dangerous, because it makes it unlawful when two or more people do something which would have been quite lawful if performed by an individual. A conspiracy to injure is simply an agreement to cause deliberate loss to another without justification. The motive or purpose of the defendants is important. If the predominate purpose is to injure the plaintiff, the conspiracy is actionable. If, on the other hand, the principal aim is to achieve a legitimate goal, the action is not unlawful, even if in so doing the plaintiff suffers injury. While it took the courts some time to accept trade union objectives as legitimate (see *Quinn* v. *Leathem*, cited above), later decisions adopted a more liberal stance (see *Crofter Hand-woven Harris Tweed Co* v. *Veitch* [1942] AC 435). As a result, this form of the tort does not pose the threat it once did to trade union activities.

Stage Two: the Immunities

The next stage of our analysis is to examine the scope of the statutory immunities from liability for the four categories of economic torts which we have just described. These are now contained in TULR(C)A 1992, s. 219.

Inducement to Breach of Contract

Under the Trade Disputes Act 1906, the immunity for inducements to breach in contemplation or furtherance of a trade dispute only extended to contacts of employment. This had allowed the courts in the 1960s to find ways of holding trade unionists liable for inducing breaches of commercial contracts (see *Stratford* v. *Lindley*, cited above).

In the mid-1970s immunity was extended to cover the breach of 'any' contract. The relevant provision states that an act performed by a person in contemplation or furtherance of a trade dispute shall not be actionable in tort on the ground only 'that it induces another person to break a contract or interferes or induces any other person to interfere with its performance' – now in TULR(C)A 1992, s. 219 (1) (a).

As we shall see, however, it is important to view this immunity in the context of subsequent legislative developments. Section 219 (1) (a) provides a prima facie immunity, but this immunity may be lost in certain instances: by taking unlawful secondary action; engaging in secondary picketing; enforcing trade union membership; or taking 'official' industrial action without first having called a secret ballot.

Interference with Contract, Trade or Business

Section 219 (1) (a) provides an immunity against the tort of interference with contract. It does not, however, offer any explicit protection against the wider 'genus' tort of interference with trade or business by unlawful means. As a result it is of crucial importance to discover whether an act which is immune by virtue of s. 219 (inducement to breach of contract, for example) may nonetheless constitute the 'unlawful means' for the tort of interference with trade or business. Before the passage of the Employment Act 1980, s. 13 (3) of TULRA 1974 (as amended) had stated that 'for the avoidance of doubt' acts already given immunity could not found the unlawful means element of other torts. When the 1980 statute repealed s. 13 (3), the legal position became confused. However, it would appear that the correct view is that the repeal of s. 13 (3) has not changed the position. According to the House of Lords in *Hadmor Productions Ltd* v. *Hamilton* [1982] IRLR 102, s 13 (3) merely confirmed what was obvious anyway from s 13 (1) – that is, inducement is 'not actionable'. So if the unlawful means are immune, then no liability in tort can arise.

Intimidation

This immunity is contained in TULRA(C)A, s. 219 (1) (b) which states that an act committed by a person in contemplation or furtherance of a trade dispute shall not be actionable in tort on the ground only

that it consists of his threatening that a contract (whether one to which he is a party or not) will be broken or its performance interfered with, or that he will induce another person to break a contract or to interfere with its performance.

Conspiracy

Section 219 (2) now provides the immunity against simple conspiracy originally contained in the Trade Disputes Act 1906.

The Trade Dispute Immunity

In order to gain the protection of the immunities the individual must be acting in contemplation or furtherance of a trade dispute. For analytical purposes you should ask yourself four questions in order to determine whether the industrial action qualifies:

(a) Is it between the correct parties? (See below.)
(b) Is there a dispute? (Note that there may still be a dispute even if the employer is willing to concede to the demands of the union [s. 244 (4)]. Thus if an employer ceases to supply another company on receiving a threat of strike action by its workforce if it continues supplies, there is still a dispute.)

(c) Is the subject matter of the dispute wholly or mainly related to one or more of the matters listed in s. 244 (1)? (See below.)

(d) Is the action in contemplation or furtherance of a trade dispute (ICFTD)?

The scope of the 'golden formula' was amended by the Employment Act 1982 and significantly narrowed in the following ways:

(i)   A trade dispute must now be 'between workers and *their* employers' (our emphasis), not between 'employers and workers' which was the previous position. Furthermore in repealing what was s. 29 (4) of TULRA, the Act no longer allowed trade unions and employers' associations to be regarded as parties to a trade dispute in their own right. Under the law as it stood before the 1982 Act, it was possible for there to be a 'trade dispute' between a trade union and an employer, even if none of the employer's workforce were involved in the dispute. In *NWL* v. *Woods* [1979] IRLR 478, for example, the House of Lords held that there was a trade dispute between the owners of a 'flag of convenience' ship and the International Transport Workers' Federation, although there was evidence that the crew did not support the union's action. As a result of the 1982 amendment, the ITF's action would not now be protected within the ICFTD formula. (See now TULR(C)A, 1992, s. 244 [1], [5]).

(ii) Disputes between 'workers and workers' are now omitted from the trade dispute definition. While this means that disputes not involving an employer are unlawful, in practice it is rare for an employer not to be party to interunion disputes. A demarcation dispute between unions will usually involve a dispute with an employer regarding terms and conditions of employment.

(iii) A trade dispute must now relate 'wholly or mainly' to terms and conditions of employment and the other matters listed as legitimate in TULRA(C)A 1992, s. 244. Under the law existing prior to the 1982 Act, the dispute merely had to be 'connected' with such matters. The amended phrase marks a return to the form of words used under the Industrial Relations Act and was inserted to overrule another aspect of the decision of the House of Lords in *NWL* v. *Nelson* (cited above). In this case it was argued that the predominant purpose behind the 'blacking' of the *Nawala* was the ITF's campaign against 'flags of convenience' shipping, and little to do with a trade dispute. The House of Lords did not agree, stating that as long as there was a genuine connection between the dispute and the subjects listed in the 1974 Act, it did not matter that other issues were predominant. The amendment wrought by the 1982 Act means that a mere connection with the matters specified in s. 244 will no longer suffice. So a dispute which is held to be predominantly a trade dispute will fall outside the trade dispute formula. In many instances it will be extremely difficult to decide which is the predominant element in the dispute and this can be illustrated by the first case which dealt with the issue: *Mercury Communications Ltd* v. *Scott-Garner* [1983] IRLR 494. Mercury had been granted a government licence to run a private telecommunications system. The Post Office Engineers Union (POEU) objected to the government's policy of 'liberalisation' and ultimate privatisation of the industry. The union instructed its members employed by British Telecom (BT) to refuse to connect Mercury's telecommunication system to the BT network. The Court of Appeal, in granting an injunction to prevent the union continuing its instruction, held that this action related wholly or mainly to opposition to the government's policy, rather than fear of future redundancies in the industry should those policies be implemented.

(iv) Since 1982, disputes relating to matters occurring outside the UK are excluded from the immunity, unless the UK workers taking action in furtherance of the dispute are likely to be affected by its outcome in terms of the matters listed in s. 244 (see s. 244 [3]). This means that sympathy action taken by British workers in order to advertise the plight of workers in countries such as South Africa will be unlawful. In any event, this sort of solidarity action would probably be regarded as a political rather than a trade dispute (*BBC* v. *Hearn* [1977] IRLR 269).

In Contemplation Or Furtherance

As we saw in chapter 17, in several cases in the mid-1970s the Court of Appeal held that individuals could not properly claim to be within the trade dispute immunity if, objectively, the action they had taken was not furthering the trade dispute because it was too remote from it. This meant that certain types of 'secondary action' – action taken against a customer or supplier of the employer in the dispute – lost their immunity.

A classic example of this approach is the case of *Express Newspapers Ltd* v. *McShane* [1980] AC 672. In the course of a dispute with provincial newspapers, the National Union of Journalists (NUJ) called on journalists employed by the Press Association (who were still supplying vital copy to the newspapers) to strike. When this call was not fully supported, the NUJ called on its members on the national newspapers to refuse to handle any copy from the Press Association. This action was restrained by the CA on the ground that it was not reasonably capable of achieving the objective of the trade dispute.

The Court of Appeal's attempt to restrict secondary action, however, was subsequently rejected by the House of Lords. The main thrust of the decision of the Lords in the McShane case was that if a person taking the action honestly believes it will further the trade dispute, then this is all that matters: there was no room for an objective test (see also *Duport Steels Ltd* v. *Sirs* [1980] 1 All ER 529).

It was, however, the approach of the Court of Appeal, and Lord Denning in particular, which most closely accorded with the newly elected Conservative government's perspective on industrial relations. As a result, the Employment Act 1980 included provisions which aimed, inter alia, to control secondary action and, to use the words of one government spokesman, to 'return the law to Denning'. This legislation commenced the new legislative policy of stripping away the immunities.

Stage Three: Removal of the Immunities

The scope of the immunities has been restricted by the legislation of the 1980s: The Employment Acts of 1980, 1982, 1988 and 1990, and the Trade Union Act of 1984. In this section we examine the restriction of secondary action; the loss of immunity for unlawful picketing; the provisions removing immunity in respect of actions aimed at enforcing the closed shop or trade union recognition on an employer; the requirements for secret ballots before industrial action; and industrial action taken in support of dismissed 'unofficial strikers' .

Statutory Control of Secondary Action

Section 17 of the Employment Act 1980 removed the protection provided by s. 13 (1) TULRA 1974 (as amended) against liability for interfering with commercial contracts by secondary action unless it satisfies conditions which enable it to pass through one of three 'gateways to legality', the most important of which is the so-called first customer/first supplier gateway. This permitted secondary action to be organised if it involved employees of persons who were in direct contractual relations with the employer involved in the primary dispute. The second gateway extended the first customer/first supplier rule to cover cases where the supply which was disrupted was between the secondary employer and an employer 'associated' with the primary employer. This gateway only applied where the supplies which were disrupted were in substitution for the goods which, but for the dispute, would have been supplied by or to the primary employer. The third gateway maintained immunity where the secondary action was a consequence of lawful picketing.

While the policy behind s. 17 is straightforward, its drafting was massively complex. Indeed, Lord Denning described it as 'the most tortuous section I have ever come across' (*Hadmor Productions* v. *Hamilton* [1981] IRLR 210). The complexity of the section was one of the reasons put forward for its repeal by s. 4 of the Employment Act 1990. The aim of s. 4 of the 1990 Act is that only direct disputes between an employer and its workers should attract immunity under s. 13 of TULRA. The only exception was to be secondary action arising out of lawful picketing – the only gateway to legality to be retained from the repealed s. 17 of the 1980 Act. The relevant law is now consolidated in TULR(C)A 1992, s. 244.

Determining whether secondary action attracts immunity is much simpler than it used to be. Ask yourself the following questions:

(i)   Is there a trade dispute within TULR(C)A, s. 244?
      If so,
(ii) Does the basic immunity contained in s. 219 apply?
      If so,
(iii) Is there secondary action as defined by s. 224?

This occurs if a person:

(a)   induces another to break a contract of employment or interferes or induces another to interfere with its performance, or
(b)   threatens that a contract of employment under which he or another is employed will be broken or its performance interfered with, or that he will induce another to break a contract of employment or interfere with its performance, and the employer under the contract of employment is not a party to the trade dispute.

At this point, we have to establish which employer is in dispute with its workers (the primary dispute). If a person acting in support of this primary dispute induces a breach of the employment contracts of the employees of a different employer, then there is secondary action.

Example

Company A's employees are on strike for higher wages. Company B supplies Company A. Company B's employees are instructed to strike in furtherance of the trade dispute with A.

The instruction to Company B's employees constitutes secondary action.

Section 224 (4) seeks to limit any attempt to extend the notion of the primary employer. The section states that an employer is not to be regarded as party to a dispute between another employer and its workers. This section would appear to confirm the thinking of the House of Lords in *Dimbleby & Sons Ltd* v. *National Union of Journalists* [1984] ICR 386, that an employer, even though associated with the employer involved in the primary dispute, was not to be regarded as party to that dispute.

If there is secondary action, then we move to the final question:

(iv) Does the case pass through the lawful picketing 'gateway' in s. 224 (1), (3)?
      If not, immunity is lost and the action is unlawful. The basic immunity of s. 219 only applies if the picket is acting lawfully within s. 220, of which the main requirement is that workers may only picket their own place of work.

Even if the workers do picket their own place of work, their actions may still amount to secondary action because they may induce a breach of the contracts of employment of employees of other employers.

Unlawful Picketing

Unlawful picketing, such as picketing a place other than your own place of work, will not attract immunity under s. 219 (see TULR[C]A, s. 219 [3] and the next chapter here).

Enforcing Union Membership

We have already referred to the fact that the EA 1988 put further curbs on the closed shop. Section 10 removed the immunities contained in s. 13 of TULRA 1974 (as amended) from primary industrial action where the reason, or one of the reasons, for the action is that the employer is employing, has employed or might employ a person who is not a member of a trade union or that the employer is failing, has failed or might fail to discriminate against such a person. As we saw in our chapter on unfair dismissal, s. 11 made it unfair for an employer to dismiss or to take action short of dismissal against an employee on the ground of the employee's non-membership of a union or a particular union. In both the situations covered by ss. 10 and 11, the fact that the closed shop may have been approved in a ballot is an irrelevancy. (See now TULR[C]A, s. 222.)

Section 14 of the EA 1982 withdrew the immunity where the reason for the industrial action is to compel another employer to 'recognise, negotiate or consult' one or more trade unions or to force the employer to discriminate in contract or tendering on the ground of union membership or non-membership in the contracting or tendering concern. (See now TULR[C]A, s. 225.)

Secret Ballots before Industrial Action (TULR[C]A, ss. 226–35)

Official industrial action will not attract the immunity offered by TULR(C)A, s. 219, unless the majority of union members likely to be called upon to take industrial action have supported that action in a properly conducted ballot. The requirements for a lawful ballot and the ways in which a union can be held to be vicariously responsible for industrial action saw considerable additions and modifications as a result of the Employment Acts of 1988 and 1990. To supplement these requirements, the Department of Employment has issued a Code of Practice on Trade Union Ballots on Industrial Action. Breach of the Code does not of itself give rise to civil or criminal liability, but any court or tribunal must, where it is relevant, take it into account as evidence of good industrial relations practice (EA 1980, s. 3). In what follows, we will try to offer some guidance through the complexities of the law in this area.

When Is a Ballot Required?

A ballot is only required in respect of an 'act done by a trade union'. An act is taken to have been authorised (beforehand) or endorsed (afterwards) by a trade union if it was done, or was authorised or endorsed, by:

- any person who is empowered by the rules so to do;
- the principal executive committee, the president, or
- any other committee of the union or any official of the union (whether employed by it or not). (TULR[C]A, s. 20[2])

The third provision, originally introduced by the EA 1990, will mean that a shop steward could render a union liable where s/he authorises or endorses action without a ballot. Moreover, by virtue of a further amendment, it is sufficient that such an official is a member of a group, the purpose of which includes organising or co-ordinating industrial action, and that *any member of that group* has authorised or endorsed the action (see now TULR[C]A, s. 20 [3] [b]). The insidious nature of this provision was highlighted by Lord Wedderburn during the House of Lords debates on the new legislation:

> under this Bill the union is at risk from an act of an unknown person, some mysterious stranger acting unilaterally after the gathering of an unknown, shadowy group to which the official, at a material time, at some point entered and became, for a few moments, a member.[13]

A union may repudiate the purported authorisation or endorsement by the third group (other committees and officials), but can *never* repudiate the actions of the principal executive committee, president, general secretary or those acting under the rules. The requirements for an effective repudiation are far more stringent and complicated as a result of changes introduced by the 1990 Act. To escape liability, the action must be repudiated by the principal executive committee or the president or the general secretary as soon as reasonably practicable. Furthermore:

- written notice of the repudiation must be given to the committee or official in question without delay, and
- the union 'must do its best' to give individual written notice of the fact and date of repudiation, without delay, (i) to every member of the union who the union has reason to believe is taking part, or might otherwise take part, in industrial action as a result of the act; and (ii) to the employer of every such member (see now TULR[C]A, s. 21[2]).

The notice given to members must also contain the following 'health warning':

Your union has repudiated the call (or calls) for industrial action to which this notice relates and will give no support to unofficial action taken in response to it (or them). If you are dismissed while taking industrial action, you will have no right to complain of unfair dismissal.

Should these requirements not be complied with, the repudiation will be treated as ineffective. In addition, there is no repudiation if the principal executive committee, president or general secretary subsequently 'behaves in a manner which is inconsistent with the purported repudiation'.

At this stage, we think it important to emphasise the fundamental point that while a properly conducted ballot is vital to maintain the protection of the immunities for any action authorised or endorsed by the union, a lawful ballot per se will not accord immunity to the action if it is unlawful for other reasons – such as secondary action or action to enforce the closed shop.

Moreover, official industrial action will only attract immunity if the following conditions are met.

Separate Ballots for Each Workplace

As originally enacted, the Trade Union Act 1984 required a single ballot of all those who were expected to take part in the industrial action. This position was, however, changed by the EA 1988; a union intending to organise industrial action, generally speaking, must organise separate ballots for each place of work. Industrial action may not be lawfully taken at a particular workplace unless a majority of members have voted in favour of the action at that workplace (see now TULR[C]A, s. 228).

The requirement of separate ballots is subject to the following major exceptions:

(i)   Where the union reasonably believed that all the members had the same workplace.

(ii) Where there is some factor:

(a) which relates to the terms, conditions or occupational description of each member entitled to vote;

(b) which that member has in common with some or all members of the union entitled to vote.

This allows a trade union to hold a single aggregated ballot covering members from different places of work if all belong to a complete bargaining unit – for instance, all electricians or all members employed by that employer. If you can make sense of this highly convoluted provision, you will also note that there does not have to be a factor which is common to all voters. There can be several factors, each of which is common to some – such as all skilled and semi-skilled grades, all part-time workers and electricians. The union must ballot *all* its members who possess the same relevant factor. So, for example, if it wishes to conduct a ballot of part-time employees employed by a particular employer, it cannot ballot those at workplace A but not those at workplace B.

Ballot Papers (TULR[C]A s. 229)

The ballot paper must ask either whether the voter is prepared to take part or continue to take part in a strike; or whether the voter is prepared to take part or continue to take part in action short of a strike; or it may ask both questions separately. The voter must be required to answer 'Yes' or 'No' to each question and the questions must not be rolled up into one (see *Post Office* v. *Union of Communication Workers* [1990] IRLR 143). Every voting paper must contain the following statement: 'If you take part in a strike or other industrial action, you may be in breach of your contract of employment'.

The ballot paper must also specify the identity of the person/s authorised to call upon members to take industrial action in the event of a vote in favour. This person need not be authorised under the rules of the union, but he or she must be someone who comes within TULR(C)A, s. 20 (2)–(4) (see above).

Section 20 (2) of TURERA provides that ballot papers must also state the independent scrutineer's name, the address for return and the date by which votes must be returned. The papers will also have to be marked with consecutive numbers.

Conduct of the Ballot

The ballot must have complied with ss. 227 and 230 as to equal entitlement to vote, secrecy and so on. The law currently offers the union a choice of voting methods: fully postal, semi-postal (voting papers are returned, but not distributed by, post) or workplace balloting (s. 230[3]). However, the Code of Practice on Trade Union Ballots on Industrial Action strongly advocates the fully postal method as the most desirable (para. 20) and TURERA makes this a legal requirement (s. 17). The Code also recommends the appointment of independent scrutineers to oversee the ballot, although there is currently no legal obligation on unions to do this (note that ss. 49 and 75 require that both executive committee and postal fund ballots must be independently scrutinised). However, you will remember that TURERA now imposes a legal requirement for postal strike ballots to be overseen by independent scrutineers.

Section 227 (1) provides that all those who the union might reasonably believe will be induced to take part, or to continue to take part, in the strike or industrial action should be entitled to vote. Section 227 (2) provides that requirement is not satisfied where a trade union member who is called out on strike 'was denied entitlement to vote in a ballot'. Section 230 (3) relates to the opportunity to vote and provides that: 'So far as is reasonably practicable, every person who is entitled to vote in the ballot must' be given an opportunity to vote.

In *British Railways Board* v. *NUR* [1989] 349, the Court of Appeal rejected the employer's argument that what is now s. 227 (2) invalidates a ballot if anyone who is entitled to vote but did not have an opportunity of voting is invited to strike. The court held that there was a profound difference between denying someone's entitlement to vote and inadvertently failing to give an individual an opportunity to vote. Wrongly denying a member's entitlement to vote is an absolute obligation with draconian consequences. However, s. 230 (3) expressly makes the opportunity to vote subject to a test of practicability. Therefore, a 'trifling error' – 200 members out of 60,000 not having an opportunity to vote – did not invalidate the ballot.

Timing of the Industrial Action

The normal rule is that the action must be called within four weeks, beginning with the date of the ballot (s. 234[1]). However, the 1989 docks dispute and the litigation surrounding it showed the harsh effect of this time limit where the union was prevented from calling industrial action during the four-week period because of an injunction. The TGWU succeeded in getting the injunction lifted but then had to reballot because it was outside the four-week limit.

Under s. 234 (2), a union may now apply for an extension of time to allow for the period during which it was prohibited from calling the action. An application has to be made 'forthwith upon the prohibition ceasing to have effect' and no application may be made after the end of a period of eight weeks, beginning with the date of the ballot.

We saw earlier the ballot paper must identify the person/s authorised to call for industrial action and, indeed, industrial action will only be regarded as having the support of the ballot if called by this 'specified person' (s. 233[1]). Finally, there must be no authorisation or endorsement of the action before the date of the ballot.

The courts have taken a realistic view of the requirement that the 'call for industrial action' must be by a specified person and have held it to include the case where the specified person authorises a subordinate (such as regional or local officials) to call for industrial action if a final 'make or break' negotiation fails: *Tank and Drums Ltd* v. *Transport and General Workers' Union* [1991] IRLR 372 CA.

In the Green Paper, 'Industrial Relations in the 1990s',[14] the government proposed that, once a ballot has produced a majority in favour of (or continuing with) industrial action, a union should be required to give the employer seven days' written notice of any industrial action to which the ballot relates. The notice would have to identify which workers were to be called upon to take industrial action, and on which specific date the industrial action would begin. Where a union proposes to call for intermittent action, such as a series of one-day strikes, it would be required to give at least seven days' notice of each day or other separate period of industrial action. Moreover, if the union suspends or withdraws its support for the action, further notice would be required before there is any subsequent call to resume the action.

The Green Paper also proposed that employers should have the right to receive the following information:

- notice of intent to hold the ballot, with details of which of the workers will be entitled to vote;
- a sample copy of the ballot paper, to enable the employer to know which questions are to be asked and what other information is to appear on the ballot paper; and
- the same details of the result as the law requires to be given to the union's members, and a copy of the report of the independent scrutineer for the ballot.

These proposals are now enshrined in clause 18 of TURERB.

The Member's Statutory Right to Prevent Unballoted Action

While the failure to hold a ballot will result in the loss of immunities, the Employment Act 1988 created an additional legal consequence. Where a trade union authorises or endorses 'industrial action' without first holding a ballot, one of its members who has been, or is likely to be, induced to take part in this may apply to the High Court for an order requiring the union to withdraw the authorisation or reverse the effect of its authorisation or endorsement (see now TULR[C]A 1992, s. 62). In bringing this action, the member may be assisted by the commissioner for the rights of trade union members.

The precise scope of the phrase 'industrial action' is unclear. But interpretation of that phrase under what is now TULR(C)A, s. 238 (dealing with the dismissal of those taking part in a strike or other industrial action) would suggest it encompasses action which does not necessarily involve a breach of contract (see *Power Packing Casemakers* v. *Faust* [1983] QB 471). The practical significance of this is not lost on the editors of *Harvey on Industrial Relations and Employment Law*.[15]

One purpose of balloting members over industrial action is to preserve the union's statutory immunity from a suit in tort brought by a plaintiff *employer*. The tort concerned will be or involve the tort of inducing a person to *break* a contract; and there is no need for any tort immunity. Therefore, for the purposes of the 1984 Act, the union does not need to ballot the members unless there is going to be a *breach* of contract. However under the 1988 Act, a member of the union can ask the court to restrain unballoted industrial action whether that industrial action involves breaches of contract or not. Ergo, the union, to be safe, needs to ballot *all* industrial action, whether or not there is going to be any breach of the member's contracts of employment.

Industrial Action in Support of Dismissed 'Unofficial Strikers'

In our earlier chapter dealing with unfair dismissal, we have described how the 1990 Act removed the limited unfair dismissal protection to 'unofficial' strikers (see now TULR[C]A, s. 237). In order to strengthen the employer's position in such a situation the 1990 Act removed the statutory immunity from any industrial action if 'the reason, or one of the reasons, for doing it is the fact or belief' that an employer has selectively dismissed one or more employees who were taking unofficial action (see now TULR[C]A, s. 223).

Civil Remedies and Enforcement

Currently, if a trade union organises industrial action which is unlawful, it can be restrained by an injunction from the courts on an application from the employer involved in the dispute, or from any other party whose contractual rights have been infringed. Union members also have the right to restrain industrial action if they are, or are likely to be, induced to participate in industrial action which does not have the support of a ballot. TURERB will extend the right of action to members of the public who suffer, or are likely to suffer, disruption from unlawful industrial action.

Injunctions

An injunction is either an order requiring the defendant to cease a particular course of action (a negative injunction) or, in its mandatory form, an order requiring the defendant to do something. The most frequent form of order in industrial disputes is the interlocutory injunction requiring the organisers to call off the industrial action pending full trial of the action. Employers who succeed at this stage rarely proceed to full trial: they have achieved their aim of halting the action. They know the suspension of the industrial action, although theoretically on a temporary basis, will defeat the strike in practical terms because the impetus will be lost. Given the crucial effect the obtaining of injunctive relief will have on the outcome of a dispute, the principles on which the court's discretion is based are of great importance. It used to be the case that in order to be granted interim relief the plaintiff had to establish a prima facie case. However, in *American Cyanamid Co* v. *Ethicon Ltd* [1975] AC 396 (a case involving patents law), the House of Lords substituted a less arduous test: namely, whether there is 'a serious issue to be tried'.

Moreover, the plaintiff must show that the defendant's conduct is causing him or her irreparable harm: harm that cannot be remedied by a subsequent award of damages (the status quo concept).

Finally, the plaintiff must convince the court that the harm being suffered by him or her is greater than will be incurred by the defendants if they are ordered to cease their activities pending full trial (the 'balance of convenience' test).

The application of these tests generally produced a favourable result for the plaintiff employer. In determining the status quo and balance of convenience tests, it is easy to quantify the economic loss to an employer as a result of a strike but far more difficult to assess the enormous damage that can be done to a union's bargaining position if an injunction is granted. This, together with the fact that interlocutory relief can be obtained on affidavit evidence, at very short notice and without the defendants even having an opportunity to answer the complaint, meant that the process was very much tilted in favour of management.

TULR(C)A s. 221 contains two provisions which seek to do something to redress the imbalance:

(a) Section 221 (1) requires reasonable steps to be taken to give notice of the application and an opportunity to be heard to a party likely to put forward a trade dispute defence.

(b) Section 221 (2) provides that where a party against whom an interlocutory injunction is sought claims that he or she acted in contemplation or furtherance of a trade dispute, the court shall have regard to the likelihood of that party succeeding in establishing a trade dispute defence. This was an attempt to mitigate the effects of *Cyanamid* in labour injunction cases.

In *NWL* v. *Woods* [1979] 3 All ER 614, Lord Diplock was of the view that the provision was intended as a reminder to judges that, in weighing the balance of convenience, they should consider a number of 'practical realities', particularly the fact that the interlocutory injunction stage generally disposes of the whole action. However, in *Dimbleby & Sons Ltd* v. *NUJ* [1984] ICR 386, his Lordship revised his view of the practical realities, given that in the interim period the Employment Act 1982 had made it possible to pursue actions for damages against trade unions themselves and therefore it was wrong to assume that the matter would be disposed at the interlocutory stage. Lord Diplock appeared to suggest that this should make a judge more willing to grant an interim injunction. But surely this factor should weight the balance of convenience *against* the granting of an injunction, given that the employer is now able to recover damages and costs at full trial from a solvent defendant.

You will find suggestions in several cases (*NWL Ltd* v. *Woods*; *Express Newspapers* v. *MacShane* [1980] AC 672; and *Duport Steels Ltd* v. *Sirs* [1980] ICR 161) that the courts have a residual discretion to grant an injunction. Consequently, in cases where a strike poses serious consequences to the employer, a third party or the general public, what is now s. 221 (2) might be overridden. This possibility is of much less practical importance in the 1980s, given the considerable narrowing of the scope of the immunities which has taken place (for a detailed discussion of this highly complex area see Wedderburn, *The Worker and the Law* pp.681-717).

Damages

Probably the most significant change in the structure of labour law during the 1980s was made by the Employment Act 1982, enabling a trade union itself to be sued for unlawful industrial action. In doing so, the Act 'broke the mould' of British labour law which had held sway, but for the brief interlude of the Industrial Relations Act, since 1906.

We have already seen that a union will be held vicariously liable for the unlawful industrial action of its membership where such action was authorised or endorsed by those identified in the TULR(C)A, s. 20 (2) (see pp. 358–9 for a full discussion and the circumstances in which a trade union may repudiate a purported authorisation or endorsement).

Limits on Damages Awarded against Trade Unions in Actions in Tort

The TULR(C)A, s. 22 places limits on the amounts which can be awarded against trade unions in actions brought against them where they have authorised or endorsed unlawful industrial action. The limits, which depend on the size of the trade union, have been as follows since 1982 (although the secretary of state does have power to vary them – s. 22[3]):

(a) £10,000 for unions with less than 5,000 members.
(b) £50,000 for unions between 5,000 and less than 25,000 in membership.
(c) £125,000 for unions with more than 25,000 but less than 100,000 members.
(d) £250,000 if the union has 100,000 or more members.

These limits apply in 'any proceedings in tort brought against a trade union'. The effect of this phrase is that where a union is sued by various plaintiffs (for example, the employer in dispute, customers, or suppliers) for the damages caused to them by the unlawful action, then the maximum will be applied to them separately. In this way a large union, such as the TGWU, could find it will be liable to pay well over the £250,000 in damages arising from any one dispute. You should also note these maxima do not apply in respect of the size of any fine imposed for contempt of court where there is a failure to comply with the terms of the injunction. Nor do the limits on damages include the legal costs the defendant union may have to pay. Hepple and Fredman cite the example of the *Stockport Messenger* action in 1983 against the National Graphical Association as a result of which the union lost one-tenth of its assets.

The damages against the union were assessed at £131,000 plus interest (which included aggravated and exemplary damages in relation to proved losses). When this was added to the £675,000 fines for contempt of court for non-compliance with an injunction, and legal costs of sequestration, it was estimated in December 1985 that the union had lost over £1 million.[16] [see also *Messenger Newspapers Group Ltd* v. *National Graphical Association (1982)* (1984) ICR 345]

Workers whose Right Lawfully to Withdraw Their Labour is Wholly or Partly Restricted

The Armed Forces

Industrial action would constitute desertion or mutiny and those who organised a strike would commit the crime of incitement to disaffection or sedition.

The Police

Following the abortive strike in 1919, it was made a criminal offence to take any actions likely to cause disaffection or breach of discipline among members of the police force. This law is now contained in the Police Act 1964, s. 53. This statute also forbids police officers the right to join a trade union, though, if they are already union members when they enlist, permission may be granted to retain that membership. The police may join the Police Federation but that is not a trade union as such and it is not affiliated to the TUC.

Merchant Seafarers

The Merchant Shipping Acts create a variety of criminal offences which could be used against those who organise or take part in industrial action *while the ship is at sea* – for example, in breach of duty endangering a ship, life or limb (Merchant Shipping Act 1988, s. 32). The 1970 Merchant Shipping Act, however, does allow merchant seafarers to strike where they have given 48 hours' notice to terminate their employment *and* the ship is safely berthed in the UK (s. 42[2]).

Communications Workers

The Post Office Act 1953 makes it a criminal offence for postal workers wilfully to delay or detain any postal packet (ss. 58, 68; see also Telecommunications Act 1984, ss. 44, 45). The 1984 Act also created a new civil liability of inducing a breach of the licensed operator's duty to operate the telecommunications system or to interfere with the performance of that duty. Liability is established when the action is taken wholly or partly to achieve such a result (s. 18[5]–[7]). Industrial action by telecommunications workers could clearly fall foul of this form of liability and, in this context, it will be irrelevant if they are acting in contemplation or furtherance of a trade dispute.

Aliens

The Aliens Restriction (Amendment) Act 1919, s. 3(2) makes it a crime punishable by three months' imprisonment for an alien to promote industrial unrest unless engaged bona fide in the industry for at least two years. This piece of xenophobic legislation owes its place on the statute book to the panic which followed the Russian Revolution of 1917 and the fear that foreign agitators were plotting a similar insurrection in Britain.

Endangering Life

Any worker who breaks a contract of service or hiring knowing or having reasonable cause to believe that the probable consequence of so doing, either alone or in combination with others, will be to endanger human life, cause serious bodily harm or expose any property to destruction or serious injury, commits a crime (originally enacted as Conspiracy and Protection of Property Act, s. 5; now TULR[C]A, s. 240). The offence is punishable by a fine of up to £100 or three months' imprisonment.

This offence might be relevant to a wide range of occupations engaged in industrial action, such as hospital workers, firefighters, refuse collectors, but there is no record of this mid-Victorian provision ever being used.

Emergency Powers

In the event of a national emergency, the government possesses extremely wide powers to intervene in an industrial dispute. The Emergency Powers Acts of 1920 and 1964 empower the government to proclaim a state of emergency and make regulations where there have occurred 'events of such a nature as to be calculating by interfering with the supply and distribution of food, water or light, or with the means of locomotion, to deprive the community of a substantial proportion of the essentials of life'. The proclamation must be renewed after one month and Parliament must approve the regulations made by the government. While the Act gives almost unlimited power to the government to make regulations, it cannot make it an offence to take part in a strike or to persuade others to do so and it cannot introduce military or industrial conscription. An emergency has been proclaimed 12 times since 1920 (including the seamen's strike in 1966, the docks strike in 1972, the miners' strike in 1972 and coal and electricity workers in 1973).

In addition, the government has the power to call in the armed forces to be used on 'urgent work of national importance' and this power may be exercised without any proclamation or consultation with Parliament (see the Defence [Armed Forces] Regulations 1939, now made permanent by the Emergency Powers Act 1964, s. 2).

More recently, the legislation which privatised the electricity and water industries provides ministers with wide powers to issue confidential directions to the relevant operators for purposes which include 'mitigating the effects of any civil emergency which may occur'. The secretary of state must lay a copy of every direction s/he gives before Parliament unless s/he 'is of the opinion that disclosure of the direction is against the interests of national security' or, in the case of electricity supply, s/he 'considers that it would be against the commercial interests of any person'.[17]

On the assumption that industrial action could come within the definition of a 'civil emergency', Gillian Morris has observed:

> In the event of industrial action taking place, the powers to regulate supplies which previously would have required approval under the Emergency Powers Act 1920 may now be exercised without the need for parliamentary involvement. At the same time as privatizing these services, therefore, the Government has increased considerably its scope for taking measures on a wholly unaccountable basis to counter the impact of industrial action.'[18]

Proposals to Ban Strikes in Essential Services

The increasing militancy of workers in essential services during the 1970s, particularly during the so-called winter of discontent of 1978/9, brought calls from certain sources for a general constraint to be placed on industrial action by such workers. However, the promise of legislation, though contained in both the 1979 and 1983 Conservative election manifestos, has not come to fruition at the time of writing. The matter was last mooted by the government in 1989, following the 'summer of discontent' and the disruption on the railways and London Underground. Once again, no legislation was forthcoming. One difficulty is in coming up with a definition of what constitutes an 'essential service'. No doubt it would cover those working in health and burial services, the fire brigade and those in gas, water, sewage and electricity. But what about the railways, docks, air and road transport? As the Green Paper, 'Trade Union Immunities', observed in 1981: so interdependent and interconnected are firms and industries that there is almost no major strike which will not ultimately affect the interests of the economy or community as a whole.'[19]

An alternative reason for the lack of legislation is offered by Gillian Morris, who speculates that financial considerations may have played some part:

Prominent advocates of restrictions all recognized the need for some form of pay guarantee or alternative method of dispute resolution, such as compulsory binding arbitration, in return. To the Government such suggestions were anathema; from an early stage it made clear its antipathy to unilateral arbitration, and it refused to countenance any index-linking arrangement beyond those already in existence for the police and fire service. In the light of this attitude, it was unlikely to pay a price for limiting recourse to industrial action in essential services.[20]

But Morris' central argument is that even though the government has not acted directly to outlaw industrial action in essential services, it has severely constrained the freedom to strike in these areas by more subtle means. First, as we have already seen, the privatisation legislation contains new and enhanced powers to defeat industrial action. Second, there are elements of the general legislation on industrial action which will have a particular impact on unions proposing to organise industrial action in essential services. The structural and organisational changes which have taken place in a number of essential services, such as water, electricity and the health service, with the decentralisation of the employer function could make action taken by workers taken in support of those employed in the same service unlawful 'secondary action'. In addition, the complexities surrounding the appropriate constituency for a lawful ballot on industrial action would pose particular difficulties for essential service unions who wished to preserve emergency cover during disputes.

In April 1993, according to a leaked letter from Mrs Gillian Shepherd, then employment secretary, to John Patten, education secretary, the government had been considering outlawing any industrial action aimed at frustrating the carrying out of a specific statutory duty. Such a change would affect all 5 million public sector staff and thousands of others working on services contracted out to public companies.

Mrs Shepherd's letter, written against the background of the teachers' boycott of tests under the national curriculum, alleged that the boycott was 'clearly designed to frustrate the carrying out of a specific statutory duty', namely that of schools to deliver the national curriculum.

On this occasion at least, the government received no help from the courts, with both the High Court and a unanimous Court of Appeal declaring that the tests boycott was against the workload caused by the curriculum and testing arrangements, and that it therefore was a lawful trade dispute.[21]

The Citizen and the Control of Industrial Action

The Green Paper, 'Industrial Relations in the 1990s', while not proposing an outright ban on strikes in the public services, did advocate further legal constraints. It proposed that customers of public services within the scope of the so-called Citizen's Charter should have the right to bring proceedings to prevent or restrain the unlawful organisation of industrial action in, or affecting, any such service.

The proposed right would be exercised where:

(a) a relevant public service was, or would be affected by, unlawful industrial action; and

(b) the unlawful industrial action had not been restrained by proceedings brought by an employer or union member.

The new right would be available to anyone who was, or was likely to be, a customer of the relevant public service when it was affected by industrial action. Proceedings could be brought if unlawfully organised industrial action either brought the service to a total standstill or resulted in its operating at a reduced level. Failure to comply with the resultant court order would put the union or strike organisers in contempt of court and fines and sequestration of assets might then follow.

While the Green Paper concerned itself solely with industrial action in the public services, TURERA extends this to cover *all* industrial action, whether it takes place in either the public or private sector (s. 22). Moreover, unlike the Green Paper, the Bill does not make the exercise of the right conditional on no employer or union member having sought to challenge the legality of the industrial action in the courts.

The Act also creates a new commissioner for protection against unlawful industrial action, who is to have the power, on application, to grant assistance for proceedings against a trade union under the new right.

These proposals are presented by the government as complementing the proposals for extending consumer protection through the Citizen's Charter (Cm. 1599), but they could have potentially disastrous effects on industrial relations. Even with the legal power which has been handed to employers in the 1980s and beginning of the 1990s, there will still be occasions when an employer will judge it more appropriate to pursue further negotiations rather than to go rushing to the courts. These proposals rob the employer of that choice and allow individuals backed by such right wing-groups as the Freedom Association to get involved, risking an increase in the bitterness of the dispute.

CHAPTER 21

Industrial Conflict II: Picketing

Introduction

The practice of picketing a place of work in order to persuade other workers not to enter the workplace has been traditionally perceived by trade unions as an essential weapon when they are involved in disputes. The vast majority of pickets lines are conducted in an entirely peaceful and orderly manner, often without the need for a police presence.[1] During the 1970s and 1980s, however, we witnessed the practice of 'mass-picketing' and instances of violent confrontation between strikers and the police – for example, the miners' strikes of 1972, 1974 and 1984/5, Grunwick in 1977 and Wapping in 1986. Such atypical 'cause célèbres' provided the rationale for statutory intervention aimed at controlling more closely the conduct of picketing through the use of both the civil and criminal law.

While it is true that picketing is one area of industrial conflict where the criminal law plays a significant part in regulation in addition to the civil law, it should be stressed that secondary picketing – picketing a workplace other than your own – is not in itself a criminal offence. Since the early 1980s there has been a blurring of the distinction between the civil and the criminal law in the case of picketing and this causes confusion in the minds of trade unionists themselves. Welch's survey of active trade unionists found that nearly 80 per cent of the sample believed that they would automatically commit a criminal offence if they peacefully picketed the premises of a supplier of their employer. Commenting on this legal mystification, Welch argues:

> This has important ideological connotations, particularly when the participants in such an activity are not aware that at a factual level they may be able to counter claims by employers, the media and the police that they are acting illegally or committing the 'offence' of secondary picketing. Moreover, such misconceptions of the criminal law may result in pickets obeying police instructions to leave or disperse even when they are within their strict legal rights.[2]

The law's approach to picketing raises the question of whether there is an adequate recognition of an individual right of assembly.

371

The Freedom to Picket

As with strike action, the law provides no right to picket. Instead it offers an extremely limited immunity from civil and criminal liability. This is now contained in TULR(C)A 1992, s. 220. Section 220 (1) (a) states that:

> It shall be lawful for a person in contemplation or furtherance of a trade dispute to attend –
>
> (a) at or near his own place of work; or
> (b) if he is an official of a trade union, at or near the place of work of a member of that union whom he is accompanying and whom he represents, for the purposes only of communicating information or peacefully persuading any person to work or abstain from working.

Notice that picketing will only receive the protection of the immunities if the pickets are attending at or near their own workplace. So-called secondary picketing was rendered unlawful by the amendments made by the Employment Act 1980. There is no statutory definition of 'place of work'. However, the Code of Practice on Picketing, published in 1980 to accompany the amendments to the statute and revised in 1992, offers the following guidance:

> The law does not enable a picket to attend lawfully at an entrance to, or exit from any place of work other than his own. This applies even, for example, if those working at the other place of work are employed by the same employer, or are covered by the same collective bargaining arrangements as the picket. (para. 18)

In *Rayware Ltd* v. *TGWU* [1989] IRLR 134, pickets assembled on the public highway at an entrance to an industrial estate which included the factory unit where they worked. They were actually three-quarters of a mile from their factory unit. The majority view of the Court of Appeal was that the pickets were 'near' their workplace and therefore acting lawfully.

The statute provides three exceptions to the 'own place of work' requirement:

(i) If workers normally work at more than one place (mobile workers) or if it is impractical to picket their place of work (for instance, an oil rig), then the section allows them to picket the place where their work is administered by the employer (s. 220[2]).

(ii) Workers who are dismissed during the dispute in question are permitted to picket their former place of work (s. 220[3]).

(iii) As you will see from s. 220 (1) (b), a trade union official may attend at any place of work provided that:

(a) s/he is accompanying a member or members of his/her trade union who are picketing at their own place of work; and

(b) s/he personally represents those members within the trade union. An official – whether lay or full-time – is regarded for this purpose as representing only those members s/he has been specifically appointed or elected to represent. So it is lawful for a regional official to attend a picket at any place within that region, whereas a shop steward can only picket the workplace of the work group s/he represents (see s. 220[4]).

Civil Liabilities

The Economic Torts

Without the protection of the immunities, picketing will generally result in an economic tort being committed. If workers assemble at the entrance to a workplace and attempt to persuade other employees not to work, the pickets could be liable for inducing a breach of contracts of employment. However, provided the picketing is lawful within s. 220, the general immunity provided by s. 219 in respect of tortious liability applies (see s. 219 [3]).

Private Nuisance

Private nuisance is an unlawful interference with an individual's use or enjoyment of his or her land. Unreasonable interference with that right by, for example, blocking an access route to the employer's property may give rise to a cause of action. So, even if the pickets stand outside the employer's premises they may be liable for the tort of private nuisance.

Picketing which exceeds the bounds of peacefully obtaining or communicating information may involve liability for private nuisance. However, there is still doubt whether peaceful picketing *itself* amounts to a nuisance when not protected by the 'golden formula'. In the case of *Lyons* v. *Wilkins*, the Court of Appeal held that peaceful picketing which involved persuasion went beyond mere attendance for the purpose of informing, and was a common law nuisance. In *Ward Lock & Co* v. *Operative Printers' Assistants' Society* [1906] 22 TLR 327, a differently constituted Court of Appeal thought otherwise. In this case it was said that picketing a person's premises is not unlawful unless it is associated with conduct which constitutes nuisance at common law: some independent wrongful act such as obstruction, violence, intimidation, molestation or threats.

In *Hubbard* v. *Pitt* [1975] ICR 308 (a rare non-industrial picketing case), Lord Denning sided with the view of the Court of Appeal in *Ward Lock*, stating:

Picketing is not a nuisance in itself. Nor is it a nuisance for a group of people to attend at or near the plaintiff's premises in order to obtain or communicate information or in order to peacefully persuade. It does not become a nuisance unless it is associated with obstruction, violence, intimidation, molestation or threats.

The majority of the Court of Appeal, on the other hand, merely affirmed the exercise of the High Court judge's discretion to grant an interlocutory injunction to the plaintiffs whose premises were being picketed and had little to say on the substantive issue. However, Lord Justice Orr did feel that the defendants' intentions and states of mind formed what he called 'a crucial question' in this matter and he was satisfied that in this case the pickets intended to interfere with the plaintiff's business.

This sort of reasoning was applied subsequently in *Mersey Dock & Harbour Co Ltd* v. *Verrinder* [1982] IRLR 152, where the High Court held that the picketing of the entrances to container terminals at Mersey Docks amounted to private nuisance despite the fact that the picketing was carried out in an entirely peaceful manner by a small group of pickets.

On the basis of this approach, it would appear that if the intention of the pickets is to achieve more than the mere communication of information and actually to interfere with the picketed employer's business, then the picket will be tortious.

As you can see, the conflict between the *Lyons* and *Ward Lock* approaches is unresolved, though you will find the weight of academic opinion favouring the *Ward Lock* approach.[3]

You will also find that the tort of nuisance was interpreted to be considerably broader in scope in *Thomas* v. *NUM (South Wales Area)* [1985] IRLR 136, a case arising out of the protracted miners' strike of 1984/5. In this case, a group of working miners obtained injunctions restraining the area union from organising mass picketing at the collieries where they worked. While Mr Justice Scott expressed his agreement with the *Ward Lock* approach that picketing per se does not amount to a common law nuisance, he held that it could be tortious if it amounted to an unreasonable interference with the victims' rights to use the highway. This was the situation in the case before the court:

> the picketing at the colliery gates is of such a nature and is carried out in a manner that represents an unreasonable harassment of the working miners. A daily congregation on average of 50 to 70 men hurling abuse in circumstances that require a police presence and require the working miners to be conveyed in vehicles does not in my view leave any room for argument.

Two important points arise from this decision

- Private nuisance is concerned with interference with the use or enjoyment of land in which the plaintiff has an interest. In this case, a species of the tort was held to extend to interference with the right to use the highway.
- The terms of the injunction granted by the court restricted picketing at the collieries to communicating and obtaining information peacefully and in numbers not exceeding six. This number is not a purely arbitrary figure; it comes from the Code of Practice on Picketing which at para. 51 advises that: 'pickets and their organisers should ensure that in general the number of pickets does not exceed six at any entrance to a workplace; frequently a smaller number will be appropriate.'

This would suggest that the judge was using the guidance in the Code to fix the parameters of lawful picketing. If this view is correct, then any picketing numbering more than six will lose the immunity offered by s. 220 and will be tortious.

Trespass
Section 220 tells us that picketing is lawful where pickets attend 'at or near' their own place of work. To mount a picket *on* the employer's land without consent will mean that the immunity will be forfeited and that the tort of trespass has been committed (see *British Airports Authority* v. *Ashton* [1983] IRLR 287).

Criminal Liability

While it is important to grasp the range of possible civil liabilities which may attach to certain types of picketing, it is the criminal law which is of the greatest practical significance in terms of the control of the activity. This can be clearly seen from the employment of the criminal law during the miners' strike, where over 11,000 charges were brought in connection with incidents arising out of the dispute. These ranged in gravity from the serious offences of riot and unlawful assembly to the less serious charges of obstruction of the highway. Additional criminal offences which may be relevant to the conduct of picketing have been created by the Public Order Act 1986. We shall offer you a brief survey of the potential criminal liability of pickets.[4]

Obstructing a Police Officer

If a police officer reasonably apprehends that a breach of the peace is likely to occur, the officer has the right and duty at common law to take reasonable steps to prevent it. If the officer is obstructed in the exercise of this duty then an offence is committed (s. 51[3] of the Police Act 1964). In practice, this gives the police a wide discretion to control picketing. While there must be an objective apprehension that a breach of the peace is a real as opposed to a remote possibility, the courts tend to accept the officer's assessment of the situation. The leading case on this question is *Piddington* v. *Bates* [1960] 1 WLR 162, where the officer's decision to restrict the number of pickets at an entrance to a workplace to two was held to be legally justified. (You should note that the Code of Practice on Picketing makes it clear that its recommended number of six pickets does not affect in any way the discretion of the police to limit the number of people on any one picket line – para. 47).

The common law duty to preserve the peace also allows the police to set up roadblocks to prevent pickets joining picket lines some distance away, provided that there is a reasonable apprehension that the risk to the peace is 'in close proximity both in time and place' (see *Moss* v. *McLachlan* [1985] IRLR 76 and the commentary on the case by Morris).[5] Under s. 4 of the Police and Criminal Evidence Act 1984, police officers may also operate 'road checks' for purposes which include ascertaining whether a vehicle is carrying a person intending to commit an offence which a senior officer has reasonable grounds to believe is likely to lead to serious public disorder.

Obstruction of the Highway (s. 137 of the Highways Act 1980)
Under this provision, it is an offence wilfully to obstruct free passage along a highway without lawful authority or excuse. Before the offence is established, there must be proof of an unreasonable user of the highway. This is a question of fact and depends upon all the circumstances, including the length of time the obstruction continues, the place where it occurs, its purpose and whether it causes an actual as opposed to potential obstruction (*Nagy* v. *Weston* [1965] 1 All ER 78). It would appear that peaceful picketing carried out in the manner envisaged by s 15. TULRA and within the numbers advised by the Code will be held to be a reasonable user. If, however, these boundaries are crossed an offence will be committed, as, for example, where pickets stood in front of a vehicle in order to stop it entering the employer's premises (*Broome* v. *DPP* [1974] AC 587) or walked in a continuous circle in a factory entrance (*Tynan* v. *Balmer* [1967] 1 QB 91).

Public Nuisance

This offence derives from common law and is committed where members of the public are obstructed in the exercise of rights which are common to all Her Majesty's subjects, including the right of free passage along the public highway. As with the more frequently charged offence under the Highways Act, it is necessary for the prosecution to prove unreasonable user.

Where an individual suffers special damage, over and above that suffered by the rest of the public, an action in tort for public nuisance may also be brought.

The Conspiracy and Protection of Property Act 1875

This Victorian statute made the following five acts criminal if they are done 'wrongfully and without legal authority' with a view to compelling any person to do or abstain from doing any act which that person has a legal right to do (the gender-biased language follows the wording in the Act):

(i)   using violence or intimidating that person or his wife or children or injuring his property;
(ii) persistently following that person about from place to place;
(iii) hiding any tools, clothes or other property owned or used by such other person, or depriving him or hindering him in the use thereof;
(iv) watching or besetting his house, residence or place of work, or the approach to such house, residence or place, or wherever the person happens to be;
(v)   following such a person with two or more other persons in a disorderly manner in or through any street or road. (Now TULRA(C)A s.241)

Until relatively recently, it was assumed that this quaintly worded provision was only of historical interest and virtually obsolete in practical terms. During the miners' strike of 1984/5, however, at least 643 charges were brought under what is now TULRA, s. 241, mainly to deal with 'watching and besetting' working miners' homes. In the view of the government, the section had demonstrated its continued efficacy in the circumstances of the strike and should not only be retained but strengthened (see White Paper, 'Review of Public Order Law').[6]

Consequently, the Public Order Act 1986 increased the maximum penalty of three months imprisonment and a £100 fine to six-months imprisonment and a £2,000 fine. The Act also made breach of what is now s. 241 an arrestable offence.

Of the five offences listed in s. 241, watching and besetting is the one which is most likely to arise out of the course of picketing. As we have seen earlier in this chapter, the weight of authority would suggest that the watching and besetting must be of such a nature as to amount in itself to tortious activity before it can give rise to liability under s. 241. If peaceful picketing is not tortious, then it cannot amount to a criminal watching and besetting either.

One final point in this section concerns the question of whether mass picketing amounts to intimidation. In *Thomas* v. *NUM(South Wales Area)* (cited above), Mr Justice Scott was of the view that not only was mass picketing a common law nuisance but it also amounted to intimidation under what is now s. 241, even where there was no physical obstruction of those going to work.

The Public Order Act 1986

In putting forward the proposals which were later largely translated into the provisions of the Public Order Act, the White Paper of 1985 stated:

The rights of peaceful protest and assembly are amongst our fundamental freedoms: they are numbered among the touchstones which distinguish a free society from a totalitarian one. Throughout the review the Government has been concerned to regulate those freedoms to the minimum extent necessary to preserve order and protect the rights of others.[7]

A number of commentators, however, have expressed a general concern that the provisions contained in the Act impose a dangerous restriction on the civil liberties of assembly and protest and, particularly in the light of events during the 1984/5 miners' strike, make it increasingly more difficult for the police to be seen to maintain a position of neutrality in the policing of industrial disputes.[8]

Part I of the Public Order Act contains five new statutory offences which may have a relevance in the context of picketing. Sections 1–3 of the Act contain the offences of riot, violent disorder and affray, and replace the common law offences of riot, rout, unlawful assembly and affray whose ambit was confused and uncertain. Sections 4 and 5 contain the more minor offences of causing fear or provocation of violence and causing harassment, alarm or distress.

Riot (s. 1)

Where 12 or more people are present together and use or threaten violence for a common purpose and their conduct (taken together) is such that a person of reasonable firmness – if present – would fear for his or her safety, each person using the violence is guilty of riot an liable on conviction to a maximum possible penalty of 10 years' imprisonment.

Violent Disorder (s. 2)

Where three or more people who are present together use or threaten violence and their conduct, taken together, would cause a person of reasonable firmness – if present – to fear for his or her safety, each person using or threatening violence is guilty of the offence and liable on conviction to a maximum of five years' imprisonment.

Note the contrast with the more serious offence of riot: less people are required; the accused need only threaten violence as opposed to using it; and there is no requirement for a common purpose.

Affray (s. 3)

The offence is committed if a person uses or threatens unlawful violence towards another and his or her conduct is such as would cause a person of reasonable firmness – if present – to fear for his or her personal safety. The maximum sentence on conviction is three years.

You should note that 'violence' is given a wide definition by s. 8 of the Act and, except in the context of affray, includes violent conduct to property as well as towards persons. In addition, the term is not restricted to conduct intended to cause injury or damage: it covers any 'violent conduct'. Rather unusually, the section provides us with an example of what it means – throwing at or towards a person a missile of a kind capable of causing injury which does not hit or falls short.

Note also that it is not necessary for the prosecution to prove that anyone actually did fear for their safety: the fear of a hypothetical bystander is sufficient.

Causing Fear of or Provoking Violence (s. 4)

The most frequently charged public order offence prior to the passage of the 1986 Act was that contained in s. 5 of the Public Order Act 1936. This section made it an offence to use threatening, abusive or insulting words or behaviour with intent to cause a breach of the peace or whereby a breach of the peace was likely to be occasioned. During the miners' strike in 1984/5, some 4,107 prosecutions were brought under this section.

Section 4 of the 1986 Act replaces s. 5 of the 1936 Act with a modified and extended version of the offence. A person is guilty of the offence if s/he:

(a) uses towards another person threatening, abusive or insulting words or behaviour; or

(b) distributes or displays any writing, sign or other visible representation which is threatening, abusive or insulting, with intent to cause that person to believe that immediate unlawful violence will be used against him/her or another by any person, or to provoke the immediate use of unlawful violence by that person or another, or whereby that person is likely to believe that such violence will be used or it is likely that such violence will be provoked.

The new provision is broader in scope than its predecessor in two respects. First, the new offence can be committed in either a public or a private place. The limitation of s. 5 of the 1936 Act to conduct in public places meant that during the miners' strike a number of summonses were dismissed where people charged with threatening words or behaviour were able to show they were on National Coal Board or other private property at the time of the alleged offence. (Indeed, the extension of coverage to both public and private places applies in respect of all five of the statutory public order offences contained in the Act.) Second, case law suggested that s. 5 did not cover a situation where the victim (for example, an elderly person) was someone who was not likely to be provoked to breach the peace. Under the new provision, a belief that immediate violence will be used against oneself or another is sufficient.

The maximum penalty on conviction is six-months' imprisonment and a £2,000 fine.

Causing Harassment, Alarm and Distress (s. 5)

This 'catch-all' and controversial offence is committed where a person:

(a) uses threatening, abusive or insulting words or behaviour, or disorderly behaviour, or
(b) displays any writing, sign or other visible representation which is threatening, abusive or insulting, within the hearing or sight of a person likely to be caused harassment, alarm or distress thereby.

The maximum penalty is a £400 fine.

It is easy to foresee that this offence will be readily employed to control the conduct of picketing. Shouts of abuse to workers as they cross the picket line, offensive gestures and insulting placards or banners may all fall foul of this section.

One of three defences provided by s. 5 (3) is if the accused can prove that his or her conduct was reasonable. The scope of this defence for the picket is untried and uncertain, though Bowers and Duggan are not optimistic:

A picket might claim that his conduct was reasonable when he called the strikebreaker names such as 'scab', because it is in the collective interest that the strike is successful and his conduct ought to achieve that result. One cannot, however, imagine the courts being very sympathetic to such a plea.[9]

Marches and Assemblies

Part II of the Public Order Act 1986 imposes new controls over the conduct of marches or processions and static assemblies.

Section 11 imposes a new national requirement for organisers of 'public processions' to give at least six clear days' notice of their intention to the police. The notice must specify the date of the procession, its proposed starting time and route, and the name and address of one of the organisers.

Picketing, by definition, is a static assembly outside the entrance of a workplace. However, protest marches are now a relatively frequent feature of larger industrial disputes, for instance the protest marches held in support of the striking miners in 1984/5 and the marches, culminating in a mass picket outside the Wapping plant of News International, during 1986 in protest at the dismissal of some 5,500 printworkers (see *News Group Newspapers Ltd* v. *SOGAT 82* [1986] IRLR 337). In future such marches will have to comply with the terms of s. 11, though you should note that the notice requirement does not apply to processions 'commonly and customarily held' – for example a march by trade unionists on May Day.

A notice may be delivered by post but only if it is by recorded delivery; otherwise it must be delivered by hand to a police station in the police area in which it is proposed the procession will start. The Act allows an exception to the six-day notice requirement in the case of a delivery by hand where it is not reasonably practicable to give that amount of advance notice. An example where this exception may be relevant in an industrial dispute would be the need for a rapid protest response to the summary dismissal of a shop steward or management's announcement of immediate plant closure and redundancies.

Failure to give the appropriate notice renders the organisers liable to a fine of up to £400. It is also made an offence to organise a march which differs in terms of start and route from the information given in the notice. Defences are available if it is proved that the accused did not know of, and neither suspected nor had reason to suspect, the failure to satisfy the requirements or the different date, time or route. In relation to a march being held on a different date or time, or along a different route, it is also a defence to prove that the difference arose from circumstances beyond the control of the accused or from something done with the agreement of a police officer.

The Power to Impose Conditions on Processions (s. 12)
This section enables the most senior police officer present to impose conditions, including route and timing, on processions when the officer reasonably believes that it may result in serious public disorder, serious damage to property or serious disruption to the life of the community, or that the purpose of the organisers is to intimidate others. Where a march or procession is *intended* to be held, 'the senior police officer' with the power to impose conditions is the chief officer of police.

The organiser of a march who knowingly fails to comply with a condition imposed under this section commits an offence, whose maximum punishment is three months' imprisonment and/or a £1,000 fine. In addition, those who participate in a march who knowingly fail to comply with any imposed condition commit a summary offence punishable with a fine not exceeding £400. Finally, those who incite marchers to break a condition are also guilty of a summary offence and are liable on conviction to a maximum of three months' imprisonment or a fine not exceeding £1,000.

Bans on Marches
The power to ban marches for up to three months under the Public Order Act on the grounds of reasonable belief that it will result in 'serious public disorder'

is retained. The major change is that the 1986 Act makes it an offence to participate in a banned march, punishable with a maximum fine, in addition to organising or inciting others to participate in one.

Static Assemblies

The Act provides the police with the power for the first time ever a clear *statutory* power to impose conditions which prescribe the location, size and maximum duration of 'public assemblies' (defined as assemblies of 20 or more people in a 'public place' which is wholly or partly open to the air). As with processions, the most senior officer present will be able to impose such conditions where s/he reasonably believes that it may result in serious disorder, serious damage to property, serious disruption to the life of the community or the 'intimidation of others with a view to compelling them not to do an act they have a right to do, or to do an act they have a right not to do'.

This provision has the clearest relevance for pickets and provides a potent additional weapon of control for the police. As the White Paper 'Review of Public Order Law' observed: 'at Grunwick's or Warrington, for example, the police could have imposed conditions limiting the numbers of demonstrators, or moving the demonstration in support of the pickets further away from the factory.'[10] Where conditions are imposed in advance of the assembly, then they may only be imposed by the chief officer of police or that officer's deputy or assistant. The organisers of a static assembly which fails to abide by the conditions or those who incite disobedience face a maximum penalty of three months' imprisonment and/or a £1,000 fine. The participants in such an assembly risk a £400 fine.

PART SEVEN

Legal Action

CHAPTER 22

Tribunal and Court Claims

Depending on the kind of issue involved, and the size of the claim (if it is a claim in the courts for damages), there are four different courts in which an employment claim can begin. Each one then has a possible appeal route, if an appeal is made, as shown in figure 22.1.

The industrial tribunal (IT) deals with most of the EPCA and other statutory issues discussed in the previous chapters. These include unfair dismissal, redundancy, discrimination and most wages problems. The IT also hears appeals against improvement and prohibition notices. The jurisdiction of the IT will, in addition, be extended to include employment contracts and certain other matters which are currently dealt with by the courts.[1] Until that happens it may still be necessary for contract issues to be dealt with either by the county court or by the High Court.

As well as the important area of personal injuries, the courts also deal with other civil claims based on torts (civil wrongs). They also deal with disputes over post-termination contract restrictions or intellectual property rights involving court action for injunctions and the like (see chapter 9 above). The High Court will usually be the relevant court in such cases. Collective issues, including actions by employers to get court orders, are also usually dealt with by the High Court.

As a comment on the present system, there is obviously a strong argument for moving to a less fragmented and more integrated labour court structure. Ideas on this, and on a generally more 'autonomous' employment law system, have been discussed extensively.[2] The proposal for a 'labour court' begs the question, though, of what sort of system that should be. The Conservative government's National Industrial Relations Court in the 1970s was regarded by the labour movement as highly pro-employer, and there is still a significant distrust of judicial involvement in industrial relations issues since that era.[3] There are, in any case, quite a few different possible models, including those operating in Europe, which could be adopted (with varying degrees of integration into their general court systems and appeal structures).

Starting a Tribunal Claim

There are no difficult formalities in starting a tribunal claim. To begin the claim it is always advisable to fill out a Form IT1 (copies are obtainable from Department of Employment offices). Although this is not essential, filling one out will ensure

Figure 22.1: Different Courts Applicable to Different Types of Claim

EPCA/OTHER STATUTORY RIGHT	CIVIL CLAIM (1)		CRIMINAL (1)
Industrial Tribunal	High Court (5)	County Court (5)	Magistrates (or Crown Court)
Employment Appeal Tribunal		Crown Court (1) (Trial Court and Appeals from Magistrates)	Divisional Court (Queen's Bench Division of High Court)
	Court of Appeal		
	House of Lords (4)		
European Court of Human Rights (3) (ECHR)	European Court of Justice (2) (EJC)		

Notes:

(1) Criminal cases can begin in the magistrates or crown court, depending on how serious they are. In Scotland the Sheriff's Court deals with criminal cases, and the Court of Session with civil claims.

(2) The ECJ is the highest court on EC employment points, and cases can also be 'referred', to decide preliminary EC points, by lower courts.

(3) Employment issues involving infringements of the European Convention on Human Rights can be taken to the ECHR (normally only after UK courts have failed to implement the Convention's requirements).

(4) In some cases it is possible to appeal directly from the High Court to the House of Lords (leap-frogging the Court of Appeal).

(5) Whether a claim begins in the High Court or the county court depends principally on its size. Claims for breach of contract, or tort, for amounts under £25,000 will generally be dealt with in a county court and those of over £50,000 in the High Court. Cases are, however, allocated in accordance with rules which allow for transfer of cases between courts and which, among other things, allow the parties to agree on where a case should be dealt with.

you provide the details about the complaint, and the compensation, relief and so on being claimed which are legally required before the claim will be heard. A specimen copy showing the sort of information required is shown in appendix II below.

The important sections are those where you are asked to state the *point* that you want dealt with, and the *grounds* which are relied on. Assistance with this is provided in the information you are given with Form IT1 (including 'Industrial Tribunals Procedure' – booklet IT L1), but it is always advisable to get assistance, before filling it in, from a union, solicitor, or Advice Bureau.

The IT has the power to give interim relief, if this is appropriate, to preserve the 'status quo'.

Unfortunately, Legal Aid is not available, although basic preliminary advice can be obtained under the Green Form scheme from local solicitors. This does not entitle you to representation, however; and without guidance and representation your chances of success are reduced.[4]

Eligibility and Time Limits

Most employment rights are subject to eligibility requirements; in particular, two years' continuous service is required for unfair dismissal claims. Service requirements are referred to earlier in the relevant subject chapters. In addition, there are procedural conditions which must be carefully followed. The most important of these is that claims should be presented as quickly as possible, and *within the statutory time limits.*

A time limit of three months from the date of the act or omission in question applies in several cases, but limits can be shorter than that – for instance, within seven days from dismissal for union victimisation cases where reinstatement, and so forth, is claimed as interim relief (see p. 228 above). Or they can be longer, as in the case of redundancy payments where the limit is six months (see p. 256). A tribunal has only very limited scope for allowing an extended period in which to claim, so it is vital to check what the relevant limit is, and comply with it. The IT could allow an extension, but only in exceptional circumstances and if it can be shown that it was not 'reasonably practicable' to present the claim in time. The exact meaning of reasonably practicable (which is the phrase used in relation to most time limits) is not always clear, but cases show that it is interpreted very strictly. It is usually only where something actually prevents you from putting in a claim that you may be allowed to proceed.

Processing the Claim

Copies of the claim are sent to the employer and to the ACAS conciliation officer who may conciliate and try to settle the claim. Assistance at this stage from a conciliation officer (who also sees the employer's response) can be very useful, and may well avoid the need to pursue tribunal proceedings. If a claim is formally settled, tribunal proceedings will normally not be possible.[5] If the claim is to be defended, the employer must send a completed Form IT3 ('Notice of Appearance') within 14 days, although extensions can be obtained.

If, on receipt of the IT1, the tribunal secretary can decide that the tribunal does not have power to make an award, applicants are notified of this and if, despite this, the claim is maintained, there is a risk of a 'costs' award being made. Unlike the courts, costs are not something you need to worry about in the IT, at least under present legislation. A costs award can be made against you, but only if you bring a case (or conduct it) frivolously, vexatiously, 'or otherwise unreasonably', and if you are obviously abusing the system – for example, by bringing the case for malicious motives, or by forcing unnecessary adjournments. There is also the possibility that a pre-hearing assessment could be ordered (usually if a respondent employer asks for one, but it is available at either side's request, or if the tribunal chair orders one to be held). This involves a hearing where the issues are considered in outline. If the IT thinks the case has no reasonable prospect of success a costs 'warning' could be issued. If the case proceeds after a costs warning it will be before a different tribunal. The warning is not referred to until after the result of the case, whereupon costs can be considered.

Preliminary hearings may also be held to decide whether the case can go ahead. In particular, a hearing may be necessary if there is doubt about the claim being presented within the time limits, or whether the qualifying service and other requirements for bringing a claim are satisfied.

Under provisions in the Employment Act 1989[6] which have not been implemented pre-hearing 'reviews' will be possible. The procedure is controversial because it will allow ITs to require deposits of up to £150 to be paid by parties as a condition of continuing a claim. Such a requirement could obviously be a powerful disincentive to continue, especially as there will also be a risk of paying costs if these exceed the deposit amount. Employers' organisations, who argue that ITs are abused by employees, are pressing for the speedy implementation of this procedure, and for the £150 limit to be raised (which can easily be done by ministerial order).

Tribunal rules[7] govern parties' rights and procedures at tribunals, but ITs have considerable discretion in how cases are dealt with. A detailed discussion of industrial tribunal procedure is not possible,[8] but the key points are:

- A party (or the IT) can require the other party to provide 'further and better' particulars to clarify their case.
- The IT can be asked to order disclosure of documents which a party has if these are necessary to decide the case fairly.
- Witness orders can be made, requiring witnesses to attend (if their evidence could be useful).

After hearing both parties' cases (including documentary evidence, witnesses, cross-examination, and closing statements by the parties), the IT will make a decision. This will normally be a brief verbal decision, and fuller reasons are posted to the parties later. The IT can order:

- compensation; or
- reinstatement or re-engagement (in unfair dismissal cases); or
- a declaration of rights (which is not legally enforceable).

Appeals

The losing party can ask the IT to review its own decision in some cases. This must be requested at the hearing, or within 14 days of the decision being recorded. The grounds are limited. They might include, for example, the decision being made when a party is not present, or where important new evidence becomes available after the hearing. The IT can order a review if this is required in 'the interests of justice', but such reviews are rarely allowed except where there has been an obvious mistake or procedural error.

Appeal to the EAT is possible, and the appeal must be lodged within 42 days of the IT decision being entered on the register. Appeals are normally only allowed on a point of law (as the IT decides factual points). However, this could include misunderstanding the facts or making a decision that is 'perverse' or not supported by evidence. A copy of the IT chair's notes should be requested as a matter of course. The IT's full written reasons will need to be obtained for the appeal. Legal Aid is available for representation in the EAT and legal advice should be obtained.

Court Claims

It is possible to initiate or defend legal claims in the courts without professional assistance, but there are many good reasons why you should not do so (unless you have no choice). The first step should be to get assistance, if possible, through support organisations like unions, law centres or CAB, and if you think you are eligible for Legal Aid you should obviously get advice from a solicitors' firm that does legal aid work.

Small claims in the county court, that is to say claims worth less than £50,000 (which might cover a variety of employment disputes) are often pursued without legal help, and these provide the opportunity of getting a claim dealt with by informal arbitration at minimal costs.[9] Even for these claims advice is worth getting.

Legal Actions against Unions

A controversial part of the Trade Union and Labour Relations (Consolidation) Act provides for the appointment of a commissioner for the rights of trade union members. The legislation enables trade unionists to get financial help to take court action against their union or its officers; for example, if industrial action is called without following legal procedures or the union's rules being properly followed. The matters which the commissioner may consider when deciding whether to support an action include, by virtue of s. 20 of the Employment Act 1988, situations where a case 'raises a question of principle'; where it is unreasonable 'having regard to the complexity of the case' to expect an applicant to deal with a case unaided; and where, in the oppinion of the commissioner, the case involves a matter of 'substantial public interest'.

Appendices

Useful Addresses

Advisory Conciliation and Arbitration Service (ACAS)
27 Wilton Street
LONDON SW1X 7AZ
(Tel: 071-210 3000)
For regional offices in other cities, see local telephone directory

Central Arbitration Committee (CAC)
39 Grosvenor Place
LONDON SW1X 7BD
(Tel: 071-210 3738)

Central Office of the Industrial Tribunals (England & Wales)
Southgate Street
BURY St. EDMUNDS
Suffolk IP33 2AQ
(Tel: 0284-762300)

Central Office of the Industrial Tribunals (Scotland)
St. Andrew House
141 West Nile Street
GLASGOW G1 2RU
(Tel: 041-331 1601)

Commission for Racial Equality (CRE)
Elliott House
10–12 Allington Street
LONDON SW1E 5EH
(Tele: 071-828 7022)

Commissioner for the Rights of Trade Union Members
Bank Chambers
2A Rylands Street
WARRINGTON
Cheshire WA1 1EN
(Tel: 0925-415771)

Data Protection Registrar
Springfield House
Water Lane
WILMSLOW
Cheshire SK9 5AX
(Tel: 0625-535777)

Department of Employment
(Redundancy Payments Office)
Arena House
North End Road
WEMBLEY HA9 0NF
(Tel: 081-900 1966)
For regional offices in other cities, see local telephone directory

Department of Social Security
Alexander Fleming House
Elephant and Castle
LONDON SE1 6BY
(Tel: 071-407 5522)

Employment Appeals Tribunal
4 St. James Square
LONDON SW1
(Tel: 071-210 3000)

Equal Opportunities Commission
Overseas House
Quay Street
MANCHESTER M3 3HN
(Tel: 061-833 9244)

Greater Manchester Hazards Centre
23 New Mount Street
MANCHESTER M4
(Tel: 061-953 4037)

Health and Safety Advice Centre
Unit 304
Argent Street
60 Frederick Street
BIRMINGHAM B1
(Tel: 021-236 0801)

Health and Safety Executive (HSE)
Public Enquiry Point
Baynards House
1 Chepstow Place
Westbourne Grove
LONDON W2 4TE
(Tel: 071-221 0870)
Addresses of HSE area offices are under 'Health and Safety Executive' in local telephone directories.

Labour Research Department
78 Blackfriars Road
LONDON SE1 8HF
(Tel: 071-928 3649)

London Hazards Centre
308 Gray's Inn Road
LONDON WC1
(Tel: 071-837 5605)

Lothian Trade Union and Community Resource Centre
12a Picardy Place
EDINBURGH
(Tel: 031-556 7318)

National Council for Civil Liberties
21 Tabard Street
LONDON SE1 4LA
(Tel: 071-403 3888)

United Kingdom Immigration Advisory Service
Central Office
190 Great Dover Street
LONDON SE1 4YB
(Tel: 071-357 6917)

Wages Inspectorate
93 Ebury Bridge Road
LONDON SW1W 8RE
(Tel: 071-730 9161)

Form IT1 – Application to an Industrial Tribunal

FOR COIT USE ONLY

Received at COIT

Case Number

Code

Initials

ROIT

Application to an Industrial Tribunal

Please read the notes opposite before filling in this form

1. Say what type of complaint(s) you want the tribunal to decide *(see note opposite)*.

2. Please give your name and address in CAPITALS

Mr ☐   Mrs ☐   Miss ☐   Ms ☐

Surname

First name(s)

Address

Postcode

Telephone

Date of birth

3. Please give the name and address of your representative. if you have one.

Name

Address

Postcode

Telephone

4. Please give the details of the employer or body (the respondent) you are complaining about *(see note opposite)*.

Name

Address

Postcode

Telephone

Please give the place where you worked or applied for work. if different from above.

Name

Address

Postcode

Telephone

5. Please say what job you did for the employer (or what job you applied for). If this does not apply, please say what your connection was with the employer.

IT 1 and IT 1(Scot) (Revised Feb 1991) —————————————————— Over ▶

6. Please give the number of normal basic hours you worked per week.

Hours [   ] per week

7. Basic wage/
salary   £ [   ] per [   ]

Average take
home pay   £ [   ] per [   ]

Other bonuses
or benefits   £ [   ] per [   ]

8. Please give the dates of your employment.
(if applicable)

Began on [   ]

Ended on [   ]

9. If your complaint is not about dismissal. please give the date when the action you are complaining about took place (or the date when you first knew about it).

Date [   ]

10. Please give full details of your complaint *(see notes attached)*:

11. Unfair dismissal claimants only *(Please tick a box to show what you would want if you win your case)*

[ ] **Reinstatement:** to carry on working in your old job as before. ————

[ ] **Re-engagement:** to start another job. or a new contract, with your old employer. ————

Orders for re-instatement or re-engagement normally include an award of compensation for loss of earnings.

[ ] **Compensation only:** to get an award of money.

You can change your change your mind later. The Tribunal will take your preference into account. but will not be bound by it.

12. Have you already sent us a copy of this application by facsimile transmission (fax)?

Yes [ ]   No [ ]

Signed [   ]   Date [   ]

Application to an Industrial Tribunal

Notes for Guidance

Before filling in this form please read:
* these guidance notes
* Leaflet ITL1 which you were given with this form
* the correct booklet for your type of case

Information

There are many things you can complain to a Tribunal about. Leaflet ITL1 tells you what they are, which law (an Act of Parliament) covers your complaint and which booklet you should get. Each of the booklets explains the law in simple terms. You can get the booklets free from any employment office, Jobcentre or Unemployment Benefit Office. If you are in doubt, your Trade Union or a Citizens' Advice Bureau may be able to give you further advice or information.

Time Limits

You must send in your application form so that it arrives at the Central Office of the Industrial Tribunals within the time limit. The time limit depends on which complaint you are making; for example, for unfair dismissal complaints it is three months beginning with the date of dismissal. So if you were dismissed on 10th January, the form must arrive by 9th April.

Qualifying periods

There are rules about how long you have to work for an employer before you can bring a case to a Tribunal. These rules are explained in the booklets.

If you are in any doubt about the time limits or qualifying periods, please contact your local employment office, Jobcentre or Unemployment Benefit Office; or get in touch with the Advisory Conciliation and Arbitration Service (ACAS) - see leaflet ITL1 for addresses and telephone numbers.

Representatives

You can present your own case at the Tribunal. If you want someone else to present your case, try to consult him or her before you complete your application form, but remember your form must arrive within the **time limit**. **If you name a representative, all future dealings will be with him or her and not with you.** If you name a representative, you should ask him or her any questions you have about the progress of your case and when the Tribunal hearing will be.

If your complaint concerns equal pay or sex discrimination. you may wish to contact the Equal Opportunities Commission for advice or representation. If your complaint is about racial discrimination, you may wish to contact the Commission for Racial Equality for advice or representation.

Help for people with disabilities

If you, or anyone who needs to visit a Tribunal, are disabled and may have difficulty getting in or out of the office. or using normal seating or toilets. please inform our staff at the office where your case is being handled. They will do all they can to help.

Data Protection Act 1984

We may put some of the information you give in this form on to a computer. This helps us to monitor progress and produce statistics. We may also give information :

- to the other party in the case;

- for the same purposes, to other parts of the Employment Department Group and organisations such as the Advisory, Conciliation and Arbitration Service (ACAS), the Equal Opportunities Commission or the Commission for Racial Equality.

Filling in the form

Help

Your Trade Union or local Citizens' Advice Bureau may be able to help you fill in the form if you have any problems, but make sure your form arrives within the **time limit.**

Questions to answer

Try to complete all the boxes that apply in your case. You must answer the questions in boxes 1, 2, 4, 8 and 10.

Be clear

This form has to be photocopied, so please use black ink, or type your answers, and use **CAPITAL LETTERS** for names and addresses. Where boxes appear in this form which give you a choice of answer(s), please tick those that apply. If there is not enough space for your answer, please continue on a separate sheet of paper and attach it to this form.

Box 1

Put here the type of complaint you want the Tribunal to decide (for example, unfair dismissal, redundancy payment, equal pay etc). A full list of types of complaint is given in leaflet ITL 1. If there is more than one complaint you want the Tribunal to decide, please say so. Give the details of your complaints in Box 10.

Box 2

Give your name and address and date of birth, and if possible a telephone number where the Tribunal or ACAS can contact you during the day about your application.

Box 4

Give details of the employer, body or person (the "respondent") you wish to complain about. In the second box, give the place where you worked or applied for work, if different from that of the respondent you have named. (For example, complete both boxes if you have named a liquidator, the Secretary of State for Employment, or your employer's Head Office as the respondent).

Box 10

Give full details of your complaint. If there is not enough room on the form, continue on a separate sheet and attach it to the form. Do NOT send any other documents or evidence in support of your complaint at this stage. Your answer may be used in an initial assessment of your case, so make it as complete and accurate as you can. (See **Help** above).

When you have finished:
- **sign and date the form**
- **keep these guidance notes and a copy of your answers**
- **send the form to:**

ENGLAND AND WALES	SCOTLAND
The Secretary of the Tribunals,	The Secretary of the Tribunals,
Central Office of the Industrial Tribunals,	Central Office of the Industrial Tribunals (Scotland),
100 Southgate Street,	St Andrew House,
Bury St Edmunds,	141 West Nile Street,
Suffolk,	Glasgow,
IP33 2AQ.	G1 2RU.
Telephone 0284 762300	Telephone 041 331 1601

Notes and References

Chapter 1: Employment Rights: Past, Present and Future

1. For a comprehensive discussion of the evolution of legal policy in this area and the impact of deregulation see Roy Lewis, 'The Role of Law in Employment Relations', in Lewis (ed.), *Labour Law in Britain* (Oxford: Blackwell, 1986) and Roy Lewis, 'Reforming Labour Law: Choices and Constraints', *Employee Relations* (1987) vol. 9, no. 4, pp. 28–31. The authors gratefully acknowledge the influence of these works in preparing this chapter.
2. H. Phelps Brown, *The Growth of British Industrial Relations*, quoted in Lord Wedderburn of Charlton, *The Worker and the Law*, 3rd edn., p. 1 (Harmondsworth: Penguin, 1986).
3. See F. Von Hayek, *1980s Unemployment and the Unions* (London: Institute of Economic Affairs, 1980). For a more detailed analysis of the views of Hayek, see Wedderburn, 'Freedom of Association and Philosophies of Labour Law', *ILJ*, vol. 18 (1989), pp. 1–38.
4. A survey by the National Association of Citizens Advice Bureaux found that some employers routinely dismiss staff weeks or even days before they complete two years in the job and thereby qualify for unfair dismissal protection. The report recommends cutting the qualifying period for employment protection from two years to six months, regardless of the number of hours worked each week ('Job Insecurity: CAB Evidence on Employment Problems in the Recession', London: National Association of Citizens Advice Bureaux, March 1993, pp. 1–55).
5. A campaign and 'Charter for Pension Fund Democracy' was launched by the TUC in September 1992. On the issues involved in protecting pension rights, see Richard Nobles, *Controlling Occupational Pension Schemes* (London: Independent Institute of Employment Rights, 1992).
6. See S. Evans, 'The Use of Injunctions in Labour Disputes', *BJIR*, vol. 25 (1987), p. 419.
7. Evans found that injunctions resulted in an immediate lifting of the industrial action or withdrawal of official support in three-quarters of the cases surveyed; unions ignored injunctions in approximately 25 per cent of cases – see endnote 5 in ibid.
8. See W.W. Daniel and E. Stilgoe, *The Impact of the Employment Protection Laws* (London: Policy Studies Institute, 1978); A. Clifton and C. Tatton-Brown, 'The Impact of Employment Protection on Small Firms', Department of Employment Research Paper 7 (London: HMSO, 1979).
9. S. Evans, J. Goodman and L. Hargreaves, 'Unfair Dismissal Law and Employment Practice in the 1980s', DES Research Paper 53 (London: HMSO, 1985).

401

10. D. Wood and P. Smith, 'Employers' Labour Use Strategies: First Report on the 1987 Survey', Department of Employment Research Paper 63 (London: HMSO, 1989).
11. In practice, companies do involve workers' representatives in the introduction of 'environment plans' and other measures, but there has been no requirement to do so to date.
12. *Employment Gazette*, December 1991, pp. 681–4.
13. B. Hepple, 'Individual Employment Law' in G.S. Bain (ed.), *Industrial Relations in Britain* (Oxford: Blackwell, 1983), pp. 393–417 at p. 393.
14. Department of Employment, Cmnd 5034 (London: HMSO, 1986).
15. Department of Employment, Cmnd 540 (London: HMSO, 1988).
16. Department of Employment, Cm. 1810 (London: HMSO, 1992).
17. The UK government's policy of deregulation has also forced it to denounce four International Labour Organisation (ILO) conventions. These included Convention no. 94 (Labour Clauses [Public Contracts] Convention 1949) and Convention no. 95 (Protection of Wages Convention 1949). The denunciation of Convention no. 94 enabled the government to rescind the Fair Wages Resolution, while the denunciation of Convention no. 95 enabled it to introduce the Wages Act 1986 and to repeal the Truck Acts. In addition, the UK has been held to have breached other ILO conventions dealing with Freedom of Association and the Right to Organise (see chapter 17 below).

Chapter 2: The Gateways to Employment Rights

1. In 1951, only 4 per cent of employees worked fewer than 30 hours a week.
2. Labour Force surveys show that 60 per cent of all part-timers are found in retail distribution, hotels and catering, education and other services.
3. Women working part-time earn 75 per cent of average full-time female hourly earnings and about 57 per cent of average male full-time hourly earnings. The Low Pay Unit has calculated that 4.2 million workers (about 80 per cent of all part-time workers) in 1989 earned below two-thirds median male earnings (Low Pay Unit, 'Part-time Work: Double Bad Deal', *Low Pay Review*, no. 8, Feb/March 1991.
4. House of Lords, Select Committee on the European Communities, 'Voluntary Part-time Work', session 1981–1982, 19th report (London: HMSO, 1982).
5. The spring 1988 Labour Force survey indicates that 55 per cent of all part-time workers are not covered by the main employment protection rights through a combination of the hours and service requirements, compared with the 29 per cent of full-timers who are disqualified because they lack two years' service.
6. N. Meager 'Temporary Work in Britain: Its Growth and Changing Rationales', *IMS Report*, no. 106, September 1985.
7. See EPCA 1978, s. 142.
8. EPCA 1978, s. 153 defines an employee as 'an individual who has entered into or works under … a contract of employment'; a contract of employment is defined as 'a contract of service or apprenticeship, whether express or implied, and (if it is express) whether it is oral or in writing'.

9. See *Ready Mixed Concrete (South East) Ltd* v. *Minister of Pensions and National Insurance* [1968] 1 All ER 433, *Market Investigations* v. *Minister of Social Security* [1969] 2 QB 173 and *Lee* v. *Chung and Shun Sing Construction and Engineering Co Ltd* [1990] IRLR 236.

10. See the EC Directive on Acquired Rights (77/187); *Dr Sophie Redmond Stichting* v. *Bartol and Others* [1992] IRLR 366, ECJ and *Rask and Christensen* v. *ISS Kantineservice A/S* [1993] IRLIB 464, ECJ.

11. For a detailed analysis of the issues see L. Dickens, *Whose Flexibility? Discrimination & Equality Issues in a Typical Work*, (London: Institute of Employment Rights, 1992).

12. B. Hepple, 'Restructuring Employment Rights', *ILJ*, vol. 15, p. 69.

13. Patricia Leighton, 'Marginal Workers', in R. Lewis (ed.), *Labour Law in Britain* (Oxford: Blackwell, 1986), ch. 18

14. *R* v. *Secretary of State for Employment ex parte Equal Opportunities Commission* [1993] IRLR 10 CA.

15. R. Disney and E. Szyszczak, 'Protective Legislation and Part-time Employment in Great Britain', *BJIR*, vol. 20, (1984), pp. 78–100.

16. *R* v. *Secretary of State for Employment ex parte Equal Opportunities Commission* [1993] IRLR 10 CA.

Chapter 3: Job Applications and Recruitment

1. *Allen* v. *Flood* [1898] AC 1. One reason for this has been the law's refusal to force a party to enter into a contract against their will; D. Newell *Understanding Recruitment Law* (London: Waterlow, 1984), p.1.

2. Department of Employment offices can advise, and complaints can be taken to the Wages Inspectorate. Unlike other EC countries the UK does not have a national minimum wage yet.

3. Non-payment of the correct rate is a criminal offence (see DE booklet, *Wages Councils and Statutory Pay Rates*) and arrears of pay can be claimed in the IT as an unlawful deduction, or in the county court for non-payment. It is also grounds for a constructive dismissal claim; *Reid* v. *Camphill Engravers* [1990] IRLR 268.

4. Employment Agencies Act 1973; Conduct of Employment Agencies and Employment Businesses Regulations 1976.

5. *E. Pascoe* v. *Hallen & Medway* [1975] IRLR 116 (asthma attack at work).

6. The UK has not implemented measures to give effect to the EC's 1986 Recommendations on the Employment of Disabled People, notably on access to employment and training opportunities. The EC Charter, clause 26, also states that 'All disabled persons, whatever the origin and nature of their disablement, must be entitled to additional concrete measures aimed at improving their social and professional integration.' Health and safety requirements are often used to justify discriminatory practices; B. Doyle 'Disabled Workers: Legal Issues' (in M. Davidson and J. Earnshaw (eds), *Vulnerable Workers: Psychosocial and Legal Issues* (Chichester: Wiley, 1991), ch. 4.2.

7. Section 4 (3) of the Act says non-disclosure of a spent conviction is not a ground of dismissal or exclusion from employment, or for prejudicing a person 'in any way'; *Property Guards Ltd* v. *Taylor and Kershaw* [1982] IRLR 175.

8. *Pedersen* v. *Camden London Borough Council* [1981] ICR 674.
9. If the offer, or important parts of it, are too vague (or there is no agreed means for settling details of important terms later) there will be no contract; *Loftus* v. *Roberts*, 18 TLR 532.
10. For a general guide, see Cheshire Fifoot and Furmston's *Law of Contract* (London: Butterworths, 1986).
11. *Newland* v. *Simons & Willer (Hairdressers) Ltd* [1981] ICR 521.
12. *Wishart* v. *National Association of Citizens Advice Bureaux* [1990] IRLR 393, CA.
13. *Spring* v. *Guardian Assurance plc and Others* (*The Times*, 22 December 1992, CA).
14. *Dalgleish* v. *Lothian & Borders Police* (1991); see LRD, *The Law at Work* (March 1992).
15. *Gill and Others* v. *Cape Contracts Ltd* [1985] IRLR 499.
16. *Powell* v. *London Borough of Brent* [1987] IRLR 466.

Chapter 4: The Contract of Employment

1. Unless these have been agreed the employer is likely to dictate such arrangements.
2. Legislation in the EPCA ss. 1–11 (as amended by TURERA), requiring written details of terms to be given to staff, has only partially dealt with this problem.
3. See A. Flanders 'What are Trade Unions For?', ch. 1 in W.E.J. McCarthy (ed.), *Trade Unions* (Harmondsworth: Penguin, 1985), p. 26.
4. See A. Fox, *Beyond Contract: Work, Power and Trust Relations* (1974). Appraisal systems, and job evaluation and analysis, are important examples of this, especially when they are linked to pay and rewards and to disciplinary systems.
5. *Associated British Ports* v. *Palmer and Others* [1993] IRLIB 464. The Court of Appeal reversed this; and TURERA then restored the position again!
6. *Associated Newspapers* v. *Wilson* (*The Times*, 2 July 1992; and see J. McMulley and P. Kaufmann, *Labour Law Review 1992* (London: Institute of Employment Rights, 1992). The case was joined with *Associated British Ports* v. *Palmer and Others* (note 5 above) and therefore had the same history thereafter.
7. On employees' rights (and employers' powers) in the transfer process, see J. McMullen, *Business Transfers and Employees' Rights* (London: Butterworths, 1992); and S. Anderman, *Labour Law: Management Decisions and Workers' Rights* (London: Butterworths, 1992).
8. It has been convincingly argued, for example, that employment contracts can be used to strengthen job security, by including 'no compulsory redundancy' clauses and restrictions on dismissal powers; K.D. Ewing, 'Job Security and the Contract of Employment', *ILJ* vol. 18 (1989), p. 217.
9. Unfair Contract Terms Act 1977.
10. Unions' freedom to negotiate rights at a *collective* level has not received such warm support. Government policy is full of contradictions; see particularly 'Employment Rights for the 1990's' (Department of Employment 1988).
11. White Paper, 'People, Jobs and Opportunity' (February 1992).
12. See M. Freedland, *The Contract of Employment* (Oxford: Clarendon Press, 1976); 'Trends in the Flexible Workforce' (*DE Gazette*, November 1987); *Attitudes Towards Employment* (London: CBI, 1985).
13. 'Labour Flexibility in Britain' (ACAS Paper 41).

14. Even if details of wages have not been agreed the court can pay you what would be reasonable.
15. *Eagland* v. *British Telecommunications plc* [1990] ICR 248.
16. EPCA sections 1–6, as substituted by TURERA, s. 26 and schedule 4. Part I of the EPCA also deals with supplementary rights, including tribunal complaints. The changes made by TURERA are supposed to comply with the EC Directive on Proof of Employment Relationships (EC 91/533) which requires workers to receive details of 'essential aspects' of their employment relationship within two months of starting work.
17. *Gascol Conversions Ltd* v. *J.W. Mercer* [1974] IRLR 155 at 156–7.
18. If, for example, your original letter of appointment says you will be entitled to a bonus, but the statement says something different (and this prompts the employer to cancel that bonus) it might be open to you to argue that the employer is not entitled to do so; *Robertson* v. *British Gas Corporation* [1983] ICR 351.
19. EPCA section 2 (3). This is likely to be amended by TURERB so that details of collective agreements are in the statement itself.
20. *Cadoux* v. *Central Regional Council* [1986] IRLR 131. Public sector workers may in certain circumstances be able to take advantage of a public law requirement to consult before action is taken which removes established employment rights; *Council of Civil Service Unions* v. *Civil Service Minister* [1985] IRLR 29.
21. *Robertson* v. *British Gas Corporation* [1983] ICR 351. In another case, *Marley* v. *Forward Trust Group Ltd* [1986] IRLR 369, it was held that the terms of a collective agreement on redundancy had become incorporated into a person's individual contract. Those terms could therefore be relied upon when the employer tried to invoke the requirements of the original 'mobility' clause. Cases can go the other way, though, as in *Alexander* v. *Standard Telephones and Cables plc* [1990] IRLR 55 (discussed below).
22. TULRA section 18 (now in TULR(C)A). It is possible, but uncommon, for agreements to state that they *will* be enforceable; *NCB* v. *NUM* [1986] IRLR 439 at 449.
23. *Maclea* v. *Essex Line Ltd* [1933] Lloyd's Report vol. 45, p. 254.
24. *Alexander* v. *Standard Telephones and Cables plc* [1990] IRLR 55.
25. Kahn-Freund, critically discussed in Paul Davies and Mark Freedland, *Kahn-Freund's Labour and the Law* (London: Stevens, 1983), pp. 168 et seq.
26. *Singh* v. *British Steel Corporation* [1974] IRLR 131.
27. *Petrie* v. *MacFisheries Ltd* [1940] 1 KB 258.
28. In *Meek* v. *Port of London Authority* [1918] 1 Ch 415, it was suggested that such knowledge was necessary; but cf. *Sagar* v. *H. Ridehalgh & Son Ltd* [1931] 1 Ch 310.
29. *F.G.Samways* v. *Swan Hunter Shipbuilders Ltd* (1975) IRLR 190.
30. *Scally* v. *Southern Health and Social Services Board* [1992] IRLR 523.
31. *Howman & Son* v. *Blyth* [1983] ICR 416.
32. *Murco Petroleum Ltd* v. *Forge* [1987] IRLR 50.
33. *Miles* v. *Wakefield District Council* [1987] 1 All ER 1089, House of Lords, where it was held that employees are only entitled to be paid if they are willing to carry out their contractual obligations.
34. *Secretary of State for Employment* v. *ASLEF* (no.2) [1972] 2 All ER 949.

35. *Johnstone* v. *Bloomsbury Area Health Authority* [1991] 2 All ER 293, CA; discussed in chapter 16 below.

Chapter 5: Workplace Change

1. See LRD, *Works Councils: The Door Opens*, April 1991, p. 10; and Lord Wedderburn of Charlton, *The Social Charter: European Company and Employment Rights* (London: Institute of Employment Rights, 1990).
2. The UK government opposes the directive on the basis it would undermine the UK's 'voluntary' arrangements; see *People and Companies*, Department of Employment (1989).
3. Paul Davies and Mark Freedland, *Kahn-Freund's Labour and the Law* (London: Stevens, 1983); A. Flanders, *Management and Unions* (London: Faber & Faber, 1970).
4. Works councils' arrangements can leave union representatives in a minority, even in unionised companies.
5. *Associated British Ports* v. *Palmer and Others* [1993] IRLIB 464. See also chapter 4, note 5.
6. Draft EC Fifth Company Directive on Company Law 1972 (amended proposal 1983, *Official Journal*, vol. 26, ch. 240).
7. *Hollister* v. *National Farmers Union* [1979] ICR 542; and *Woods* v. *W.M. Car Services (Peterborough) Ltd* [1982] IRLR 413, CA.
8. *Smith* v. *Stockport Metropolitan Borough Council*, 8 August 1979, Stockport County Court; [1979] CLY 905.
9. For example, where an employer's arrangements for transferring staff are in breach of the implied duty to act fairly (the 'fair dealing' requirement); *Newns* v. *British Airways plc* [1992] 575, CA.
10. *Haden Ltd* v. *Cowen* [1982] IRLR 315.
11. *Cresswell and Others* v. *Board of Inland Revenue* [1984] IRLR 190.
12. *United Bank Ltd* v. *Akhtar* [1989] IRLR 507, where a bank's insistence on an employee moving job locations without adequate notice or financial assistance was held to be a constructive dismissal.
13. *White* v. *Reflecting Roadstuds Ltd* [1991] IRLR 331.
14. *Waine* v. *Olivier (Plant Hire) Ltd* [1977] IRLR 434.
15. See chapter 4 on statutory written statements; note that the tribunal has power to decide the terms you are working on (including any new terms) if they have not been provided or are incorrect.
16. *Burdett Coutts and Others* v. *Hertfordshire County Council* [1984] IRLR 91.
17. *Rigby* v. *Ferodo Ltd* [1987] IRLR 516.
18. Alterations in the way pay is calculated may also be a breach of contract; see *R.F. Hill Ltd* v. *Mooney* [1981] IRLR 258
19. *Chubb Fire Security Ltd* v. *Harper* [1983] IRLR 311.

Chapter 6: Reductions in Work

1. *Bond* v. *CAV Ltd*; *Neads* v. *CAV Ltd* [1983] IRLR 360.
2. *Millbrook Furnishing Ltd* v. *McIntosh* [1981] IRLR 309.
3. *K. MacRae & Co Ltd* v. *Dawson* [1984] IRLR 5.

4. EPCA ss. 12–18.
5. For guidance on payments, see *Guarantee Payments* (DE booklet PL 724).

Chapter 7: Pay

1. On pay, see A.M. Bowey, *Handbook of Salary and Wages Systems* (London: Gower, 1982); ACAS advisory booklet no. 2, *Introduction to Payments Systems*; and K. Puttick, R. Painter, I. Henn, S. Evans, *Wages and the Law* (London: Shaw & Sons, 1989).
2. WA ss. 8 (1), (2), 26 (1).
3. See M. White, *Payment Systems in Britain* (London: Gower, 1981); and A.M. Bowey, *Handbook of Salary and Wages Systems* (London: Gower, 1982).
4. See I.Smith, *The Management of Remuneration: Paying for Effectiveness* (London: IPM/Gower, 1983)
5. It is also one aspect of the trend towards personal contracts; see *Personal Contracts – Protecting Yourself*, LRD bargaining report, October 1991. Not surprisingly, the changeover to personal contracts is often accompanied by the removal, by employers, of rights to union representation. See *Associated British Ports* v. *Palmer and Others* [1993] IRLIB 464.
6. *Pedersen* v. *Camden LBC* [1981] IRLR 173. On job advertisements, and their effects on wages, see D. Newell, *Understanding Recruitment Law* (London: Waterlow, 1984); and see chapter 3 above.
7. *Robertson* v. *British Gas Corporation* [1983] ICR 351 (letter promising incentive bonus created a contractual right).
8. In *Re Famatina Development Corporation Ltd* [1914] 2 Ch 271.
9. *Way* v. *Latilla* [1937] 3 All ER 759.
10. *Gaumont British Picture Corporation Ltd* v. *Alexander* [1936] 2 All ER 1686. The exception to this is where the pay is regulated by a Wages Council order fixing the minimum rate. This can be checked with the Wages Inspectorate or Department of Employment offices. For guidance, see *Wages Councils and Statutory Pay Rates*, DE booklet. Wages Councils will be abolished, and the Wages Inspectorate phased out, by TURERB 1993.
11. See *State Benefits*, LRD Booklet, April 1992.
12. *Gill* v. *Cape Contracts Limited* [1985] IRLR 499.
13. *R.F. Hill Ltd* v. *Mooney* [1981] IRLR 258.
14. *Bauman* v. *Hulton Press Ltd* [1952] All ER 1121. In the case of performance-related pay, such as piecework, there is an implied duty on employers to give workers the opportunity to earn; *Devonald* v. *Rosser & Sons* [1906] 2 KB 728.
15. *A. Hanlon* v. *Allied Breweries (UK) Ltd* [1975] IRLR 321.
16. *Adams* v. *C. Zub Associates Ltd* [1978] IRLR 551.
17. *Bond* v. *CAV Ltd* [1983] IRLR 360.
18. *Bridgen* v. *Lancashire County Council* [1987] IRLR 58.
19. A feature of personalised contracts and performance-related pay is the movement away from across-the-board pay rises, and to greater management discretion in awarding increases.
20. *Murco Petroleum Ltd* v. *Forge* [1987] IRLR 50.
21. *F.C. Gardner Ltd* v. *Beresford* [1978] IRLR 63; *Murco Petroleum Ltd* v. *Forge*.

22. See 'Personal Contracts – Protecting Yourself', LRD bargaining report, p. 13.
23. *Lavarack* v. *Woods of Colchester Ltd* [1967] 1 QB 278.
24. *Smith* v. *Stockport Metropolitan Council* 8 August 1979, Stockport County Court [1979] CLY 905.
25. EPCA ss. 8–10, and 146 (as modified by TURERA, section 27). This only applies to staff working more than 8 hours a week. There is an exemption if the employer has fewer than 20 employees.
26. Section 1. For guidance, see *The Law on the Payment of Wages and Deductions – A Guide to Part I of the Wages Act 1986*, Department of Employment booklet PL810; and F. Davidson, *A Guide to the Wages Act 1986* (London: Blackstone, 1986).
27. Section 7.
28. Section 8 (3) (4).
29. *Delaney* v. *Staples* [1991] IRLR 112 CA; [1992] IRLR 191, HL. The jurisdiction of tribunals to deal with contract problems is due to be extended under TURERA.
30. Section 1 (5).
31. TULR(C)A ss. 68 and 68A as substituted by TURERA, s. 15. Increases in dues can only be deducted if they have been notified one month in advance by the employer with a reminder that authorisation can be withdrawn by written notification to the employer.
32. Sections 2–4.
33. This can amount to a 'double indemnity'; see R.W. Painter and P. Leighton, 'The Wages Act: A Critical Guide' in *Employee Relations* (1986) vol. 8, no. 6, p. 27.
34. Section 3.
35. Section 5. TULR(C)A, s. 68A, as inserted by TURERA, s. 15, provides for IT complaints for unauthorised deductions of union dues.
36. *Avon County Council* v. *Howlett* [1983] 1 All ER 1073.
37. *Clayton Newbury* v. *Findlay* [1953] 2 All ER 826.
38. The TUC in 1992 started a campaign for changes and has backed a Charter for Pensions Fund Democracy. For a critical analysis of UK pensions law, which put forward recommendations for reform, see Richard Nobles, *Controlling Occupational Pensions Schemes* (London: Institute of Employment Rights, 1992).
39. For a comprehensive guide, see R. Ellison, *Pensions: Law and Practice* (London: Longman, 1992); and J. Seres, *Pensions: A Practical Guide* (London: Longman, 1992).

Chapter 8: Holidays, Sickness and Time Off

1. In addition, clause 8 of the EC Social Charter states: 'Every worker of the European Community shall have a right to a weekly rest period and to annual leave.'
2. Details of collective agreements' provisions on holidays are published in the *Department of Employment Gazette* and in LRD's *Collective Bargaining* series.
3. *Tucker and Others* v. *British Leyland Motor Corporation Ltd* [1978] IRLR 493.
4. Sickness benefit and invalidity benefit can be claimed when contract benefits or statutory sick pay are not paid.
5. *Mears* v. *Safecar Security Ltd* [1982] ICR 626.
6. See also *State Benefits*, LRD, April 1992.

7. The rules are in the Social Security and Housing Benefits Act 1982 and the Statutory Sick Pay (General Regulations) 1982. On invalidity benefit, which can be claimed after SSP entitlement ends after 28 weeks (and other benefits), see *State Benefits*, LRD.
8. See DHSS Guidance '*How to Appeal*'.
9. UK policy is to encourage employers rather than legislate; White Paper 'People, Jobs and Opportunity' (February 1992).
10. EC Directive 92/85 improves pregnancy-related rights and has required the UK, in TURERA, to amend its maternity rights legislation.
11. *Warner* v. *Barbers Stores* [1978] IRLR 109.
12. TULR(C)A, s. 168.
13. TULR(C)A, s. 169.
14. TULR(C)A, s. 170.
15. See also *The Safety Reps' Action Guide*, LRD, 1991.
16. Safety Representatives and Safety Committees Regulations 1977, SI 1977 no. 500, reg. 4 (2) (6), and Code of Practice 'Time Off for the Training of Safety Representatives' (available from HSE).
17. EPCA, s. 29.
18. EPCA, s. 31.
19. EPCA, s. 31A.

Chapter 9: Conflicts of Interest, Competition and Confidentiality

1. Theft Acts 1968 and 1978.
2. *Janata Bank* v. *Ahmed* [1981] IRLR 457, CA.
3. *Sinclair* v. *Neighbour* [1967] 2 QB 279.
4. *Hivac Ltd* v. *Park Royal Scientific Instruments Ltd* [1946] Ch 169.
5. *Nova Plastics Ltd* v. *Froggatt* [1982] IRLR 146.
6. *Provident Financial Group plc* v. *Hayward* [1989] IRLR 84.
7. *Spafax Limited* v. *Harrison* [1980] IRLR 442.
8. *Wessex Dairies Ltd* v. *Smith* [1935] 2 KB 80.
9. *R. Bullivant Ltd* v. *Ellis* [1987] IRLR 491.
10. *Faccenda Chicken Ltd* v. *Fowler and Others* [1986] IRLR 69.
11. *Reiss Engineering Co Ltd* v. *Harrison* [1985] IRLR 232.
12. Copyrights, Designs and Patents Act 1988, s. 11.

Chapter 10: Equal Pay

1. This decision is perhaps less important than it would be given the subsequent ruling of the ECJ in *Francovich* v. *Italian Republic* [1992] IRLR 84. In *Francovich* the ECJ ruled that when an individual suffers damage as a result of a *member state's* failure to correctly implement a directive which confers rights for the benefit of the individual, the individual can sue the state directly under European law for the damage suffered by the state's failure. This ruling considerably strengthens the position of private sector workers.
2. *Mirror Group Newspapers Ltd* v. *Gunning* [1986] ICR 145.

3. *Meeks* v. *National Union of Agricultural and Allied Workers* [1976] IRLR 198.
4. *Ainsworth* v. *Glass Tubes and Components Ltd* [1976] IRLR 74.
5. A.E.M. Holmes and R.W. Painter, *Employment Law*, 2nd edn (London: Blackstone, 1991).
6. Anne E. Morris and Susan M. Nott, *Working Women and the Law: Equality and Discrimination in Theory and Practice* (London: Routledge, 1991), p. 128.
7. Michael Rubenstein, 'Highlights' [1988] IRLR 324.
8. Michael Rubenstein, 'Highlights' [1991] IRLR 43.
9. Tables 10.1 and 10.2 are taken from 'Equal Pay for Men and Women: Strengthening the Acts' (EOC, 1990), p. 26.
10. EOC, 'Equal Pay for Men and Women Strengthening the Acts' (London, 1990), p. 6.
11. Ibid.

Chapter 11: Race and Sex Discrimination

1. C. Brown and P. Gay, *Racial Discrimination 17 Years after the Act* (London: Policy Studies Institute, 1985). For a survey of the literature see P. Iles, and R. Aulick, 'The Experience of Black Workers' in M.J. Davidson and J. Earnshaw (eds), *Vulnerable Workers: Psychosocial and Legal Issues* (Chichester: Wiley, 1991).
2. For a detailed discussion see A.E. Morris and S.M. Nott, *Working Women and the Law: Equality and Discrimination in Theory and Practice* (London: Routledge/Sweet & Maxwell, 1991), ch. 4.
3. S.D. Anderman, *Labour Law: Management Decisions & Workers' Rights* (London: Butterworths, 1991), p. 182.
4. Under the Fair Employment (Northern Ireland) Acts 1976, 1979 it is unlawful for employers to discriminate against employees or applicants for employment on the grounds of their religious belief or political opinion.
5. Morris and Nott, *Working Women and the Law*.
6. Michael Rubenstein, *The Dignity of Women at Work: A Report on the Problem of Sexual Harassment in the Member States of the European Communities* (Luxembourg: Office for Official Publications of the European Communities, 1988), p. 16. Moreover, a survey by Alfred Marks in 1990/1 found that around two-thirds of employees surveyed had experienced some form of sexual harassment on several occasions, usually by a colleague or a senior person. Eighty-eight per cent of employers were aware of incidents of sexual harassment. However, only a quarter of those who experienced harassment reported it and many had little confidence in the employer's ability to deal with the harassment effectively (see '*Sexual Harassment in the Office: A Quantitative Report on Client Attitudes and Experiences 1990/92*', available from Alfred Marks).
7. For some examples of policy statements on sexual and racial harassment which have been issued by employers see 'Combating Harassment at Work', IDS study 513 (London: Incomes Data Services Ltd, September 1992).
8. See *Marleasing SA* v. *La Comercial Internacional de Alimentacion SA* 13/11/90 European Court of Justice case no. 106/89.
9. See [1993] IRLR 27 HL; see also the Court of Appeal's decision in *Shomer* v. *B & R Residential Lettings Ltd* [1992] IRLR 317, reaffirming the comparative approach adopted in *Webb* and *Brown* v. *Rentokil* [1992] IRLR 302, EAT.

10. A. Byre, *Indirect Discrimination* (London: EOC, 1987).

11. *Review of the Race Relations Act 1976: Proposals for Change* (London: CRE, 1985); *Equal Treatment for Men and Women: Strengthening the Acts* (London: EOC, 1988); *Second Review of the Race Relations Act 1976: A Consultative Paper* (London: CRE, 1991).

12. *Perera* v. *Civil Service Commission* [1982] IRLR 147.

13. The EOC advocated a return to the stricter test of justification in *Equal Treatment For Men And Women: Strengthening The Acts*.

14. Morris and Nott, *Working Women and the Law*, p. 88.

15. See Alice Leonard, *Pyrrhic Victories* (London: EOC, 1986).

16. *Trial by Ordeal: A Study of People who Lost Equal Pay and Sex Discrimination Cases in the Industrial Tribunals during 1985 and 1986* (London: EOC, 1989).

17. See also *Kirby* v. *MSC* [1980] 3 All ER 334.

18. Ibid.

19. See also *Wylie* v. *Dee & Co Ltd* [1978] IRLR 103.

20. This provision was inserted by the SDA 1986.

21. *Chattopadhyay* v. *The Headmaster of Holloway School* [1981] IRLR 487. For the most recent attempt to restate the approach to be taken by ITs to proof of unlawful discrimination see *King* v. *The Great Britain-China Centre* [1991] IRLR 513 CA.

22. Indeed, success rates are low in general for discrimination claims. In 1990/1, there were 1,078 claims of sex discrimination. Of these, 335 resulted in ACAS conciliated settlements and 424 were withdrawn. Of the 319 cases which proceeded to IT hearing, only 78 were successful. In the same year, there were 926 claims of race discrimination. Of these, 185 were conciliated by ACAS and 371 were withdrawn. Of the 370 cases which proceeded to IT hearing, only 47 were successful (*Employment Gazette*, December 1991, pp. 681–4).

23. See *Alexander* v. *Home Office* [1988] IRLR 190. Currently, it would appear that exemplary damages covering oppresive, arbitrary or unconstitutional action by the servants of the government, are not available in discrimination cases (see *Deane* v. *L.B. of Ealing* [1993] IRLR 209, EAT, applying *Gibbons* v. *South West Water Services Ltd* [1993] 1 All ER 609, CA.

24. See above, n. 3.

25. Alice Leonard's survey of successful sex discrimination applicants in 1980–4 found the median average award in recruitment cases was £291; Leonard, *Pyrrhic Victories*, p. 14 cited above. An *Equal Opportunity Review* survey showed that in 1987 the average award in sex and race discrimination cases was under £450 (*Equal Opportunity Review*, vol. 19, 1988, p. 7). In 1990/1, the median award in race discrimination cases was £1,749 and as little as £1,142 in those involving a finding of sex discrimination (*Employment Gazette*, December 1991, pp. 681–4).

26. In *Sharifi* v. *Strathclyde Regional Council* [1992] IRLR 259, the EAT expressed the view 'that an award of £500 for injury to feelings may be regarded as at or near the minimum'.

27. See above, n. 8.

28. It is appropriate to compare the maximum compensation award available under the race and sex discrimination legislation with the maximum of £30,000 set under the *Fair Employment (Northern Ireland) Act* 1989 for religious discrimination. In *Duffy* v.

Eastern Health & Social Services Board [1992] IRLR 251, the first award for unlawful religious discrimination made by the Northern Ireland Fair Employment Tribunal was a sum of £25,000 as compensation for injury to feeling.
29. See [1989] IRLR 459.
30. See also *British Gas plc* v. *Sharma* [1991] IRLR 101, EAT.
31. See above, n. 3.

Chapter 12: Other Forms of Discrimination

1. For an examination of five case studies of HIV in the workplace see P. Wilson, *HIV and AIDS in the Workplace: An Examination of Cases of Discrimination* (London: National AIDS Trust, 1992).
2. See K. Widdows, 'AIDs and the Workplace: Some Approaches at the National Level', *International Journal of Comparative Labour Law and Industrial Relations*, vol. 4, p. 140, 1988.
3. See *AIDs and the Workplace – A Guide for Employers* (London: Department of Employment/Health and Safety Executive, 1990).
4. B.W. Napier, 'AIDS Sufferers at Work and the Law' in M.J. Davidson and J.Earnshaw (eds), *Vulnerable Workers: Psychosocial and Legal Issues* (Chichester: Wiley, 1991).
5. For a detailed discussion of the legal position of disabled workers, see B. Doyle, 'Disabled Workers: Legal Issues' in Davidson and Earnshaw (eds), *Vulnerable Workers: Psychosocial and Legal Issues*'; B. Doyle, 'Disabled Workers, Employment Vulnerability and Labour Law' in *Vulnerable Workers in the UK Labour Market: Some Challenges For Employment Law*, R.W. Painter, *Employee Relations*, vol. 9, no. 5, 1987.
6. A draft EC directive which aims to 'facilitate the safe travel of workers with reduced mobility in order to assist them in gaining access to the place of employment' was submitted to the Council of Ministers in February 1991 but has not yet been formally discussed by the ministers. The draft requires public transport, special transport services for workers with disabilities and transport provided by employers to comply with certain minimum requirements to facilitate its use by workers who have special difficulty in using public transport because of 'a serious handicap of a physical or mental origin'.
7. See Doyle, 'Disabled Workers: Legal Issues', pp. 93–117.
8. The Bill has received the support of the Employment Law Committee of the Law Society: see *Disability, Discrimination and Employment Law* (London: Law Society, 1992).

Chapter 13: Terminating the Contract

1. The court expressed the opinion that where an offer of employment is conditional upon 'satisfactory' references, that is likely to have a subjective meaning of 'satisfactory to the defendants'. It is highly probable that no objective test is applicable and there is no obligation in law upon the employers in considering the references other than to consider in good faith whether they were satisfactory to them. Nevertheless, it is still prudent to use wording such as 'references satisfactory to us' so as to avoid any doubt.
2. See also *Waddock* v. *LB Brent* [1990] IRLR 223.

Chapter 14: Unfair Dismissal

1. See *Addis* v. *Gramophone Co Ltd* [1909] AC 488 HL and *Bliss* v. *South East Thames Regional Health Authority* [1985] IRLR 308 CA.
2. See *Ridge* v. *Baldwin* [1964] AC 40 HL.
3. In 1990/1, 56.6 per cent of cases dealt with by industrial tribunals concerned unfair dismissal. However, this proportion has been falling since 1986/7, when unfair dismissal cases represented 74.5 per cent of all complaints (*Employment Gazette*, December 1991, pp. 681–4).
4. See Kevin Williams, 'Unfair Dismissal: Myths and Statistics', *ILJ*, vol. 12, no. 3, pp. 157–65.
5. Statistical source: *Employment Gazette*, December 1991, pp. 681–4.
6. See *Irani* v. *South West Hampshire Health Authority* [1985] ICR 590; *Powell* v. *London Borough of Brent* [1987] IRLR 466 CA; *Hughes* v. *London Borough of Southwark* [1988] IRLR 55.
7. See W.R. Hawes and G. Smith, 'Patterns of Representation of the Parties in Unfair Dismissal Cases: a Review of the Evidence', DE Research Paper no. 22 (1981).
8. The following are examples of this policy of classifying issues as question of fact and thus limiting the possibility of appeals: whether a worker is an 'employee' (*O'Kelly* v. *Trusthouse Forte plc* [1983] IRLR 369 CA); whether a 'constructive dismissal' has taken place (*Pedersen* v. *Camden London Borough Council* [1981] IRLR 173 CA); whether an employee resigned or was forced to do so (*Martin* v. *Glynwed Distribution Ltd* [1983] IRLR 198 CA); whether it was reasonably practicable to present an unfair dismissal claim on time (*Palmer* v. *Southend-on-Sea Borough Council* [1984] IRLR 119 CA).
9. See *Bailey* v. *BP Oil (Kent Refinery) Ltd* [1980] IRLR 287.
10. *Dedman* v. *British Building & Engineering Appliances* [1974] ICR 53; *Walls Meat Co Ltd* v. *Khan* [1978] IRLR 499).
11. *Riley* v. *Tesco Stores Ltd* [1980] IRLR 103. Compare with *Jean Sorelle Ltd* v. *Rybak* [1991] IRLR 153 EAT where erroneous advice concerning the final date for presentation of claim by an industrial tribunal clerk provided grounds to excuse a late claim. See also *London International College* v. *Sen* [1993] IRLR 333, CA, for signs of a less rigid approach to cases where the applicant receives misleading advice as to the time limit from his/her solicitor.
12. See *Palmer* v. *Southend-on-Sea Borough Council* [1984] IRLR 119.
13. The decision in *Churchill* has recently received the approval of the House of Lords in *Machine Tool Industry Research Association* v. *Simpson* [1988] IRLR 212.
14. See EPCA ss. 55 (4), 90 (1).
15. See also *Batchelor* v. *British Railways Board* [1987] IRLR 136.
16. Even post-*Polkey*, the courts and tribunals have still shown a propensity to forgive minor procedural lapses, provided that in the overall context of the case they did not result in unfairness: see *Fuller* v. *Lloyds Bank plc* [1991] IRLR 336, EAT and *Eclipse Blinds Ltd* [1992] IRLR 133, EAT.
17. Minor or understandable breaches of procedure in ill-health dismissals may be excused: see *A Links & Co Ltd* v. *Rose* [1991] IRLR 353 and *Eclipse Blinds Ltd* v. *Wright* [1992] IRLR 133.

18. See R.W. Painter, 'Any Other Substantial Reason: A Managerial Prerogative?', *New Law Journal* (1981) p. 131; Bowers and Clark, 'Unfair Dismissal and Managerial Prerogative: A Study of 'Other Substantial Reason'', *ILJ*, vol. 10 (1981), p. 34.
19. See L. Dickens, M. Jones, B. Weekes and M. Hart, *Dismissal: A Study of Unfair Dismissal and the Industrial Tribunal System* (Oxford: Basil Blackwell, 1985).
20. P. Lewis, 'An Analysis of Why Legislation has Failed to Provide Employment Protection for Unfairly Dismissed Employees', *BJIR*, vol. XIX, no. 3, November 1981, pp. 316–26.
21. See Hugh Collins, 'Capitalist Discipline and Corporatist Law', *ILJ*, vol. 11, 1982, pp. 78, 170; also D.J. Denham, 'Unfair Dismissal Law and the Legitimation Of Managerial Control', *Capital & Class*, 41, summer 1990, p. 83 and Hugh Collins, *Justice in Dismissal* (Oxford; Oxford University Press, 1992).
22. In *Rao* v. *Civil Aviation Authority* [1992] IRLR 203, the EAT held that where a dismissal is unfair because of a procedural defect, compensation should be assessed first by deciding whether the award based on loss should be reduced on grounds of contributory fault; the resultant sum could then be further reduced to reflect the likelihood that the employee would have been fairly dismissed if the proper procedure had been followed. The EAT did not perceive this approach as imposing a double penalty. See also *Red Bank Manufacturing Co Ltd* v. *Meadows* [1992] IRLR 209.
23. On this proposal and many other aspects of the working of the law of unfair dismissal, see Dickens, Jones, Weekes and Hart, *Dismissal*.

Chapter 15: Redundancy and Insolvency Rights

1. S.D. Anderman, *Management Decisions and Workers' Rights* (London: Butterworths, 1992), pp. 138–9.
2. *Alexander and Others* v. *Standard Telephones & Cables Ltd* [1990] IRLR 550.
3. 'Capitalist Discipline and Corporatist Law', *ILJ*, vol. 11 (1982), p. 78.
4. R.H. Fryer, 'The Myths of the Redundancy Payments Act', *ILJ*, vol. 2, (1973), p. 1.
5. For example, the TUC General Council's statement 'Employment Law: A New Approach', June 1990.
6. For a discussion of this in relation to the 1984 miners' strike, see W.M. Rees, 'The Law, Practice and Procedures Concerning Redundancy in the Coal Mining Industry', *ILJ*, vol. 15 (1985), p. 203. The successful 1992 court action was based, in part, on the fact that consultation procedures had been well established, making it harder for British Coal to ignore them.
7. In *McClelland* v. *Northern Ireland General Health Services Board* [1957] 2 All ER 129 the contract said that dismissal could only be for 'gross misconduct, inefficiency, and unfitness' – this was held to prevent dismissal on any other grounds, and so the dismissal for redundancy was a breach of contract; see also K.D. Ewing, 'Job Security and the Contract of Employment', *ILJ*, vol. 18 (1989), p. 217, which discusses McClelland.
8. Redundancy rights are in the EPCA, part V, ss. 54–80 and Part VI, ss. 81–120, and in the Trade Union and Labour Relations (Consolidation) Act 1992.
9. TULR[C]A ss. 152, 153. Unfair selection for redundancy on union grounds will not be subject to a service qualification as a result of changes made by TURERA.

10. EPCA, s. 59.
11. EPCA, s. 57 (3).
12. *United Kingdom Atomic Energy Authority* v. *E.F. Claydon* (1974) IRLR 6.
13. As in *Lee* v. *Notts CC* (1980) where a teacher taken on for only temporary periods was still held to be eligible for redundancy pay.
14. *Pink* v. *White* [1985] IRLR 489.
15. *Murphy* v. *Epsom College* [1984] IRLR 271.
16. *Lesney Products & Co Ltd* v. *Nolan* [1977] IRLR 77.
17. *Macfisheries Ltd* v. *Findlay* (1985) ICR 160.
18. *Bromley & Hoare Limited* v. *Evans* (1972) 7 ITR 76, NIRC.
19. *North Yorkshire CC* v. *Fay* [1985] IRLR 247.
20. EPCA, s. 88. Constructive dismissal and/or redundancy pay is also possible if you have been kept on such working for longer than your contract allows.
21. On employees' rights in the transfer process, see Fraser Younson, *Employment Law and Business Transfers: A Practical Guide* (London: Sweet & Maxwell, 1989).
22. The Action Programme implementing the Social Charter will include rules on this and on the effects of organisational changes in transnational enterprises.
23. Sched. 13, para. 17 (2)–(5).
24. Sections 82, 94.
25. *E. Crompton* v. *Truly Fair (International) Ltd* (1975) IRLR 250.
26. *Berg and Busschers* v. *Besselsen* [1989] IRLR 447, ECJ; and *Rask and Christensen* v. *ISS Kantrineservice A/S* (1993) IRLIB no. 464, ECJ.
27. *Dr Sophie Redmond Stitching* v. *Bartol and Others* [1992] IRLR 366, ECJ. The decision is clearly important for UK workers affected in a similar way, for example when governmental grants are withdrawn or local authority services are 'contracted out' to organisations that are competing for work.
28. Regulation 3 (4), as modified by TURERA, ss. 33 (3).
29. There is official guidance on this in DE booklet PL 699, *Employment Rights on the Transfer of an Undertaking* (1987).
30. *Melon* v. *Hector Powe Ltd* (1980) IRLR 47, HL.
31. *Newns* v. *British Airways plc* [1992] IRLR 575, CA. Note that amendments by TURERA, s. 33 (4), to Regulation 5 now enable an employee to object to a transfer of his/her contract, although this will bring it to an end without there being a 'dismissal' by the transferor.
32. For discussion of this, see Hugh Collins, 'Transfer of Undertakings and Insolvency' *ILJ,* vol. 18, 1989, p. 144.
33. *Gorictree* v. *Jenkinson* (1985) ICR 51.
34. Equal pay and treatment requirements may assist though (see chapters 10 and 11).
35. EPCA ss. 82 (3)–(7) and 84.
36. *Spencer and Griffin* v. *Gloucestershire CC* (1985) IRLR 393, CA.
37. Section 84 (3)–(7).
38. *Elliot* v. *Richard Stump Ltd* (1987) IRLR 215.
39. Section 84 (6).
40. *G.W. Stephens* v. *Fish* (1989) ICR 324, EAT.
41. *Hempell* v. *W.H. Smith* (1986) IRLR 95.
42. Sections 82, 92.

43. *Lignacite Products Ltd* v. *Krollman* [1979] IRLR 22.
44. Section 82 (2).
45. Section 92 (1).
46. EPCA s. 110.
47. EPCA s. 31. See DE guidance booklet PL 703.
48. Section 90 defines this but it is usually the date when the job finishes.
49. EPCA s. 106. For guidance, see DE booklet, *Employees' Rights on Insolvency of an Employer*, PL 718 (1989).
50. Guidance on payments is also DE Booklet PL 808, *Redundancy Payments* (1989).
51. See also DE guidance booklet, *Redundancy Consultation and Notification*, PL 833.
52. *TGWU* v. *Ledbury Preserves (1928) Ltd* [1985] IRLR 492.
53. EPCA s. 123.

Chapter 16: Health, Safety and the Work Environment

1. The Robens Committee Report (Report of the Committee on Health and Safety at Work) recognised this and was the reason for the Health and Safety at Work Act 1974 formalising arrangements on employee involvement.
2. For example *Latimer* v. *AEC Ltd* [1953] 2 All ER 449.
3. Dept. of Employment papers: *Lifting the Burden* (London: HMSO, 1985); *Building Business ... Not Barriers* (HMSO, 1986); *Releasing Enterprise* (HMSO, 1988).
4. On the effects of deregulation and inadequate monitoring and enforcement, see Roger Moore, *The Price of Safety: The Market, Workers' Rights and the Law*, (London: Institute of Employment Rights, 1991).
5. Reported in *Health and Safety at Work – The Journal of the Working Environment* (March 1992), p. 8.
6. EC Directive 89/391. For commentary, see R. Eberlie 'The New Health and Safety Legislation of the European Community', *ILJ*, vol. 19 (1990), p. 81; and *1992 and Health and Safety*, LRD, January 1992.
7. *Johnstone* v. *Bloomsbury Health Authority* [1991] 2 All ER 293, CA.
8. *Ottoman Bank* v. *Chakarian* [1930] AC 277.
9. *Rogers* v. *Wicks & Wilson Ltd* (1988), IDS brief 366 HSIB 148; see also *Dryden* v. *Greater Glasgow Health Board* [1992] IRLR 469; and see R.W. Painter 'Smoking Policies – The Legal Implications', *Employment Relations*, vol. 12, no. 4, p. 17.
10. HSAWA s. 7
11. HSAWA s. 2
12. The leading case is *Wilson and Clyde Coal Co Ltd* v. *English* [1938] AC 57; discussed below.
13. The Royal Commission on Civil Liability and Compensation for Civil Injuries (1978).
14. See A. Holmes and R. Painter *Employment Law* (London: Blackstone Press, 1988), ch. 9. On the remaining Factories Act 1961 legislation, and regulations and orders under it, see HSE, *Guide to the Factories Act 1961* (London: HMSO).
15. For detailed coverage, see the *Encyclopaedia of Health and Safety at Work – Law and Practice* (London: Sweet & Maxwell, 1992). See also J. Stranks, *Handbook of Health and Safety Practice* (London: ROSPA/Pitman, 1992). Information on workplace requirements and standards is available from local HSE offices and the Public

Enquiry Point – HSE, Baynards House, 1 Chepstow Place, Westbourne Grove, London W2 4TE. Tel: 071-221 0870.

16. On companies' wider environmental obligations see S. Ball and S. Bell, *Environmental Law* (London: Blackstone Press, 1991).

17. See *Health and Employment*. ACAS, 1992.

18. See Kate Painter, 'It's Part of the Job: Violence at Work', in 'Vulnerable Workers in the UK Labour Market, ed. Patricia Leighton and Richard Painter, *Employee Relations*, vol. 9, no. 5, 1987, pp. 30–40, discussing *Dutton & Clark Ltd* v. *Daly* [1985] IRLR 363.

19. On 27 January 1993 it was announced that an employee of Stockport Council had secured an out-of-court settlement (reportedly £15,000) for the effects of smoking by other staff which, it had been claimed, caused bronchitis. The introduction of 'no-smoking' policies by employers will not normally be grounds for an employee who wants to smoke at work to leave and claim constructive dismissal (*Dryden* v. *Greater Glasgow Health Board* [1992] IRLR 469).

20. The Safety Representatives and Safety Committees Regulations 1977, SI 1977, no. 500. As a result of EC legislation, the Management of Health and Safety at Work Regulations 1992 include new requirements, including provision for the appointment of 'competent persons', to evaluate risks and assist with health and safety procedures. Greater protection from victimisation is provided in TURERA for employees with safety responsibilities. Specifically, s. 28 inserts new ss. 22A–22C and 57A in the EPCA giving representatives and other employees a right not to suffer a 'detriment' or to be dismissed for undertaking health and safety work.

21. For an excellent guide, see *The Safety Reps' Action Guide*, LRD booklets (May 1991).

22. See Eberlie, 'The New Health and Safety Legislation of the European Community'.

23. Provisions to give employees a right not to have action taken against them for exercising the rights are in the EPCA, ss. 22A–22C and 57A, as inserted by TURERA, s. 28 and schedule 5.

24. For guidance, see *VDUs and Health and Safety: A User's Guide* on safe VDU use and 1992 UK implementing legislation (LRD booklets, October 1991).

25. The most important claim possible is by dependants for their loss of financial support; Fatal Accidents Act 1976.

26. Until compensation is paid income support and other assistance must be obtained from the employer, or from state benefits. These include industrial injuries disablement benefit, reduced earnings allowance; disablement allowance, see *Sick or Disabled* (DSS booklet FB 28) and *State Benefit*, LRD booklets (April 1992).

27. A child suffering a pre-natal injury can also sue; Congenital Disabilities (Civil Liability) Act 1976.

28. *Paris* v. *Stepney Borough Council* [1951] AC 367. On the scope of the duty, see J. Munkman, *Employer's Liability at Common Law* (London: Butterworths, 1980).

29. *Pape* v. *Cumbria County Council* [1991] IRLR 463 (dermatitis caused by cleaning agents).

30. *Baxter* v. *Harland & Wolff plc* [1990] IRLR 516, CA. Under the new measures required by the EC, adequate risk-assessment procedures are now a pivotal requirement.

Chapter 17: Trade Unions, the Judges and the Law

1. Lord Justice Scrutton addressing the University of Cambridge Law Society, 18 November 1920, *Cambridge Law Journal*, vol. 1, p. 8.
2. P. Elias, B. Napier and P. Wallington, *Labour Law* (London: Butterworths, 1980), p. 210.
3. Lord Wedderburn, 'Industrial Relations and the Courts', *ILJ*, vol. 9, no. 65, p. 71.
4. See also *Barrett & Baird (Wholesale) Ltd* v. *Institution of Professional Civil Servants* [1987] IRLR 3 and the case note by Bob Simpson, *Modern Law Review*, vol. 50, p. 506.
5. See, for example, *Star Sea Transport Co of Monrovia* v. *Slater* [1978] IRLR 507; *Express Newspapers Ltd* v. *McShane* [1979] 2 All ER 760; *Associated Newspapers Ltd* v. *Wade* [1979] 1 WLR 697; *Beaverbrook Newspapers Ltd* v. *Keys* [1978] ICR 582.
6. J.A.G. Griffith, The Politics of the Judiciary, 4th edn (London: Fontana, 1991).
7. Wedderburn, 'Industrial Relations and the Courts', p. 78.
8. For some thought-provoking contributions to this debate see K.D. Ewing, 'The Right to Strike', ILJ, vol. 15, pp. 143–60; K.D. Ewing, *A Bill of Rights for Britain* (London: Institute of Employment Rights, 1990); Lord Wedderburn, *The Worker and the Law*, 3rd edn (Harmondsworth: Penguin, 1986), ch. 10; Roger Welch, *The Right To Strike: A Trade Union View* (London: Institute of Employment Rights, 1991).
9. For examples from other countries see K. Ewing, *A Bill of Rights for Britain?* (London: Institute of Employment Rights, 1990).
10. See Lord Wedderburn, *Employment Rights in Britain and Europe: Selected Papers in Labour Law* (London: Lawrence & Wishart, 1991).
11. Welch, *The Right to Strike*, p. 38.
12. For a detailed analysis of the formation of legal policy since 1979 see Simon Auerbach, *Legislating for Conflict* (Oxford: Oxford University Press, 1990).
13. Hazel Carty, 'The Employment Act 1990: Still Fighting the Industrial Cold War', *ILJ*, vol. 20 (1991), pp. 1–20 at p. 20.
14. F.A. Hayek, *1980s Unemployment and the Unions* (London: Institute of Economic Affairs, 1980).
15. ILO Committee of Experts, Observation 1989 on Convention no. 87: Freedom of Association and Protection of the Right to Organise.
16. K. Ewing, *Britain and the ILO* (London: Institute of Employment Rights, 1990), p. 24

Chapter 18: Trade Unions and Their Members

1. This embodies the EAT's approach to the trade union provision of property for use by a political party in *ASTMS* v. *Parkin* [1983] IRLR 448. In this case, the EAT upheld the decision of the certification officer that a contribution towards the Labour Party headquarters should have come out of the political fund even though it was by way of commercial investment.
2. The term 'political office' referred to in paras (c) and (d) covers MPs, MEPs, local authority councillors and any position within a political party, for example ward secretaries.
3. Section 5 (1) of the 1913 Act already provided that when a union adopted a political fund, existing members must be informed of their right not to contribute and the

CO's model rules currently contain a provision requiring that new members shall be supplied with a copy of the political fund rules. This right to be informed of exemption from the political level now appears as TULR(C)A, s. 84 (2) (b).

4. The CO's model rules state that, with the exception of new members, a member who gives notice of exemption shall be exempt from contributing to the political fund from the following 1 January. New members who give notice of exemption within one month of receiving a copy of the rules must be exempt from the date of the notice (see also TULR[C]A, s. 84 [2] [b]).

5. The statement also exhorts unions, where they do not already do so, to provide a right of access for members to the accounts of the political fund. Also unions should, in completing their returns to the CO, attach a list showing each payment over £250 made from their general funds to external bodies not falling within the 'political objects' definition, specify the source and amount of any investment income to the political fund, and show the administrative costs connected with the political fund.

6. I.T. Smith and J.C. Wood, *Industrial Law*, 4th edn. (London: Butterworths, 1989), p. 463.

7. See also *Martin* v. *Scottish TGWU* [1952] 1 All ER 691.

8. See *Lee* v. *Showmen's Guild* [1952] 2 QB 329.

9. See *Rothwell* v. *APEX* [1975] IRLR 375.

10. Ewan McKendrick, 'The Rights of Trade Union Members – Part I of the Employment Act 1988', *ILJ*, vol. 17, no. 3, September 1988, pp. 141–50 at p. 149.

11. For a penetrating analysis of the litigation during the miners' strike see K D. Ewing, 'The Strike, the Courts and the Rule-Books', *ILJ*, vol. 14, no. 3, pp 160–75.

12. See *The Lightman Report on the NUM* (Harmondsworth: Penguin, 1990).

13. McKendrick, 'The Rights of Trade Union Members', p. 152.

14. The rule has several exceptions, including the following:
    * it does not apply to actions which infringe the individual rights of the member;
    * the rule does not apply so as to prevent a member suing to restrain an ultra vires act, for that cannot be cured by a simple majority.

    The occasions upon which a member is most likely to want to sue his/her union are: first, to remedy a wrong done to him/her personally (and especially to complain of wrongful discipline or expulsion) and, second, to restrain the union from committing an ultra vires act. As we have seen, both of these are the principal exceptions where the rule does not apply anyway.

15. McKendrick, 'The Rights of Trade Union Members', p. 152.

16. John Bowers and Simon Auerbach, *Blackstone's Guide to the Employment Act 1988* (London: Blackstone Press, 1988), p. 45.

17. The appointment of a receiver of the funds of the NUM during the miners' strike was the first recorded receivership of a trade union. The NUM's trustees were also removed by the court (*Clarke* v. *Heathfield* [1985] ICR 203, 606).

18. The scheme narrows this down to: elections for executive committee, president, chair, secretary or treasurer of the union.

19. *Hansard* (House of Commons), 10 December 1992, cols 797–8.

20. Ian Smith and John Wood, *Industrial Law*, 4th edn (London: Butterworths, 1989), p. 478.

Chapter 19: Collective Bargaining

1. On collective bargaining, and the unions' role in it, see Lord Wedderburn, *The Worker and the Law* (Harmondsworth: Penguin, 1986); and W.E.J. McCarthy (ed.), *Trade Unions* (Harmondsworth: Penguin, 1985).
2. GDH Cole (1913), 'Trade Unions as Co-managers of Industry' in McCarthy (ed.), *Trade Unions*, pp. 76–82.
3. Royal Commission on Trade Unions and Employers' Associations (1965–8, Cmnd. 3623) the 'Donovan Report' (London: HMSO).
4. *In Place of Strife*, Department of Employment and Productivity (1969).
5. Bob Simpson, *Trade Union Recognition and the Law* (London: Institute of Employment Rights, 1991).
6. ACAS, *Annual Report* (1988), p. 8.
7. ACAS, *Annual Reports* (1988–91).
8. Precedents on this already exist in the case of single-employer agreements, but European unions have already started to look at multilateral bargaining arrangements that would be transnational *and* cover different employees within particular industries and economic sectors.
9. Lord Wedderburn, *The Social Charter, European Company and Employment Rights: An Outline Agenda* (London: Institute of Employment Rights, 1990).
10. Simpson, *Trade Union Recognition and the Law*, p. 7.
11. ACAS, *Industrial Relations Handbook* (London: HMSO). See also *Employment Policies*, ACAS advisory booklet no. 10.
12. *Ford Motor Co Ltd* v. *Amalgamated Union of Engineering and Foundry Members* [1969] 2 All ER 481.
13. In *National Coal Board* v. *National Union of Mineworkers* [1986] IRLR 439 the potential for legally enforceable agreements was discussed.
14. Enforceability was considered in the government's consultative document, *Industrial Relations in the 1990s* (1991).
15. Transfer of Undertakings (Protection of Employment) Regulations 1981.
16. See ACAS, *Using ACAS in Industrial Disputes* and ACAS, *The ACAS Role in Conciliation, Arbitration and Mediation*.
17. *City and Hackney Health Authority* v. *National Union of Public Employees* [1985] IRLR 252.
18. *Tadd* v. *Eastwood* [1983] IRLR 320.
19. *Gibbons* v. *Associated British Ports* [1985] IRLR 376.
20. *Joel* v. *Cammel Laird Ltd* (1969) 4 ITR 207.
21. TULR(C)A, ss. 5–7.
22. A leading case is *Squibb United Kingdom Staff Association* v. *Certification Officer* [1979] IRLR 75, CA.
23. In particular by the Employment Act 1988, ss. 10,11, which prevent action by either the union or employer to maintain union membership. See now TULR(C)A, ss. 152, 222.
24. See K. Ewing 'Trade Union Recognition: A Framework for Discussion', *ILJ*, vol. 19 (1990), p. 209.

25. See Simpson, *Trade Union Recognition and the Law*, which discusses alternative approaches.
26. *J. Wilson & Bros Ltd* v. *USDAW* [1977] ICR 530.
27. *Cleveland County Council* v. *Springett and Others* [1985] IRLR 131.
28. Employment Protection Act 1975, s. 1 (later in TULR(C)A, s. 209).
29. ACAS, *Employment Handbook* (1990), p. 9.
30. For general guidance, see paras 1–7 of the ACAS Code.
31. *Bakers Limited* v. *Allen* [1983] IRLR 329 CA.
32. See TULR(C)A s. 185; and on disclosure generally ACAS Code of Practice, 'Disclosure of Information to Trade Unions for Collective Bargaining Purposes', no. 3.

Chapter 20: Industrial Conflict I

1. For a detailed analysis of the effect of strikes and other industrial action on the contract of employment, the question of the payment of wages to those taking industrial action and the social security implications of unemployment caused by trade disputes see K.D. Ewing, *The Right to Strike* (Oxford: Oxford University Press, 1991).
2. Roger Welch, *The Right to Strike: A Trade Union View* (London: Institute of Employment Rights, 1991) p. 25.
3. *Wiluszynski* v. *Tower Hamlets London Borough Council* [1989] IRLR 259; see also *British Telecommunications plc* v. *Ticehurst* (1992) *The Times*, 18 March, CA.
4. For the purposes of the continuity provisions, the terms strike and lock-out are defined by EPCA 1978, sched. 13, para. 24 (1). A strike involves the cessation of work by a body of employees acting in combination or a concerted refusal to work. A lock-out involves the closing of a place of employment, the suspension of work or the refusal by the employer to continue to employ any number of employees. In the case of both strike and lock-out, the action taken must be in consequence of a dispute and its purpose must be to coerce the other party to accept or not accept terms and conditions of or affecting employment.
5. See J. Mesher, 'Social Security in the Coal Dispute', *ILJ*, vol. 14, 1985, p. 191.
6. Social Security Act 1986 s. 23 (5).
7. Finance Act 1981, s. 29, SI 1982 no. 66.
8. See ILO Committee of Experts, Observation 1989 on Convention 87, discussed in chapter 17 above.
9. This approach was developed by Lord Justice Brightman in *Marina Shipping Ltd* v. *Laughton* [1982] 481 at 489 and was subsequently employed by Lord Diplock in *Merkur Island Shipping* v. *Laughton* [1983] 2 All ER 189.
10. See also *Drew* v. *St Edmondsbury BC* [1980] ICR 513.
11. *Daily Mirror Newspapers* v. *Gardner* [1968] 2 All ER 163; see also *Torquay Hotels Co Ltd* v. *Cousins* (cited above).
12. I.T. Smith and J.C. Wood, *Industrial Law*, 4th edn (London: Butterworths, 1989), p. 522.
13. *Hansard* (House of Lords) 23 July 1990, col. 1272.
14. Cm. 1602 (London: HMSO, 1991).
15. London: Butterworths, 1993, II M, para. 3610.

16. B.A. Hepple and S. Fredman, *Labour Law and Industrial Relations in Great Britain* (Deventer: Kluwer, 1986), p. 212.
17. Electricity Act 1989, s. 96; Water Act 1989, s. 170. The Telecommunications Act 1984, s. 94, provides grants powers of direction.
18. Gillian Morris, 'Industrial Action in Essential Services', *ILJ*, vol. 20, 1991, p. 92.
19. Cmnd. 8218, 1981, paras 330–4.
20. Morris, 'Industrial Action in Essential Services', p. 90.
21. *Guardian* 23 April 1993; *London Borough of Wandsworth* v. *National Association of Schoolmasters/Union of Women Teachers* [1993] IRLR 344, CA.

Chapter 21: Industrial Conflict II: Picketing

1. S. Evans, 'Picketing under the Employment Acts', in P. Fosh and C. Littler (eds), *Industrial Relations and the Law in the 1980s: Issues and Trends* (Aldershot: Gower, 1985).
2. Roger Welch, *The Case for Positive Trade Union Rights* (Employment Relations Research Centre, Anglia Higher Education College, 1989).
3. See, for example, R. Lewis, 'Picketing', in R. Lewis (ed.), *Labour Law in Britain* (Oxford: Blackwell, 1986), p. 199; P.L. Davies and M. Freedland, *Labour Law: Text & Materials*, 2nd edn (London: Wiedenfeld & Nicholson, 1984), p. 852.
4. More detailed accounts of developments in this area are provided by Gillian Morris, 'Industrial Action & the Criminal Law', *Industrial Relations Legal Information Bulletin*, 5 May 1987, pp. 2–9, and J. Bowers and M. Duggan, *The Modern Law of Strikes* (London: Financial Training Publications, 1987), ch. 4.
5. Gillian Morris commentary, *ILJ*, vol. 14, p. 109.
6. Cmnd. 9510, May 1985.
7. Ibid.
8. See Lewis, 'Picketing', pp. 216–19, and Lord Wedderburn, *The Worker and the Law* (Harmondsworth: Penguin, 1986), pp. 550–3.
9. Bowers and Duggan, *The Modern Law of Strikes*, p. 44.
10. Cmnd. 9510, para. 5.7.

Chapter 22: Tribunal and Court Claims

1. EPCA, s. 131 and TURERA, s. 38. Tribunal chairs will also be able to deal with various breach of contract, the Wages Act and other matters sitting alone.
2. Lord Wedderburn 'Labour Law – From Here to Autonomy' *ILJ*, vol. 16, 1987, p. 1; the Labour Party Manifesto 1992 also proposed a labour court.
3. On the labour court issue it has been said that 'if you want to adopt a dog and would like to have a corgi, you do not want to end up with a rottweiler'; Lord Wedderburn, 'The Social Charter in Britain: Labour Law – and Labour Courts', in Wedderburn, *Employment Rights in Britain and Europe – Selected Papers*, (London: Cent, 1991) p. 375.
4. *The Effectiveness of Representation at Tribunals* (Lord Chancellor's Department, 1989); and Philip Parry, *Industrial Tribunals: How to Present your Case* (London: Industrial Society, 1991).

5. For guidance on this and on conciliation, see ACAS, *Individual Employment Rights – ACAS Conciliation between Individuals*.

6. Employment Act 1989, s. 20.

7. Industrial Tribunals (Rules and Procedure) Regulations 1985.

8. Department of Employment booklet ITL, *Industrial Tribunals Procedure* (1990) available from Job Centres covers most points; and see Parry, *Industrial Tribunals – How to Present your Case*.

9. See *Small Claims in the County Court* and the other guidance available from county court offices and CABs.

Table of Cases

Page numbers in this table are after the dash

424

Index